John Doran

**Annals of the English Stage**

Vol. II

John Doran

**Annals of the English Stage**
*Vol. II*

ISBN/EAN: 9783337280802

Printed in Europe, USA, Canada, Australia, Japan

Cover: Foto ©ninafisch / pixelio.de

More available books at **www.hansebooks.com**

"THEIR MAJESTIES' SERVANTS."

# ANNALS

OF

# THE ENGLISH STAGE,

FROM

## THOMAS BETTERTON TO EDMUND KEAN.

Actors—Authors—Audiences.

By Dr. DORAN, F.S.A.,

AUTHOR OF "TABLE TRAITS," "LIVES OF THE QUEENS OF ENGLAND OF THE HOUSE OF HANOVER," ETC., ETC.

IN TWO VOLUMES.

VOL. II.

NEW YORK:
W. J. WIDDLETON, PUBLISHER.
1865.

# "BILL OF THE PLAY."

## VOL. II.

| CHAP. | | PAGE |
|---|---|---|
| I. | Margaret Woffington | 5 |
| II. | Colley Cibber | 15 |
| III. | England and Ireland | 33 |
| IV. | Ryan, Rich, O'Brien | 41 |
| V. | Susanna Maria Cibber | 51 |
| VI. | Reappearance of Spranger Barry.—Retirement of Mrs. Pritchard | 57 |
| VII. | The last years of Garrick and Barry | 66 |
| VIII. | David Garrick | 75 |
| IX. | Spranger and Anne Barry | 96 |
| X. | Kitty Clive, Woodward, Shuter | 108 |
| XI. | Samuel Foote | 119 |
| | Supplemental Catalogue of New Plays from the retirement of Garrick to the end of the Eighteenth Century | 136 |
| XII. | Of Authors, and particularly of condemned Authors | 144 |
| XIII. | The Audiences of the last half of the Eighteenth Century | 163 |
| XIV. | Charles Macklin | 184 |
| XV. | A Bevy of Ladies;—but chiefly, Mrs. Bellamy, Miss Farren, Mrs. Abington, and "Perdita" | 197 |
| XVI. | A Group of Gentlemen | 217 |
| XVII. | John Henderson | 235 |
| XVIII. | Sarah Siddons | 241 |
| XIX. | John Kemble | 264 |
| XX. | George Frederick Cooke | 286 |
| XXI. | Master Betty | 296 |
| XXII. | Stage Costume and Stage Tricks | 302 |
| XXIII. | Prologue, Epilogue; Dedications, and Benefits | 318 |
| XXIV. | Old Stagers Departing | 337 |
| XXV. | New Ideas; New Theatres; New Authors; and the New Actors | 353 |
| XXVI. | Edmund Kean | 377 |
| XXVII. | Edmund Kean—Continued | 400 |

# DORAN'S ANNALS OF THE STAGE.

## CHAPTER I.

#### MARGARET WOFFINGTON.

THAT good-tempered woman who is looking with admiration at the pretty and delicate child who is drawing water from the Liffey, is Madame Violante. She is mistress of a booth, for rope-dancing and other exhibitions in Dame Street. As the young girl turns homeward, with the bowl of water on her head, the lady follows, still admiring.

The object of her admiration is as bright and as steady as a sunbeam. If she be ill-clad, she is exquisitely shaped, and she will live to lend her dresses to the two Miss Gunnings, to enable them to attend a drawing-room at the Castle; their first steps towards reaching the coronets of countess and duchess that were in store for them.

This child, meanwhile, enters a shabby huckster's shop, kept by her widowed mother, on Ormond Quay. The father was a working bricklayer, and married the mother when she was as hard-working a laundress. There is another child in this poor household, a sister of the water-bearer, fair, but less fair than she. When Madame Violante first saw Mary and Margaret Woffington, she little dreamed that the latter would be the darling of London society, and the former the bride of a son of one of the proudest of English earls.

Margaret Woffington, born in 1720, was very young when Madame Violante induced her mother to let her have the pretty child as a pupil. The foreign lady was of good repute, and Margaret became an apt pupil, performed little tricks while her mistress was on the rope, learned French thoroughly, and acquired graces of person, style, and carriage, by which she gained fortune, and reaped ruin.

As a child, she played Macheath, in Madame's booth, when the "Beggars' Opera" was acted there by children. From the age of seventeen to twenty, she was on the more regular Dublin stage, charming all eyes and hearts by her beauty, grace, and ability in a range of characters from Ophelia to Sir Harry Wildair. Rich at once engaged her, at a moderate salary, and, in 1740, brought her out, at Covent Garden, as Sylvia to Ryan's Plume and the younger Cibber's Brazen. A successful *coup d'éssai* emboldened her to try Sir Harry. She played it night after night, for weeks, and Wilks was forgotten. It is said she so enraptured one susceptible damsel, that the young lady, believing Sir Harry to be a man, made him an offer of marriage.

Walpole was among the last to be pleased. "There is much in vogue, a Mrs. Woffington," he writes, in 1741; "a bad actress, but she has life." Walpole's friend, Conway, confesses that "all the town was in love with her;" but to Conway's eyes, she was only "an impudent Irish-faced girl." Even these fastidious gentlemen became converted, and, at a later period, Walpole records her excellent acting in Moore's "Foundling," with Garrick, Barry, and Mrs. Cibber.

Her Lothario was not so successful as her Sir Harry; but her high-born ladies, her women of dash, spirit, and elegance, her homely, humorous females, in all these she triumphed; and triumphed in spite of a voice that was almost unmanageable for its harshness.

Margaret and Garrick were very soon on very intimate terms. In the summer of 1742, they were together in Dublin, and on their return, according to a tradition of the stage, Garrick and Mrs. Woffington, living together, alternately supplied the expenses of the household, each being at the head of the latter during a month. In Garrick's term the table is said to have been but moderately furnished; whereas during the beautiful Margaret's month, there was a banquet and brilliant company daily; all the fashionable men about town being delighted at an invitation from the Irish actress. Johnson used to be among those visitors, and he noticed the difference in the quality of the housekeeping, after his usual fashion. "Is not this tea stronger than usual, madame? It's as red as blood!" It was Margaret's month, and the liberal lady smiled.

That Garrick ever entertained thoughts of marrying Margaret, I very much doubt, despite the story, said to have been told by the lady to Murphy, that he had gone so far as to buy the wedding-ring, and try it on her finger. In the early part of the few years which elapsed between Garrick's debût in London and his marriage with Eva Maria Violetta, he lived in such affectionate intimacy with the charming Irish actress, as to address to her the song beginning with

"Once more I'll tune the vocal shell,
To hills and dales my passion tell,
A flame which time can never quell,
Which burns for you, my Peggy!"

Notwithstanding this homage, the lady's infidelities were so numerous, that whatever may have been her wrath or disappointment, she had no right to expect that of so inconstant a mistress of *one* home, Garrick was likely to make the wife of another. However this may have been, it remains undeniable that Garrick preserved, to his last days, a pair of silver buckles which once belonged to that Peggy, who, from first to last, enthralled more hearts than any actress since the days of Elizabeth Barry;—from those of young fellows with the down just budding on their lips, to what was left of those of old Owen Mac Swiney and older Colley Cibber, between which two ancient danglers, people compared Margaret to Susanna between the two Elders.

In good truth, her company was sought after by "men of the first rank and distinction;" and "persons of the gravest character, and most eminent for learning," felt honored by her acquaintance, and were charmed with her conversation. She founded her avowed preference of the company of men to that of women, on the alleged fact that the latter never talked but of satins and silks. She herself was endowed with a good understanding, which was much improved by contact with intellectual society, and by much reading. In short, it seems to have been impossible to resist this clever, vivacious, affable, and good-natured creature; one who laughed most unaffectedly at the joke which touched her own character nearest; whose errors are forgotten in her much-abounding and still-enduring charity, and who not only faithfully kept that part of the decalogue which says, "Thou shalt not covet thy neighbor's *wife*," but provided a home for her neighbors' wives, through many generations, by building the asylum for them, which still exists at Teddington. "Mes enfans, sauvez-vous par la charité!"

Margaret Woffington was the most beautiful and the least vain of the women of her day. Whatever character she had to play, she identified herself therewith; and did it happen to be that of an old or ordinary woman, she descended to the level of circumstances, and hid every natural beauty beneath wrinkles and stolidity, according to the exigencies of the part.

Her sister, Mary Woffington, whom many living persons remember well, failed comparatively as an actress; but she achieved better fortune as a woman than her more able and attractive sister. By marriage she connected herself with Walpole's family, and Walpole, whose mother was the daughter of a timber-dealer, was disgusted.

"I have been unfortunate in my own family," says Walpole to Mann, in 1746; "my nephew, Captain Cholmondeley, has married a player's sister." This last was Mrs. Woffington's sister, Mary. Captain, subsequently the Reverend Robert Cholmondeley, was the second son of the Earl Cholmondeley, who obtained Houghton, by marrying Walpole's only legitimate sister Mary. At the match between the captain and the player's sister the earl was greatly incensed, and he went to Mrs. Woffington to tell her as much. But Margaret so softened him by her winning ways, and won him by her good sense, and subdued him to her will, that he, at last, called her his "dear Mrs. Woffington," and declared that he was happy at his son's choice, in spite of his having been "so very much offended previously." This aroused Margaret's spirit a little. "Offended previously!" she exclaimed, "I have most cause to be offended now." "Why, dear lady?" asked the earl.

"Because," replied the actress, "I had one beggar to support, and now I shall have two!"

Of this marriage, Mrs. Woffington lived to see five of the nine children born. One of these, married to Sir William Bellingham, Bart., carried the Woffington blood back to one of the oldest families in Ireland. Another of Margaret Woffington's nieces was Maid of Honor to the Princess of Wales; who, when driving with her royal mistress through Leatherhead, in 1806, was killed by the upsetting of the carriage. Mary Woffington (the Hon. Mrs. Cholmondeley) survived till 1811.

To see Margaret Woffington and Smith in Sylvia and Plume was an ecstasy, *he* being so graceful and vivacious, while *she* charmed her audiences in both the dresses worn by Sylvia, rendering, says the *Dramatic Censor*, "even absurdities pleasing by the elegance of her appearance and the vivacity of her expression." Mrs. Bellamy was so overcome by her acting Jocasta in that awful drama of "Œdipus," that she fainted on the stage, when playing Eurydice to her. Some persons set this down to affectation; but George Anne was not a lady likely to affect a swoon for the sake of complimenting a rival actress.

Mrs. Woffington was the only player who acted Sir Harry Wildair with the spirit and elegance of the original—Wilks, to whom Garrick and Woodward were, in this part, inferior. She was excellent in Lady Plyant, and admirable in the representation of females in high rank and of dignified elegance. Millamant, Lady Townley, Lady Betty Modish, and Maria, in the " Nonjuror," were exhibited by her with that happy ease and gayety, and with such powerful attraction, that the excesses of these characters appeared not only pardonable, but agreeable.

Her Jane Shore did not admit of competition with Mrs. Oldfield's; but that and Hermione were full of merit, notwithstanding. In male attire, the elegance of her figure was most striking; but I cannot suppose that her Lady Randolph, of which she was the original representative in London, in any one point approached that of Mrs. Crawford (Barry), or of Mrs. Siddons. Indeed, her voice unfitted her for tragic parts. She called it her " bad voice!"

Margaret Woffington's independence was one of the great traits in her character. About six years before Mrs. Cibber left the stage she was often too indisposed to act; and at short notice Mrs. Woffington was advertised to play some favorite part of her own, instead. Once, when thus advertised, she pleaded illness, and would not go to the theatre. The next night, as Mrs. Woffington came on, as Lady Jane Grey, she was greeted with a hurricane of hisses, for having failed to appear the evening before. They even called upon her to "beg pardon!" *then* her complexion glowed with angry beauty, her eyes flashed lightning, and she walked off the stage, magnificently scornful. It was with great difficulty she was induced to return, and when she *did*, the imperious fair one calmly faced her excited audience with a "*now then!*" sort of look. She expressed her willingness to perform her duty, but it was for them to decide: "On or off; it must be as you please; to me it is a matter of perfect indifference!" The audience petted this wayward creature, and the contending parties were friends forever after.

Margaret and Kitty Clive got on as ill together as the former and Mrs. Cibber. The green-room was kept alive by their retorts, joyous by their repartees, or uncomfortable by their dissensions. But there were no two dramatic queens who hated each other so cordially within the theatre as Margaret and George Anne Bellamy. In rivalry or opposition on the stage, they entered into the full spirit of their parts, felt all or more than they said, and not only handled their daggers menacingly, but losing control of temper sometimes, used them more vigorously than law or good manners would allow.

After a career in London of undiminished popularity, she passed over to Dublin for three seasons, 1751–54, where she was equally the popular idol, drew thousands of pounds, had a salary, first of £400, then of £800, for the season, was enthroned at the Beef Steak Club by Sheridan, addressed verses, free enough to be what they were not—her own, to the Lord Lieutenant, and altogether ruled "the court, the camp, and the grove." Victor extols all her tragic parts, save Jane Shore; and Mrs. Delaney confirms his account of her Lady Townley, as being better than any the town had seen since Mrs. Oldfield's time; adding, that she pronounced well, and spoke sensibly; but that her voice was not agreeable, and that her arms were ungainly. Of her Maria ("Nonjuror"), Mrs. Delaney says that the effect in Dublin was marred by the immoderate size of Mrs. Woffington's hoops!

It was at this time she took a step which was sharply canvassed —that of forsaking the church in which she was born, and putting her arm, as it were, under that of Protestantism. She went a long way, and in strange companionship too, in order to take this step. She and Sheridan made a pleasant excursion, on the occasion, through Mullingar to Longford and Carrick on Shannon, and on, by Lough Allen and Drumshamboe, till they stood on the verge of the Pot of the Shannon.

Murphy fancies that as Roman Catholics could not then legally wear a sword, she renounced her old faith that she might carry one, in male characters, without offending the law! This is sheer nonsense. But whatever took her to the little village on the mountain side, it is impossible to conceive a more striking contrast than the one between this magnificent district, where occasionally an eagle may be seen sweeping between Quilca and Sliev na Eirin, with Covent Garden or Smock Alley! I do not know if at that period, as till lately, the Primate of Ireland had a little shooting-box on a platform of the mountain, but to the modest residence still existing of the Protestant pastor, Sheridan and Margaret took their way; and there the brilliant lady enrolled herself as a member of the church by law established. The influences which moved her to this were simply that *she* would not lose her chance of an estate for the sake of the old religion in which she had been baptized. Her ex-admirer, Mac Swiney, had left her heiress to his estate of £200 a year; and that the bequest might be legal, and the succession uncontested, the frail Margaret qualified for prospective fortune by declaring herself a Protestant, in the presence of competent witnesses.

She returned to the "Garden" in the season 1754–5, going through all her best characters in that, and the two succeeding, and her final seasons. The last male part she acted was Lothario; the last original part she created was Lady Randolph (which, however, had been previously played in Edinburgh by Mrs. Ward), and in Rosalind, paralysis put an end to her professional career. Just previously, her Lothario had not been highly esteemed; and

Barry, in the memorable suit of white-puckered satin, had produced all the effect in "Douglas." This affected her spirits. Then she was annoyed at young Tate Wilkinson, whom Foote had just brought on the stage, and who had audaciously imitated the worst parts of Margaret's voice. Almost the only unkind act that can be laid to Mrs. Woffington's charge, was her consequent attempt to induce Rich not to enter into an engagement with Wilkinson. Her scorn drove the unfortunate young gentleman, for his story was a sad one, from the green-room, despite the interference of Shuter. One night, as she was playing Clarissa in the "Confederacy," she saw Wilkinson in a stage-box with Captain Forbes, and unable to control her rage, she came close to the box, and absolutely made him shrink back by the sneering sarcasm with which she flung at him one of her speeches. A rude woman in the box above mimicked her peculiar voice so well, as Clarissa turned away, that Mrs. Woffington thought it came from Wilkinson. That night she swept through the green-room, a beautiful fury, and the next day, at Rich's levee, she assailed Tate with terrible eloquence, prophesied evil to him, wished the evil she prophesied, and altogether manifested little of the kindly nature which was, in truth, her own.

Soon followed thereon the fatal 3d of May, 1757. The play was "As You Like It," in which she acted Rosalind. Young Tate Wilkinson was standing at the wing as she passed on to the stage, and on her way she complimented him, ironically, on his recent success as a debutant. Wilkinson watched and studied her throughout the piece, till she came off early in the fifth act, and suddenly complained of being ill. Wilkinson offered his arm, leaning on which she retired to the green-room, rallied, went on, changed her dress, again trod the stage, defiantly of fate, and again yielded to the coming blow; but only for a moment. Once more she recovered, her self-will being so great, and she began the lines of the epilogue. She had just uttered, with fearful gayety, the words:—"If I were among you, I'd kiss as many of you as had beards that pleased me——," when that once saucy tongue became paralyzed. A last flash of courage impelled her to an attempt to proceed; but it was vain, and at the sense that she was stricken, she flung up her hands, uttered a wild shriek in abject terror, and staggering towards the stage-door, fell into the arms stretched to receive her; and amid indescribable confusion of cheering and commiserating cries, Margaret Woffington disappeared from the stage, forever.

In November of that year, a fine gentleman asked, "What has become of Mrs. Woffington?" "She has been taken off by Colonel Cæsar," answered another fine gentleman. "Reduced to *aut Cæsar aut nullus*," said the smart Lord Tyrawley. "She is gone to be married," said Kitty Clive; "Colonel Cæsar bought the license at the same time Colonel Mostyn bought his." At this time, poor Margaret, in the meridian of her beauty, somewhat weary of her calling, ashamed, it is said, of her life, was slowly dying at "Teddington, in Twickenhamshire," as Walpole loved to call it. So slowly, that the end did not come till 1760.

In the interval, Margaret Woffington is said to have lived to good purpose. Unreasonably exalted as her character has been, it is impossible to contemplate it at its close, without respect. Charity, good works, sorrow for the past, hope,—all the Magdalen was there in that beautiful wreck. In a playful time she and Colonel Cæsar had agreed that the survivor of the two should be the heir of the other; but Margaret would not let a jest do injury to her family and to the poor. Of her few thousands, she left the greater part to her sister; her mother she had pensioned and protected; to the poor of Teddington, among whom she reposes, she left well-endowed alms-houses. The poor, at least, may bless the memory of that once bright young creature, whom Madame Violante saw drawing water from the Liffey.

Those alms-houses form a better relic of Margaret Woffington than the poor stage-jewels which her dresser, Mrs. Barrington, a respectable actress, hoped to inherit. These were claimed by, and surrendered to, the Hon. Mrs. Cholmondeley, and were carried to Ireland by that lady's daughter, on her marriage with Sir William Bellingham.

Such is the story of one, of whom an anonymous contemporary has written,—"Mrs. Woffington is a downright cheat, a triumphant plagiary. She first steals your heart, and then laughs at you as secure of your applause. There is such a prepossession arises from her form; such a witchcraft in her beauty, and to those who are personally acquainted with her, such an absolute command, from the sweetness of her disposition, that it is almost impossible to criticise upon her." With this criticism, I leave Margaret Woffington to the tender judgment of all gentle readers.

But while Margaret Woffington is slowly dying, here is a funeral passing through Berkeley Square. "Mr. Colley Cibber," is the name often pronounced in the crowd. It is one of which we have, for some time, lost sight; let us return to it, before we pass on to that of other conspicuous men.

## CHAPTER II.

#### COLLEY CIBBER.

IN the year 1671, the coffee-house politicians, the fine gentlemen, the scholars, and the gossips, generally, were in no lack of themes for discussion. In Bow Street, the quidnuncs congratulated themselves, from April to December, at the resolution of the Commons, whose members had rebuked the Lords for daring to alter an impost laid on sugar, to the effect that in all aids given to the King by the Commons, the tax levied might be agreed to, but it could not be altered by the Lords. Knots of shabby-looking clergymen were constantly to be seen in Mr. Brent, the mercer's shop, discussing the arrangements just made for the sustenance of London incumbents, burnt out by the Great Fire. Up-stairs, in the long-room over Mr. Brent's shop, the "wit's room" at Will's, the company never wearied of hearing Major Mohun, the actor, speak of Lord Fairfax, who was just dead. There was much gossip, too, both there and about town, touching my Lord Manchester, lately deceased, the parliamentary general who had helped to restore monarchy. If he was the servant of two masters, some persons thought he had been sufficiently punished by being the husband of five wives. The critics were more genially engaged in canvassing the merits of Casaubon, the learned prebendary of Canterbury, who had recently laid aside his critical acumen with his mortal coil. The artists were canvassing the merits of a monument which was that year beginning to rear its head on Fish Street Hill. The architect was Sir Christopher Wren. A foreign sculptor from Holstein was, at that moment, preparing designs for the *basso relievo* now on the pedestal. This sculptor lived in Southampton Street, Bloomsbury, where, on the 6th of November, 1671, while arranging the completion of his figures, his lady up-stairs,—she was of a cavalier family, and had the blood of William of Wyckham in her veins,—presented him with a living figure, the counterfeit presentment of its father. The child thus born, as it were, with the London Monument, was named Colley Cibber.

How Colley fared at school, stood his own ground, and was envied by the dunces he beat, in a double sense,—how he was determined to succeed in life, and *did* succeed, and was therefore denounced, as an ass or a knave, by those who failed, or who hated him for his success, or who feared the sarcasms which he himself delivered, without fear,—is known to us all.

The success of Colley Cibber, throughout life, may be ascribed to three circumstances; the acuteness with which he detected opportunity, the electric rapidity with which he seized it, and the marvellous unerring tact by which he turned it to profit. By this he was distinguished, despite some easy negligence and luxurious idleness, from his earliest days; and from his first to his last consequent triumph, he paid for each in the malevolence of those who envied him his victories and denied his merit.

When a lad at Grantham Free School, he alone accepted the magisterial proposal to compose a funeral oration, in honor of the dead King, Charles II. He gained such glory by his achievement that his fellows sent him to Coventry. For succeeding better than any of them in writing an ode in honor of the new King, an ode which he modestly owns to have been as execrable as any thing he composed half a century later, when poet-laureate, they ostracized the bard whom they could not equal in song. Colley was satisfied with his glory, and treated his young adversaries with all the mingled good-nature and audacity with which he subsequently treated his better armed enemy, Mr. Pope.

When he "met the Revolution," in 1688, at Nottingham, failing to obtain military employment, he gladly availed himself of an opportunity to wait behind Lady Churchill's chair, as she sat at table with the Princess Anne. Half a hundred years later he refers to the friend he acquired by thus performing lackey to her; and he happily caps a climax of glorious compliment to the then Duchess of Marlborough, by flatteringly alluding to something that pleasantly distinguished her above all the women of her time,—a distinction which she received not from earthly sovereigns, but "from the Author of Nature;" that of being "*a great grandmother without gray hairs.*"

He failed, indeed, in obtaining a commission, as he did in an attempt to enter the church; but for those failures Cibber was, in no wise, responsible. Had he grasped a pair of colors we should have heard of him, honorably, in Flanders. Had he received ordination, he would at least have as well known how to push his way as the Reverend Philip Bisse, who kissed the Countess of Plymouth in the dark, affecting to take her for a maid of honor, and who thereby gained that lively widow for a wife, and through her the bishoprics, successively, of St. Davids and Hereford.

Colley being alike debarred from ascending the pulpit, or leading to the imminently deadly breach, turned to the sock and buskin, alternately donning the one or the other, for nothing; but watching his opportunity, and never failing to take advantage of it. He gladly, after a term of hungry probation, accepted the little part of the Chaplain, in the "Orphan;" and when the old comedian Goodman swore there was the stuff for the making of a good actor in the young fellow, the tears came into Cibber's eyes; but they were tears of joy, for he recognized that his good time had commenced, and he watched opportunity more indefatigably than ever.

Meanwhile, he was happy on ten, and fifteen shillings a week, with food, and raiment, and lodging, under his father's roof, and an ardent desire that he might one day play lover to Mrs. Bracegirdle. When the ambitious young fellow had induced his sire to allow him £20 a year, in addition to the £1 a week which he then gained on the stage, Colley made love to a young lady off the stage, and married at the age of twenty-two. He and his wife were as happy as any young couple that ever took a leap in the dark. This is his own testimony; but beyond that darkness he looked eagerly, watching still for opportunity. It came, when Congreve's "Double Dealer" was to be played before Queen Mary. Kynaston had fallen suddenly ill, and who could learn and play the part of Lord Touchwood in a few hours? Congreve looks at Cibber, and the young actor looks confidently at Congreve. He undertakes the task, fired by the thought of promotion, and of performing before a crowned head. His success was perfect. Congreve was delighted, and the salary of the ecstatic comedian was raised some few shillings a week. His young wife danced round him for joy at this glimpse of Golconda. The company of actors began to dislike him, after the fashion of his Grantham school-fellows.

Little recked Colley Cibber what men thought of him, provided only the thought helped him towards fortune. At a pinch, he supplied a new prologue, for the opening of a season at Drury Lane, the prosperity of which was menaced by an opposition from the new theatre in Lincoln's Inn Fields. The poet begged hard that he might have the speaking of his own piece, but he was not accounted actor good enough for that, and thus he lost, not by error of his own, a particular opportunity. But the master slipped a couple of guineas into his hand, and declared that he, Colley, "was a very ingenious young man." Cibber was consoled; he had, at all events, profited by the opportunity, of making way with his "Master." To be sure, said Colley, "he knows no difference between Dryden and Durfey;" but that also made no difference to Colley.

Some weeks subsequently the "Old Bachelor" was suddenly substituted for the previously announced tragedy of "Hamlet." When all the parts had been distributed to the principal actors, Cibber, ever vigilant, and ever ready, quietly remarked that they had forgotten one of the most telling parts in the whole play, Fondlewife. It was Doggett's great part. In it he was unapproachable. He was not a member of the company. Who could or would dare to face a public whose sides were still shaking with laughter at Doggett's irresistible performance of this character! No one knew the part; mid-day was at hand; the curtain must go up by four; the play could *not* be changed. What *was* to be done? Colley, of course, offered himself to do it, and his offer was treated with contempt; but the managers were compelled to accept it. Here was a golden chance which had golden results for Cibber. He played the part, at night, in dress, feature, voice, and action, so like to the incomparable Doggett himself, that the house was in an uproar of delight and perplexity,—delight at beholding their favorite, and perplexity as to how it could possibly be he. For there sat Doggett himself, in the very centre of a forward row in the pit; a stimulant rather than a stumbling-block to Cibber; and the astonished witness of the newly-acquired glory of this young actor, who always seemed ready to undertake any thing, and who was always sure of accomplishing whatever he undertook. "It would be too rank an affectation," he writes, "if I should not confess that to see him there, a witness of my reception, was to me as consummate a triumph as the heart of vanity could be indulged with."

Surely, this persevering fellow merited success; but still were his play-fellows like his school-fellows. They envied and decried him. If he solicited a part, he was put by, with the remark, that *it was not in his way.* He wisely replied, that any part, naturally written, should be in the way of every man who pretended to be an actor. The managers thought otherwise, and left Colley—but not to despair. He had just discerned another opportunity, and, *more suo,* he clutched it, worked it to a noble end, and with it achieved a double and a permanent triumph—triumph as author as well as actor.

For many years there had not been a comedy written but at the expense of husbands. They were the dupes and dolts of the piece; were betrayed and dishonored; cudgelled and contented in their abject debasement. Audiences had had something too much of this, and Cibber was the first to perceive it. He himself was not yet sufficiently enlightened to discover that the majority in all theatrical audiences were gasping for a general purer air of refinement, and were growing disgusted with the mire in which such writers as Ravenscroft, and others with more wit than he, plunged and dragged them. Cibber, at all events, made the first step out of this slough, by producing his "Love's Last Shift." It was not readily accepted, but it forced its way to that consummation, by the testimony borne to its merits by competent judges. It was played in January, 1695. Its grossness is scarcely inferior to that of comedies most offending in this way, and which were produced both earlier and later. Nevertheless, it marks an epoch. There was no comically outraged husband in it. The style is still that of the old, free, coarse-comedy, in all the other persons of the drama. The women lack heart and natural affection; the men are unrefined and uncivil, and both converse too much after the intolerable mode which was not yet to be driven from the sadly-abused stage. Sentiment there is, indeed, after a sort; but when it is not smart and epigrammatic, it is repulsively low and selfish. Amid the intrigues of the piece, there stands glitteringly prominent the first of the brilliant series of Cibber's fops, Sir Novelty Fashion. This character he wrote for his own acting, and his success in it established him as an actor of the first rank. The interest of the audience in Sir Novelty does not centre in him as an unprincipled rake (he is, however, sufficiently unscrupulous), as it is attracted towards him as a "beau," a man of fashion, who professes to see nothing tolerable in himself, solely in order to extort praise for his magnificence, from others. He is "ugly, by Gad!" he is a "sloven!" If he wears hundreds of yards of trimming, it is to encourage the poor ribbon-weavers. If all the eminent tailors in town besiege his house, it is to petition him for the pattern of his new coat. He is the first man who was ever called "*beau*," which title he professes to prefer to "right honorable," for the latter is inherited, while the former is owing to his surprising mien and unexampled gallantry. He does not make love to a lady; his court is paid by indicating to her why she should love *him*. He judges of a man of sense by the fashion of his peruke; and if he enters a lady's apartment in an unpowdered perriwig, she may rest assured that he has no designs on her admiration. Sir Novelty is one of those fine gentlemen who go to both theatres on the same evening; he sits with his back to the stage, and is assured that he looks like a gentleman; for, is he not endowed with a "fertile genius for dress?"

Southerne, who had read this play and liked it, was fearful of Cibber's own part in it. "Young man," said he, "I pronounce thy play a good one. I will answer for its success, if thou dost not spoil it by thine own action!" When the play was over, Nell Gwyn's old friend, Sackville, now earl of Dorset, Lord Chamberlain, and the "best good man with the worst-natured muse," declared that "Love's Last Shift" was the best play that any author, in his memory, had produced; and that for a young fellow to show himself such an actor, and such a writer, in one day, was something extraordinary." Colley, always modest, but not through vanity, nicely alludes to Dorset's known good-nature, and sets down the compliment not to his deserts, but to Dorset's wish to "encourage a young beginner." Cibber himself pronounced his comedy puerile and frothy.

It is due to Cibber to say that in this piece his own part of Sir Novelty is never so prominent as to interfere unfairly with the other personages. The piece itself, gross as it is, had a tendency towards reforming the stage. Cibber's self-imposed mission in this direction was consummated when he produced his "Careless Husband." This was one of two works of Colley which Walpole pronounced to be worthy of immortality. The other was the "Apology" for his life. The progress towards purity, made between Cibber's first comedy and the last I have named above, is nothing less than marvellous. In the "Careless Husband" he produced a piece at which the most fastidious ladies of *those* times might sit, and listen to, unmasked. I say "listen," for the comedy is a merely conversational piece, sparkling with wit, and with fewer lines to shock the purer sense than many an old play which still retains a place upon the stage. The descriptions here are as clever as the dialogue is spirited. If evil things come under notice, they are treated as people of decency would treat them, often gracefully, never alluringly. The incidents, told rather than acted, are painted, if I may so speak, with the consummate skill, ease, and distinctiveness of a most accomplished artist. The finest gentlemen are less vicious here than they are temporarily foolish; and one has not been long acquainted with Lady Easy, before the discovery is made that she is the first pure and sensible woman that has been represented in a comedy, since a world of time. There is good honest love, human weaknesses, and noble triumphs over them, in this piece. If Mr. Pope sneered at the author as a "dunce," which he was not, Mr. Pope's neighbor, Horace Walpole, has registered him rightly as a "gentleman," and traced his great success in describing gentlemen, to the circumstance of his constant and familiar intercourse with that portion of "society."

In this piece, there is the most perfect of Cibber's beaux, written for his own acting; and it is to be observed, that as time progressed and fashion changed, so did he observe the progress, and in his costume illustrate the change. Lord Foppington is a different man from Sir Novelty Fashion; my lord *does* make love to a lady. With a respectful leer, he stares full in her face, draws up his breath, and cries, "Gad, you're handsome!" He is married, too, and has just sufficient regard for his wife to wish himself sunburnt if he does not prefer her to his estate. He talks French enough to cite an *à la* what d'ye call it; has Horace enough at his memory's ends to show his breeding, by an apt quotation; and evidences his gentlemanly feeling, albeit a *fine*-gentlemanly feeling, on witnessing the happy union of the two wayward lovers,—Lord Morelove and Lady Betty Modish,—by the very characteristic exclamation;—"Stap by breath, if ever I was better pleased since my first entrance into human nature!"

The example of comparative purity, set in this piece, was not immediately followed; but for that, Cibber is not to blame. The "Careless Husband" was produced in 1704, and nearly seventy years elapsed before the period when Garrick positively refused to pollute the boards of Drury Lane, by reproducing thereon, on Lord Mayors' Days, one of the most filthy of the filthy plays of Ravenscroft. The critics of Cibber's time were unreasonable. Because he was sometimes an adapter, they called him an adapter always; and the reviewers, sick, sorry, nay maddened at his success, declared of his most original comedy, that it was "not his own." But they never had the wit to discover whence he had stolen it.

He took the adverse criticism with philosophy and good humor, —as he took most things. By the last, he once saved ten shillings a week of his salary. Rich announced the intended reduction to him, with the remark, that even then he would have as much as Goodman ever had,—whose highest salary was forty shillings a week. "Aye!" said Cibber, laughing, "and Goodman was forced to go on the highway, to help him to live!" To save Colley from the same desperate course, Rich made no reduction in his salary.

We obtain from Croker's *Boswell*, an instance of Cibber's care in perfecting a piece, and his readiness in adapting passing incidents to suit his purpose. Mrs. Brett, the divorced Countess of Macclesfield, and long thought to be the mother of Savage, the poet, was the second wife of that Colonel Brett, whose opinion as to what would best please the town was eagerly sought after by authors and actors. His first wife, a great leader of fashion, had taken the handsome fellow from the hands of bailiffs, married him, and ultimately left him a wealthy widower. For the taste and judgment of the second Mrs. Brett, Cibber had the highest respect; and he consulted her on every scene of the "Careless Husband," as he wrote it. At some one of these consultations, he probably heard of the too great civility of the Colonel to his wife's maid, both of whom, Mrs. Brett once found fast asleep in two chairs. The lady was satisfied to leave token of her presence, by casting her lace handkerchief over her husband's neck. Of the otherwise painful incident she never took any notice; and let us hope that the Colonel profited by the silent rebuke, as Sir Charles Easy did. However this may be, Cibber incorporated the incident into his play, where it heightens the interest of one of the most interesting scenes.

Cibber was essentially a comic actor. His Richard partook very much of the manner of his Sir Novelty Fashion; and his "A horse! a horse!" used to excite the hilarity of his audience. He avows, gracefully enough, that his want of a strong and full voice soon cut short his hopes of making any figure in tragedy. He adds, with some conceit, and more affected modesty, "I have been many years since convinced, that whatever opinion I might have of my own judgment or capacity to amend the palpable errors that I saw our tragedians most in favor to commit, yet the auditors who would have been sensible of such amendments (could I have made them) were so very few, that my best endeavor would have been but an unavailing labor, or what is yet worse, might have appeared, both to our actors and to many auditors, the vain mistake of my own self-conceit; for so strong, so very near indispensable, is that one article of voice, in the forming of a good tragedian, that an actor may want any other qualification whatsoever, and yet will have a better chance for applause than he will ever have, with all the skill in the world, if his voice is not equal to it." Colley admirably explains this, by adding, . . "I say, for *applause* only;—but applause does not always stay for, nor always follow, intrinsic merit. Applause will frequently open, like a young hound upon a wrong scent: and a majority of auditors, you know, are generally composed of babblers, that are profuse of their voices, before there is any thing on foot that calls for them. Not, but I grant, to lead, *or mislead, the many*, will always stand in some rank of a necessary merit; yet, when I say a good tragedian, I mean one, in opinion of whose real merit the best judges would agree."

Cibber is so perfect as a critic, he so thoroughly understands the office, and so intelligibly conveys his opinions, that it were well if all gentlemen who may hereafter aspire to exercise the critical art, were compelled to study his *Apology* as medical students are to become acquainted with their *Celsus*. No one should be admitted to practice theatrical criticism who has not got by *heart* Cibber's descriptions of Betterton and Mrs. Oldfield; or who fail on their being examined as to their proficiency in the *Canons of Colley*.

Then, if there be one circumstance more than another for which Cibber merits our affectionate regard, it is for the kindly nature with which he tempers justice, and the royal generosity which he displays in attributing certain alleged excellencies in his own acting, to his careful study of the acting of others. If Cibber played Sparkish and Sir Courtly Nice with applause, it was entirely owing, so he nobly avows, to the ideas and impressions he had received from Mountfort's acting of those characters. Although his Richard was full of defects, yet he attracted the town by it. He assigns this attraction to the fact of his attempting to reproduce the style and method of one of the greatest of *Richards*, —Sandford.

While praising others he is ever ready to disparage himself; and he as heartily ridicules his insufficient voice, his meagre person, and his pallid complexion, as any enemy might have done for him. He exalts the spirit, ease, and readiness of Vanbrugh, and denounces the puerility and frothy stage-language of his own earlier dramas, accepting heartily Congreve's judgment on "Love's Last Shift," which "had in it a great many things that were like wit, that in reality were *not* wit." He courageously pronounces the condemnation of his "Love in a Riddle," to be the just judgment of an enlightened audience. In the casting of a play, Colley was contented to take any part left to him, after the other great men had picked, chosen, rejected, and settled for themselves; and a couple of subordinate characters in the " Pilgrim" were as readily undertaken by him and as carefully acted as his Richard, Sir Francis, or Master Slender.

To his own alteration of Shakspeare's "Richard III," he alludes with some diffidence. There is no trace of self-complacency in his remarks. Colley's adversaries, however, have denounced him for this act as virulently as if he had committed a great social crime. But whatever may be said as to our old friend's "mangling of Shakspeare," the piece which he so mangled has ever since kept the stage, and it is Cibber's and not Shakspeare's "Richard" which is acted by many of our chief players who have the coolness, at the same time, to protest that their reverence for Shakspeare's text is a pure homage rendered to a divine inspiration.

There were actors of Cibber's days who disliked to play villains like Richard, lest the audience should mistake the counterfeit for the real character. But if people thought Cibber vicious because he played a vicious fellow to the life, he took it as a compliment. His voice was certainly too weak and piping for tragedy, but as he philosophically remarks, "If the multitude were not in a roar, to see me in Cardinal Wolsey, I could be sure of them in Alderman Fondlewife. If they hated me in Iago, in Sir Fopling they took me for a fine gentleman. If they were silent at Syphax, no Italian Eunuch was more applauded than I when I sung in Sir Courtly. If the morals of Esop were too grave for them, Justice Shallow was as simple and as merry an old rake as the wisest of our young ones could wish me."

Cibber had a fine perception of the good and the true. That the "Beggars' Opera" should beat "Cato" by a run of forty nights does not induce him to believe that any man would be less willing to be accounted the author of the tragedy than of the opera, the writer of which, he says, with some humor: "I knew to be an honest, good-natured man, and who, when he had descended to write more like one in the cause of virtue, had been as unfortunate as others of that class."

Colley had quite as just a perception of the different value of fair and unfair criticism. Of theatrical criticism, in the proper sense of the word, there was, in those days, none. But this lack of effective criticism was not caused by incapacity for the task on the part of writers; as may be seen in the admirable critical sketches in Cibber's "Life." Indeed, the capability existed from a remote period,—a fact acknowledged by those who have read Sir Thomas Overbury's finished summary of the character of an "Actor."

In place of criticism, however, there was a system of assault by the means of unfounded reports. *Mist's Journal* was foremost in attacking Cibber and his colleagues, but "they hardly ever hit upon what was *really* wrong in us," says Colley, who took these would-be damaging paragraphs, founded upon hearsay, with perfect indifference. Wilks and Booth were much more sensitive, and preferred that public answer should be made; but Cibber, secure, perhaps too secure, he says, in his contempt for such writers, would not consent to this. "I know of but one way to silence authors of that stamp," he says, "which was, to grow insignificant and good for nothing, and then we should hear no more of them. But while we continued in the prosperity of pleasing others, and were not conscious of having deserved what they said of us, why should we gratify the little spleen of our enemies, by wincing to it, or give them fresh opportunities to dine upon any reply they might make to our publicly taking notice of them?"

Cibber cared not for *Mist's Journal* while such a man as Sheffield, Duke of Buckingham, made a friend of him. To this Duke, a dull Earl once expressed his opinion that Mr. Cibber was not sufficiently "good company" for his grace. "He is good enough for me," said the Duke; "but I can believe that he would not suit *you*." A peer who, at least, had wit enough to enjoy Quin's society, had the ill-manners to say, "What a pity it is, Mr. Quin, you are an actor!" "Why," said ever-ready James, "what would you have me be?—A lord?" Cibber, like Quin, was proud of his vocation. Colley originated nearly eighty characters during his career, from 1691 to his retirement in 1733. Among them are the grand old fops, the crafty or the inane old men, the dashing soldier, and the impudent lackey. In tragedy, he was nearly always wrong. Of middle size, fair complexion, and with a shrill voice, apt to crack, and therefore to make him ridiculous in serious parts, he was, of "shape, a little clumsy," says one sketcher of his character,—while, "his shape was finely proportioned," is the account of a second. Mr. Urban says that when Cibber had to represent ridiculous humor, there was a mouth in every nerve, and he was eloquent, though mute. "His attitudes were pointed and exquisite; his expression was stronger than painting; he was beautifully absorbed by the character, and demanded and monopolized attention; his very extravagances were colored with propriety." That the public highly appreciated him is clear from the enthusiasm with which they hailed his occasional returns to the stage, between 1733 and 1745, when he finally withdrew, after acting Pandulph in his "Papal Tyranny." His Shallow, in those occasional days, was especially popular. "His transition from asking the price of ewes, to trite but grave reflections on mortality, was so natural, and attended by such an unmeaning roll of his small pig's-eyes, that perhaps no actor was ever superior in the conception and execution of such solemn insignificancy."

The general idea of Cibber has been fixed by the abuse and slander of Pope. In the dissensions of these two men, Cibber had the advantage of an adversary who keeps his temper while he sharpens his wit, and maintains self-respect while courteously crushing his opponent; but even Pope, who so hated Cibber, could praise the "Careless Husband;" and a man, lauded by Pope, who detested him; by Walpole, who despised players; and by Johnson, who approved of his "Apology," must have been superior to many of his contemporaries. He wrote the best comedy of his time, was the only adapter of Shakspeare's plays whose adaptation survives—to show his superiority, if not over the original poet, at least over all other adapters; and of all borrowers from the French, not one reaped such honor and profit as he did by his "Nonjuror," which also still lives in "The Hypocrite." Of all English managers, he was the most successful and prosperous—only to be approached in later days by Garrick. Of all English actors, he is the only one who was ever promoted to the laureateship, or elected a member of White's Club. None laughed louder than he did at the promotion, or at those friends of his to whom it gave unmixed dissatisfaction. If a sarcasm was launched at him from the stage, on this account, he was the first to recognize it, by his hilarity, in the boxes. Further, when necessity compelled him to plead in person in a suit at the bar, his promptitude, eloquence, and modest bearing, crowned by success, demonstrated what he might have accomplished, had he been destined to wear the wig and gown. To sum up all—after more than forty years of labor, not unmixed by domestic troubles, he retired, with an ample fortune, to enjoy which he had nearly a quarter of a century before him. Such a man was sure to be both hated and envied—though only by a few.

Of Cibber's being elected to White's Club House, Davies sneeringly remarks:—" and so, I suppose, might any man be who wore good clothes, and paid his money when he lost it. He fared most sumptuously with Mr. Arthur (the proprietor), and his wife, and gave a trifle for his dinner. After he had dined, when the clubroom door was opened, and the laureate was introduced, he was saluted with the loud and joyous acclamation of 'Oh, King Coll! come in, King Coll! Welcome, King Colley!' And this kind of gratulation," adds Davies, " Mr. Victor thought was very gracious and very honorable!" Considering the time, about 1733, such a greeting had nothing offensive in it. If there had been, Cibber was just the man to resent it, at the sore cost of the offender, whether the latter were Chesterfield or Devonshire, Cholmondeley or Rockingham, Sir John Cope, Mrs. Oldfield's General Churchill, or, the last man likely to be so audacious—Bubb Doddington himself.

Among them all, Colley kept his own to the last. A short time before that last hour arrived, Horace Walpole hailed him, on his birthday, with a good morrow, and "I am glad sir, to see you looking so well." "Egad, sir," replied the old gentleman—all diamonded, and powdered, and dandified, " at eighty-four, it's well for a man that he can look at all." Therein lay one point of Cibber's character,—the making the best of circumstances.

And now he crosses Piccadilly, and passes through Albemarle Street, slowly, but cheerfully, with an eye and a salutation for any pretty woman of his acquaintance, and a word for any " good fellow" whose purse he has lightened, or who has lightened his, at dice or whist. And so he turns into the adjacent square, and as his servant closes the door, after admitting him, neither of them wots that the master has passed over the threshold for the last time, a living man.

In December, 1757, I read in contemporary publications, that there "died at his house in Berkeley Square, Colley Cibber, Esq., Poet Laureate." The year of his death was as eventful as that of his birth. In its course, Byng was shot, and Calmet died; the Duke of Newcastle became prime minister, Clive won the battle of Plassy, and the Duke of Cumberland surrendered Hanover and a confederate army to the French, by the treaty of Closter-seven. Within Cibber's era the Stuart had gone, Nassau had been, and the House of Brunswick had succeeded. This house was never more unpopular than at the time of Cibber's death, for one of its sons had permanently tarnished his military fame; but great as the public indignation was at the convention of Closter-seven, there was a large fraction of the London population, at least, who ceased to think of it, while Colley Cibber was carried to sleep with kings and heroes, in Westminster Abbey. The general conclusion arrived at, seems to have been that he was a well-abused man, who would speedily be forgotten.

To this, it may be replied, that in spite of the abuse, often little merited, he was an eminently successful man throughout life; and accomplished a career, achieved (and scattered) a fortune, and built up a fame which will always render him an object of interest.

A little too careless, perhaps; rather too much given to gambling and philandering; somewhat more than might be of the young beau about him, even in his old days, when, however, he was happy and resigned under a burden of years which few men bear with content or resignation.

At the period of Colley Cibber's death, his daughter-in-law, Mrs. Susanna Cibber, was enchanting the town with her Isabella, played to Garrick's Biron; and Barry and Mrs. Bellamy were raising melodious echoes within the walls of Covent Garden. His son, Theophilus Cibber, was hanging about town, without an engagement, and in a fine suit of clothes. Colley had, once, thus seen him, and had saluted him with a contemptuous "I pity you!" "You had better pity my tailor!" said the son, who was then challenging Garrick to play with him, the same parts alternately!

Then, while the body of the Poet Laureate was being carried to Westminster Abbey, there was, up away in a hut in then desolate Clerkenwell, and starving, Colley's own daughter, Charlotte Charke. Seven and twenty years before, she had first come upon the stage, after a stormy girlhood, and something akin to insanity strongly upon her. Her abilities were fair, her opportunities great, but her temper rendered both unavailable. She appears to have had a mania for appearing in male characters on, and in male attire off, the stage. By some terrible offence she forfeited the recognition of her father, who was otherwise of a benevolent disposition; and friendless, she fought a series of battles with the world, and came off in all more and more damaged.

She starved with strollers, failed as a grocer in Long Acre, became bankrupt as a puppet-show proprietor in James Street, Haymarket; remarried, became a widow a second time, was plunged into deeper ruin, thrown into prison for debt, and released only by the subscriptions of the lowest, but not least charitable, sisterhood of Drury Lane. Assuming male attire, she hung about the theatres for casual hire, went on the tramp with itinerants, hungered daily, and was weekly cheated, but yet kept up such an appearance that an heiress fell in love with her, who was reduced to despair when Charlotte Charke revealed her story, and abandoned the place.

Her next post was that of valet to an Irish Lord, forfeiting which, she and her child became sausage-makers, but could not obtain a living; and then Charlotte Charke cried " Coming, coming, sir!" as a waiter at the King's Head Tavern, Mary-le-Bone. Thence she was drawn by an offer to make her manager of a company of strolling players, with whom she enjoyed more appetite than means to appease it. She endured sharp distress, again and again; but was relieved by an uncle, who furnished her with funds, with which she opened a tavern in Drury Lane, where, after a brief career of success, she again became bankrupt. To the regular stage she once more returned, under her brother Theophilus, at the Haymarket; but the Lord Chamberlain closed the house, and Charlotte Charke took to working the wires of Russell's famous puppets in the Great Room, still existing in Brewer Street. There was a gleam of good fortune for her; but it soon faded away, and then for nine wretched years this clever, but most wretched of women, struggled frantically for bare existence, among the most wretched of strollers, with whom she endured unmitigated misery.

And yet Cibber's erring and hapless daughter contrived to reach London, where, in 1755, she published her remarkable autobiography, the details of which make the heart ache, in spite of the small sympathy of the reader for this half-mad creature. On the profits of this book she was enabled to open, as *Landlord*, a tavern at Islington; but, of course, ruin ensued; and in a hut, amid the cinder heaps and worse refuse in the desolate fields, she found a refuge, and even wrote a novel, on a pair of bellows in her lap, by way of desk! Here she lived, with a squalid handmaiden, a cat, dog, magpie, and monkey. Humbled, disconsolate, abandoned, she readily accepted from a publisher who visited her, £10 for her manuscript. This was at the close of the year 1755, and I do not meet with her again till 1759, two years after her father's death, when she played Marplot, in the "Busy Body," for her own benefit, at the Haymarket, with this advertisement:—" As I am entirely dependent on chance for a subsistence, and desirous of settling into business, I humbly hope the town will favor me on the occasion, which, added to the rest of their indulgences, will be ever gratefully acknowledged by their truly obliged and obedient servant, Charlotte Charke."

She died on the 6th of April, 1760. Her father was then sleeping in Westminster Abbey; her brother Theophilus was at the bottom of the Irish Sea, with a shipful of Irish Peers, English players, pantomimists, and wire-dancers; and her sister-in-law, Susanna Cibber, was playing Juliet to Garrick's Romeo, and approaching the time when she was to be carried to Westminster also.

Cibber had other daughters besides that audacious Charlotte, who is said to have once given imitations of her father on the stage; to have presented a pistol at, and robbed him on the highway, and to have smacked his face with a pair of soles out of her own basket. Again may it be said, happy are the women who have no histories! Let us part kindly with this poor woman's father,—a man who had many virtues, and whose vices were the fashions of his time. Of him, a writer has sarcastically remarked, that he praised only the dead, and was forever attacking his contemporaries! He who refrained from evil-speaking against those who could no longer defend themselves, and who flung the shafts of his wit and satire only at those who had tongues wherewith to reply, was in that much a true and honest fellow. "Mr. Cibber, I take my leave of you with some respect!" It is none the less for the satire of the "Craftsman," who ordered the players to go into mourning for the defunct manager; the actresses to wear black capuchins, and the men of the company "dirty shirts!"

## CHAPTER III.

ENGLAND AND IRELAND.

THE season 1757-8 was the last of the series during which Barry opposed Garrick. At the close of it, Spranger proceeded to Dublin, taking with him from Drury Lane, versatile Woodward, to retain whom Garrick would not increase his salary.

At Drury, Garrick brought out Home's "Agis," with a cast including himself, Mossop, and Mrs. Cibber; Mrs. Pritchard and Mrs. Yates! The piece failed notwithstanding. Walpole would not praise it, and the angry author would never speak, or even bow to him, afterwards. Gray compared this piece to an antique statue which Home had painted white and red, and dressed in a negligée, made by a York mantua-maker! Other critics found in "Agis," Charles I. treacherously dealt with by the Scots, whereby the author had intended to punish his nation for its bigotry with regard to the drama generally, and "Douglas" in particular. Walpole added that Home was a goose for writing a second tragedy at all, after having succeeded so well with the first. It was unfortunate for this critic that "Agis" was written *before* "Douglas," though it followed in succession of representation.

Murphy, who had been a student at St. Omer's, a clerk in a city bank, an unsuccessful actor, and a political writer; who, moreover, was refused a call to the bar by the benchers of the Temple and Gray's Inn, on the ground of his having been a player! but who was admitted by the less bigoted benchers of Lincoln's Inn,—feeling his way towards comedy illustrative of character, by farces descriptive of foibles, very humorously satirized the quidnuncs who then abounded, in his "Upholsterer, or What Next?" in which Garrick acted Pamphlet, as carefully as he did Ranger or King Lear.

But Garrick's chief concern was to replace Woodward, and in this he as nearly succeeded as he could expect, by engaging an

Irish actor, O'Brien, who, in the early part of 1758-9 made his appearance as Captain Brazen, and, by the graceful way in which he drew his sword, charmed all who were not aware that his father was a fencing master. He exulted in light comedy and young tragic lovers, for half a dozen years, after which he became the hero of a romance in life, and began to be ashamed of his calling.

The great incident of the season was the acting of Anthony, by Garrick, to the Cleopatra of Mrs. Yates, but they gained even more laurels as Zamti and Mandane in the "Orphan of China," a tragedy, wherein small matters are handled in a transcendental style. But Mandane lifted Mrs. Yates to an equality with Mrs. Cibber; and Walpole, who spoke of Murphy, sneeringly, as a "writing actor," did him the justice to add that he was "very good company."

Then, Foote played Shylock! Wilkinson delighted everybody by his imitations, save the actors whom he mimicked, and Garrick took the "Pupille" of the Gallo-Irish Fagan, and polished it into the pretty little comedietta, the "Guardian," in which his Heartly showed what a man of genius could make of so small a part. Mozeen, who had left the law for the stage, found a bright opportunity for Miss Barton in his "Heiress;" and Dr. Hill showed the asinine side of his character by describing his farce of the "Route" as by "a person of honor!"

> "For physic and farces, his equal there scarce is;
> His farces are physic, his physic a farce is!"

So wrote Garrick of Hill, who was a clever man, but one who lacked tact and judgment, and got buffeted by men who had not a tithe of his zeal and industry. His chief defect lay in his intolerable conceit.

Dodsley's "Cleone," rejected by Garrick, became the distinction of the Covent Garden season of 1758-9. Ross played Sifroy, and Mrs. Bellamy the heroine. As a counter-attraction, Garrick essayed Marplot, in vain. "Cleone" is a romantic tragedy. The time is that of the Saracenic invasion of the south of France, and the story bears close resemblance to the legend of St. Genevieve, where a faithful young wife and mother suffers under unmerited charges of treason to her absent husband and her home. The author extended his drama from three acts to five, at the suggestion of Pope. Dr. Johnson subsequently looked upon it as the noblest effort made since the time of Otway! and Lord Chesterfield contributed advice which shows that stage-French was not of the best quality in those days. "You should instruct the actors," he said, "not to mouth out the *oy* in the name of Sifroy as though they were crying *oysters.*" "People," writes Gray to Mason, " who despised 'Cleone' in manuscript, went to see it, and confess '*they cried so!*'" Dodsley, after some flatness, "piled the agony," skilfully, and Mrs. Bellamy made hearts ache and eyes weep, for many successive glorious and melancholy nights.

The stage lost Mrs. Macklin this year, such an "old woman" as it was not to see again till the period of Mrs. Davenport. In October, 1759, too, Theophilus Cibber satisfied people that he was not born to be hanged. With Lord Drogheda and his son, Harlequin Mattocks, Miss Wilkinson the wire-dancer, and a ship-load of frippery, he was crossing the Irish Sea from Parkgate to Dublin, when the vessel was caught in a gale, and went down with all on board. Such was the end of a fair player and a sad rogue. Somewhere off the Scottish coast, whither the ship had been blown, perished Ancient Pistol, and the original George Barnwell. His sire, wife, and sister bore the calamity which had fallen upon him, with philosophical equanimity.

On the retirement of Barry from London, Garrick travelled abroad, for a year, to recruit his health. All the intervening time, till Barry returned, has the appearance of a season of truce. No great tragic actor arose to seize the wreath of either of the absent tragedians, though the town was seduced from its respective allegiances, for a moment, by the advent and bright promise of young Powell; and Walpole was eager to recognize a greater than Garrick in the aspiring city clerk.

Walpole was accustomed to describe Garrick as a mere machine, in whom the power to express Shakspeare's words with propriety, was absurdly held to be a merit! "On the night of Powell's first appearance, the audience," says Walpole, "not content with clapping, stood up and shouted." Walpole adds, that Powell had been clerk to Sir Robert Ladbroke, and "so clever in business, that his master would have taken him in as a partner; but he had an impulse for the stage. His figure is fine, and voice most sonorous, as they say, but I wait for the rebound of his fame, and till I can get in, but at present all the boxes are taken for a month." Walpole suppresses the fact that Garrick had not only selected Powell as his substitute, in his absence, but had carefully instructed him in the part of Philaster, and thereby helped him to the triumphant position which the young actor, then twenty-eight years of age, held during the first of his few seasons, from 1763 to 1768, the year of poor Powell's death.

No new tragic poet of eminence now arose, nor did any old one increase his reputation. Home is supposed to have been thinking of the siege of Berwick when, in his "Siege of Aquileia," he portrayed our Edward under the figure of Maximin. Brookes's boasted purity of language and sentiment in *his* "Earl of Essex" was playfully crushed by Johnson. "Who rules o'er freemen should himself be free," was a line cited for its beauty, by Sheridan, the actor. "Who drives fat oxen should himself be fat," was the stupid comment of the lexicographer.

Farce flourished within this period,—supplied by the Rev. Mr. Townley, Garrick, Foote, Colman, and Murphy, the last of whom increased his fame by such comedies as the bustling, and yet monotonously bustling, "All in the Wrong," and the "Way to Keep Him." The authors of this period sought to correct faults and not to laugh at them. This, perhaps, gives a didactic turn to the plays of Murphy and Mrs. Sheridan, which renders them somewhat heavy when compared with the comedies of those who were rather among the wits, than the teachers, of their days. But a new brilliancy, too, was to be found in the later writers. Colman's "Jealous Wife," in which Garrick and Mrs. Pritchard were the Mr. and Mrs. Oakley, and the "Clandestine Marriage," principally Colman's, but in which Garrick had a share, were full of this brilliancy. With the exception of Hoadley's "Suspicious Husband," no modern comedy had such success as these. Every great actor still tries Mr. Oakley, and the noblest of old beaux has been the heritage only of the most finished of our comedians, from King, with whom it originated, down to Farren, with whom it seems to have died.

While the insolence of servants and the weaknesses of masters were satirized in "High Life below Stairs," a piece which George

Selwyn was the gladder to see, as he was weary of low life above stairs—the disinterestedness of Irish wooers was asserted in Macklin's "Love á la Mode;" rascality, generally, was pummelled in Foote's "Minor;" novel-reading was proved to be perilous, in "Polly Honeycomb;" sharpers were exposed in Reed's "Register Office;" Platonic love was shown to be not without its dangers, in "The Deuce is in Him," and so on, with other pieces, than which none raised more laughter than the "Mayor of Garratt," in which Weston exhibited in Jerry Sneak, the type of hen-pecked husbands, and Foote in Matthew Mug, a portrait of the Duke of Newcastle. Then Whitehead, in his "School for Lovers," wrote a dull play on society to show that society was dull; and Mrs. Sheridan, in the "Discovery," pointed to the absurdity of young married people being unhappy. Opera was making way at both houses, but especially at Covent Garden, where, with a few other novelties of no note, Arne's "Artaxerxes," superbly set, was as superbly sung, by Tenducci, Beard, and Arne's famous pupil, Miss Brent. Bickerstaffe's "Love in a Village" followed, warbled by Beard and Miss Brent, as Hawthorne and Rosetta, and made joyous by Shuter's Justice Woodcock. The same writer's "Maid of the Mill" succeeded, in which Mattocks played Lord Aimworth; Beard, Giles; and Miss Brent, Polly, the latter with a joyousness that never dreamed of the coming penury and hunger.

Managers, however, catered drolly for the public. Thus, on the 12th of October, 1758, when Mossop acted Richard III., Signor Grimaldi relieved the tragedy, by dancing comic dances between the acts! Garrick, nevertheless, was not idle. During Barry's absence, David added to his original characters, Lovemore, in "The Way to Keep Him," Æmilius ("Siege of Aquileia"), Oakley ("Jealous Wife"), Sir John Dorilant ("School for Lovers"), Farmer ("Farmer's Return"), Alonzo ("Elvira"), and Sir Anthony Branville ("Discovery"). In the last, he exhibited a new style, in a new character. "He seemed utterly to have extinguished his natural talents, assuming a dry, stiff manner, with an immovable face, and thus extracted from his pedantic object (who assumed every passion, without showing a spark of any in his action or features) infinite entertainment." Barry, meanwhile in Ireland, found that Sheridan had had a checkered time of it there. At one period, a course of prosperity; at another, he was the victim of gentlemen, from whose rude wooing he protected his actresses. The wooers called him "scoundrel-player." Sheridan answered that he was "as good a gentleman" as those who called him scoundrel; and, consequently, his life was not safe from these ruffians, who interrupted the performances, but against whom the collegians took side with the player. It was not till some blood was spilled, and the Lord Chief Justice, Ward, had condemned a young savage, named Kelly, to pay £500 fine and suffer three months' imprisonment, that peace was restored. At this trial, Kelly's counsel remarked, he had seen a gentleman-soldier and a gentleman-tailor, but had never seen a gentleman-player. "Sir," said Sheridan, with dignity, "I hope you see one, now."

Sheridan lost money, year after year, by paying excessive salaries to Woodward, the Macklins, and to operatic companies. Macklin and Mossop, together, nearly drove Sheridan mad; he was glad to be rid of both, and to find greater attraction in the beautiful Mrs. Woffington who used to petition for kisses, once a year, and must have found little difficulty in procuring what she asked for, on her benefit nights.

At that time, nearly one hundred persons in the Lord Lieutenant's household claimed free admission, the government allowing £100 a year, as the price for which it was purchased! But prosperity attended Sheridan's management, nevertheless, till he neglected the stage for claret, toasts, songs, and aristocratic fellowship. Therewith came a quarrel with his public. The latter had *encored* a speech delivered by Digges, in "Mahomet," which contained a passage applicable, in a hostile sense, to the vice-regal court. Sheridan forbade Digges repeating this speech a second time, on the next representation, and Digges declining to do so, when the audience demanded it, the latter, in inconceivable rage, pulled the interior of the house to pieces, destroyed all the properties they could reach, broke up the wooden fittings, and flinging the box-doors upon them, set fire to the whole mass! The building was rescued with difficulty.

After a time it was repaired, and Sheridan let it to Victor and Snowden, who in the season of 1754-5 engaged Barry and Miss Nossiter; and it is to be remarked that of all the characters he played, Macbeth was the most, and Henry V. the least, attractive. Romeo stood midway in profit, between those two. Mossop was the hero of the succeeding season, with profit to the management, after which Sheridan resumed the control; but not till he had been compelled to undergo a great humiliation. Fearing for the safety of his house, he consented to make public apology for his previous conduct to the management, and Sheridan was then patronized by the public, till Barry and Woodward, in October, 1758, opened a new theatre in Crow Street, and divided the patronage and the passions of the town. At Crow Street, there were Barry, young Mrs. Dancer, whom he afterwards married, Mossop, King, Woodward, and others. At Smock Alley Mrs. Abington alone was a sufficient counter-attraction. But when Mossop passed over to manage Smock Alley, and the Countess of Brandon patronized him, in return for his permitting her to cheat him at cards, and Mrs. Bellamy joined the same troop, then Barry was put on his mettle; he secured Mrs. Abington and Shuter; and the town became as divided, and as furious and unreasonable, as if they were at issue on some point of religious belief. Mrs. Bellamy was arrested by a partisan of the adverse house, simply that she might be prevented from acting at the other; and the players were so often seduced from their engagements by the respective managers, that the performers were sometimes called to go on the stage of one theatre, when they were actually dressing at another! If Mossop choose "Othello" for his benefit one night, Barry was sure to have it for his own, on the same, or the following evening. In short, the rival managers went on ruining each other. They exerted themselves, however, indefatigably, Barry playing even Macheath, and other operatic characters. He and Mossop formed extravagant engagements with every great actor, save Garrick, whom they could win over, down to clever dogs, and intelligent monkeys. At the end of a seven years' struggle, Barry found that Dublin could not support two theatres, and leaving Mossop in possession of the field, he returned to London, having ruined himself and Woodward, and lost every thing he possessed but his gentle humor, his suavity, his plausibility, and his hopes.

As a sample of Dublin theatrical life, in Barry's time, I cite the following passage from Gilbert's *History of Dublin*, and therewith close the subject for the present. "Dublin was kept in a state of commotion by the partisans of the rival theatres. As already noticed, the Countess of Brandon, with her adherents, attended constantly at Smock Alley, and would not appear at Crow Street; but Barry's tenderness in making love on the stage, at length brought the majority of the ladies to his house. Of the scenes which commonly occurred during this theatrical rivalry, on nights when some leading lady had bespoken a play, and made an interest for all parts of the house, particularly by pit and gallery tickets among her tradespeople, we have been left the following notice :—The lady of the night goes early into the box-room to receive her company. This lady had sent out pit and gallery tickets to all her tradespeople, with the threatenings of the loss of her custom if they did not dispose of them; and the concern she was under, when the time was approaching for the drawing up of the curtain, at the sight of a thin pit and galleries, introduced the following entertainment. The lady was ready to faint; and after smelling bottles were applied, she cried out, 'She was ruined and undone! She never would be able to look dear Mr. B. in the face any more, after such a shocking disappointment.' At many of these repeated lamentations, the box-keeper advanced, and said: 'I beg your ladyship will not be so disheartened; indeed, your ladyship's pit will mend, and your ladyship's galleries too, will certainly mend, before the play begins!' At which the lady cried, 'Out, you nasty flattering fellow! I tell you I'm undone, ruined and undone! that's all. But I'll be revenged. I am resolved. I'll pay off M——. I'll turn off all my saucy tradespeople to-morrow morning.'"

During Barry's absence, some excellent actors took their last farewell of the English stage. Of these I will speak in the next chapter.

## CHAPTER IV.

### RYAN, RICH, O'BRIEN.

PERHAPS the last of the players who had been contemporary with Betterton, died when Richard Ryan departed this life, at his house in Crown Court, Westminster, in August, 1760. Westminster claims him as born within the Abbey precincts, Paul's School for a pupil, and a worthy old Irish tailor for a son, of whom he was proud. Garrick confessed that Ryan's Richard was the one which, in its general features, he took as the model of his own, and Addison especially selected him to play Marcus in his "Cato."

He was but a mere boy when he first appeared with Betterton (who was playing Macbeth) as Seyton, wearing a full-bottomed wig, which would have covered two such heads as his. Between this inconvenience, and awe at seeing himself in presence of the greatest of English actors, the embarrassed boy hesitated, but the generous old actor encouraged him by a look, and young Ryan became a regularly engaged actor.

From first to last he continued to play young parts, and his Colonel Standard, in 1757, was as full of the spirit which defies age, as his Marcus, in 1713, was replete with the spirit which knows nothing of age. Easy in action, strong, but harsh of voice, careless in costume and carriage, but always earnest in his acting, he obtained and kept a place at the head of actors of the second rank, which exposed him to no ill feeling on the part of the few players who were his superiors.

Quin loved him like a brother: and it is singular that there was blood on the hands of both actors. Quin's sword dispatched aggressive Bowen and angry Williams to Hades; and Ryan, put on his defence, slew one of the vaporing ruffians of the day, to the quiet satisfaction of all decent persons.

On June 20th, 1718, the summer season at the Lincoln's Inn

Fields house had commenced with "Tartuffe." After the play, Ryan was supping at the Sun, in Long Acre; he had taken off his sword, placed it in the window, and was thinking of no harm to any one, when he saw standing before him, flushed with drink, weapon in hand, and all savagely a-thirst for a quarrel and a victim, one Kelly, whose pastime it was to draw upon strangers in coffee-houses, force them to combat, and send them home more or less marred in face or mutilated in body. Kelly stood there, not only daring Ryan, but making passes at him, which meant deadly mischief. The young actor took his sword from the window, drew it from the scabbard, and passing it through the bully's body, stretched him on the floor, with the life-blood welling from the wound. The act was so clearly one induced by self-protection, that Ryan was called to no serious account for it.

He had like to have fared worse on that later occasion, when, after playing Scipio, in "Sophonisba," he was passing home down Great Queen Street, and a pistol-shot was fired at him, by one of three or four footpads, another of whom seized his sword. In this fray his jaw was shattered. "Friend, you have killed me; but I forgive you," said Ryan, who was picked up by the watch, and committed to surgical hands, from which he issued, after long suffering, something the worse for this serious incident in his life.

Ryan was "the esteemed Ryan" of numerous patrons, and when a benefit was awarded him, while he yet lay groaning on his couch, Royalty was there to honor it, and an audience in large numbers, the receipts from whom were increased by the golden guerdons forwarded to the sufferer from absent sympathizers. Perfect recovery he never reached, but he could still portray the fury of Orestes, the feeling of Edgar, the sensibility of Lord Townley, the grief and anger of Macduff, the villany of Iago, the subtilty of Mosca, the tipsyness of Cassio, the spirit of young Harry, the airiness of Captain Plume, and the characteristics of many other parts, with great effect, in spite of increasing age, some infirmities, and a few defects and oddities.

I have already noticed how Quin, in his old days, declined any longer to play annually for Ryan's benefit, but offered him the £1,000 sterling, Quin had bequeathed to him in his will. Brave old actor! Dr. Herring, who was then Archbishop of Canterbury, had not in him a truer spirit of practical benevolence than James Quin manifested in this act to Dick Ryan—who died in 1760.

In the following year, died Rich, the father of Harlequins, in England. He has never been excelled by any of his sons, however agile the latter may have been. Rich (or Lun, as he called himself) was agile, too, but he possessed every other qualification, and his mute Harlequin was eloquent in every gesture. He made no motion, by head, hand, or foot, but something thereby was expressed intelligibly. Feeling, too, was pre-eminent with this expression; and he rendered the scene of a separation from Columbine as graceful, to use the words of Davies, as it was affecting. Not only was he thus skilled himself, but he taught others to make of silent but expressive action the interpreter of the mind; Hippisley, Nivelon, La Guerre, Arthur, and Lalause, are enumerated by Davies, as owing their mimic power to the instructions given to them by Rich, whose action was in as strict accordance with the sentiment he had to demonstrate, as that of Garrick himself. The latter, in his prologue to "Harlequin's Invasion," in which Garrick introduced a speaking Harlequin, thus alluded to the then defunct hero:—

> "But why a speaking Harlequin? 'tis wrong,
> The wits will say, to give the fool a tongue.
> When Lun appeared, with matchless art and whim,
> He gave the pow'r of speech to ev'ry limb.
> Though mask'd and mute, convey'd his quick intent,
> And told, in frolic gestures, all he meant.
> But now the motley coat, and sword of wood,
> Require a tongue, to make them understood."

To introduce the speaking Harlequin was, however, only to restore to speech one of the most loquacious fellows who ever wore motley. For, as Colman had it, poor Harlequin—

> "Once spoke,
> And France and Italy admired each joke.
> But Roundhead England, all things who curtails,
> Who cuts off monarchs' heads and horses' tails,
> By malice led, by rage and envy stung,
> Put in his mouth a gag, and tied his tongue."

Rich thought himself so much a better actor than mimic, that he was ten times happier when giving foolish instruction to a novice training for Hamlet, than when he was marshalling his corps of pantomimists, and admirably teaching them to say every thing, and yet be silent.

A man like John Rich, of course had his little jealousies. He was angry when the combination of Garrick and Quin filled his house and treasury, and when the season of 1746–7 yielded him a profit of nearly £9,000, to which his wand of Harlequin had contributed little or nothing. He was wont to look at the packed audience, through a hole in the green curtain, and then murmur, "Ah! you are there, are you? much good may it do you!"

The avidity of the old public, however, to witness harlequinades, was even more remarkable than that of the present day. Then, pantomimes went through, not merely a part of one, but several seasons. Theobald's "Harlequin Sorcerer," which had often filled "Lincoln's Inn Fields," was even more attractive at "Covent Garden," above a quarter of a century later. The company assembled at mid-day, and sometimes broke the doors open, unless they were opened to them, by three o'clock, and so took the house by storm. Those who could not gain admittance, went over to Drury Lane, but Garrick found them without heart for tragedy; the grown-up masters and misses had been deprived of their puppet show and rattle, and were sulky accordingly.

Booth, Wilks, and Cibber, came under the somewhat dirty censure of Hogarth, who ridiculed them in a well-known unsavory engraving, for producing Harlequin Jack Sheppard. Booth tolerated these harlequinades, and Garrick acted in like fashion; remarking—"If you won't come to Lear and Hamlet, I must give you Harlequin;" and he perhaps gave them the best the stage ever had, save Rich, in Woodward, who had worn the party-colored jacket before, but who, in "Queen Mab," and in speaking Harlequins, exhibited an ability, the effect of which is illustrated in a contemporary print, wherein you see all the great actors of the day in one scale, and Harlequin Woodward in the other, who makes them kick the beam.

From the very first, however, the poets made protest against the invasion of the stage by foreign dancers and home-born Harlequins; and Cibber quotes Rowe as complaining, or asking, in a prologue to one of his first plays—

"Must Shakspeare, Fletcher, and laborious Ben,
Be left for Scaramouch and Harlequin?"

One of the most curious features connected with pantomime, and which certainly dignified Harlequin, was the assumption of that character by such sterling actors as Woodward and O'Brien. The *London Magazine*, a century ago, wished "that so eminent an actor as Woodward might never be permitted to put on the fool's coat again." Rich thought himself, indeed, as good an actor as they; but, though the son of a gentleman, he was illiterate: sometimes said turbot for *turban*; talked of *larning* Wilkinson to be a player; told Signora Spiletta always to lay her emphasis " on the *adjutant*;" and said to Tate, " You should see *me* play Richard!"

Nevertheless, John Rich was supreme, in his own particular line. His " catching the butterfly," and his " statue scene" were salient portions of his Harlequin, which people went to see because of their excellence. Still finer was that in which Harlequin is hatched from the egg by the heat of the sun. Jackson calls it a masterpiece in dumb show; " from the first chipping of the egg, his receiving of motion, his feeling of the ground, his standing upright, to his quick harlequin trip round the empty shell, through the whole progression, every limb had its tongue, and every motion a voice which spoke with most miraculous organ to the understandings and sensations of the observers."

There was this difference between Rich and Garrick in their conduct towards authors. Garrick would decline with courteous commendation a manuscript he had never looked at; but Rich kept a drawer full of such copy, and when an author demanded his piece, Rich would tell him to take which he liked best, he would probably find it better than his own.

Rich's good humor seldom failed him, though he was warm of temper; he was less witty than Foote, but he was of a better nature. One night, during his proprietorship of Covent Garden, a man, rushing down the gallery, fell over into the pit. He was nearly killed; but Rich paid all the medical and other expenses, and the poor fellow, when his broken bones were whole again, called on the manager and expressed his gratitude for the kindness shown to him. "Well, sir," said Rich, "you must never think of coming into the pit, in that manner, again!" and, to prevent it, Rich gave him a free admission.

We should altogether misjudge Rich if we looked on him as the founder of the modern, miserable, purposeless, storyless harlequinade. This sort of entertainment deteriorated soon after his death. In 1782, Walpole saw the pantomime of "Robinson Crusoe," and his comment is, "how unlike the pantomimes of Rich, which are full of wit, and coherent, and carried on a story." Rich left Covent Garden to his son-in-law, Beard, the vocalist. Beard's first wife was Lady Henrietta Herbert, daughter of the Earl of Waldegrave, and this match was a happy one, though Lord Wharncliffe incorrectly recorded of Beard that he was "a man of indifferent character." Beard held Covent Garden, for himself and second wife, under a not unpleasant restriction. Rich directed that the property should be sold, whenever £60,000 could be got for it; and for that handsome sum the house was, ultimately, made over to Colman, Harris, and their partners.

Beard and Lady Herbert remind me of another *mesalliance*. In the studio of Catherine Read, the portrait painter, a good deal of love-making was carried on. Here is a February morning of 1764, and a young couple, all the handsomer for a bracing-walk through the eager and nipping air, are conversing confidentially in one corner of the room while discreet Miss Read plies her work in another. The lady is Lady Susan Fox Strangways; the gentleman owns a villa at Dunstable, and is one of the airiest actors of the Theatre Royal, Drury Lane, Mr. O'Brien.

Subsequently, the lady's father, Stephen Fox, the first Earl of Ilchester, opening his post-bag, hands a letter to Lady Susan from Lady Sarah Bunbury, his daughter's dearest friend. The letter was really from O'Brien, who imitated Lady Sarah's writing. The intrigue was discovered, and the father's wrath was so overwhelming, that Lady Susan promised that the affair should proceed no further, if she were only permitted to take a last farewell. She waited a few days for this final meeting, till she became of age, when, released from lock and key, she went on foot, escorted by a lackey, to breakfast with Lady Sarah, and to call on Miss

Read by the way. In the street she sent the footman back, for a particular cap in which she was to be painted; a few moments after she was out of sight, a couple of chairmen were carrying her to Covent Garden Church, where Mr. O'Brien was waiting for her, and, the wedding ceremony being performed, the happy and audacious pair posted down to the bridegroom's villa at Dunstable. Only the night before he had played Squire Richard, in the "Provoked Husband."

This ended O'Brien's brief theatrical career of about eight years; and therewith departed from the stage the most powerful rival Woodward ever encountered upon it; the original actor of Young Clackit, in the "Guardian," Lovel, in "High Life below Stairs," Lord Trinkett, in the "Jealous Wife," Beverley, in "All in the Wrong," Colonel Tamper, in the "Deuce is in Him," &c.

In one character O'Brien must have exhibited extraordinary humor,—Sir Andrew Aguecheek. He was playing it on the 19th of October, 1763, a period when it was the custom to have two sentinels posted on either side of the stage, and one of these fellows was so overcome by Sir Andrew's comicality, that he laughed till he fell, to the infinite amusement of all who witnessed the circumstance.

O'Brien's marriage caused a sensation in the Fashionable World, and brought sorrow to some parties. On April the 9th, 1764, Walpole writes to Mann :—" A melancholy affair has happened to Lord Ilchester; his eldest daughter, Lady Susan (Strangways), a very pleasing girl, though not handsome, married herself, two days ago, at Covent Garden Church, to O'Brien, a handsome young actor. Lord Ilchester doated on her, and was the most indulgent of fathers. 'Tis a cruel blow!" Three days after, Walpole writes to Lord Hereford, "Poor Lady Susan O'Brien is in the most deplorable situation, for her Adonis is a Roman Catholic, and cannot be provided for out of his calling." Sir Francis Delaval, one of the rich amateur actors of his time, touched by her calamity, "made her a present of—what do you think!" asks Horace, "of a rich gold stuff! The delightful charity! O'Brien comforts himself, and says it will make a shining passage in his little history!"

As O'Brien had not the means whereby to live without acting, his wife's noble family thought it would be no disgrace, to *hide* the disgrace which had fallen upon it, by providing for the young couple—at the public expense. Accordingly, a grant of lands in America was procured for them, and thither they went. On Christmas Day, 1764, Charles Fox writes of his cousin, to Sir George Macartney:—" We have heard from Lady Susan since her arrival at New York. I do not think they will make much of their lands, and I fear it will be impossible to get O'Brien a place." When Charles Fox wrote this, he was about fifteen, and looked as handsome as he does in the famous picture at Holland House, which contains also the portraits of Lady Susan, who married the actor, and Lady Sarah Lennox (Bunbury), who did *not* marry the king.

The Board of Ordnance ultimately provided for O'Brien, and the player and his aristocratic wife were away between seven and eight heavy years, beyond the Atlantic. Weary of their banishment, they returned to England, without leave asked of the Board. O'Brien was not the only officer in England without leave. In the *Last Journals of Horace Walpole*, which I edited in 1858, the Journalist says:—" General Conway was laboring to reform that department (the Board of Ordnance), and had ordered all the officers under it to repair to their posts, those in America particularly, who had abandoned their duty. O'Brien received orders among the rest, to return, but he refused. Conway declared they would dismiss him. Lord and Lady Holland interposed ; but Conway was firm, and he turned out O'Brien."

Lord Ilchester, albeit ashamed of his son-in-law, was not ashamed to write to Lord North, soliciting a place for O'Brien ; but Lord North did not even reply to the letter. It is just possible that the player was a proximate cause of Fox's withdrawal from the administration, and his becoming in permanent opposition to the Court. Fox had spoken against Lord North, and the latter endeavored to conciliate him. "He weakly and timidly called him aside, and asked him if he had seen Maclean, who had got the post which had been asked for O'Brien, and who would make O'Brien his deputy ; but this Fox received with contempt."

Let me remark here, that in "blood" young O'Brien was the equal of Lady Susan. In the days of Charles I., Stephen Fox, her ancestor, was bailiff to Sir Edward Nicolas, the King's secretary, at Winterbourne, Wilts; where Stephen (not yet *Sir* Stephen), occasionally officiated as clerk of the parish. At that time the direct ancestor of our lucky actor was a member of that ancient family of those O'Briens, who generally contrived to take opposite sides in every quarrel. William O'Brien's grandfather was faithful to the cause of James II., and on the capitulation of Limerick, made his way to France, where he served in the Irish brigade, under O'Brien, Viscount Clare. That brigade, many of whose members "took to the road" in France, in order to support themselves, turned out first-rate fencing masters, who lived by teaching. Such was the father of our O'Brien, and such was the family history of the actor; and surely the descendant of King Brien of the Tributes, was of as good blood as the daughter of a house, the first worthy, that is to say fortunate member, of which was parish clerk in a Wiltshire village.

O'Brien failing to obtain a post, or to enjoy the laborious luxury of a sinecure, turned his attention to writing for the stage, and on the night of December 8, 1772, he produced two pieces—at Drury Lane, his comedy of "The Duel;" at Covent Garden his *comedietta*, "Cross Purposes." The first is an adaptation of the "Philosophe sans le savoir," in which Barry did not more affect his audience than I have seen Baptiste *ainé* do, on the French stage. "The Duel," however, failed, through the mawkish, sentimental scenes which the adapter worked in, at the suggestion of some of his noble relatives, who spoiled his play, but made him pecuniary compensation for its ill-fortune.

"Cross purposes," also an adaptation—from "Les trois frères rivaux," was more lucky. It was levelled at the follies of the day, and every one was amused by the light satire. In the first piece, Barry was sublime in his affectation of cheerfulness, on his daughter's wedding-day, while his son is engaged in a duel fought under paternal sanction. In the second, Shuter as Grub, and Quick as Consol, made the house as hilarious, as Barry, in the scenes in which he was engaged, made his audience sympathetic.

Mrs. Cibber, addressing Mrs. Woffington, in the "Dialogue in the Shades," speaks of O'Brien and Powell as the only actors of eminence who had appeared since Margaret's time. O'Brien was entirely in Woodward's line, from Mercutio to Harlequin. I collect from Genest, that after his aristocratic connections made a placeman of him, O'Brien grew ashamed of his vocation. "If we may judge from . . . . what I was told in 1803, when I resided in his neighborhood, O'Brien had, since he left the stage, wished to sink the player, and to bury in oblivion those years of his life which are the most worth being remembered—ashamed, perhaps, of a profession which is no disgrace to any one who conducts himself respectably in it, and in which to succeed, is, generally speaking, a proof of good natural abilities, and a diligent application of them —*Ex quovis ligno non fit Mercurius.* It is not everybody that can make even a moderate actor."

O'Brien left the stage after playing Squire Richard, and subsequently he became "William O'Brien, of Swinsford, County of Dorset, Esq." His wife died on the 9th of August, 1827, on which night the Haymarket company acted the "Poor Gentleman!"

Before Barry reappeared in London, the stage suffered more serious losses than these. At one, Garrick uttered a cry—as of anguish, at the falling away of the brightest jewel of the stage.

## CHAPTER V.

### SUSANNA MARIA CIBBER.

"Mrs. Cibber dead!" said Garrick, "then tragedy has died with her!" When he uttered this, on the 31st of Janury, 1766, he little knew that a young girl, named Sarah Kemble, then in her twelfth year, was a strolling actress, playing juvenile tragedy, and light opera, was reciting or singing between the acts, and was preparing herself for greatness.

Let us look back to the early time and the room over the upholsterer's shop, in King Street, Covent Garden, where Tom Arne and his sister, Susanna Maria, are engaged in musical exercises. Tom ought to have been engrossing deeds, and that fair and graceful, and pure-looking girl, to be thinking of any thing but coming out in Lampe's opera, "Amelia," the words by Carey. The old Roman Catholic upholsterer had been sorely tried by the heterodox inclinations of his children. They lived within sound of the musical echoes of the theatres, and thereof came Dr. Arne, the composer, and his sister, the great singer, the greater and ever youthful actress.

In 1732, Susanna Maria Arne appeared successfully in Lampe's serious opera, "Amelia," which was "set in the Italian manner," and brought out at what was called the "French Theatre," in the Haymarket. Miss Arne was then about twenty years of age, with a symmetry of figure and a sweetness of expression which she did not lose during the four-and-thirty years she continued on the stage. In the Venus of her early days, she was as beautiful as the Venus Popularia, whose mother was Dione, and her Psyche was as timid, touching, and inquiring, as she who charmed the gods from the threshold of Olympus.

It is not pleasant to think that on a young creature so fair, bright, pure, and accomplished,—an honest man's honest daughter, such a sorry rascal as Ancient Pistol,—Theophilus Cibber, in fact, should have boldly cast that one of his two squinting eyes, which he could bring to bear with most effect upon a lady. When, as a newly-married couple, they stood before Colley Cibber, they must have looked like Beauty and the Beast!

Beauty soon overcame the elder Cibber's antipathy. Colley could not withstand the new magic to which he was subjected; and when it was first proposed that the brilliant vocalist should become a regular actress, Colley, however much he may have shaken his head, at first, favored the design, and gave all necessary instructions to his winning, beautiful, and docile daughter-in-law. Can you not see the pair in that first floor in Russell Street? Half the morning, she has been repeating Zara, never wearied by Cibber's frequent interruptions. Perseverance was ever one of her great characteristics; and she carries herself, and sweeps by with her train, and speaks meltingly or sternly, in grief or in anger, her voice silvery and, with its modulation, under command,—a voice in the very sound of which there were smiles or tears, sunshine or storm :—all this she does, or exercises, at Colley's sole suggestions, you suppose. Not a bit of it! Susanna Cibber has a little will of her own: and she is quite right, for she has as much intellect as will, and docile as she is when she sees the value of Colley's teaching, she supports her own views when she is satisfied that these are superior to the ideas of the elderly gentleman, who, standing in an attitude for imitation, to which she opposes one of her own, lets the frown on his brow pass off into a smile, as he protests, "foregad!" that the saucy thing could impart instruction to himself.

On the 12th of January, 1736, the great attempt was made, and Mrs. Cibber came out as Zara, to the Lusignan of Milward, the Nerestan of her husband, and the Selima of Mrs. Pritchard, who had not yet reached the position which this young actress occupied at a bound, but beyond which Mrs. Pritchard was destined yet to go.

For fourteen consecutive nights, Susanna drowned houses in tears, and stirred the very depth of men's hearts, even her husband's, who was so affected that he claimed, and obtained, the doubling of the salary first agreed on for his wife. Theophilus, of course, did not keep the money; he spent it all, to his great, temporary, satisfaction. His wife's next appearance was in come dy,—Indiana ("Conscious Lovers"), where the neat simplicity of her manners, and the charm which she seemed to shed on even common-place expressions, formed a strong contrast to the more solemn but stilted dignity of her tragedy queens, the glory of which faded before the perfection of her Ophelia. For this character, her voice, musical qualities, her figure, and her inexpressibly sweet features, all especially suited her. Wilkinson states that no eloquence could paint her distressed and distracted look, when she said: "Lord, we know what we are, but know not what we may be!" Charming in all she undertook, all her critics pronounced her unapproachable in Ophelia, and through all the traditions of the stage, there is not one more abiding than that which says that Mrs. Cibber was identified with the distraught maiden. Her Juliet, Constance, Belvidera, exhibited rare merits, while as Alicia, in the mad scene, "the expression of her countenance, and the irresistible magic of her voice, thrilled to the very soul of her whole audience," says Murphy. Wilkinson was powerless when attempting to mimic the voice and expression of Mrs. Cibber. The tone, manner, and method of Garrick, Quin, Mrs. Bellamy, Mrs. Crawford (Barry), nay, even the very face of Mrs. Woffington, he could reproduce with wonderful approach to exactness. But Mrs. Cibber's excellence baffled him. He remembered her and it, but he could not do more than remember. "It is all in my mind's eye," he would say, with a sigh at his incapacity.

In fine ladies and in sprightly comedy,—save in the playful delivery of epilogues,—Mrs. Cibber comparatively failed. Among her original characters were the Lady, in "Comus," Sigismunda, Aspasia, in Johnson's "Irene," Zaphira, in "Barbarossa," and Cœlia, in Whitehead's comedy, the "School for Lovers." In these, as in all she played, I collect from various sources, that Mrs. Cibber was distinguished for unadorned simplicity, artless sensibility, harmony of voice, now sweetly plaintive, now grandly powerful, and eyes that in tender grief seemed to swim in tears; in rage, to flash with fire; in despair, to become as dead. Her beauty did not so much consist in regularity of feature as in variety and power of expression; with this, she had symmetry of form; and this, indeed, is true beauty. She preserved these gifts which age lightly touched, and to the last it was impossible to look at her figure and not think her young, or view her face and not consider her handsome.

Mrs. Cibber would, perhaps, have been one of the happiest women of her day, had she not been cursed with a husband who was no more made for her than Caliban for Miranda. Theophilus could not appreciate her but as a gold winner, and he so abused the treasure, of which he was every way unworthy, as to expose her to temptations by which that unhanged villain hoped to profit; but by yielding to which she got rid of her "most filthy bargain," lost nothing in the public esteem, and acquired a protector and a home,—neither of which she ought to have wanted. There she enjoyed all the becomingnesses of life, save one; and she continued to act with better heart, but under physical infirmities, which her physicians could not understand nor her applauding audiences believe in, till death struck her down in the very midst of her labors.

She was not only of good heart to the last, but apparently as little affected by age as by her domestic trials. She wore spectacles? Yes! I confess that much. There she sits, somewhat past fifty, at Garrick's house, spectacles on nose, reading her part of Cœlia, in the "School for Lovers." Now Cœlia is but sixteen, and some one suggests, only seeing those spectacles, that it would be better to call her at least twenty-three. Mrs. Cibber looked up smilingly through her "glasses," quietly dissented, and when the piece was acted, she played the young and gentle Cœlia with such effect, that no one present thought of Mrs. Cibber being older than the part represented her to be.

King George III. has the reputation of having killed Mrs. Cibber, indirectly. His Majesty commanded the "Provoked Wife," in which she was to play Lady Brute. Ill health, for which physicians could not account, had reduced her strength; but the Roman Catholic actress was determined to perform the duty expected from her, to that most Protestant King. But she never trod the stage again. The career which had commenced in 1732, closed in January, 1766; and in the month following all that was mortal of this once highly, but, perhaps, fatally-gifted lady, was entombed in the cloisters of Westminster Abbey, not within the edifice, like Mrs. Oldfield's, opposite Congreve's monument, but in the cloisters, whither had preceded her Aphra Behn, Mrs. Bracegirdle, and the father of the restored English stage, "Mr. Betterton, gentleman." Rather more than seven years had then elapsed since Theophilus Cibber had gone down, twelve fathoms deep, to the bottom of the Irish sea; and about the same time, short of a month or so, had gone by since Colley Cibber had been brought hither to rest in the neighborhood of defunct, but once real, kings and queens.

The voice of Mrs. Cibber, the soul of Mrs. Pritchard, and the eye of Garrick, formed a combination which in one actor would, according to Walpole, render him superior to all actors the world had seen or could see. Hitherto it has *not* been seen.

Gentle as Mrs. Cibber was, she could master Garrick himself. "She was the greatest female plague belonging to my house," he once said, with the memory on him of the strong language of Kitty Clive, and the rough thrusts of other heroines. These he could parry, but not Susanna Cibber. "Whatever her object, a new part or a new dress, she was always sure to carry her point by the acuteness of her invention, and the steadiness of her perseverance."

Her misfortunes in life brought some affronts upon her. Thus, in October, 1760, she was at Bath, with Mr. Sloper, the "protector" of whom I have spoken, and their daughter, "Miss Cibber." The whole party went to the Rooms, where the young lady was led out to dance. She was followed by another couple, of whom, the lady protested against Miss Cibber being allowed to dance there at all. There would have been more modesty in this second young lady if she had been silent. There ensued a fracas, of course. Mrs. Delaney, in a letter to Mrs. Dewes, says that "Mr. Cibber" collared Mr. Collett, abused him, and asked if he had caused this insult to be put *on his daughter?* Mr. "Sloper" must be meant, for Theophilus was then dead. The affront was the result of directions given by that very virtuous personage. Beau Nash, then being wheeled about the room. Some discourse was held with the shattered beau, but nothing came of it; and pretty Miss Cibber never danced, or was asked to dance, at Bath again. This brings us back to the mother, from whom I am pleased to part with a pleasanter incident. Dr. Delaney once sat enraptured, as he listened to her at Dublin, singing in the "Messiah;" and, as she ceased, he could not help murmuring on behalf of the accomplished singer, "Woman, thy sins be forgiven thee!" *Amen!* And so passes away "the fair Ophelia," in that character, at least, never to be equalled.

From Scotland Yard, where she died, the way was not long to Westminster Abbey Cloisters. With what rites she was committed to the earth, I cannot say; but a paper on the doors of the Roman Catholic Chapel, in Lincoln's Inn Fields, that day, requested you, "of your charity," to "pray for the soul of Mrs. Susanna Maria Cibber!"

*Amen* again! She was a woman more sinned against than sinning, and so well respected, that Mr. and Mrs. Garrick visited her and Mr. Sloper, at the country-house of the latter, at Woodhay; where Ophelia taught her parrot snatches of old tragedy, and exhibited the bird to her laughing friends. The highest salary this "Tragic Muse" ever received was £600 for sixty nights; and this £10 per night was often earned under such tremor and suffering, that Mrs. Cibber would exclaim, with the applause ringing in her ears, "Oh! that my nerves were made of cart-ropes!" But, we must leave her, for an actor who re-enters, and an actress who departs.

## CHAPTER VI.

REAPPEARANCE OF SPRANGER BARRY.—RETIREMENT OF MRS. PRITCHARD.

AFTER playing some nights at the Opera House, in 1766, and with Foote at the little house in the Haymarket, where Thalia and Melpomene reigned on alternate nights, in 1767, Barry and Mrs. Dancer,—the former after an absence of ten years,—appeared at Drury Lane, in October of the last-named year. Direct rivalry with Garrick, there was none: for the latter and Mrs. Pritchard acted together on one night; Barry and Mrs. Dancer played their favorite characters the next; while King, Dodd, Palmer, Parsons, Mrs. Abington, Mrs. Clive, and Miss Pope, led in comedy. The two great tragedians acted in the same company till 1774, when Barry passed to Covent Garden, where he remained till his death, in 1777,—a few months only before that of Woodward, and about half a year subsequent to the retirement of Garrick, from Drury Lane and the stage.

"I hear the stage in England is worse and worse," wrote Fox to Fitzpatrick, from Nice, in 1768. I do not know what foundation there was for such a report, save that the school of sentimental comedy had then come in and established itself,—the founder being Kelly, an honest, clever, Irish ex-staymaker, and his essay being made with "False Delicacy" (Cecil, King; Lady Betty Lambton, Mrs. Abington). Mrs. Pritchard, too, had then just retired, leaving the tragic throne to be contended for by Mrs. Yates and Mrs. Dancer, who subsequently reigned as Mrs. Barry, and who, as Mrs. Crawford, was finally superseded by Mrs. Siddons.

So firmly as well as suddenly had sentimental comedy come into fashion, that when Goldsmith's "Good Natured Man" (Croaker,

Shuter; Honeywood, Powell—who disliked his part; Miss Richland, Mrs. Bulkley) was produced in 1768, at Covent Garden, it nearly failed, through the scene of the bailiffs, which was considered too farcical for genteel comedy! The age was rapidly becoming almost too fastidious. The reaction was carrying it too far; and the moral Mrs. Sheridan's first comedy, "The Dupe," was condemned, for offences which it was said to contain against decorum. Even Johnson disapproved of the bailiffs, in Goldsmith's comedy, though he was the first to enjoy the rich humor of the lower characters in "She Stoops to Conquer." The sage did not spare sarcasm. "Are you going to make a scholar of him?" asked Goldsmith, in reference to the petted boy who waited on Johnson. "Aye, Sir," was the reply, "scholar enough to write a bailiff scene in a comedy!"

Garrick now rested entirely on his old triumphs; but he acted repeatedly with Mrs. Barry. Romeo dropped from the repertory of Garrick and Barry; but Lear and Macbeth were played by each of them to the Cordelia and Lady of Barry's wife, whose versatility was remarkable; for she was the first, the best, and the richest-brogued of Widow Bradys, as she was the most touching and dignified of Lady Randolphs. As Lord and Lady Townley, the Barrys drew great houses; but Garrick was not disturbed, for his Ranger and his Hamlet drew greater still; and none of the original characters played by Barry during this, his last engagement at Drury Lane, reached a popularity which could ruffle Garrick's peace of mind. These were Rhadamistus, in "Zenobia;" Roman, in "Fatal Discovery;" Tancred, in "Almida;" Timon, in Cumberland's version of "Timon of Athens;" Aubrey, in the "Fashionable Lover; Evander (to his wife's Euphrasia), in the "Grecian Daughter;" Melville, in the "Duel;" and Seraphis, in "Sethona." Of these, Evander showed the actor's mastery over the feelings of his audience; Aubrey was distinguished for its grave, and Melville for its touching, dignity. With his admirers, he was still the "silver-tongued Barry," and the "silver-toned lover;" but the thick-and-thin adherents to Garrick repeated these phrases satirically, in allusion only to the *silversmith*, who was Spranger Barry's father.

Voltaire had written a criticism against Shakspeare's Hamlet, which Garrick adopted; and, mangling the bard whom he professed to love, he put "Hamlet" on the stage without the Gravediggers and without Osrick! This mutilation passed for Shakspeare, until John Bannister restored the original, on playing the Dane, for his own benefit, in 1780. Yet, so irreverend to the spirit of Garrick, did this proceeding seem to old Wrighton, that when Bannister came off the stage, the elder player said to him: "Well, sir, if ever you should meet with Mr. Garrick in the next world, you will find that he will never forgive you for having restored the Grave-diggers to Hamlet!"

The most serious event, however, of this time, was the retirement of Mrs. Pritchard,—a more serious loss to the stage, perhaps, than the death of Mrs. Cibber. She had well earned repose, after five and thirty years of most arduous labor.

In 1733, Mrs. Pritchard, a young, and well-reputed married woman, was acting at our suburban fairs, but how much earlier, as Miss Vaughan, does not appear. Her slender cultivation, or rather her total want of education, is no proof that she was not of a respectable family; and the pertinacity of her brother, a clever low comedian, Henry Vaughan, in pursuing a claim to property left by a relative, Mr. Leonard, of Lyon's Inn, shows that there was one quality connected with the family, which the world respects.

Mrs. Pritchard did not at once win, but long worked for, her fortune. Her husband held a subordinate post in the theatre, till her talents raised him above it. Her history, in one point, resembles Betterton's; it was a life of pure, honest, unceasing labor; she was too busy to afford much material for further record. In another point, it resembled Mrs. Betterton's, in the unobtrusive virtue of her character. While Margaret Woffington was pretending to lament over the temptations to which she yielded, and George Anne Bellamy yielded without lamenting, honest Mrs. Pritchard neither yielded nor lamented. It is true, she was not so inexpressibly beautiful as Margaret, not so saucily seductive as George Anne, but she carried with her the lustre of rectitude, and the beauty of honesty and truth; living, she was welcomed wherever virtue kept home; and dying, she left fairly-acquired wealth, a good example, and an irreproachable name to her children.

At first she fought her way very slowly, but played every thing, from Nell to Ophelia; and throughout her career she originated every variety of character, from Selima, in "Zara," to Tag, in "Miss in her Teens," from Mrs. Beverly, in the "Gamester," to Clarinda, in the "Wedding Day;" from Hecuba to Mrs. Oakley.

We are so familiar with the prints of her as Hermione and Lady Macbeth, and to hear of her awful power in the latter, as well as of the force and dignity of her Merope, Creusa, and Zara, her almost too loud excess of grief in Volumnia, and the absolute perfection of her two queens, Katherine and Gertrude, that we are apt to remember her as a tragedian only. Her closet-scene, as the Queen in "Hamlet," was so fine and finished in every detail, that its unequalled excellence remains a tradition of the stage, like the Ophelia of Mrs. Cibber. There was a slight tendency to rant, and some lack of grace in her style, which, according to others, marred her tragedy. On the other hand, there is no dispute, as to her excellence in comedy, particularly before she grew stout; and, indeed, in spite of her becoming so, as in Millamant, in which, even in her latest years, her easy manner of speaking and action, charmed her audience, though elegance of form and the beauty of youth were no longer there.

As a perfectly natural actress, she was admirable in such parts as Mrs. Oakley, Doll Common, and the Termagant, in the "Squire of Alsatia." With such characters she identified herself. I find her less commended in artificial ladies like Clarissa and Lady Dainty; and for queens of fashion, like Lady Townley and Lady Betty Modish. Yet, although she only pleased in these high-bred personages, she was "inimitably charming" in Rosalind and Beatrice, in Estifania and Clarinda, in Mrs. Sullen and Lady Brute; and in all characters of intrigue, gayety, wit, playfulness, and diversity of humor. I may sum up all by repeating that her distinguishing qualities were natural expression, unembarrassed deportment, propriety of action, and an appropriateness of delivery which was the despair of all her contemporaries, for she took care of her consonants, and was so exact in her articulation, that, however voluble her enunciation, the audience never lost a syllable of it. Mrs. Pritchard and Mrs. Abington were selected, at various periods, to represent the Comic Muse, and nothing can better indicate their quality and merits.

Garrick, Quin, Mrs. Cibber, and Mrs. Pritchard, acting in the same piece, at Covent Garden! No wonder that Walpole, in 1746, says, "Plays only are in fashion," and calls the company, which included Woodward, Ryan, and Mrs. Horton, as "the best company that, perhaps, ever were together." In Mrs. Pritchard's Beatrice, as in Mrs. Clive's Bizarre, Garrick, as Benedict to the first, and Duretete to the second, had an antagonism on the stage which tested his utmost powers. Each was determined to surpass the other; but Walpole intimates that Mrs. Pritchard won in *her* contest, and states that Garrick hated her because her Beatrice (which he preferred to Miss Farren's) had more spirit and originality than his Benedict. Walpole also praised her Maria (" Non juror"), and only smiled at her Jane Shore when she had become so fat, that for her to talk of the pangs of starvation, seemed ridiculous. But the highest mark of his, never easily-won, estimation of this great actress consisted in his refusal to allow his "Mysterious Mother" to be acted, as Mrs. Pritchard was about to leave the stage, and there was no one else who could play the Countess.

Walpole knew her as a neighbor as well as a player, for Mrs. Pritchard purchased Ragman's Castle, a villa on the Thames, between Marble Hill and Orleans House, which she bought against an opposing bidder, Lord Lichfield, and resided in it till Walpole took it of her, for his niece, Lady Waldegrave. The actress was occasionally his guest, and he testifies to the becomingness and propriety of her behavior; but sneers a little at that of her son, the Treasurer of Drury Lane, as being better than he had expected.

Johnson said that it was only on the stage Mrs. Pritchard was inspired with gentility and understanding; but Churchill exclaims,

> "Pritchard, *by Nature* for the stage designed,
> In person graceful, and in sense refined,
> Her wit, as much as Nature's friend became,
> Her voice as free from blemish as her fame,
> Who knows so well in majesty to please,
> Attempted with the graceful charms of ease?"

And contrasting her great qualities with the increasing figure which, perhaps, offended, in her later years, "the eye's too curious sense." Churchill adds,

> "But when perfections of the mind break forth,
> Honor's chaste sallies, judgment's solid worth,
> When the pure, genuine flame by Nature taught,
> Springs into sense and every action's thought,
> Before such merit all objections fly,
> Pritchard's genteel, and Garrick six feet high."

I believe that the French actress, Rachel, was so ignorant of the true history of that which she represented, that, to her, all the events, in the various pieces in which she played, happened in the same comfortable chronological period "once upon a time." One of the greatest actresses of the Garrick period, in some respects, perhaps *the* greatest, was equally ignorant. Mrs. Pritchard, it is said, had never read more of the tragedy of "Macbeth" than her own part, as it was delivered to her in manuscript, by the prompter, to be got "by heart." Quin was nearly as ignorant, if a questionable story may be credited. Previously to Garrick's coming, the "Macbeth" which was played as Shakspeare's was really Davenant's, with Locke's music. When Garrick announced that, for the future, he would have Shakspeare's tragedy and not Davenant's opera acted, no man was more surprised than Quin; "Why!" he exclaimed, "do you mean to say that we have not been playing Shakspeare all this while?" Quin had less excuse than Mrs. Pritchard,—for how was that poor lady,—"the inspired idiot," Johnson styled her,—a strange sort of person, who called for her "gownd," but whose acquired eloquence was beautiful and appropriate,—how was poor Mrs. Pritchard to know any thing of the chronology of the story, when Garrick played the Thane in a modern gold-laced suit, and she herself might have called on the Princess Amelia in her dress for the Thane's wife? Nevertheless, the incomparable two were as triumphant as if they had been dressed according to time and place. Nor were they less so in two other characters which they dressed to the full as much out of propriety, though not of grace,—namely, Benedict and Beatrice.

I have alluded to the essay made by Miss. Pritchard. Let me

add that when the young lady first appeared as Juliet, Mrs. Pritchard as her mother, Lady Capulet, led her on the stage. The scenes between them were heightened in interest, for Lady Capulet hovered about Juliet with such maternal anxiety, and Juliet appealed by her looks so lovingly to her mother, for a sign of guidance or approval, that many of the audience were moved to tears.

The house was moved more deeply still on an after night, —the 24th of April, 1768,—the night of Mrs. Pritchard's final farewell, when Garrick played Macbeth in a brown court suit, laced with gold, and she the "lady," with a terrible power and effect such as even the audiences of those days were little accustomed to. Her "Give *me* the dagger?" on that night was as grand as her "Are you a man?" and when the curtain descended, such another intellectual treat was not looked for in that generation.

There was a "tremendous house," to which she tremblingly delivered a poetical address, written by Garrick, in which she said—

"In acted passion tears must seem to flow,
But I have that within that passeth show."

Her old admirers stood by their allegiance, and even Mrs. Siddons's Lady Macbeth, in long after years, could not shake it. Lord Harcourt, no lukewarm friend of Mrs. Siddons, missed in *her* Lady Macbeth "the unequalled compass and melody of Mrs. Pritchard." In the famous sleep-walking scene, his lordship still held Mrs. Siddons to be inferior,—there was not the horror in the sigh, not the sleepiness in the tone, nor the articulation in the voice, as in Mrs. Pritchard's, whose exclamation of, "Are you a man?" was as much superior in significance to that of Mrs. Siddons's, as the "Was he alive!" of Mrs. Crawford's (Barry's) Lady Randolph was, in depth of anxious tenderness.

Mrs. Pritchard retired to Bath to enjoy her hard-earned leisure; but met the not uncommon fate of those who withdraw from toil, to breathe awhile, and repose, in the autumn of their days. A trifling accident to her foot took a fatal turn, and in the August of the year in which she withdrew, she closed her honored and laborious career. Her name, her example, and her triumphs,—all deserve to be cherished in the memory of her younger sisters, struggling to win fame and resolved not to tarnish it. Garrick's respect for her was manifested in the remark once made at the mention of her name; "*She* deserves every thing we can do for her."

Mrs. Pritchard's daughter failed to sustain the glory of her mother's name. The season of 1767-8 was the last for both ladies, as it was for Mrs. Pritchard's son-in-law, the first and more coxcombical of the two John Palmers. Mrs. Palmer was short, but elegant and refined; unequal to tragedy, except, perhaps, in the gentle tenderness of Juliet; she was a respectable actress in minor parts of comedy, such as Harriet ("Jealous Wife"), and Fanny ("Clandestine Marriage"), of which she was the original representative. Palmer died three months before his mother-in-law, at the early age of forty, leaving bright stage memories as the original representative of the Duke's servant, in "High Life below Stairs," Sir Brilliant Fashion, Brush ("Clandestine Marriage"), &c. His widow re-married with Mr. Lloyd, a political writer, and a *protégé* of Lord North.

The inheritance of Mrs. Cibber and Mrs. Pritchard was to be won by a young girl, who, about the time of Mrs. Pritchard's death, was playing Ariel and other characters in barns and hotel-rooms,—namely, Sarah Kemble,—subsequently Siddons. Miss Seward saw the three great actresses; the first two in her younger days. She never forgot the clear, distinct, and modulated voice of Mrs. Pritchard, nor the pathetic powers, the delicate, expressive features, and the silvery voice, sometimes too highly pitched, of Mrs. Cibber. Mrs. Pritchard's figure, we are told was then "coarse and large, nor could her features, plain even to hardness, exhibit the witchery of expression. She was a just and spirited actress; a more perfectly good speaker than her more elegant, more fascinating contemporary. Mrs. Siddons has all the pathos of Mrs. Cibber, with a thousand times more variety in its exertion, and she has the justness of Mrs. Pritchard, while only Garrick's countenance could vie with hers in those endless shades of meaning which almost make her charming voice superfluous, while the fine proportion and majesty of her form, and the beauty of her face, eclipse the remembrance of all her consummate predecessors." Tate Wilkinson states, in his memoirs, that Mrs. Siddons always reminded him of Mrs. Cibber, in voice, manner, and features.

But before we address ourselves to Sarah Kemble, we have to chronicle the last years of two great actors, with whose period she is connected by having played with the greater of the two,—Garrick and Barry.

## CHAPTER VII.

#### THE LAST YEARS OF GARRICK AND BARRY.

DURING the remainder of the period that Garrick and Barry continued at the same house, the stage seemed to languish as their career drew to a close. Barry's energies slackened, and Garrick studied no new part. Within the same period old Havard died, after a service of utilities and some authorship, which extended to nearly threescore years. If power may be judged by effects, Havard was a powerful writer, for his "Charles I.," when acted at York, excited such painful emotions in a young lady named Terrot, that she died of it. Kitty Clive now retired, and Holland died, it is said, of small-pox; but he was more affected by Powell's death. After this event, he was standing in the green-room, talking mournfully of his comrade. "The first time we played together, in private," he said, "I acted Iachimo to his Posthumus. When I first appeared in public, we performed the same characters; and they were the last we ever played together!" "And you are dressed for Iachimo, as you tell it," added a listener. Holland smiled sadly; and soon after he slept with his old playfellow, Posthumus; dying at the age of forty. Love, in Falstaff only inferior to Quin, died also about this time. Under that pseudonym he saved his father, the city Architect, it was supposed, the disgrace that might attach to him, if his son called himself by his proper name (Dance) on the stage. Covent Garden, in losing Powell, lost one who was as ignorant as Mrs. Pritchard, but he had fine stage inspirations. Of the acquisitions made at this time, the most notable was that of Lewis, who first appeared at Covent Garden, in the season of 1773-4 as Belcour, and in light tragic parts.

Play-goers felt that the old school of actors was breaking up, and the poets did little to render the finale illustrious. It was the dramatic era of Kelly and Goldsmith, both of them needy Irishmen, and hard-working literary men, having many things in common, except talent, but being especially antagonistic as the upholders,—Kelly of sentimental, Goldsmith of natural comedy. Kelly was the victor at first, for his "False Delicacy," of which few now know any thing, brought him a little fortune, while Goldsmith's "Good-natured Man" would have made shipwreck but for Shuter's energy and humor. As I look over the records of this time, I cannot but remark how many of the dramatic poets toiled in vain. Taking, for instance, the tragic writers,—Hoole, the watch-maker's son, is still an honored name as a translator of the Italian poets, but his "Cyrus" and "Timanthes" are wrapped in oblivion. Some among us may still read the story of *Hindostan*, written by one whose own story was as strange as that of *Gil Blas*, and who, driven upon the world as an adventurer, in consequence of a duel, in which he was a principal, rose from the condition of a common sailor to be Secretary to the Governor of Bencoolen, and a Lieutenant-Colonel. I allude to the Scotchman, Dow, at whose "Zingis" the public laughed, more than they shuddered, and whose "Sethona" even the two Barrys could not render endurable, despite magnificent acting.

Home fared as badly as Dow. There was a strong prejudice at this season against Scotchmen, and Home was obnoxious as a client of Lord Bute's. His "Fatal Discovery," an Ossianic subject, was mounted with Roman costumes and Greek scenery, and the audience threatened to burn the house down if the piece was not withdrawn! The silver tongue of Barry could not charm them into patience. Equally unsuccessful was Home's "Alonzo," the hero of which does not appear till the play is half over. Home sat by Barry's bedside as the tragedy was being acted, and Mrs. Barry sent every half hour to say how she was, hoping the best and doing her utmost. But what could even that great actress do for a piece of which the story, as Walpole remarks, is that of David and Goliath, worse told than it would have been if Sternhold and Hopkins had put it into metre? His criticism is made in his happiest vein: "A gentlewoman embraces her maid, when she expects her husband. He goes mad with jealousy, without discovering what he ails, and runs away to Persia, where the post comes in from Spain, with news of a duel that is to be fought, the Lord knows when. As Persian princes love single combat as well as if they had been bred in Lucas's coffee-house, nobody is surprised that the Prince of Persia should arrive to fight a duel, that was probably over before he set out. The wife discovers the Prince to be her own husband, and the lad her own son, and so, to prevent mischief, stabs herself, and then tells the whole story, which it was rather more natural to do first. The language is as poor as the plot. Somebody asked me what prose Home had ever written. I said I knew none but his poetry."

Then, to a version of Voltaire's "Orestes," Mrs. Yates, as Electra, could not give life; and when Craddock gave to her all the profits he derived from his tragedy of "Zobeide," he showed his sense of that lady's value. Kelly could give her nothing, for he gained nothing by his "Clementina," at which the audience yawned more than they hissed. Managers seemed to understand little of the requirements of the public taste; and Colman still kept the Fool from "King Lear," as being "such a character in tragedy as would not be endured on the modern stage." In our own time, however, it has been not only endured, but enjoyed. One of the pleasantest of stage memories is connected with the Fool, as acted by Miss P. Horton, now Mrs. German Reed.

Garrick taxed all Barry's powers, for he imposed on him the part of Tancred, in perhaps the most insufferable of the tragedies of this time, the "Almida" of Mallett's daughter, Madame Celisia, which Garrick brought out only because her husband had been hospitable to him in Italy! Cumberland laid as heavy a charge on him in his emendation of "Timon," in which there was more of Cumberland and less of Shakspeare than the public could welcome. Walpole let pass Murphy's imbroglio of "Alzuma," and his over-rated "Grecian Daughter," the success of which was due to the Barrys alone, as Evander and Euphrasia; but he records his impression of Mason's "Elfrida," which may joyously close the tragic register of this period.

"It is wretchedly acted," he writes to the author (Mason), in February, 1773, "and worse set to music. The virgins were so inarticulate, that I should have understood them as well if they had sung choruses of Sophocles. Orgar (Clarke) had a broad

Irish accent. I thought the first virgin, who is a lusty virago, called Miss Miller, would have knocked him down; and I hoped she would. Edgar (Bensley) stared at his own crown, and seemed to fear it would tumble off." Miss Catley looked so impudent, and so *manifestly* unlike the British virgin whom she was supposed to represent, "you would have imagined she had been singing the 'Black Joke,' only that she would then have been more intelligible. Smith did not play Athelwold ill. Mrs. Hartley is made for the part (Elfrida), if beauty and figure would suffice for what you write; but she has no one symptom of genius. Still, it is very affecting, and does admirably for the stage, under all these disadvantages. The tears came into my eyes, and streamed down the Duchess of Richmond's lovely cheeks." Those great folk must have been easily moved, or Mrs. Hartley must have had more talent than Walpole will acknowledge.

Of her beauty, there is no doubt, nor of its effects. In Hull's poor tragedy, "Henry II.," she played Rosamond to the Henry of Smith; and this handsome couple went on making love to one another, on the stage, till they believed in it, and fairly ran away together. When Smith, in his older and wiser days, was living in well-endowed retirement, at Bury St. Edmunds, a remark made by him, affirming the fidelity of his married life, caused his excellent wife to look up at him. He blushed; murmured something of having forgotten "*one* slip," and never boasted again. He had the grace of repentance.

Of comedies, and operas and farces, that have been forgotten, I will say nothing. Mrs. Lennox showed more dramatic power in her novels, and Mrs. Griffiths more good purpose in her hints to young ladies, than they did in their plays. O'Brien found his pieces condemned, through his adoption of the suggestions of his aristocratic friends. Bickerstaffe, ex-page to Lord Chesterfield, in Dublin, and an ex-officer of marines, not yet compelled to fly the country in dishonor, gained less renown by "Lionel and Clarissa" (Mattocks and Miss Macklin), of the entire originality of which he boasted, than he did by the "Padlock" (Mungo, by Dibdin), which he borrowed from the Spanish; or by the "Hypocrite" (Cantwell, by King), which was a refitting of Cibber's "Nonjuror," with the addition of Maw-worm. Kelly's sentimental comedies were only tolerated by the Wilks party, whom he had offended by his political writings, when they were brought forward under an assumed name, but they had not merit enough of their own to live. Even Cumberland's "West Indian" (Belcour, King; Major O'Flaherty, Moody), and his "Fashionable Lover" (Lord Aberville, Dodd; Aubrey, and Augusta Aubrey, by the Barrys), have departed from the scene, with his "Brothers." All Cumberland's *dénoûements* may be conjectured before the curtain falls on his second acts. Of the "Brothers," George Montagu writes to Walpole: "I am glad it succeeds, as he has a tribe of children, and is almost as extravagant as his uncle, and a much better man." Cumberland lacks that most at which he most aims,—facility to delineate character. He has less power of style than purity of sentiment. Of his fifty-four pieces, one alone, the "Wheel of Fortune," survives. In all, he exhibits more regard for modesty than he furnishes matter for amusement.

But the one comedy of this period, which has gloriously survived all the rest, and which is being acted as I write, is Goldsmith's "She Stoops to Conquer." There is nothing in it of the mawkishness of Kelly nor of the pompous affectation of Cumberland. It was *so natural*, that those who did not despair, doubted of it; and the author himself had not the courage to believe in its success, though Johnson and a faithful few alone augured triumph. After a world of difficulty, the night of performance arrived at last,—the 15th of March, 1773. From the Shakspeare tavern, Johnson led a band of friends to Covent Garden, where he sat in the front of a side box; and as he laughed, the applause increased. But the friendly approvers were occasionally indiscreet, despite the instructions of Cumberland, who very kindly asserts, that the success of the comedy was owing to the exertions of those *claqueurs*,—predetermined to secure a triumph!

It came, that triumph,—and to a rare son of genius; one, who showed that drollery was compatible with decency, and that high comedy could exist without scoundrelly fine gentlemen to support it. It gave good opportunities, also, to rising actors, who, on the refusal of Smith to play Young Marlow, and of Woodward to play Tony Lumpkin, were cast for those parts,—namely, Lee Lewes and little Quick. Goldsmith did not venture to go down to Covent Garden till the fifth act was on, and then he heard the one solitary hiss, which was the exception to the universal applause, and which has been variously ascribed as issuing from the envious lips of Kelly or of Kenrick.

Sentimental comedy, ridiculed by Foote at the Haymarket, in his "Handsome House Maid, or Piety in Pattens," was dethroned, for a period, by Goldsmith's comedy. It was time. Sentiment had been carried to its utmost limits a month or two before, in a little piece called "Rose." In this operatic drama, we find Lord Gainlove (Vernon) celebrating his twenty-first birthday, by inviting every marriageable lady within five miles. Each of them is to bring a rose; and my lord is to marry her who brings one that cannot decay. The roses are brought by all, save Serina (Mrs. Smith), who, on being questioned, remarks, that the only rose which never decays is virtue; and that *she* brings the imperishable flower! She is raised to the rank of Lady Gainlove, forthwith!

To a similar school belongs the "Maid of Kent," of Francis Godolphin Waldron. The piece has more of talk than of action in it. Waldron was a respectable actor, a worthy bookseller, and an honest treasurer of the Theatrical Fund. A simple man—he once announced, in the country, that he would play Richard, in humble imitation of the inimitable Mr. Garrick! Waldron was a Roman Catholic, and on publishing an appendix to his edition of Ben Jonson's "Sad Shepherd," he had the courage to recall public attention to the poems of Father Southwell, the martyr, of which he gave some specimens. Through him, and later editors, Southwell has become as one of those true and familiar friends who are cherished for their virtues, and are not questioned on account of their creeds.

Perhaps one of the most important improvements in stage arrangements was made at Covent Garden, on the 23d of October, 1773, when Macklin first appeared as Macbeth. The taste of the nation, according to Whitehead, depended on Garrick; but Garrick, like his predecessors, had been accustomed to dress the Thane in the uniform of a modern military officer. Shakspeare, in his mind's eye, saw the persons of this drama all in native costume, for Malcolm recognizes Rosse, at a distance, for his countryman, by his dress. Macklin, bearing this in mind, dressed all the characters in Scottish suits; but unfortunately, he himself is said to have looked more like a rough old Scotch bagpiper, than the Thane of Cawdor, and King of Scotland. He hoped to snatch a triumph from Garrick, from Barry, and from Smith; and indeed, in his scene with the witches, his interview with his wife, his hypocrisy after the king's death, his bearing with the murderers, and in contrasts of rage and despondency, he gained great applause. In the other scenes he failed. On the first two nights there was occasionally a little sibilation, which Macklin attributed to Reddish and Sparks, whose friends headed a riot, which was ended by Macklin, on his third appearance in the character, being driven from the stage, with much attending insult.

A few nights later he was announced for Shylock and Sir Archy Mac Sarcasm; but he could not obtain a hearing. Bensley, Woodward, and Colman, treated with the enraged audience, in obedience to whose commands Mr. Macklin was declared to be discharged from the theatre. Against five of the rioters Macklin entered an action, and Lord Mansfield intimated that a jury would give heavy damages against men who had gone to the theatre with a preconceived resolution, not of judging of the merits, but of ruining an actor. Lord Mansfield ordered the case to be referred to a Master, with directions that liberal satisfaction be made; but Macklin interposed, offering to stop all further proceedings, if the defendants would pay the costs, spend £100 in tickets for his daughter's benefit, the same sum for his own, and a third for the advantage of the manager. And this was agreed to. "You have met with great applause to-day, Mr. Macklin," said Lord Mansfield; "you never acted better."

Let us now follow Garrick and Barry to the close of their professional courses, in 1776 and 1777, and make record of the principal productions which were brought forward during the last brilliant years of the first, and the majestic decline of the latter. At Drury Lane, came first Burgoyne's "Maid of the Oaks," as "fine as scenes could make it, and as dull as the author could not help making it," says Walpole. This was followed by Cumberland's "Choleric Man," the author of which, when accused of stealing a portion of it from Shadwell's "Squire of Alsatia," protested he had never seen that play! Dr. Franklin was as reluctant to acknowledge how much his "Matilda" owed to Voltaire's "Duc de Foix." All Walpole's affirmations that a better tragedy than Jephson's "Braganza" had not been seen for fifty years, could not give life to a heavy tragedy, by a man of such a comic turn of mind, that he was called "the mortal Momus." These pieces, with others of less note, were brought forward at Drury Lane, where Garrick appeared for the last time as Don Felix, in the "Wonder," on the 10th of June, 1776.

He had been accustomed to take his share in the country dance with which this comedy used to end, with unabated vigor, down to the latest period; and he delighted in thus proving that his strength and spirits were unimpaired. On this final night the dance was omitted, and Garrick stepped forward, in front of a splendid and sympathizing audience, to take his one and final farewell. For the first time in his life he was troubled, and at this emotion, the house was moved too, rather to tears than to applause. He could pen farewell verses for others, but he could neither write nor deliver them for himself. In a few phrases, which perhaps were not so unpremeditated as they appeared to be, he bade his old world adieu! They were rendered in simple and honest prose. "The jingle of rhyme, and the language of fiction, would but ill-suit my present feelings," he said; and his good taste was duly appreciated.

Of this season at Drury Lane, I will only notice here a link which connects this old time with the present, in the fact, that in the course of it the name of *Kean* (Moses Kean, the uncle of Edmund) appears to Glumdalca, and Mrs. Siddons made her first appearance in London, as Portia, to King's Shylock.

Meantime, at Covent Garden, the town damned, condoned, and finally crowned the "Rivals" of Sheridan; who showed that a young fellow of twenty-three could write a comedy, remarkable for wit, good arrangement of plot, and knowledge of men and manners. Hoole's dull "Cleonice," and Hull's as dull adaptation of Thomson's "Edward and Eleonora," were followed by the gayest and most popular of operas—Sheridan's "Duenna," which was acted seventy-five times in one season, eclipsing the glory even of the "Beggars' Opera." But the audiences were dulled again by

Mason's "Caractacus," the acting of which Walpole styles "a barbarous exhibition." The chief part (given to Clarke), he cruelly says, "will not suffer in not being sputtered by Barry, who has lost all his teeth."

In Garrick's last season, he *looked* youthful parts as well as ever he did. It was the reverse with Barry, who gave up Douglas for Old Norval, and who was so ill, while dressing for Jaffier, that acting it seemed impossible; and yet the great player, at whom Walpole sneers, entered on the stage only to be inspired; he was warmed by the interest of the scene, and, brightening with the glow of love and tenderness, communicated his feelings to all around—but he fell almost into insensibility on reaching the greenroom. He played Evander to Mrs. Barry's Euphrasia, on the 28th of December, 1776—the last time on which his name appeared in the bills. Death took him, and Shuter, and Woodward, close upon one another; but Garrick and Kitty Clive retired to enjoy a season of luxurious rest—Garrick at Hampton, and Mrs. Clive, between Margaret Woffington's grave, and Horace Walpole's mansion at Teddington.

The great actor, in his retirement, used to smile, when his friends told him he had surpassed Betterton. Whether the smile showed he accepted the flattery or differed from the opinion, I do not know; but Garrick would remark, that Booth, in "Cato," had never been excelled; and yet, when Quin first played the part, the pit rang with, "*Booth outdone!*" and *encored* the famous soliloquy —an honor never enjoyed by either Betterton or Garrick. Let us now accompany the latter to Hampton, and, sojourning with him there, look back over his past career.

## CHAPTER VIII.

### DAVID GARRICK.

WHEN Garrick commenced his career as actor, he was twenty-five years of age, and, according to Pond's portrait, a very handsome fellow. In the first burst of his triumph, Cibber thought the new player "well enough," but Foote, with the malice that was natural to him, remarked, "Yes, the hound has something clever, but if his excellence was to be examined, he would not be found in any part equal to Colley Cibber's Sir John Brute, Lord Foppington, Sir Courtly Nice, or Justice Shallow." This was said, not out of justice to Cibber, but out of ill-will against Garrick. How he affected the town may be seen in the criticism of the *Daily Post*. "His reception was the most extraordinary and great that was ever known upon such an occasion, and we hear that he obliges the town this evening, with the same performance." The figure of Betterton looking down upon him from between Shakspeare and Dryden, on the ceiling of the theatre, may have stimulated him. Garrick's Hamlet placed him indisputably at the head of his profession, and his Abel Drugger and Archer fixed his pre-eminence in both low and light comedy. In the former comic part, he "extinguished" Theophilus Cibber, whose grimaces had been the delight of the gallery. Garrick's Abel was awkward, simple, and unobtrusive; there was neither grimace nor gesticulation in it, and he "convinced those who had seen him in Lear and Richard that there was nothing in human life that such a genius was not able to represent."

Walpole never liked him ; and he laughed at the "airs of fatigue which Garrick and other players give themselves after a long part;"—comparing their labor with that of the Speaker and of some members of the House of Commons. The fine gentleman depreciated the fine actor systematically, but at the close of a score of years' familiarity with his acting, he rendered a discriminating judgment on him. "Good and various," the player was allowed to be, but other actors had pleased Walpole more, though "not in so many parts." "Quin, in Falstaff, was as excellent as Garrick in Lear. Old Johnson far more natural in every thing he attempted. Mrs. Porter surpassed him in passionate tragedy. Cibber and O'Brien were what Garrick could never reach, coxcombs and men of fashion. Mrs. Clive is, at least, as perfect in low comedy, and yet, to me, Ranger is the part that suited Garrick the best of all he ever performed. He was a poor Lothario, a ridiculous Othello, inferior to Quin in Sir John Brute and Macbeth, and to Cibber in Bayes; and a woeful Lord Hastings and Lord Townley. Indeed, his Bayes was original, but not the true part; Cibber was the burlesque of a great poet, as the part was designed, but Garrick made it a Garretteer. The town did not like him in Hotspur, and yet I don't know if he did not succeed in it beyond all the rest. Sir Charles Williams and Lord Holland thought so too, and they were no bad judges." It was less fair criticism when Walpole wrote, with reference to Garrick, "I do not mention the things written in his praise;—because he writes most of them himself."

This last charge was also made in a pamphlet, said to have been by Foote. It is there asserted that Garrick had considerable share in the property, and great influence in the management, of the *Public Advertiser*, the *Gazetteer*, the *Morning Post*, and the *St. James's Chronicle*. The critical and monthly reviews, he found *means* (we are told) to keep in his interest. The *Gentleman's Magazine* and *London Review* alone withstood him. Quin and Mossop, living,—he is said to have hated; dead,—to have offered to bury their remains with unusual honors. The Barrys, King, Lee, Mrs. Abington, and others, he is said to have mimicked in private; by similar mimicry in public, he is accused of having broken Delane's heart, and he is also charged with having ruined Powell, by binding him to beggarly-paid service, under a bond of £1,000, and by exacting the heavy penalty when the terms were infringed. He is charged with damning his brethren with faint praise, and ridiculing the monotony of Mrs. Cibber's action; *he* who said that tragedy had died with her! It was laid as a meanness on him that he would not engage great actors,—at a time both the Barrys were in his company, drawing houses as great as could be drawn by his own powers. Wilkinson has asserted the youthfulness of his look and action to the last, but his anonymous detractors, while they allowed that as Ranger, he mounted the ladder nimbly, professed to see that he was old about the legs. Is he a lover? they mock his wrinkled visage and lack-lustre eye, in which softness, they say, was *never* enthroned; his voice is hoarse and hollow, his dimples are furrows, his neck hideous, lips ugly, "the upper one, especially, is raised all at once like one turgid piece of leather." In such wise, was he described just before he left the stage; and to embitter his retirement, he is told that his worst enemy has got famous materials for his " Life!"

Garrick was proud of his Abel Drugger, but he was ready to acknowledge the superiority of Weston in that part, whose acting was described by Garrick as the finest he ever saw. To this pleasant piece of criticism was added a £20 note, on Weston's benefit night.

And yet, from first to last, did his enemies deny that Garrick was influenced by worthy motives. Walpole describes him, unjustly, as jealous (even after his retirement) of rising young players; and Horace writes, in 1777, " Garrick is dying of yellow jaundice, on the success of Henderson, a young actor from Bath. *Enfin donc desormais*, there must never be a good player again! As Voltaire and Garrick are the god and goddess of envy, the latter would put a stop to procreation, as the former would annihilate the traces of all antiquity, if there were no other gods but they."

I have quoted what Walpole said of the actor in his first year;—this is what he says of him in his last: " I saw Lear the last time Garrick played it, and as I told him, I was more shocked at the rest of the company than pleased with him,—which I believe was not just what he desired; but to give a greater brilliancy to his own setting, he had selected the very worst performers of his troop; just as Voltaire would wish there were no better poets than Thomson and Akenside." This is not true. Garrick played with gentlemen Smith and Bensley; Yates, Parsons, and Palmer; Mrs. Abington, Mrs. Yates, and, for a few nights, Mrs. Siddons.

Because Garrick never allowed his judgment to be overpowered by his emotions, intense as they were, Johnson thought there was all head and no heart in his acting. While David was once playing Lear, Johnson and Murphy were at the wing, conversing in no subdued tone. As Garrick passed by them, he observed, "You two talk so loud, you destroy my feelings." "Punch has *no* feelings," growled Asper, contemptuously.

By pen, as well as by word of mouth, did Johnson wound the self-esteem of his friend. Although Boswell asserts that Garrick never forgave the pointed satire which Johnson directed against him, under the pseudonym of Prospero, the records of the actor's life prove the contrary. That it was something he could never entirely forget is true, for the assault was made under circumstances by which its bitterness was much aggravated. Garrick had, just before, manfully exerted himself to render Johnson's "Irene" successful. And on the 15th February, 1752, on the morning of the night on which Garrick was to play Tancred, there appeared a paper in the *Rambler*, from Johnson's pen, in the two personages of which, no one could be mistaken. They are described as coming up to town together to seek a fortune, which had been found by one of them, Prospero, who was "too little polished by thought and conversation to enjoy it with elegance and decency."

Asper then describes a visit he reluctantly pays to Prospero's house. He is tardily admitted, finds the stairs matted, the best rooms open, that he may catch a glance at their grandeur, while his friend conducts him into a back room, suited for inferior company—where Asper is received with all the insolence of condescension. The chairs and carpets are covered, but the corners are turned up that Asper may admire their beauty and texture. He did "not gratify Prospero's folly with any outcries of admiration, but coldly bade the footman let down the cloth."

The host gives his guest inferior tea, talks of his jeweller and silversmith, boasts of his intimacy with Lord Cofty, alludes to his chariot, and ladies he takes in it to the Hark, and exhibits his famous Dresden china, which he "always associates with his chased tea-kettle." "When I had examined them a little," says Asper, "Prospero desired me to set them down, for they who were accustomed only to common dishes seldom handled china with much care." Asper takes credit for much philosophy in not dashing Prospero's "baubles to the ground;" and when the latter begins to affect a preference for the less distinguished position of one with whom he was "once upon a level," Asper quits the house in disgust.

This attack was ungracious and cowardly, on one side, as it was undeserved on the other. I can fancy it disturbed Garrick's performance of Tancred on that night; the *Rambler* was universally read, and the application could not fail. But it disturbed nothing else. Years later, when Johnson visited Garrick at his Hampton villa, the spirit of Asper was softened in his breast, and he was justified in the well-known remark he made, as he contemplated the beauty and grandeur around him:—"These are the things Davy, that make death terrible!" It must not be forgotten, however, that Johnson, at last, allowed no one to abuse Davy but himself, and he then always mentioned that "Garrick was the most liberal man of his day."

So great, indeed, was his honesty, too, that Garrick, having entered thoughtlessly into some bargain, carried it out with the remark, that "terms made over our cups must be as strictly observed as if I had agreed to them over tea and toast." His gallantry, also, was indisputable. When Mrs. Yates invited him to her house to discuss a treaty touching " £800 a year, and finding her own clothes," he answered, "I will be as punctual as I ought to be, to so fine a woman, and so good an actress."

One of the critical years in the life of Garrick,—of whom Chesterfield always strangely asserted, that although he was the best actor the world had ever seen, or could see, he was *poor in comedy!*—was 1746, when he and Quin first appeared together, at Covent Garden, in the "Fair Penitent," the night was that of the 14th of November. "The 'Fair Penitent,'" says Davies, "presented an opportunity to display their several merits, though the balance was as much in favor of Quin as the advocate of virtue is superior in argument to the defender of profligacy. . . . The shouts of applause when Horatio and Lothario met on the stage together, in the second act, were so loud and so often repeated, before the audience permitted them to speak, that the combatants seemed to be disconcerted. It was observed that Quin changed color, and Garrick seemed to be embarrassed; and it must be owned that these actors were never less masters of themselves than on the first night of the contest for pre-eminence. Quin was too proud to own his feelings on the occasion; but Mr. Garrick was heard to say, "Faith, I believe Quin was as much frightened as myself."

Davies, who praises Mrs. Cibber in the heroine, states that competent judges decided that Quin found his superior on this occasion. By striving to do too much, he missed the mark at which he aimed. "The character of Horatio is compounded of deliberate courage, warm friendship, and cool contempt of insolence. The last, Quin had in a superior degree, but could not rise to an equal expression of the other two. The strong emphasis which he stamped on almost every word in a line, robbed the whole of that ease and graceful familiarity which should have accompanied the elocution and action of a man who is calmly chastising a vain and insolent boaster. When Lothario gave Horatio the challenge Quin, instead of accepting it instantaneously, with the determined and unembarrassed brow of superior bravery, made a long pause, and dragged out the words, 'I'll meet thee there!' in such a manner as to make it appear absolutely ludicrous." He paused so long before he spoke, that somebody, it was said, called out from the gallery, "Why don't you tell the gentleman whether you will meet him or no?"

But there is no one who gives us so lively a picture of the principal actors in this piece, as Cumberland, who tells us that "Quin presented himself, upon the rising of the curtain, in a green velvet coat, embroidered down the seams, an enormous full-bottomed periwig, rolled stockings, and high-heeled, square-toed shoes. With very little variation of cadence, and in a deep full tone, accompanied by a sawing kind of action, which had more of the senate than the stage in it, he rolled out his heroics with an air of dignified indifference that seemed to disdain the plaudits that were showered upon him. Mrs. Cibber, in a key high pitched, but sweet withal, sang, or rather recitatived, Rowe's harmonious strain. But when, after long and eager expectation, I first beheld little Garrick, then young and light, and alive in every muscle and every feature, come bounding on the stage, and pointing at the wittol Altamont and the heavy-paced Horatio (heavens! what a transition), it seemed as if a whole century had been swept over in the space of a single scene; old things were done away, and a new order at once brought forward, bright and harmonious, and clearly destined to dispel the barbarisms and bigotry of a tasteless age too long attached to the prejudices of custom, and superstitiously devoted to the illusions of imposing declamation." Foote's imitation of Garrick's dying scene in Lothario was an annoyance to Garrick and a delight to the town, particularly at the concluding words:—" adorns my tale, and che-che-che-che-che-cheers my heart in dy-dy-dy-dying."

Garrick was again superior to Quin, when playing Hastings to his Gloucester, in "Jane Shore." Davies describes Quin as "a good commonwealth-man," for taking an inferior character, one which the actor himself used to designate as one of his "whiske parts,"—a phrase which shows that he dressed the duke as absurdly as he did Horatio.

Quin had his turn of triumph when he played Falstaff to Garrick's Hotspur. The former character he kept as his own, as long as he remained on the stage; but after a few nights, Garrick resigned Hotspur, on the ground of indisposition, to careful Havard. The two great actors agreed to appear together as Orestes and Pyrrhus, and Cassius and Brutus; but Garrick did not like the old costume of Greece or Rome, and the agreement never came to any thing.

It was long the custom to compare the French actor Lekain with Garrick. The two had little in common, except in their resolution to tread the stage, and achieve reputation by it. Lekain was born in 1729, the year in which Baron departed the stage. He was the son of a goldsmith, and had gained wide notice as a maker of delicate surgical instruments, when a passion for the stage led him, as in Garrick's case, to playing frequently in private, especially in Voltaire's little theatre, in the Rue Traversière, now known as the Rue Fontaine Molière.

On this stage Lekain exhibited great powers, with defects, which were considered incurable; but he was only twenty years of age, and he could then move, touch, and attract the coldest of audiences. Voice, features, and figure were against him, and yet ladies praised the beauty of all, so cunning was the artist. He
4*

played Orosmane, in "Zaire," before Louis XV., and the King was angry, to find that the actor could *compel* him to weep! When Voltaire first heard him, he threw his arms around Lekain, and thanked God for creating a being who could delight Voltaire by uttering bad verses! And yet Voltaire dissuaded him from taking to the stage; but when Voltaire saw in him the hero of his own tragedies, then poet and player lived but for one another, thought themselves France, and that the eyes of the world were upon them. Voltaire addressed Lekain as "Monsieur le Garrick of France, in merit though not in purse!" and as "My very dear and very great support of *expiring tragedy!*" When he wrote this in 1770, there was a boy seven years old in Paris, who, seventeen years later, began the most splendid career ever run by French actor,—as Seïde, in Voltaire's "Mahomet,"—Talma!

Garrick and Lekain equally respected the original text of an author; but the former, more readily than the latter, adapted so-called "emendations." When Marmontel *improved* the bold phrases of old Rotrou's "Venceslas," Lekain repeated the improvements, at rehearsal; but at night, he kept to the original passages of the author, and thus created confusion among his fellow actors, who lost their *cues*. In this, Garrick deemed him unjustifiable.

Lekain, like Betterton, never departed from the quality of the part he was playing, even when off the stage. Garrick, like Charles Young, would forget Lear, to set a group in the green-room laughing at some good story. Lekain treated his Paris audiences with contempt. He would affect fatigue after playing less than a dozen times in a single winter, and then pass from one country town to another, acting twice a day! He received a salary from Paris while he was acting at Brussels. He could not play a hundred different parts like Garrick, who identified himself with all; but he carried about with him a repertory of eight or nine characters, with half that number of costumes and a turban; and, with these parts, painfully learnt and elaborately acted, he enthralled his audiences. Voltaire protests that Lekain's means were as great, and his natural truthfulness of acting as undeniable as Garrick's; "but, oh! sublime Garrick!" exclaims Mercier, "how much more extended are thy means; how different thy truthfulness!"

This truthfulness was the result of anxious care. Garrick spent two whole months in rehearsing and correcting his Benedict, and when he played it, all the gayety, wit, and spirit seemed spontaneous. In Fribble, he imitated no less than eleven men of fashion, so that every one recognized them; and in dancing, Mrs. Woffington could not excel him. "Garrick," says Mrs. Delaney, "is the genteelest dancer I ever saw."

One of Garrick's distinguishing characteristics was his power of suddenly assuming any passion he was called on to represent. This often occurred during his continental travels, when in the private rooms of his various hosts,—princes, merchants, actors,—he would afford them a taste of his quality; Scrub or Richard, Brute or Macbeth, and identify himself on the instant with that which he assumed to be. Clairon, the famous French actress, almost worshipped him for his good nature, but more for his talent, particularly on the occasion when, in telling the story of a child falling from a window, out of its father's arms, he threw himself into the attitude, and put on the look of horror, of that distracted father. The company were moved to honest tears, and when the emotion had subsided, Clairon flung her arms round his neck, kissed him heartily, and then, turning to Mrs. Garrick, begged her pardon, for "she positively could not help it!"

Of the French players, Garrick said that Sophie Arnould was the only one who ever touched his heart. To a young Englishman of French descent, subsequently Lord North's famous antagonist, Colonel Barré, whom he met in Paris, he said, on seeing him act in private, that he might earn a thousand a year, if he would adopt playing as a profession.

French *ana* abound with illustrations of Garrick's marvellous talent, exercised for the mere joke's sake. How he deceived the driver of a *coucou* into believing his carriage was full of passengers, Garrick having presented himself half a dozen times at the door, each time with a different face; how he and Preville, the French actor, feigned drunkenness on horseback; and how Garrick showed that his rival, drunk everywhere else, was not drunk enough in his legs. But the greatest honor Garrick ever received was in his own country, and at the hands of Parliament. He happened to be sole occupant of the gallery in the Commons, one night of 1777, during a very fierce discussion between two members, one of whom, noticing his presence, moved that the gallery should be cleared. Burke thereupon sprang to his feet, and appealed to the House; was it consistent with becomingness and liberality to disturb the great master of eloquence? one to whom they all owed so much, and from whom he, Burke, had learned many a grace of oratory? In his strain of ardent praise, he was followed by Fox and Townshend, who described the ex-actor as their great preceptor; and ultimately, Garrick was exempted from the general order that strangers leave the house! Senators hailed him as their teacher, and the greatest of French actors called him *Master!*"

It was Grimm's conclusion, that he who had not seen Garrick, could not know what acting was. Garrick alone had fulfilled all that Grimm's imagination could conceive an actor should be. The player's great art of identification astounded him. In different parts he did not seem the same man; and Grimm truly observed, that all the changes in Garrick's features arose entirely from inward emotion;—that he never exceeded truth; and that, in passion alone, he found the sources of distinction. "We saw him," he says, "play the dagger scene in 'Macbeth,' in a room, in his ordinary dress, without any stage illusion; and as he followed with his eyes the air-drawn dagger, he became so grand, that the whole assembly broke into a general cry of admiration. Who would believe," he asks, "that this same man, a moment after, counterfeited, with equal perfection, a pastry-cook's boy, who, carrying a tray of tartlets on his head, and gaping about him at the corner of the street, lets his tray fall in the kennel, and, at first stupefied by the accident, bursts at last into a fit of crying?" Such was he who fairly frightened Hogarth himself, by assuming the face of the defunct Fielding!

Garrick's assertion, that a man must be a good comic actor to be a great tragedian, gave M. de Carmontelle the idea of a picture, in which he represented Garrick in an imposing tragic attitude, with a comic Garrick standing between the folding doors, looking with surprise, and laughing at the other. While the ever-restless actor was sitting for this, he amused himself by passing through imperceptible gradations, from extreme joy to extreme sadness, and thence to terror and despair. The actor was running through the scale of the passions.

Grimm approvingly observed, that Garrick's "studio" was in the crowded streets. "He is always there," writes Grimm; and, no doubt, Garrick perfected his great talents by the profound study of nature. Of his personal appearance, the same writer remarks: "his figure is *mediocre ;* rather short than tall; his physiognomy agreeable, and promising wit; and the play of his eyes prodigious. He has much humor, discernment, and correctness of judgment; is naturally *monkeyish,* imitating all he sees; and he is always graceful!" Such is the account of a member of a society, whose kindness was never forgotten by the English actor. The desire to see him there again was as strong as Mrs. Woffington's, who, being reminded by Sir C. Hanbury Williams, that she had seen Garrick that morning, exclaimed," "but that's an age ago!"

St. Petersburg caught from Paris the Garrick fever; but the offer of the Czarina Catherine, to give Garrick two thousand guineas for four performances could not tempt him to the banks of the Neva. Denmark was fain to be content with his counterfeit presentment; and a portrait, painted in London, by order of the King was hung up in the royal palace, at Copenhagen.

I have alluded to some things his enemies laid to his charge. They are small matters when they come to be examined; and the more they are examined, the less obnoxious does Garrick seem to censure.

I find more instances of his generosity than of his meanness,—more of his fairness of judgment than of his jealousy. He was ever ready to play for the benefit of his distressed brethren. When Macklin lost his engagement under Fleetwood, Garrick offered to allow him £6 per week out of his own salary, till he found occupation. He saw, when his own triumph was in its first freshness and brilliancy, the bright promise of Barry; and pointed out his great merits, and predicted his future success. To ensure that of young Powell, he gave him frequent instruction; and when he brought the soon forgotten Dexter from Dublin, he not only gave him "first business," and useful directions, but expressed his convictions that, with care and diligence, he would stand in the foremost rank of actors.

The commonest incidents have been tortured, to depreciate Garrick's character. When, in 1775, Sheridan's "Duenna" was in the course of its run of seventy-five nights, the name of the autho.' was extraordinarily popular. At this juncture, Garrick did further honor to that name, by reviving the "Discovery," by Sheridan's mother, and acting the principal part in it himself. The carpers immediately exclaimed, that the mother had been revived in opposition to the son. They did not even take the low ground of the revival being adopted as a source of profit, on acccount of the author's family name.

Even Mrs. Siddons's disparagement of Garrick, tells in his favor. She played two or three nights with him, but her first appearances were comparatively failures. Garrick observed some awkward action of the lady's arms, and he gave her good advice how to use them. But Mrs. Siddons, in telling the story, used to say: "He was only afraid that I should overshadow his nose." Years subsequently, Walpole remarked this very action of the arms, which Garrick had endeavored to amend!

To those who object that Garrick was personally vain, it may suffice to point out that he was the first to allude to his own defect of stature. In the prologue to the tragedy of "Hecuba," written and spoken by himself, he mentions the high-soled buskins of the ancient stage, and adds:—

> "Then rais'd on stilts, our play'rs would stalk and rage,
> And at three steps stride o'er a modern stage;
> Each gesture then would boast unusual charms,
> From lengthen'd legs, stuff'd body, sprawling arms!
> Your critic eye would then no pigmies see,
> But buskins make a giant e'en of me."

If he esteemed little of himself personally, he had, on the other hand, the highest estimation of his profession. In this he bears a resemblance to Montfleury, who, being asked, when his marriage articles were preparing, how he wished to be described, answered: that ancestry conferred no talent, and that the most honorable title he desired to be known by, was, that of "*Actor to the King.*"

Garrick was often severe enough with conceited aspirants, who came to offer samples of their quality, to whom he listened while he shaved, and whom he often interrupted by imitative *yaw, yaws!* But when convinced there was stuff in a young man, Garrick helped him to do his best, without thought of rivalry. It is pleasant thus to contemplate him preparing Wilkinson, in 1759, for his attempt at tragedy, in Bajazet, to the Aspasia of Mrs. Pritchard. Garrick heard him recite the character in his own private room; gave him some valuable advice; presided at the making up of his face; and put the finishing strokes of the pencil, to render the young face of one and twenty as nearly like that of the elder Oriental, as might be.

It may be said that this was a cheap sort of generosity, but it was characteristic of kindliness of heart. He could make other and nobler sacrifices; on the last night he ever trod the stage, with a house crammed, with a profusely liberal audience, Garrick made over every guinea of the splendid receipts, not to his own account at his bankers, but to that of the Theatrical Fund. After this his weaknesses may surely be forgotten. He may have been as restless and ignorant as Macklin has described him; as full of contrasts and as athirst for flattery as the pencil of Goldsmith has painted him; as void of literary ability as Johnson and Walpole asserted him to be; and as foolish as Foote would have us take him for; his poor opinion of Shuter and Mrs. Abington may seem to cast reproach upon his judgment; and his failure to impress Jedediah Buxton, who counted his words rather than attended to his acting, may be accepted as proof that he was a poor player (in Jedediah's eyes); but the closing act of his professional life may be cited in testimony of a noble and unselfish generosity. It was the crowning act in a career marked by many generous deeds, but marred by many crosses, vexations, and anxieties.

Colman, even before he quarrelled with Garrick, assailed him as a " grimace-maker," a " haberdasher of wry faces," a " hypocrite who laughed and cried for hire," and so forth; but Garrick, in return, wrote verses in praise of Colman's translation of *Terence;* and when these had softened the translator's resentment, Garrick chose the most solemn and most joyous day, Christmas, 1765, to write better verses, in which he states that failing in health, assailed by enemies, treated with ingratitude, and weary of his vocation as he is, that joyous season is made doubly joyous by the restoration of their friendship.

Garrick could yield, too, to the most exacting of his rivals.

When Barry rather unjustly complained that Garrick only put him up to play on unlucky days,—when operas, or concerts, or lady's drums, were a counter attraction, David kindly bade him select his own days; he himself would be content to play singly on the others. "Well, sir!" said Barry, "I certainly could not ask more than you grant!"

Vanity, it has been said, was one of Garrick's weak points; but he was not so proud of the Prince of Hesse talking with him at Ranelagh, as people were of Mr. Garrick telling them what the Prince had said. His courtesy, discretion, justice, and firmness, are illustrated in a thousand ways, in his correspondence. His best actresses vexed him to the heart; but he never lost his temper or his politeness with the most vexing or capricious of them all. His counsel to young actors grasping at fame, was of the frank and useful nature which was likely to help them to seize it; and his reproof to foolish and impertinent players,—like the feather-brained Cautherley,—was delivered with a severity which must have been all the more stinging, as its application was as dignified as it was merciless. As for Garrick's professional jealousy, he seems to me to have had as little as was consonant with human nature. I know of no proprietor of a theatre, himself an actor, who collected around him such a brilliant brotherhood of actors as Garrick did; yet, when any one of these left him, or was dismissed by him, the partisans of the retiring player raised the cry of "*jealousy!*"

When Mallet was writing his *Life of the Duke of Marlborough*, he dexterously enough intimated to Roscius that he should find an opportunity of noticing in that work the great actor of the later day. The absurdity of this must have been evident to Garrick, who immediately replied, "My dear friend, have you quite left off writing for the stage?" As Mallet subsequently offered to Garrick his reconstruction of the masque of "Alfred," which he had originally written in conjunction with Thomson, and Garrick produced the piece, it has been inferred that the latter took the bait flung for him by the wily Scot. It seems to me that Garrick perceived the wile, but produced the play, notwithstanding.

There was, perhaps, weakness of character rather than frankness, in the way he would allude to his short stature,—in his obviating jokes on his marriage, by making them himself, or getting his friend, Edward Moore, to make them, not in the most refined fashion. Sensitive to criticism no doubt he was; but he was more long-suffering under censure than Quin, who pummelled poor Aaron Hill in the Court of Requests, because of adverse comments in the *Prompter*. Sensitive as Garrick was, he could reply to criticism merrily enough. Another Hill, the doctor and dramatist, had attacked his pronunciation, and accused him of pronouncing the *i* in *mirth* and *birth* as if it were an *u*. On which Garrick wrote:—

> "If 'tis true, as you say, that I've injured a letter,
> I'll change my note soon, and I hope, for the better.
> May the just rights of letters as well as of men,
> Hereafter be fixed by the tongue and the pen;
> Most devoutly I wish that they both have their due,
> And that I may be never mistaken for U."

Again, if he were vain, he could put on a charming appearance of humility. Lord Lyttleton had suggested to him that as a member of Parliament, he might turn his powers of eloquence to patriotic account. Such a suggestion would have fired many a man's ambition—it only stirred Garrick to write the following lines:

> "More than content with what my labors gain;
> Of public favor, though a little vain;
> Yet not so vain my mind, so madly bent,
> To wish to play the fool in Parliament;
> In each dramatic unity to err,
> Mistaking TIME, and PLACE, and CHARACTER!
> Were it my fate to quit the mimic art,
> I'd 'strut and fret' no more in *any* part;
> No more in public scenes would I engage,
> Or wear the cap and mask, on any stage."

Burke said of Garrick, that he was the first of actors, because he was the most acute observer of nature that Burke ever knew. Garrick disliked characters in which there was a "lofty disregard of nature;" yet he resembled Mrs. Siddons in believing that if a part seemed at all *within* nature, it was not to be doubted but that a great actor could make something out of it.

Garrick's repertory extended to less than one hundred characters, of which he was the original representative of thirty-six. Compared with the half century of labor of Betterton, and the number of his original characters, Garrick's toil seems but mere pastime. In his first season, on that little but steep stage at Goodman's Fields, so steep, it is said, that a ghost in real armor, ascending on a trap, once lost his balance and rolled down to the orchestra, Garrick seems to have been uncertain whether his vocation lay more with tragedy or with comedy. In that season he repeated his comic characters eighty-four times; he appeared but fifty nights in a repetition of half a dozen tragic parts. In the sum of the years of his acting, the increase of number is slightly on the side of the latter, while, of his original characters, twenty belonged to tragedy, and sixteen to comedy. After he had been two-and-twenty years on the stage, Garrick undertook no new study.

Of his original characters, the best remembered in stage traditions are, Sharp, in the "Lying Valet," Tancred, Fribble, Ranger, Beverley, Achmet ("Barbarossa"), Oronooko (in the altered play), Lovemore ("Way to Keep Him"), and Oakley, in the "Jealous Wife." Of these, only Beverley and Oakley can be said to still survive.

Of Garrick and his labors I have now said enough; let us follow him thither where he found repose from the latter, in company with one whom many of us, who are not yet old, may remember to have seen in our early youth, the Mrs. Garrick who is said to have told Edmund Kean that he could not play Abel Drugger, and to have been answered by Edmund, "Dear madam, I know it!"

In June, 1749, Lord Chesterfield, who, in his Irish vice-royalty had neglected Garrick, just as in London he ignored Sheridan whom he had patronized in Dublin, wrote to his friend Dayrolles, "The parliament is to be prorogued next Tuesday, when the ministers will have six months' leisure to quarrel, and patch up and quarrel again. Garrick and the Violetti will likewise, and about the same time, have an opportunity of doing the same thing, for they are to be married next week. They are, at present, desperately in love with each other. Lady Burlington was, at first, outrageous; but, upon cooler reflection upon what the Violetti, if provoked, might say or rather invent, she consented to the match, and superintends the writings." Later in June, Walpole touches on the same subject to Mann, announcing the marriage itself, "first at a Protestant, then at a Roman Catholic chapel. The chapter of this history," he adds, "is a little obscure, and uncertain as to the consent of the protecting countess, and whether she gives a fortune or not."

This Eva Maria Violetti was a dancer, who, three years previously to this marriage, was enchanting the town with her "poetry of motion." The sister Countesses of Burlington and Talbot competed for her with "sullen partiality." The former carried her to Chiswick, wore her portrait, and introduced her to her friends. Lady Carlisle entertained her; and the Prince of Wales paid his usual compliment, by bidding her take lessons of Desnoyers, the dancing master, and Prince's companion,—which Eva Maria did not care to do.

The public were curious to know who this beautiful young German dancer was, in whom Lord and Lady Burlington took such especial interest. That she was nearly related to the former was a very popular conjecture. However this may have been, she was, in many respects, Garrick's good genius, presiding gracefully over his houscholds in the Adelphi and at Hampton.

"Mr. Garrick," whose early residence was, according to the addresses of his letters, "at a periwig maker's, corner of the Great Piazza, Covent Garden," saw good company at Hampton where Walpole cultivated an intimacy with him, for Mrs. Clive's sake, as he pretended. Here is the actor at home, on August 15th, 1755. "I dined to-day at Garrick's," writes Walpole to Bentley; "there were the Duke of Grafton, Lord and Lady Rochfort, Lady Holdernesse, the crooked Mostyn, and Dabreu, the Spanish minister; two regents, of which one is Lord Chamberlain, the other Groom of the Stole, and the wife of a Secretary of State. This being *sur un assez bon ton*, for a player. Don't you want to ask me how I liked him? Do want, and I will tell you. I like *her* exceedingly; her behavior is all sense and all sweetness, too. I don't know how, he does not improve so fast upon me; there is a great deal of parts, and vivacity, and variety, but there is a great deal, too, of mimicry and burlesque. I am very ungrateful, for he flatters me abundantly, but, unluckily, I know it."

Fifteen years later, Mrs. Delaney describes a day at Garrick's house at Hampton, and speaks as eulogistically of the hostess. "Mr. Garrick did the honors of his house *very respectfully*, and, though in high spirits, seemed sensible of the honor done them. Nobody else there but Lady Weymouth and Mr. Bateman. As to Mrs. Garrick, the more one sees her, the better one must like her; she seems *never* to depart from a perfect propriety of behavior, accompanied with good sense and gentleness of manners; and I cannot help looking on her as a *wonderful creature*, considering all circumstances relating to her." The above words referring to Garrick are held by Lady Llanover, the editor of Mrs. Delaney's correspondence, to be "high testimony to Garrick's tact and good-breeding, as few persons in his class of life know how to be '*respectful*,' and yet in '*high spirits*,' which is the greatest test of real refinement." This is severe, oh, gentlemen players; but the lady forgot that Mr. Garrick was the son of an officer and a gentleman.

Walpole warned people against supposing that he and Garrick were intimate. When the actor and his wife went to Italy:— "We are sending to you," wrote Horace to Mann, "the famous Garrick and his once famous wife. He will make you laugh as a mimic; and as he knows *we* are great friends, will affect great partiality to me; but be a little upon your guard, remember he is an *actor*." It is clear that Garrick, down at his villa, insisted on being treated as a gentleman. "This very day," writes Walpole to Mason, September 9, 1772, "Garrick, who has dropped me these three years, has been here by his own request, and told Mr. Raftor how happy he was at the reconciliation. I did not know we had quarrelled, and so omitted being happy too."

Lord Ossory's intimacy with Garrick was one of the strictest friendship. Lord Ossory speaks of him, Gibbon, and Reynolds, who were then his guests, as all three delightful in society. "The vivacity of the great actor, the keen, sarcastic wit of the great historian, and the genuine pleasantry of the great painter, mixed up well together, and made a charming party. Garrick's mimicry of the mighty Johnson was excellent."

Garrick was the guest of Earl Spencer,—Christmas, 1778, when he was attacked by his last and fatal illness. He was carried to his town house, No. 5, Adelphi Terrace,' where Dr. Cadogan asked him if he had any affairs to settle. Garrick met the intimation with the calm dignity of Quin: "I have nothing of that sort on my mind," he said, "and I am not afraid to die."

Physicians assembled around him out of pure affection and respect; Haberden, Warren, and Schomberg. As the last approached, Garrick, placidly smiling, took him by the hand, faintly murmuring, " though last, not least in our dear love." But as the crowd of charitable healers increased, the old player who—wrapped in a rich robe, himself all pale and feeble, looked like the stricken Lusignan, softly repeated the lines in the " Fair Penitent," beginning with,

"Another and another still succeeds."

On January 20th, 1779, Garrick expired. Young Bannister, the night before, had played his old part of Dorilas to the Merope of Miss Younge. The great actor was solemnly carried to Westminster Abbey by some of the noblest in the land, whether of intellect or of rank. Chatham had addressed him living, in verse, and peers sought for the honor of supporting the pall, at his funeral. The players, whose charitable fund he had been mainly instrumental in raising to near £5,000, stood near their master's grave, to which the statue of Shakspeare pointed, to do him honor. Amid these, and friends nearer and dearer still, the greatest of English actors, since Betterton, was left in his earthly sleep, not very far from his accomplished predecessor.

They who had accused him of extravagance, were surprised to find that he had lived below his income. They who had challenged him with parsimony, now heard of large sums cheerfully given in charity, or lent on personal security; and the latter often forgiven to the debtor. "Dr. Johnson and I," says Boswell, "walked away together. We stopped a little while by the rails of the

Adelphi, looking on the Thames, and I said to him with some emotion, that I was now thinking of two friends we had lost, who once lived in the buildings behind us. Topham Beauclerk and Garrick." "Ay, sir," said he tenderly, "and two such friends as cannot be supplied!"

And Mrs. Garrick? She wore her long widowhood till 1822, dying then in the same house on the Adelphi Terrace. She was the honored guest of hosts whom all men honored; and at the Bishop of London's table held her own, against the clever men and women who held controversy under Porteus's roof. Eva Maria Garrick twice refused Lord Monboddo, who had written a book to show that humanity was merely apedom without the tail. The widow of Roscius was higher in the social scale than the wife of a canny Scotch Lord of Session, with an uncanny theory.

As I take leave of Garrick, I remember the touching scene which occurred on the last night but one of his public performances. His farewell to the stage was made in a comic character; but he and tragedy parted forever the night before. On that occasion he played Lear to the Cordelia of Miss Younge. As the curtain descended, they lay on the stage hand in hand, and hand in hand they rose and went, Garrick silently leading, to his dressing-room; whither they were followed, by many of the company. There stood Lear and Cordelia, still hand in hand, and mute. At last Garrick exclaimed, "Ah Bessie, this is the last time I shall ever be your father; the *last time!*" and he dropped her hand. Miss Younge sighed too, and replied affectionately, with a hope that before they finally parted he would kindly give her a father's blessing. Garrick took it as it was meant, seriously; and as Miss Younge bowed her head, he raised his hands, and prayed that God would bless her! Then slowly looking round, he murmured, "May God bless you all!" and divesting himself of his Lear's dress, tragedy, and one of her most accomplished sons, were dissevered forever!

In New Drury, such compliment was not paid to Garrick as was offered to Betterton in New Lincoln's Inn Fields Theatre; on the ceiling of which house was painted a noble group of poets—Shakspeare, Rare Ben, Beaumont, Fletcher, and some of later date. These were on a raised terrace, and a little below them, looking up, stood Betterton, with whom they were holding conference. Worthier homage was never rendered to departed merit! From him to whom it was rendered, and from Garrick who deserved no less, let us now turn to one who, lingering somewhat longer on the stage, yet earlier passing from the scene of life, claims a parting word,—silver-toned Barry.

## CHAPTER IX.

#### SPRANGER AND ANNE BARRY.

OUTSIDE the five and thirty years of Barry's professional life, little is known of him. As of Betterton, it may be said, he labored, loved, suffered losses, and died. It is the sum of many a man's biography.

Spranger's professional career is traced in preceding pages; but I may add to it, that Dublin is to this day, and with reason, proud of Spranger Barry, and of Margaret Woffington; for mere human beauty they have never been surpassed; for talents and for genius, with respect to their profession, they have not often been equalled. Spranger of the silver tongue, was the only actor who ever shook Garrick on his throne; but lacking the fulness of the perfection of Garrick, Barry only shook him for an instant; he never dethroned him. He is remembered as the vanquished wrestler is remembered, who has wrestled his best, given a heavy fall or two, has succumbed in the last grapple, and is carried from the arena on loving arms, amid the acclamations of the spectators, and with the respect of his conqueror.

In the Irish silversmith's accomplished son, born in 1719, there was very good blood, with some of the disadvantages attached to that possession. Of fine personal appearance and bearing, an aristocratic expression, and a voice that might win a bird from the nest, Spranger Barry had expensive and too magnificent tastes. He was a gentleman; but he lived as though he were the lord of countless thousands, and with an income on which an earl might have existed becomingly, with moderate prudence, Spranger Barry died poor.

From the very first, Barry took foremost ground; and Mrs. Delancy may well expatiate on the delight of seeing Garrick, Barry, and Sheridan, together in one piece. Such a triad as those three were, when young, in the very brightest of their powers, and achieving triumphs which made their hearts beat to accomplish something higher still, perhaps, never rendered a stage illustrious.

From 1747 to 1758, Barry was, in some few characters, the best actor on our stage. After the above period, came the brilliant but ruinous Irish speculation with Woodward. During the time of that disastrous Dublin management, Barry's powers were sometimes seriously affected. He has been depicted as reckless; but it is evident that anxieties were forced upon him, and a proud man liable to be seized by sheriffs' officers, ere he could rise from simulated death upon the stage, was not to be comforted by the readiness of his subordinates to murder the bailiffs. Mrs. Delaney had been enraptured with him in his earliest years; but she found a change in him, even as early as 1759. The gossiping lady thus exhibits to us the interior of Crow Street, one night in February, of the year just named, when, despite the lady's opinion, the handsome and manly fellow was not to be equalled in the expression of grief, of pity, or of love.

"Now what do you think? Mrs. Delaney with *ditto* company went to the *Mourning Bride* to see the new playhouse; and Mrs. Fitzhenry performed the part of Zara, which I think she does incomparably. The house is very handsome, and well lighted; and there I saw Lady Kildare and her two blooming sisters,—Lady Louisa Conolly (the bride) and Lady Sarah Lennox,"—(the latter lady reckoned among the first loves of George III.),—"who, I think the prettiest of the two. Lord Mornington" (afterwards father of the Duke of Wellington) "was at the play, and looked as *solemn* as one should suppose the young lady he is engaged to" (Miss Hill) "would have done! ... The play, on the whole, was tolerably acted, though I don't like *their celebrated* Mr. Barry; he is tall and ungainly, and does not speak sensibly nor look his part well: he was Osmyn. Almyra was acted by a very pretty woman, who, *I think*, might be made a *very good actress.* Her name is Dancer."

Barry *did* make her an excellent actress, and his wife to boot. Nevertheless, the Dublin speculation failed; and I find something characteristic of it among the properties enumerated in the inventory of articles made over by Barry to his successor, Ryder. For instance:—"Chambers, with holes in them;" "House, very bad;"

"One stile, broke;" "Battlements, torn;" "Garden wall, very bad;" "Water-fall, in the Dargle, very bad." The same definition is applied to much more property; with "woods, greatly damaged;" "clouds, little worth;" "wings, with holes, in the canvas;" or, "in bad order." "Mill, torn;" "elephant, very bad;" and Barry's famous "Alexander's car," is catalogued as "some of it wanting." Indeed, the only property in good order, comprised eighty-three thunder-bolts!

Of Barry's wardrobe, he seems to have parted only with the "bonnet, bow, and quiver, for Douglas;" but Mrs. Barry's was left in Crow Street. It consisted of a black velvet dress and train; nine silk and satin dresses, of various hues, all trained; numerous other dresses, of inferior material; and "a pair of shepherd's breeches," which Boaden thinks were designed "for the dear woman's own Rosalind, no doubt."

The only known portraits of Barry represent him as Timon and Macheath. They were taken before he entered upon his last ten years, in London;—years of gradual, noble, but irresistible decay. Like Betterton, Barry suffered excruciatingly from attacks of gout; but, like Betterton, and John Kemble in this respect resembled them both,—he performed in defiance of physical pain: mind triumphing over matter.

On the 8th of October, 1776, he played Jaffier to the Pierre of Aikin, and the Belvidera of his wife. He was then only fifty-seven years of age; but there was a wreck of all his qualities,— save indomitable will. The noble vessel only existed in ruins, but it presented a majestic spectacle still. Barry, on the stage, was almost as effective as he had ever been; but, off the charmed ground, he succumbed to infirmity and lay insensible, or struggling, or waiting mournfully for renewal of strength, between the acts. He continued ill for many weeks, during which his chief characters passed into the hands of Lewis, the great grandson of Harley's secretary, Erasmus Lewis, but himself the son of a London linen-draper. Lewis, who had now been three years on the London stage, played Hamlet, and Norval, Chamont, Mirabel, Young Bevil, and Lord Townley; but on the 28th of November, Barry roused himself, as if unwilling that the young actor, who had excelled Mossop in Dublin, should overcome, in London, the player who had competed, not always vainly, with Garrick. On that night, as I have already recorded, he played Evander to his wife's Euphrasia, in the "Grecian Daughter;" but he never played or spoke on the stage again. On January 10th, 1777, he died, to the great regret of a world of friends and admirers, and to the awakening of much poetry of various quality. One of the anonymous sons of the Muse, in a quarto poem, remarks:—

> "Scarcely recovered from the stroke severe,
> When Garrick fled from our admiring eyes,
> Resolv'd no more the Drama's sons to cheer,
> To make that stroke more fatal,—Barry dies."

> "He dies: and with him sense and taste retreat;
> For, who can now conceive the Poet's fire?
> Express the just? the natural? the great?
> The fervid transport? or the soft desire?"

The poet then fancies gathering around the player's tomb, led thither by the Tragic Muse,—the Moor, "with unrivall'd grace;" ill-fated Anthony; injured Theseus; feeble Lusignan; woe-stricken Evander; heart-bleeding Jaffier; and, chief of all, Romeo, with "melting tears," "voice of love, and soothing eloquence." Thalia, too, brings in Bevil and Townley;—

> "And oh! farewell she cries, *my graceful son!!*"

Graceful, but pathetic as he was graceful. This was specially the case when, in his younger days, he played with Mrs. Cibber,—Castalio to Monimia,—at which a comic actor, once looking on, burst into tears, and was foolish enough to be ashamed of it. No two (so critics thought) played lover and mistress, wife and husband, as they did. Mrs. Cibber, said these critics, who forgot her Beatrice to Garrick's Benedick, could, with equal, though different effect, be only the daughter or sister to Garrick;—Cordelia to Garrick's Lear, but a Juliet to Barry's Romeo, a Belvidera to his Jaffier. When Mrs. Bellamy acted with him, the effect was less complete. Colley Cibber was in the house on the night of his first appearance as Othello—did what he was not accustomed to do,—applaud loudly; and is said to have preferred Barry, in this character, to either Betterton or Booth. In Orestes, Barry was so incomparable, that Garrick never attempted the part in London. His Alexander lost all its bombast, in his hands, and gained a healthy vigor; while, says Davies, "he charmed the ladies repeatedly, by the soft melody of his love complaints, and the noble ardor of his courtship." The grace of his exit and entrance was all his own; though he took lessons in dancing, from Desnoyers, to please the Prince of Wales.

Barry was a well-informed man, had great conversational powers, and told an Irish story with an effect which was only equalled by that with which he acted Sir Callaghan O'Brallaghan. In that accomplishment and this character, Garrick owned that Barry was not to be approached; but, said the former, "I can beat Barry's head off in telling all stories, but Irish ones."

It was in pathos on the stage, not in humor off of it, that Barry excelled. "All exquisitely tender or touching writing," says an anonymous contemporary, "came mended from his mouth. There was a pathos, a sweetness, a delicacy, in his utterance, which stole upon the mind, and forced conviction on the memory. Every sentiment of honor and virtue, recommended to the ear by the language of the author, were riveted to the heart by the utterance of Barry." Excessive sensibility conquered his powers. His heart overcame his head; but Garrick never forgot himself in his character. Barry felt all he uttered, before he made his audience, feel; but Garrick made his audience feel, and was not overcome by his own emotions.

Churchill describes the lofty and admired Barry as possessing a voice too sweet and soft for rage, and as going wrong through too much pains to err. The malignant bard alludes to the "well-applauded tenderness" of his Lear; to the march of his speeches, line by line; to his preventing surprise by preparatory efforts; and to his artificial style, manifest alike in his passions as in his utterance. This dark portrait was limned with the idea that it would please Garrick, whom it could *not* please. The two actors respected each other. "You have already," writes Barry, in 1746, to Garrick, "made me happy by your friendship, It shall be the business and pleasure of my life to endeavor to deserve it; and I would willingly make it the basis of my future fortune." This feeling never waned. Above a score of years later, Barry writes: "I hear you are displeased with me, which I beg leave to assure you, I shall feel much more than all the distresses and disappointments that have happened to me."

Previous to the earlier date, Lord Chesterfield had said of Barry, "He is so handsome, he will not be long on the stage; some rich widow will carry him off." At the later date, Barry was in London, with the widow, but not a rich widow, he had brought from Dublin. The only good result of his otherwise unlucky sojourn there as theatrical manager, was in his second marriage, with Mrs. Dancer. The lady was admirably trained by him; and when Garrick saw Mrs. Barry play the Irish Widow, in his own farce, after superbly enacting a tragic part, he could not help exclaiming, sincerely as he admired Mrs. Cibber, Pritchard, and Yates,—"She is the heroine of heroines!"

In his later days, when infirmity pressed him painfully, Barry occasionally lost his temper, for a moment. Once this occurred when Miss Pope's benefit interfered with that of Mrs. Barry, and he wrote an angry letter to Garrick, the ill-temper in which is indicated by Garrick's indorsement: " —from Barry; he calls Miss Pope ' *trumpery !*' "

Lacy told Davies that the Barrys' salary was £1,500 a year (but the cost of their dresses fell heavily on them). "Mr. Barry is only paid when he plays," said Garrick to Miss Pope; and this explains Barry's own remark: "I have lost £48 by the death of the Princess Louisa."

In costume and in stage diet, Barry was the reverse of Mossop. Near ninety years ago, the former played Othello in a gold-laced scarlet suit, small cocked hat, and knee breeches, with silk stockings, which then displayed his gouty legs. His wife, as Desdemona, wore, more correctly, a fascinating Italian costume, and looked as captivating as the decaying actor looked grotesque. Barry did not vary his diet according to the part he had to play.

It was his invariable custom, after acting, to sup on boiled fowl. His house, first in Broad Street, then in Norfolk, and lastly in Cecil Street, was visited by the good among the great. Such was Henry Pelham, himself an inelegant, but frank speaker in Parliament, who had a great admiration for Barry's graceful elocution.

The actor was in possession of all his powers, and his voice was at its sweetest, when he had this honest statesmen for friend. Henry Pelham died in 1754, when Barry and Miss Nossiter were playing Romeo and Juliet, with the relish of real lovers. Long before that, however, player and minister had been friends, but it was the player, the Mark Anthony of the stage, whose vain glory made wreck of their friendship. Pelham invited himself to sup with Barry, and the actor treated his guest as one prince might another. He invariably did the honors of his table with great elegance; but on this occasion there was a magnificent ostentation which offended Pelham. "I could not have given a more splendid supper myself," he remarked; and he would never consent to be Barry's guest again.

Of the nineteen characters, of which he was the original actor, there stand out, more celebrated than the rest, Mahomet, in Johnson's "Irene;" Young Norval, in London (in the white puckered satin suit); and Evander, in the "Grecian Daughter." The last was a master-piece of impersonation, and Barry drew tears as copiously in this part as ever his great rival did in King Lear, in which, by the way, Garrick's too frequent use of his white pocket-handkerchief was looked upon by the critics as bathos, with respect to the act; and an anachronism, with regard to the article!

"Were interred, in a private manner, in the cloisters, Westminster, the remains of Spranger Barry, late of Covent Garden Theatre." Such is the simple farewell, a week after his death, of the public papers, to young Douglas, old Evander, the silver-toned actor. Macklin was one of the funeral procession from Cecil Street to the cloisters. Looking into the grave, he murmured, "Poor Spranger!" and when some one would fain have led the old man away, he said mournfully, "Sir, I am at my rehearsal. Do not disturb my revery!"

Mrs. Barry survived her great husband, nearly a quarter of a century. Although that great husband did not found a school of acting, he had his imitators. A Barry school required a manly beauty, and an exquisitely-toned voice, such as fall to the lot of few actors. Nevertheless, in 1788, a successor was announced in the person of an Irish player, Middleton, whose real name was

Magann. He had abandoned the medical profession for the stage, some obstacles to his reaching which had actually rendered him partially and temporarily insane. He had fine powers of elocution, and in Romeo and Othello reminded the old friends of Barry—perhaps, painfully, of their lost favorite. The imitation was, no doubt, strong; but it was stronger off the stage than on; for, with 30s. a week, Middleton strove to live in Barry's sumptuous style. Thereby, he soon ceased to live at all, ending a brief career in abject misery, and leaving his body to be buried by the charity of his fellow-players.

Mrs. Barry was sufficiently recovered from the grief of losing her husband, to be able to play Viola, for her benefit, two months after his decease. When she resumed her great part of Lady Randolph, she spoke a few lines, written by Garrick, in memory of the first and the most elegant and perfect of young Norval. In those lines Barry is thus alluded to:—

"Of the lov'd pilot of my life bereft,
Save your protection, not a hope is left.
Without that peace your kindness can impart,
Nothing can calm this sorrow-beaten heart.
Urged by my duty, I have ventur'd here;
But how for Douglas can I shed the tear?
When real griefs the burden'd bosom press,
Can it raise sighs feigned sorrows to express?
In vain will art, from nature, help implore,
When nature for herself exhausts her store.
The tree cut down on which she clung and grew,
Behold, the propless woodbine bends to you;
Your soft'ning pow'r will spread protection round;
And, though she droops, may raise her from the ground."

I will not divide the sketch of the story of Mrs. Spranger Barry from that of the greatest and most worthy of her three husbands. Her father was a gay, well-to-do, but extravagant apothecary in Bath, whose daughter, Miss Street, was one of the belles there, celebrated for her graceful figure, expressive beauty, and rich auburn hair. The handsome and clever girl was jilted by a lover, whose affection for the apothecary's daughter cooled, on a sudden accession of fortune occurring to himself. Poor Ariadne went for solace to the North, where, after some while, she found a Bacchus in a hot-headed, jealous, but seductive actor, named Dancer, who married her, and placed her, nothing loath, upon the stage.

Her friends were scandalized, and her widowed mother bequeathed her a trifling annuity, only on condition of her ceasing to be an actress. Mrs. Dancer declined; and the honest man to whom the annuity was thereby forfeited, surrendered the whole to her, and bade her prosper!

Prosperity, however, only came after long study and severe labor, and many trials and vexations. When Barry assumed the management of the Dublin Theatre, he found Mrs. Dancer a most promising actress, and her lord the most jealous husband in Ireland. Youth, beauty, genius, were the endowments she had brought to that husband; and he, on his death, left her in full possession of all she had brought with her, and nothing more. But these and a liberal salary were charms that attracted many admirers. An Irish Earl was not ashamed, indeed, to woo the young, fair, and accomplished creature, with too free a gallantry; but all the earls in the peerage had no chance against the manly beauty and the silver tone of Spranger Barry.

Hand-in-hand with her new husband, she came to London. Garrick sat in the pit, at Foote's theatre, to witness her *début*. He approved; and forthwith she took a place at the head of her profession,—equal almost with her great namesake of the previous century, not inferior to Mrs. Pritchard or Mrs. Cibber, superior to Mrs. Yates, and not to be excelled till, in the evening of her days, Sarah Siddons came, to wish her gone, and to speed the going.

Mrs. Barry was otherwise remarkable: she had "a modest gayety in her manners and address; and though in Belvidera, Lady Randolph, Rutland, Euphrasia, Monimia, and Desdemona, she defied rivalry, she really preferred to act Lady Townley, Beatrice, the Widow Brady, Rosalind, and Biddy Tipkin. She acted tragedy, to gratify the house; comedy, to please herself; and she had a supreme indifference for the patronage of Ladies of Quality if she could only win the plaudits of the public at large. In the "Jubilee," however, she represented the *Tragic* muse.

Two years after Barry's death, his widow met with and married a scampish young Irish barrister, named Crawford, who spent her money, broke her heart, and was the cause of her theatrical wardrobe being seized by a Welsh landlord, for debt. The General who married the widow of Napoleon treated her with respect, but young Crawford only regarded the middle-aged but handsome and accomplished widow of Spranger Barry as a means whereby he might live. There is something supremely melancholy in the story of Mrs. Barry, after this time. She raised her young husband to such efficiency that in London, he played Pierre, to her Belvidera; and the bad fellow might have respected a woman who did this, and could also earn £1,100 in sixteen nights of acting, in Ireland. In the latter country, whither Mrs. Crawford, as I regret to call her, went, after playing Zara, in 1781, thereby leaving a long-desired opening to Mrs. Siddons,—Mr. Crawford acquired a reputation for shabbiness. On his benefit night, in a supper scene, he provided no refreshments on the table, for the actors seated round it, and this omission produced a scene of unrehearsed effects, —of exposure of Crawford's meanness, on the part of the players, and indignation against him on the part of the audience. When he became lessee, after Ryder, his own unhappy wife could not trust him, and often refused to go on, till Crawford had collected the amount of her salary from the doorkeepers,—if they had taken as much. He was reduced to such straits that one night, on the desertion of his unpaid band, he himself, and alone, played the violin in the orchestra, dressed as he was for Othello, which he acted on the stage. The Irish audience enjoyed the fun, and even Mrs. Crawford was so attached to him, that when Jephson's "Count of Narbonne" was first produced, in which, from her age, she should have played the Countess, she chose to act Adelaide, that her husband might still make love to her, as Theodore!

All that she earned, Crawford squandered. Fortunately, the small annuity left by her mother was secured to her, and this Crawford could not touch. What became of this unworthy Irishman I cannot say; but he helped to spoil Mrs. Crawford, as an actress. Her health and spirits failed, and her acting grew comparatively languid. The appearance of Mrs. Siddons, in the best of her years, strength, beauty, and ability, quickened the jealous pulses of the older actress's heart, and she once more played Lady

Randolph, with such effect, that the *Morning Chronicle* asserted no competitor could achieve a like triumph. The younger actress at last outshone Mrs. Crawford, whose very benefits became unprofitable. Her last appearance on the stage was at Covent Garden, on the 16th of April, 1798, in Lady Randolph, a character which Mrs. Siddons did not play that season,—her Mrs. Haller being the peculiar triumph of that glorious year.

Mrs. Barry, the original Euphrasia, died in 1801, having reaped honor enough to enable her to be free from envy of others, and having means sufficient to render her closing days void of anxiety. The Grecian Daughter, the Widow Brady, and Edwina, in Hannah More's "Percy," were the best of her original characters; of her other characters, Lady Randolph is the most intimately connected with her name. As between her and Mrs. Siddons, the judgment seems well founded which declares that Mrs. Crawford was inferior to Mrs. Siddons in the terrific, but superior in the pathetic. At Mrs. Crawford's "Is he alive?" in Lady Randolph, Bannister had seen half the pit start to their feet. Mrs. Siddons was but a "demi-goddess," as Walpole has it, in comedy, where Mrs. Barry was often inimitable. Walpole saw both actresses in "Percy," and he most admired Mrs. Siddons's passionate scenes. When, years before, he saw Mrs. Barry in the same play, his mind was preoccupied with politics, and he thought less of the actress than of passing events, of which he was reminded by passages in the play.

Mrs. Crawford, to take leave of her in her last name, was no admirer of the great actress by whom she was displaced; and albeit somewhat smartly, the old lady did not ill distinguish between the school to which she belonged and that founded by her comparatively young rival. "The Garrick school," she said, "was all *rapidity* and *passion;* while the Kemble school is so full of *paw* and *pause* that, at first, the performers, thinking their new competitors had either lost their cues, or forgotten their parts, used frequently to prompt them.

As we associate the name of Barry with that of Garrick, so do we that of Mossop with Spranger Barry. Mossop, whose career on the stage commenced in 1749, with Zanga,—type of characters in which alone he excelled,—died in 1773, at the age of forty-five.

He was the ill-fated son of an Irish clergyman, and he was always on the point of becoming a great actor, but never accomplishing that end. His syllables fell from him like minute-guns, even in or-din-a-ry con-ver-sa-tion, and the nickname of the "teapot actor," referred to his favorite attitude with one arm on his hip and the other extended. In London, an evanescent success in Richard and similar characters, almost made of him a rival of Garrick. In Dublin, he ruined Barry by his opposing management, which also brought down ruin on himself. Of this "monster of perfection," or the "pragmatical puppy," as he was variously called, we learn something from the *Dublin Journal* of May 8th, 1772, which says, " A few days ago, the celebrated tragedian, Mossop, moved to his new apartments in the Rules of the Fleet." When Mossop repaired to London, his powers had failed. He could not obtain "first business," declined to accept "second," and proudly died in poverty, at Chelsea, leaving for all fortune, one poor penny.

Garrick offered to bury him, but a kinsman who would have nothing to say to the actor, claimed the satisfaction of consigning him to the grave, whither, after all, his brother actors carried him. So ended the promising player who combined gastronomy with his study of the drama, and ordered his dinner, according to the part he had to act; sausages and Zanga; rump-steaks and Richard; pork-chops and Pierre; veal-cutlets and Barbarossa; and so forth! The antagonism of the two Irish actors seems to have wearied the Dublin people, who, at last,

"Did not care a toss-up,
If Mossop beat Barry, or Barry beat Mossop."

Of some other actors who left the stage about the same period, I will speak in the next chapter.

## CHAPTER X.

#### KITTY CLIVE, WOODWARD, SHUTER.

As Mr. Wilks passes along, to or from rehearsal, there are two young girls of about sixteen years of age, who gaze at him admiringly. Day after day, the graceful actor remarks this more graceful couple, the name of the brighter of whom is Raftor. If not Irish, she is of Irish parentage, and of good family. Her father, a native of Kilkenny, had served King James, and got ruin for his wages. When Catherine Raftor was born, in 1711, she was born into a poor household, and received as poor an education as many countesses, her contemporaries; and here we come upon her, some sixteen years afterwards, watching *Sir Harry Wildair* entering or issuing from that gate of Elysium, the stage-door of the Theatre Royal, Drury Lane. If she but knew the "Sesame!" that would give admission to *her*, she would be as happy as a houri!

She had the potent magic in her voice which won access for her to the elder Cibber, who awarded the young thing fifteen shillings a week, and then intrusted to her the little part of Ismenes, in "Mithridates." In such solemn guise commenced the career of the very queen of hoidens and chambermaids. As for her companion in the occupation of gazing at Wilks, in the street, —a Miss Johnson, she was appropriated to himself by Theophilus Cibber, who made of her his first wife; but she failed to attain the celebrity of Miss Raftor, who charmed audiences by the magic of her voice, and authors by the earnestness with which she strove to realize their ideas. She had achieved a great reputation as a comic actress, when, in 1732, Miss Raftor married Mr. Clive, the brother of Mr. Baron Clive. In the following year Fielding thus writes a paragraph of her biography, in his manly dedication to her of the "Intriguing Chambermaid," in which she played Lettice: "As great a favorite as you are at present with the audience, you would be much more so were they acquainted with your private character, could they see you laying out great part of the profits which arise to you from entertaining them so well, in the support of an aged father; did they see you who can charm them on the stage with personating the foolish and vicious characters of your sex; acting in real life the part of the best wife, the best daughter, the best sister, and the best friend."

"Kitty Clive," however, and her not very courteous husband could not keep household together, and they separated. The lady was a little vivacious, and stood undauntedly persistent for her rights, whether at home or on the stage—against her husband, or against Mrs. Cibber, or Edward Shuter, or Garrick himself, who stood in more awe of her than she of him. She alone dared take a liberty with him, and, by a witty word well applied, to so incline him to irrepressible laughter as to render speaking impossible. None other dared to interfere with Roscius. But it was all done out of good nature, in which Mrs. Clive was steeped to the lips, and of which she was lavish even to young actresses who came, in her later days, to dispute the succession to her parts. To the most formidable and triumphant of these, good Miss Pope, she gave excellent counsel, warning, and encouragement, for which "Pope" never ceased to be grateful.

Mrs. Cibber and Mrs. Clive, as Polly and Lucy, in the "Beggars' Opera," must have exhibited a matchless combination of singing and acting. Mrs. Clive was as ambitious as Mrs. Cibber, and would fain have played, like her, leading parts with Garrick. Her most successful attempt in this way was her Bizarre to his Duretete, in the "Inconstant." One effect of her careful, earnest, but perfectly natural and apparently spontaneous acting was to put every other player on his mettle. That done, Mrs. Clive took care the victory should not be lost to her for want of pains to gayly secure it. She was a capital mimic, particularly of the Italian signoras, whom she did not call by nice names. For a town languishing for the return of Cuzzoni, she had the most unqualified contempt. She herself was inimitable; she wrung from Johnson the rarest and most unqualified praise; and over her audiences she ruled supremely; they felt with her, smiled with her, sneered with her, giggled, tossed their heads, and laughed aloud with her. She was the one true Comic Genius, and none could withstand her.

She had that power of identification which belongs only to the great intellectual players. She was a born buxom, roguish chambermaid, fierce virago, chuckling hoiden, brazen romp, stolid country girl, affected fine lady, and thoroughly natural old woman, of whatever condition in life. From Phillida, in "Love in a Riddle," her first original character, to Mrs. Winnifred, in the "School for Rakes," her last, with forty years of toil and pleasure between them, she identified herself with all. *But*, in parts like Portia and Zara, which Mrs. Clive essayed, she fell below their requirements, though I do not know how the most beautifully expressive voice in the world could have been "awkwardly dissonant" in the latter part. Her Portia was too flippant, and in the trial scene it was her custom to mimic the most celebrated lawyer of the day. The laughter raised thereby was uncontrollable, but it was as illegitimately awakened as Doggett's when he played Shylock as a low comedy part.

After forty years' service, Mrs. Clive took leave of the stage, April 24, 1769, in Flora, in the "Wonder," and the Fine Lady, in "Lethe." Garrick played Don Felix; King, Lissardo; and Mrs. Barry, Violante; a grand cast, in which, we are told, Mrs. Clive made Flora, in the estimation of the audience, equal to Felix and Violante. Drury Lane, had it been capacious enough, would have held twice the number that gained admittance. From these she took leave, in an epilogue, weak and in bad taste, written by her friend Walpole, who affected to despise the writers of such addresses, and, in this case, did not equal those whom he despised.

Mrs. Clive has the reputation of being the authoress of two or three insignificant farces, produced at her benefits, to exhibit some peculiar talent of her own. They had no other merit. Such was her theatrical, let us now accompany her to her private, career. The last editor of Walpole's Letters states, that to a youth of folly succeeded an old age of cards. This statement is most gratuitous. Isaac Reed says: "Notwithstanding the temptations to which a theatre is sometimes apt to expose young persons of the female sex, and the too great readiness of the public to give way to unkind suppositions in regard to them, calumny itself has never seemed to aim the slightest arrow at her fame."

She was quick of temper, especially if David attempted to fine her for absence from rehearsals; and no wonder, since for one hundred and eighty nights' performance this charming actress received but £300! but, as she said, "I have always had good health, and have ever been above subterfuge." When about to retire, she wrote to Garrick, with some obliviousness as to dates: —" What signifies 52 ? They had rather see *the* Garrick and *the* Clive at 104 than any of the moderns. The ancients, you know, have always been admired. I do assure you, I am at present in such health and spirits, that, when I recollect I am an old woman, I am astonished."

In her retirement, Mrs. Clive passed many happy years, in the house which Walpole gave up as a home for herself and brother, next to his own at Strawberry, and which he playfully called "Clive-den." A green lane, which he cut for her use between the house and the common, he proposed to call *Drury Lane.* Here, at Clive-den, the ex-actress gave exquisite little suppers after pleasant little card parties, at which, in Walpole's phrase, she made miraculous draughts of fishes. Men and women of "quality" and good character, married and unmarried,—actors, authors, artists, and clergymen,—met here; where the brother of the hostess, a poor ex-actor, ill-favored and awkward, told capital stories, and found the company in laughter and Walpole in flattery.

Of an evening, in summer-time, trim Horace and portly Clive might be seen walking in the meadows together; or Walpole and a brilliant company, gossiping, laughing, flirting, philandering, might be noted on their way across the grass to Strawberry, after a gay time of it at "*Little* Strawberry Hill." Not always without mishap, as Walpole himself has recorded in his narrative of his perilous passing of the stile with Miss Rich; and not invariably in the very sunniest of humors, for Miss Pope had seen Horace "gloomy of temper and dryly sarcastic of speech." The place was, perhaps, at its pleasantest, when Walpole, Mrs. Clive and her brother, sat together in the garden, and conversed playfully of old dramatic glories. *She* was so joyous, that Lady Townshend said, —her face rose on Strawberry and made it sultry. And Walpole himself remarked, in 1766, "Strawberry is in perfection; the verdure has all the bloom of spring · the orange-trees are loaded with blossoms: the gallery is all sun and gold; and Mrs. Clive all sun and vermilion." When Hounslow powder-mills blew up, Walpole described the terrific power of the explosion, by remarking, that it "almost shook Mrs. Clive!" Only the death of the last Earl of Radnor, of the Robartes line, made her *almost* look sad. The earl left her £50 as a memorial of his respect; and what with the heat of the summer of 1757, the unexpected legacy, and her assumption of respectful. grief, she made up one of the drollest faces imaginable. One of her dear delights was to play quadrille with George Montagu, from dinner to supper; and then to sing Purcell, from supper to breakfast time. She left the place, even for short intervals, with reluctance; but her brilliant face was seen for a whole day in Palace Yard, where she sat to see the coronation procession of George III., with her *great* friends around her, —Lady Hertford, Lady Anne Conway, Lady Hervey, Lady Townshend, Miss Hotham, Mr. Chute, and also her brother. Her only trials were when the tax-gatherer ran off, and she was compelled to pay her rates twice; or when the parish refused to mend her ways, as she said; or her house was broken into by burglars; or when she was robbed in her own lane by footpads. "Have you not heard," she wrote to Garrick, in June, 1776, " of your poor Pivy? I have been rob'd and murder'd, coming from Kingston. Jimey" (her brother) "and I in a post chey, at half-past nine, just by Teddington church was stopt. I only lost a little silver and my senses; for one of them came into the carriage with a great horse-pistol, to search for my watch, but I had it not with me." And then Garrick and other actors, with Governor Johnstone and his wife, met at Little Strawberry at dinner, and laughed over past perils.

In 1784 she came up to London to see Mrs. Siddons act. Mrs. Clive was born in the life-time of Elizabeth Barry, who had acted before Charles II.; she had seen Mrs. Porter, Mrs. Oldfield, Mrs. Cibber, Mrs. Pritchard, Mrs. Yates, and Anne Barry; and finally, she saw Mrs. Siddons. Mrs. Clive listened to the new actress with profound attention; and on being asked, at the conclusion of the performance, what she thought of it: "Think!" said the vivacious old lady, in her ready way; "I think it's all truth and daylight!"

In the December of the following year, the long career of this erst comic muse came to a close. Walpole tells it briefly, unaffectedly, and well. "It did not much surprise me," he says; "and the manner comforts me. I had played at cards with her, at Mrs. Gostlings, three nights before I came to town, and found her extremely confused, and not knowing what she did; indeed I had seen something of this sort before, and had found her much broken this autumn. It seems, that the day after I saw her, she went to General Lister's burial, and had got cold, and had been ill for two or three days. On the Wednesday morning, she rose to have her bed made; and while sitting on the bed, with her maid by her, sank down at once, and died without a pang or a groan." So departed the actress, of whom Johnson said, that she had more true humor than any other he had ever seen. She originated nearly fourscore characters; among others, Nell, in the latter "Devil to Pay;" Lappet ("Miser"); Edging ("Careless Husband"); half a dozen Kittys; but chief of all, the Kitty of "High Life Below Stairs;" Muslin ("Way to Keep Him"); and Mrs. Heidelberg, in the "Clandestine Marriage."

HARRY WOODWARD: to think of him, is to think of Captain Bobadil,—in which he never had equal,—and of Harlequin, in which he was second only to Rich. To remember Harry Woodward, is to remember the original French Cook, in Dodsley's "Sir John Cockle," wherein Woodward turned to good account the French he had learned at Merchant Tailors' school. He was also the first Beau, in "Lethe;" and his Flash, in "Miss in her Teens," his Jack Meggot, in the "Suspicious Husband," his Dick, in the "Apprentice," his Block, in the "Reprisal," his Lofty, in the "Good-Natured Man," his Captain Ironsides, in the "Brothers," and his Captain Absolute, in the "Rivals,"—were all original and brilliant creations, in acting which, the best of his many brightly-endowed successors lacked something possessed by *him*, whose Slender and Petruchio are described as being perfect pictures of simplicity and manliness.

Look at him in his boyhood;—he is a tallow-chandler's son, *rien que ça!* living close by the Anchor brewery, in Southwark; —Mr. Child's brewery, whose daughter married with his clerk, Halsey; and then it was Halsey's brewery; and Halsey's only daughter married Lord Cobham; and from this pair, the brewery was bought by Halsey's manager and nephew, Ralph Thrale, on the death of whose son, Henry, it passed by purchase to his chief clerks, Barclay and Perkins. The brewery, now, is no more like what it was in Woodward's days than Drury Lane theatre is like the Curtain, the Fortune, or the Globe. As Woodward played beneath the Anchor gateway, there was probably little uneasiness in his mind at the idea of his helping and succeeding his sire in candle-making; but when Woodward became a pupil at Merchant Tailors', I think it may have been otherwise. How young Woodward was ever sent thither, I cannot guess; but I conclude that his father, "the *tallow*-chandler," was not aware, that among the statutes of the institution there was one which said that, "in the schoole at noe time of the yere, they shall use tallow candle in noe wise, but wax candles onely." Perhaps, old Woodward supplied them to order.

I think if Woodward had never gone to Merchant Tailors', he never would have added lustre to the British stage. He was born about the last year of Queen Anne's reign, and was in Lawrence Pountney when he was some ten years old. The quick lad became a very good classical scholar, and in after years, he used to astonish and gratify the society which he most loved, by the aptness and beauty of his quotations; not for effect, for Harry Woodward, look you, was as modest as he was clever.

Well, learning to enjoy Horace, you will say, was no specific for turning a boy into a player. Perhaps not; but there were less satisfactory customs then prevailing among the *Mercatores Scissores.* The masters treated the boys who missed their election to St. John's, with canary and cake, as if to teach them that drinking was a solace for disappointment. Then the discipline was lax, and young Merchant Tailors of the Bench were seduced by the rather older Merchant Tailors of the Table, to taverns, and to ordinaries, where gaming was practised, and to the playhouse, where they learned something new from the Vizard Masks in the pit. Then, there was young Beckingham, the linen-draper's son, and a Merchant Tailor of the Table, who wrote a tragedy, "Scipio Africanus," to see which the whole school occupied a greater portion of the Lincoln's Inn Fields' pit, and sent up applauding shouts for Quin, who acted Scipio, as well as for their school-fellow, the author. These practices and the traditions of others may have influenced a lively and thoughtless boy, who was proud to play Peachem in the juvenile company, who acted the "Beggars' Opera," under the elder Rich, at Lincoln's Inn Fields. I cannot find exactly the date when Woodward commenced as a professional actor; but he was not more than a mere youth. There was a boy of his name, at Goodman's Fields, who played pantomime parts before Harry Woodward appeared there in 1730, —commencing then a career with Simple, in the "Merry Wives of Windsor," which ended at Covent Garden, on the 13th of January, 1777, with Stephano, in the "Tempest." On the 10th of April, the then new comedy, "Know your own Mind," was acted, for his benefit, and on that day week, the lad who used to play under the gateway of the Anchor brewery,—to trudge, in all weathers, over old London Bridge, to Merchant Tailors' School, and who preferred the life of a player to that of a candle-maker, died; and with him, it was said, as Wildair with Wilks, Captain Bobadil died too.

Woodward was one of the most careful dressers on the stage; not as regards chronology, but perfection of suit; of fitness, no one then made account. Woodward played Mercutio in the full dress of a very fine gentleman of Woodward's day; it was unexceptionable as a costume, though not fitting in the play. Then, he was one of the few lucky actors who never seem to grow old. After nigh upon half a century of labor, his Fitzpatrick, in "News from Parnassus," was as young in look and buoyant in manner as the Spruce of his earlier days. He was also among one of the few judicious and generous actors, when in the highest favor with the town; at which season, he did not disdain, when it was needful, to go on as a soldier, to deliver a message; but then he delivered it like a soldier, and the frequenters of the joyous rooms under and over the "Piazza," made approving reference to that "clever little bit of Woodward's, last night."

Woodward always found a defender in Garrick. Foote, who abused hospitality by mimicking his host, called Woodward a "contemptible fellow," when he heard that the latter was about to dress Malingene so as to look like Foote. "He cannot be contemptible," said Garrick, "since you are afraid of him in the very line in which you, yourself, excel."

Of course, being naturally a comic actor, Woodward had an affection for tragedy; but it was not in him to utter a serious line with due effect. His scamps were perfect in their cool impudence; his modern fops shone with a brazen impertinence; his fops of an older time glistened with an elegant rascality; his mock heroes were stupendously but suspiciously outrageous; his every-day simpletons, vulgarly stolid; and his Shaksperian light characters brimful and running over with Shakspearian spirit. Graceful of form, his aspect was something serious off the stage, but he no sooner passed the wing than a ripple of funny emotion seemed to roll over his face, and this, combined with a fine stage-voice, never failed to place him and his audience in the happiest sympathetic connection. "Bobadil was his great part, in which he acquired a vast increase of reputation, and gave a striking proof of his genius;" but there were two other characters in which Woodward could hardly have been inferior, for it may be gathered from Wilkinson, that in Marplot, he was every thing author or audience could wish, and that in Touchstone, he excelled at least all his contemporaries, and had no equal in it till Lewis came.

Woodward was at one time a *good man*, in the mercantile view of the phrase, for he was a rich man. Unfortunately, he was induced by Spranger Barry to become partner with him in the Dublin Theatre,—in which venture, Woodward lost all he had saved; and Barry, too, made shipwreck of his fortune. Garrick passed from the stage to years of repose and enjoyment. Barry and Woodward could not quit it till, having had more than enough of labor, Death summoned them to a, perhaps, not unwelcome rest.

Little is known of the origin of Edward Shuter. Small trust can be placed in the report that he was the son of a clergyman— not because he himself was, at one time, only a billiard-marker, or that he could with difficulty read his parts, and had much perplexity in even signing his own name; but because Ned himself never boasted of it. What is certain of him is, that he was an actor entirely of the Garrick period, commencing his vocation as

Catesby, at Richmond, in 1744, and concluding as Falstaff, to the Prince, in "Henry IV.," of Lewis, played for his own benefit, at Covent Garden, in May, 1776.

I suppose Chapman, who directed the theatre at Richmond, was struck by the rich humor of the billiard-marker; but it was strange that a low comedian should make his *début* in so level a part as Catesby. He was then, however, a mere boy. In June, 1746, when he acted Osrick and third Witch in "Macbeth," Garrick playing Hamlet and the Thane, he was designated "Master Shuter." Thence, to the night on which he went home to die, after playing Falstaff, his life was one of intense professional labor, with much jollification, thoughtlessness, embarrassment, gay philosophy, hard drinking, and addiction to religion, as it was expounded by Whitfield.

He played through the entire range of a wide comic repertory, and among the characters which he originated are Papillon, in the "Liar," Justice Woodcock, Druggett, Abrahamides, Croaker, Old Hardcastle, and Sir Anthony Absolute. His most daring effort was in once attempting *Shylock!* There are few comic actors who have had such command over the muscles of the face as Shuter. He could do what he liked with them, and vary the laughter as he worked the muscles. Not that he depended on grimace; this was only the ally of his humor, and both were impulsive—as the man was, by nature; he often stirred the house with mirth, by saying something better than the author had put down for him. Off, as on the stage, it was Shuter's characteristic that he pleased everybody—and ruined himself. I never pass his old lodgings in Denzil Street, without thinking kindly of the eccentric but kind-hearted player. Some laughed at him, perhaps, for taking to serious ways, without abandoning his old gay paths of delight; but the former was of his sincerity, the latter of his weakness. That he should choose to follow Calvinistic Whitfield rather than Arminian Wesley, does seem singular; but poor Ned felt that if salvation depended on works, "Pilgarlick," as Whitfield called him, was lost; whereas, faith rescued him, and Shuter could believe. He did something more; works he added to his faith, though he made no account of them. Of all the frequenters of Whitfield's Tabernacle in Tottenham Court Road, there was no more liberal giver than the shattered, trembling, laughing, hoping, fearing, despairing—in short, much perplexed actor and man, who oscillated between Covent Garden stage and the Tabernacle pulpit, and meditated over his pipe and bottle in Drury Lane, upon the infinite varieties of life. And therewith, *exit*, Shuter: and *enter*, Mr. Foote!

## CHAPTER XI.

### SAMUEL FOOTE.

"ONE Foote, a player," is Walpole's contemptuous reference to him who was otherwise designated as the "British Aristophanes." But, as often happens, the player was as good a man by birth, and at least as witty a man by nature, as he who despised him. His father was a Cornish gentleman, and an M. P.; his mother a daughter of Sir Edmund Goodere, Bart., through whom Foote called cousins with the ducal family of Rutland. A lineal successor of this baronet followed Mrs. Clive, as Walpole's tenant at Little Strawberry Hill, and Horace called him "a goose."

Young Sam Foote, born at Truro, in 1720, became a pupil at the Worcester Grammar School. His kinsfolk on the maternal side used to invite him to dinner on the Sundays, and the observant, but not too grateful guest, kept the Monday school hilarious and idle, by imitations of his hospitable relatives. The applause he received, helped to make Foote, ultimately, both famous and infamous.

Later in life he entered Worcester College, Oxford, and quitted both with the honors likely to be reaped by so clever a student. Having made fun of the authorities, made a fool of the provost, and made the city turn up the eye of astonishment at his audacity in dress, and way of living, he "retired," an undergraduate, to his father's house. There, by successfully mimicking a couple of justices who were his father's guests, he was considered likely to have an especial call to the Bar. He entered at the Temple, and while resident there, a catastrophe occurred in his family. His mother had two brothers; Sir John Goodere and Captain Samuel Goodere. The baronet was a bachelor, and the captain in the royal navy, being anxious to enjoy the estate, strangled his elder brother on board his own ship, the *Ruby*. The assassin was executed. Shortly after, Cooke introduced his finely-dressed friend Foote, at a club in Covent Garden, as "Mr. Foote, the nephew of the gentleman who was lately hung in chains for murdering his brother!"

Foote succeeded as ill at the Temple as at Oxford; and his necessities, we are told, drove him on the stage. As, when those necessities were relieved, he preferred buying a diamond ring, or new lace for his coat, to purchasing a pair of stockings, we may fairly conclude that the stage was a more likely place wherein he might succeed than the back benches of a court of law. Indeed, he did not live to make, but to break, fortunes. Of these he " got through" three, and realized the motto on his carriage, "*Iterum, iterum, iterumque.*"

His connection with those great amateur actors, the Delavals, was of use to him, for it afforded him practice, and readier access to the stage, where, as a regular player, he first appeared at the Haymarket, on the 6th of February, 1744, as Othello, "dressed after the manner of the country." He failed; yet "he perfectly knew what the author meant," says Macklin. Others, again, describe his Moor as a master-piece of burlesque, only inferior in its extravagance and nonsense to his Hamlet, which I do not think he ever attempted. His Pierre and Shylock were failures, and even his Lord Foppington, played in his first season, indicated that Cibber was not to depart with the hope that he was likely to have in Foote an able successor.

Nevertheless, it is difficult to assign Foote's position exactly. According to Davies, he was despicable in all parts, but those he wrote for himself; and Colman says he was jealous of every other actor, and cared little how any dramas but his own were represented. Wilkinson ascribes to him a peculiar excellence.

In Dublin, 1744-5, he was well received, and drew a few good houses; and thence came to Drury Lane. He played the fine gentlemen,—Foppington, Sir Novelty Fashion, Sir Courtly Nice, Sir Harry Wildair; with Bayes, and Dick; Tinsel, and the Younger Loveless, in Beaumont and Fletcher's "Scornful Lady;" but he could not reach the height of Cibber, Booth, or Wilks. He had the defects of all three, and nothing superior to either, but in the expression of the eye and lip. His thick-set figure, and his vulgar cast of features, he had not yet turned to purpose. He was conscious of a latent strength, but knew not where it lay. He had failed in tragedy, and was pronounced unfit for comedy; and he asked, almost despairingly, "What the deuce then *am* I fit for?" As we find him the next three years, 1747, 8, 9, at the Haymarket, giving his "Diversions of the Morning," his "Tea," his "Chocolate," and his "Auction of Pictures;" it is clear that he soon discovered where his fitness lay.

At the outset, he combined the regular drama with his "Entertainment," Shuter, Lee, and Mrs. Hallam, being with him. The old wooden house being unlicensed, Foote got into difficulties, for a time, but he surmounted them by perseverance. He drew the town, morning after morning, and then night after night, with imitations of the actors at other houses, of public characters, and even of members of private clubs. Some of the actors retaliated, Woodward particularly. Their only strong point was that Foote, in striving to enrich himself, was injuring the regular drama. His Cat Concerts did really constitute fair satire against the Italians. But people paid, laughed, and defied law and the constables; and Foote continued to show up Dr. Barrowby, the critic; Chevalier Taylor, the quack oculist; Cocks, the auctioneer; Orator Henley; Sir Thomas De Veal, the Justice of the Peace; and other noted persons of the day.

How these persons were affected by the showing-up, I cannot say; but Foote objected to being himself shown up by Woodward. Whereon, Garrick asked, "Should he dress at you in the play, how can you be alarmed at it, or take it ill? The character, exclusive of some little immoralities which can never be applied to you, is that of a very smart, pleasant, conceited fellow, and a good mimic."

For a few years Foote was engaged alternately at either house, on a sort of starring engagement, during which he produced his "Englishman in Paris" (Buck, by Macklin; Lucinda, by his clever daughter); "Englishman Returned from Paris" (Buck, by Foote); "Taste" (Lady Pentweazle, by Worsdale); and the "Author" (Cadwallader, by Foote). In the first two satires, was scourged the alleged folly of sending a young fellow to travel, by way of education; but in this instance the satire fails, for Buck, who leaves home a decided brute, returns in an improved form as only a coxcomb. "Taste" satirized the enthusiasm for objects of *vertù*, the gross humbug of portrait painters, and the vanity of those who sat to them. Worsdale was himself an artist, and a scamp. He kept, half-starved, and kicked Letitia Pilkington, the very head of all the house of hussies, obnoxious to such treatment. In the "Author" Foote did not so much satirize writers, or care for improving their condition, as he did to caricature one of his own friends, Mr. Ap Rice (or Apreece), a patron of authors, who sat open-mouthed and silly, in the boxes, to the delight of the audience, and mystified by the reflection of himself, which he beheld on the stage.

In 1760, Foote brought out his "Minor" in Dublin, he playing Shift, and Woodward, Mrs. Cole. In the summer of the same year he reproduced it at the Haymarket, playing Shift, Smirk, and Mrs. Cole. After occasionally acting at the two larger theatres, and creating Young Wilding, in the "Liar," he finally went to the Haymarket, where, from 1762 to 1776, he acted almost exclusively.

In the "Minor," the author pilloried Longford, the plausible auctioneer, Mother Douglas, a woman of very evil life, and, in Shift, the Rev. George Whitfield, who was nobly, and with much self-abnegation, endeavoring to amend life wherever he found it of an evil quality. Here was Foote's weakness. He did not care for the suppression of vice; but if he who attempted to suppress it had a foible, or a strongly-marked characteristic, Foote laid hold of him, and made him look like a fool or a rascal, in the eyes of a too willing audience.

The "Minor" failed in Dublin, very much to the credit of an Irish audience, if they condemned it on the ground of its grossness and immorality. To the credit of English society, there was strong protest made against it here; and also in Scotland—in and out of the pulpit; but the theatres were full whenever it was represented, nevertheless! The injury it effected must have been incalculable, for the wit was on a par with the blasphemy; but when Saving Grace and the work of the Holy Ghost are employed to raise a laugh of derision, the edification of the hearers is as little to be expected as it was hoped or cared for by the author. Foote, nevertheless, protested that in this piece, which brought back the coarseness of Aphra Behn, with a deeper irreligious tint, he meant no offence against the pious, but only against hypocrites. He was merely driven to that excuse. It is one, I think, that cannot be accepted, for Foote was not a truthful man. When he was taxed with ridiculing the Duchess of Kingston as Kitty Crocodile, in the "Trip to Calais," he assured Lord Hertford, the Chamberlain, that he had no idea that the allusions in that piece could apply to the duchess; and when he failed in procuring a license to play it, he had the impudence to assert as the grounds of failure, that he had refused to put Lord Hertford's son on the box-keeper's free list—or as a more improbable story has it, to make the young gentleman box-keeper; and—hence, denial of the license ! Lady Llanover, in a note in her *Memoirs of Mrs. Delaney*, roundly asserts that when Foote had completed his caricature of the duchess, " he informed her of it, in the hopes of extorting a large bribe for its suppression ;" but from this assertion I dissent; though it is not improbable, as Walpole has recorded, that the duchess offered him a bribe "just as if he had been a member of parliament!"

Foote's fourteen years of summer seasons at the Haymarket, formed an era of their own. There had never been any thing resembling it, nor has any thing like it succeeded. In his first year, 1762, he produced the "Orators." "There is a madness for oratories," writes Walpole, alluding to Macklin's school, and Foote's lectures. In the satire on public speakers, Foote caricatured Faulkner, the Irish publisher; a fact which Chesterfield was the first to joyfully proclaim to the victim, whose infirmity—he had but one leg—should have saved him from what otherwise may have been due to his conceit, if personal caricature be justifiable at all.

In the "Mayor of Garratt," the more general caricature of a class—the Sneaks and the Bruins, has been more lastingly popular; the individual, however, is included in Matthew Mug, aimed at the Duke of Newcastle.

In the "Patron," the general satire was levelled at the enthusiasm of antiquaries, men capable of falling in love with a lady, because her nose resembled that of the bust of the Empress Poppœa. The individual pilloried in this piece was Lord Melcombe, under the form of Sir Thomas Lofty, played by Foote;

who also laughed at the English Nabob of that day, in Sir Peter Pepperpot, acted by him, in the same piece. Foote considered this his best play; but in this, as in all his pieces, with much original wit, there was rank, though judicious plagiarism, from the stores of other writers.

In the "Commissary," Foote, as Zachary Fungus, aimed his shafts at the gentility of the vulgar; hitting Dr. Arne, personally, in the character of Dr. Catgut. In 1766, Foote met with the accident which reduced him to the condition of one-legged George Faulkner, whom he held up to ridicule in the "Orators," and he did not play; but in 1767 he opened the Haymarket Theatre, after reconstructing the interior. He wrote no new piece; but he had the Barrys for a few nights, and brought out that burlesque-tragedy, the "Tailors," which was said to have been left anonymously at Dodsley's shop, and which kept its vitality down to the days of John Reeve. The fault of this piece is not in having tailors instead of persons of consequence in a burlesque, but—that the tailors talk seriously, and like people of consequence, well brought up.

His great success in 1768, was with his "Devil on Two Sticks," by which he cleared between three and four thousand pounds—a golden harvest, of which scarcely a grain was left at the close of the year. The satire here is generally laid against medical quackery, in the person of Dr. Last, by Weston; but Foote, as the Devil, in disguise, took upon him the burden of individual caricature. As Dr. Squib, he rendered ridiculous Dr. Brocklesby; and as the President of a College of Physicians, he exposed to derision Sir William Browne, who had taken an active part in a professional controversy, now without interest. Sir William's wig, coat, contracted eye firmly holding an eye-glass, and his remarkably upright figure, were all there; but the caricaturist had forgotten Sir William's special characteristic—his muff, which the good-tempered doctor sent to Foote, to make the figure complete!

In 1769, Foote produced nothing new of his own; but the general business was good, and Sheridan drew good houses in tragedy, both this season and the next, though Foote described him as "dwindled down into a mere *Cock and Bottle* Chelsea Pensioner." In 1770, Foote, in his "Lame Lover," in which he acted Sir Luke

Limp (Vandermere and Weston played Sergeant and Jack Circuit), made a miss in aiming at "those maggots of the law, who breed in the rotten parts of it." In the following year, the groundwork of his expected annual play, was the ungallant conduct of Mr. Walter Long to Miss Linley, afterwards Mrs. R. B. Sheridan. In the "Maid of Bath," Long is severely handled under the name of Flint, and Bath society is roughly illustrated. The taste, in using a private, domestic story for such a purpose, is questionable. The satire, however, did not kill Long, who lived till 1807, and bequeathed then, to the already wealthiest heiress in England, Miss Tilney, daughter of Sir James Tilney, Bart., nearly a quarter of a million of money. It was this heiress's hard fate to marry a more worthless personage than he who only wooed and was false to the Maid of Bath; and the small wreck of her fortune is now being saved—or lost amid the breakers and breakwaters of the Court of Chancery.

Foote, characterizing himself as a "popularity-monger," produced in the course of his next season the "Nabob," in which he made a combined charge on antiquaries and Anglo-East-Indians generally, in the person of Sir Matthew Mite, in which was involved the individual caricature of General Richard Smith, whose father had been a cheesemonger. Some irascible Anglo-Indians called at Foote's house in Suffolk Street, behind the theatre, to administer personal chastisement; but he bore himself with such tact, convinced them so conclusively that he had not had Smith in his mind, and persuaded them, by reading the play, that it was only naughty old Indians generally against whom he wrote, that they who came to horsewhip remained to dine, and make a night of it. The piece was afterwards supported by the *good* old ladies, to show their antagonism to Anglo-Indian naughtiness.

Foote's "Nabob" afforded Walpole an excuse for withdrawing his name from the Society of Antiquaries. In the play, Mite is made an F. S. A.; and reads a foolish address to the Society, on Whittington and his Cat. This was in ridicule of Pegge, who had touched on the subject of the illustrious lad, but who was "gravelled" by the then inexplicable *Cat.* Walpole, affecting to see that Pegge and Foote had rendered the Society for ever ridiculous, took his name off the books; but not on that account.

The true ground was that, in his own words :—" I heard that they intended printing some more foolish notes against my " Richard III."

In 1773, Foote produced his Puppet-show-droll, " Piety in Pattens, or the Handsome Housemaid." In this he committed a mistake, not unlike that he had committed in the " Minor," by taking unworthy means to a certain end. In a dull and occasionally indecent introductory address, he professed to have chosen puppets for his actors, because the contemporary players were marked by inability. This was said to a densely crowded house, while Garrick and Barry were still at the head of their profession ! In the piece itself, played by excellently contrived puppets, Foote intended to ridicule sentimental comedy, by professedly playing one, showing " how a maiden of low degree, by the mere effects of morality and virtue, raised herself to riches and honors." The sentiment here involved is, of course, made fun of; but, in fact, the author failed to render it ridiculous, for the housemaid declines the riches and honors which she might have taken as the rewards of her morality and virtue. There ensued a riot, and some damage, after which Foote resorted to the novel process of resting the approbation of his piece, on a show of hands; but though there was a majority in his favor, the piece was not permanently successful. The author found compensation in his "Bankrupt," which was chiefly aimed at a speculating Baronet, but generally at all who were concerned in cheating their creditors. In 1774 a better, but a more cruel piece of wit was produced by " Foote, the celebrated buffoon," as Walpole had called him the year before. This was the " Cozeners." Mrs. Grieve, the woman who had extorted money, on pledge of procuring government appointments, and who had not only deceived Charles Fox, by pretending to be able to marry him to an heiress, but had lent him money rather than miss his chariot from her door, was fair game, and was well exposed, in Mrs. Fleecem. This was delicate ground, however, for Foote, who was very generally accused of having earned an annuity from Sir Francis Delaval, by bringing about a marriage between Sir Francis and the widow Lady Nassau Powlett, who had been a very intimate friend of Foote's. The cruelty of the satire lay in the character of Mrs. Simony, in which the vices of the once fashionable and lately hanged preacher, Dodd, were transferred to his then living widow. It was an insult to that poor woman, and a brutality against the Rev. Richard Dodd, brother of the criminal, and the estimable Vicar of Camberwell. The ridicule of Lord Chesterfield's advice to his son is in far better taste. But Foote was now beginning to lose spirit, and he produced only one more piece, the " Capuchin," in which he played O'Donovan, in 1776. This piece was merely an alteration of the unlicensed " Trip to Calais," in which Foote had gibbeted the Duchess of Kingston. In the " Capuchin" he more rudely treated her Grace's Chaplain, Jackson, under the name of Viper; but the farce had small merit, and the only thing in connection with it, deserving of record is, that Jackson, while on trial for treason, in the time of the Irish Rebellion, destroyed himself.

Such are the dramatic works of the English satirist, to compare whom with Aristophanes is an injustice to the Athenian, whose works Plato admired; and even St. Chrysostom kept them under his pillow! In the eleven extant comedies, of the fifty-four written by Aristophanes, we find the inequality of the distribution of riches pointed at in " Plutus ;" in the " Clouds" the poet is in jest, not in earnest, in denouncing vice; in the " Frogs," we have a humorous review of both, Euripides and Æschylus; in the " Knights," a satire against Cleon, which is unequalled for fun and effect. The " Inhabitants of Acharnæ" is a " screaming farce," chiefly in favor of peace-makers. The " Wasps" caricatures the Athenian disposition to go to law. The " Birds," is made a vehicle to convince the audience of the necessity of a change in the government. " Peace," in which the heroine, so called, never utters a word, was written to bring about the much-desired end of the Peloponnesian war. The " Female Orators" exposes the absurdity of women desiring to be beyond their vocation. The " Feast of Ceres" demonstrates that the women can both say and act to the purpose, when called upon; and this is more seriously shown in " Lysistrata." All these, however, are original, plot and wit are the poet's own (which is far from being the case with Foote); and the chief end seems to be the public good, and not the satirizing of particular individuals. Aristophanes, however, goes in this latter direction, even farther than Foote; his abuse of Socrates, a great and good reformer, is not palliated by the wit which accompanies it; a daring wit, which was carried to such excess that the downfall of the old comedy ensued, and Alcibiades forbade that any living person should be, thenceforth, attacked by name upon the stage.

The descriptions of Aristophanes are true, however coarse they may be. He was a patriot and philosopher, as well as a poet, and fearless in attacking every obstruction to the well-being and improvement of society. Foote laughed at individuals, denied the personality, and cared nothing at all as to who might be the better or the worse for his sarcasm. It has been said that the satire of Aristophanes killed Socrates. It really did so no more than that of Foote killed Whitfield. In this one respect, the two men *are* alike.

Such exhibition of character as Foote made was described by Johnson, as *vice;* and he, like Churchill, denied the actor's powers. The former maintained that Foote was never like the person he assumed to be, but only unlike Foote; and that he failed altogether, except with marked characteristics. He was as a painter who can portray a wen; and if a man hopped on one leg, Foote could do that to the life. Foote himself acknowledged that he pursued folly, and not vices, but he never mimicked in others the follies which were the most strongly marked in himself; such as extravagance in dress. He did not aim at improvement of character; his motives in this respect were of the very lowest: " Who the devil !" he said, " will give money to be told Mr. Such-a-one is wiser and better than himself . . . Demolish a conspicuous character and sink him below our level . . . *there* we are pleased, there we chuckle and grin, and toss the half-crown on the counter." Now, bad examples which lower our standard of right and wrong do infinite harm. At this sinking of men below our level, the Archbishop of Dublin has glanced, when he says : " For *one* who is corrupted by becoming as bad as a bad example, there are ten that are debased by becoming *content* with being better."

If there was little honesty in Foote's method of dealing with human weaknesses, so was there small courage in the spirit of the satirist. He could annoy Garrick by saying that his puppets would not be so large as life, " not larger in fact than Mr. Garrick," and could mimic him as refusing to engage Punch and his wife,—Mr. and Mrs. Barry,—for he could do so with impunity. But Barry, six feet high, he never assailed, and he was deterred from bringing Johnson on the stage, by a threat from the latter that he would break every bone in his body.

Johnson, personally, disliked Foote, yet was forced into admiration by Foote's wonderful powers of wit and laughter-compelling humor. Johnson, probably, was trying to excuse himself when he said that if the grave Betterton had come into the room where Foote was, the latter would have driven him from it by his broad-faced, obstreperous mirth. But Foote's conversational powers and wide knowledge, which charmed Fox, would have charmed Betterton too, and I do not think either could have been like Johnson's imaginary hostler, who, encountering Foote in a stable, thought him a comic fellow, but parted from him without a feeling of respect. Johnson thought less of Foote's conversation than Fox did; he described it as between wit and buffoonery, but admitted that Foote was a "fine fellow in his way," and he hoped somebody would write his life with diligence. Walpole tersely described him as "a Merry Andrew, but no fool." So the black boy thought, who hated the small beer which Foote (who sneered at Garrick for having been a wine-merchant) at one time brewed and sold, through a partner. The boy was so delighted with Foote's wit, as he waited on him at dinner, that he declared, in the kitchen, he could drink his bad beer forever, and would certainly never complain of it again.

Foote had so little moral courage, and was so thin-skinned, that attacks upon him in the newspapers caused him exquisite pain, and he stooped so far to the Duchess of Kingston as to offer to suppress his "Trip to Calais," if she would put a stop to the assaults made on him through the press. The notorious lady, who was tried for bigamy, called him the "descendant of a Merry Andrew," and Foote informed her that though his good mother had lived to fourscore, she had never been married *but once.* Something, however, is to be said for this well-abused person. She did not marry the Duke of Kingston till the Ecclesiastical Court had broken her marriage with Lord Hervey. The House of Lords reversed the decree of the Ecclesiastical Court, after the lady had married a second time, and it was this reversal of an old judgment which exposed her to the penalties of bigamy. When these facts are remembered, half the jokes against Foote's adversary fall to the ground.

Neither the claims of friendship nor a sense of courtesy could restrain Foote from a brutal jest when opportunity offered to make one. He had no more intimate friend than Charles Holland, who was at Drury Lane, from 1755 to 1769; and whose father was a baker, at Chiswick. Foote attended the funeral there, and on his return to town, he gayly remarked, that he "had seen Holland shoved into the family oven!" As for his courtesy, it was on a par with his sense of friendship and fellowship. When down at Stratford, on the occasion of the Shakspeare Jubilee, Garrick's success embittered Foote's naturally bitter spirit. A well-dressed gentleman there, civilly spoke to him on the proceedings. "Has Warwickshire, sir," said Foote, "the advantage of having produced you as well as Shakspeare?" "Sir," replied the gentleman, "I come from Essex." "Ah!" rejoined Foote, remembering that county was famous for calves,—"from Essex. Who drove you?"

The better samples of Foote's wit are to be found in his own comic pieces. In his "Lame Lover," how admirable is Mr. Sergeant Circuit's remark when his wife asks for money, and protests she must have it, as her honor is in pawn! "How a century will alter the meaning of words!" cries the Sergeant. "Formerly, chastity was the honor of women, and good faith and integrity the honor of men; but now, a lady who ruins her family by punctually paying her losses at play, and a gentleman who kills his best friend in a ridiculous quarrel, are your only tip-top people of honor! Well, let them go on! It brings grist to our mill; for while both sexes stick firm to their honor, we shall never want business either at Doctors' Commons or the Old Bailey!" Again, in the "Nabob," a hard hit is made at the bold profligacy of the period, in the words of Touchet (Baddeley) to Sir Matthew Mite (Foote), both of whom had been talking of hanging, or worse, hereafter, to the bribe-taking members of an election-club; —"That's right, stick to that! for though the Christian Club may have some fears of the gallows, they don't value damnation a farthing!"

Some of Foote's apologists have almost worshipped him as the reformer of abuses, the scourge of hypocrites, and the terror of evil-doers. But Foote does not seem to have been moved by any higher principle than gain. If Mrs. Salmon had a Chamber of Horrors, the more murders that were committed, the better she was pleased, for the more she made by the crime. Foote endeavored to crush Whitfield by personal ridicule; but Whitfield was a far more useful man in his very wicked generation than Foote, who did not denounce the wickedness, but mimicked the peculiarities of the reformer. "There is hardly a public man in England," says Davies, "who has not entered Mr. Foote's theatre with an aching heart, under the apprehension of seeing himself laughed at."

Foote certainly read the pieces offered him for presentation. He kept Reed's "Register Office" for months, and thought so well of it as to turn its Mrs. Snarewell into Mrs. Cole, in his "Minor." That was little compared with his stealing a whole farce from Murphy; and the last was nothing compared with his return for the hospitality bountifully afforded him by Lord Melcombe, at his villa, at Hammersmith. Foote there studied the peculiarities of his good-natured host, and then produced him on the stage, in the character of the Patron!

Foote, again, read old pieces, with a purpose, quite as attentively as he did new. When he produced his "Liar," in 1762, he professed to have taken it from Lopez de Vega,* that is, from the original source from which Corneille took his "Menteur." From the latter, Steele took his "Lying Lover," and a comparison of the language of the two pieces will show that Foote plundered Steele, and hoped to escape by acknowledging obligations to an older author, whom he could not read. There is least of plagiarism in the "Mayor of Garratt," yet even there Foote is detected in borrowing from "Epsom Wells," but with judgment. If he was a picker-up of unconnected trifles, he chose only those of value, and he polished and reset them with tact and taste. He has done this in the "Commissary," in which there is a theft from

[* This is an error; the play, Verdad Loepedia, is by Alascon, and not by "Lopez de Vega.]—Ed.

"Injured Love," in a joke which Hook stole, in his turn, from the "Commissary," to enliven his "Killing no Murder."

Except in ceasing to mimic Whitfield on the stage, after the death of that religious reformer, I can scarcely find a trait of delicacy in Foote's character. He seems to have been as unscrupulous in act, as he was cruel in his wit. One may forgive him, however, for his remark to John Rich, who had been addressing him curtly, as "*Mister.*" Perceiving that Foote was vexed, Rich apologized by saying, "I sometimes forget my own name." "I am astonished you could forget your own name," said Foote, "though I know very well that you are not able to write it!"

Foote, who spared nobody, was angry with Dr. Johnson for saying that he was an infidel, as a dog was an infidel; he had never thought of the matter. "*I*, who have added sixteen new characters to the drama of my country!" said Foote. When he left hospitable General Smith's house, after a longer sojourn than usual, Foote's only comment was: "I can't miss his likeness now, after such a good sitting." When Digges first appeared in Cato, we are told that Foote occupied a place in the pit, and raising his voice above the sound of the welcome given to the new actor, exclaimed, "He looks like a Roman chimney sweeper on May-day." That Foote "deserved to be kicked out of the house for his cruelty," is a suggestion of Peake's, in which all men will concur. But did he deserve it? Chronology tends to disprove this story. Foote played for the last time on the 30th of July, 1777. His name does not appear in the bills after that day. Digges made his first appearance in London, as Cato, on the 14th of the following August, and if Foote went into the pit on that occasion, his envy and malevolence must have supplied him with the energy of which he had been deprived by paralysis and other infirmities.

Foote's vanity was as great as his cruelty. To indulging in the former he owed the loss of his leg. Being on a visit to Lord Mexborough, where the Duke of York and other noble guests were present, Foote foolishly boasted of his horsemanship; being invited to join the hunt the next day, he was ashamed to refuse, and at the very first burst the boaster was thrown and his leg broken in two places. Even when his leg was amputated, he was helped, by the incident, to an unworthy thought, namely, that he would now be able to mimic the one-legged George Faulkner, of Dublin, to the life! This, however, may have been said out of courage.

He bore, with fortitude, a visitation which gained for him a license to open the Haymarket, from the 15th of May to the 15th of September. It opened his way to fortune; and though what O'Keefe says may be true, that it was pitiable to see him leaning against the wall of his stage dressing-room, while his servant dressed his cork leg, to suit the character in which his master was to appear, I can well believe what O'Keefe adds, that "he looked sorrowful, but instantly resuming all his high comic humor and mirth, he hobbled forward, entered the scene, and gave the audience what they expected, their plenty of laugh and delight."

Among the fairest of Foote's sayings was the reply to Mr. Howard's intimation that he was about to publish a second edition of his *Thoughts and Maxims.* "Ay! second thoughts are best." Fair, too; was his retort on the person who alluded to his "game leg." "Make no allusion to my weakest part! Did I ever attack your head?" Then Garrick once took as a compliment, that his bust had been placed by Foote in the private room of the latter. "You are not afraid, I see, to trust me near your gold and bank-notes." "No," retorted the humorist, "you have no hands!"

Foote was sometimes beaten with his own weapons. After he had leased the Edinburgh Theatre from Ross, for three years, at five hundred guineas a year, a dispute arose, followed by a lawsuit, in which Foote was defeated. The Scottish agent for the vanquishing side, called on Foote, in London, with his bill of costs, which the actor had to defray. The *amari aliquid* having been got through, the player remarked that he supposed the agent was about to return to Edinburgh, like most of his countrymen, in the cheapest form possible. "Ay, ay," replied the agent, dryly, tapping the pocket in which he had put the cash, "I shall travel—*on foot!*" Foote himself is described as looking rueful at the joke. Again, Churchill only said of him that he was in self-conceit an actor, and straightway Foote, who lived by degrading others, was "outrageously offended." Foote wrote a prose lampoon on

Churchill and Lloyd, but did not publish it. Churchill, the bruiser, was not a safe man for Foote to attack, and the actor was fain to be satisfied with calling him the "clumsy curate of Clapham."

Foote took Wilkinson to Dublin in 1757, where they appeared as instructor and pupil, in one of Foote's entertainments, called a "Tea." Wilkinson imitated Luke Sparks as Old Capulet; convulsed the house, instead of being "stoned," as Mrs. Woffington expected, with his imitation of the two Dublin favorites, Margaret herself and Barry, in "Macbeth," and, emboldened by the applause, he imitated Foote in his own presence. Foote's audacity was tripped up by the suddenness of the action; and he looked foolish,—wishing to appear pleased with the audience, but not knowing how to play that difficult part. Subsequently, however, Foote called on Wilkinson, and threatened him with a duel, or chastisement, if he ever dared take further liberties with him on the stage. Wilkinson laughed at the impotently-angry ruffian, and all his brother actors laughed with him. The malignity of Foote found satisfaction in his writing the part of Shift, in the "Minor" (as it was first represented, in Dublin), as a satire on Wilkinson; and he knowingly misrepresented Wilkinson's origin, in order to bring him into contempt.

There is no doubt that Foote loved some of those he jested at. He heard of Sir Francis Delaval's death, with tears; but he smiled through them, when he was told that the surgeons intended to examine the baronet's head. He remarked that it was useless; he had known the head for nearly a quarter of a century, and had never been able to find any thing in it! But the wit's testimony to character is never to be taken without reserve. "Why does he come among us," he said of Lord Loughborough. "He is not only dull himself but the cause of dulness in others!" This is certainly not true, for this Scottish lawyer was remarkable in society for his hilarity, critical powers, and his store of epigrams and anecdotes. Lord Loughborough, moreover, merited the respect of Foote, as an old champion of the stage. When he was Mr. Wedderburn, and represented Dunfermline, in the General Assembly of Scotland, he resisted the motion for an act to prohibit the presence of either lay or clerical members of the church, at dramatic representations. The Assembly had just before been shaken by the fact that the clergy had been to witness Home's "Douglas," and it had smiled grimly at the palliative plea of one offender, "that he had ensconced himself in a corner, and had hid his face in a handkerchief to *avoid scandal*." Wedderburn opposed the motion in one of the best speeches which he ever delivered in Scotland, and which ended with these words: " Be contented with the laws which your wise and pious ancestors have handed down to you for the conservation of discipline and morals. Already have you driven from your body its brightest ornament, who might have continued to inculcate the precepts of the Gospel from the pulpit, as well as embodying them in character and action. Is it, indeed, forbidden to show us the kingdom of heaven by a parable? In all the sermons produced by the united genius of the Church of Scotland, I challenge you to produce any thing more pure in morality, or more touching in eloquence, than the exclamation of Lady Randolph :—

"'Sincerity!
Thou first of virtues, let no mortal leave
Thy onward path, although the earth should gape,
And from the gulf of hell, destruction cry
To take dissimulation's winding way.'"

Johnson rightly *pooh-poohed* this passage. Foote was admirable in impromptu. When he once saw a sweep on a blood-horse, he remarked : "There goes Warburton on Shakspeare!" When he heard that the Rockingham Cabinet was fatigued to death and at its wit's end, he exclaimed, that it could not have been the length of the journey which had tired it! Again, when Lord Caermarthen, at a party, told him his handkerchief was hanging from his pocket, Foote replaced it, with a "Thank you, my lord; you know the company better than I." How much better does Foote appear thus, than when we find him coarsely joking on Lord Kelly's nose, while that lord was hospitably entertaining him; or sneering at Garrick for showing respect to Shakspeare, by a "jubilee."

After all, the enemies he had provoked killed him. His fire and his physical powers were decaying when some of those enemies combined to accuse him of an enormous crime. He did not fly, like guilty Isaac Bickerstaffe, under similar circumstances, but manfully met the charge, and proved his innocence. The anxiety, however, finished him. He had an attack of paralysis, played for the last time, on the 30th of July, 1777, in his " Maid of Bath," and after shifting restlessly from place to place, died on the 21st of October, at Dover. A few months previously, he had made over the Haymarket Theatre to Colman, for a life annuity of £1,600, of which Foote lived but to receive one half-year's dividend. After the age of fifty-six, he thus passed away,—an emaciated old man,—and on Monday, the 27th of October, he was carried, by torchlight, to the cloisters of Westminster Abbey, whither Betterton, Barry, Mrs. Cibber, and others of the brotherhood of players, had been carried before him.

The Haymarket season of that year indicated a new era, for in 1777, Edwin, as Hardcastle, Miss Farren, as Miss Hardcastle; Henderson, as Shylock, and Digges, in Cato, made their first appearance in London. The old Garrick period,—save in some noble relics (Macklin, the noblest of them all),—was clearly passing away.

What the dramatic poets produced from the period of Garrick's withdrawal to the end of the century will be best seen by a reference to the Supplement, which I append to this part of my volume.

## SUPPLEMENT TO CHAPTER XL.

LIST OF THE PRINCIPAL DRAMATIC PIECES PRODUCED AT THE PATENT THEATRES, FROM THE RETIREMENT OF GARRICK TO THE END OF THE EIGHTEENTH CENTURY :—

1776-1777.—*Drury Lane.*

"Trip to Scarborough" (altered by Sheridan from Vanbrugh). Miss Hoyden, Mrs. Abington.

"School for Scandal" (Sheridan). Sir Peter Teazle, King; Charles Surface, Smith; Lady Teazle, Mrs. Abington.

1776-1777.—*Covent Garden.*

"Caractacus" (Mason). Caractacus, Clarke; Evelina, Mrs. Hartley.

## LIST OF NEW PLAYS. 137

"Know Your Own Mind" (Murphy). Millamour, Lewis; Lady Bell, Mrs. Mattocks.

### 1777-8.—*Drury Lane.*

"Battle of Hastings" (Cumberland). Edgar Atheling, Henderson; Elvina, Mrs. Yates.

### 1777-8.—*Covent Garden.*

"Percy" (Hannah More). Percy, Lewis; Douglas, Wroughten; Edwina, Mrs. Barry.
"Alfred" (Home). Alfred, Lewis; Ethelswida, Mrs. Barry.
"Poor Vulcan" (Dibdin). Vulcan, Quick; Venus, Miss Brown.

### 1778-9.—*Drury Lane.*

"Camp" (Tickell, falsely attributed to Sheridan).
"Fathers, or the Good-natured Man" (newly-discovered Comedy, by Fielding). Sir George Boncour, King.
"Law of Lombardy" (Jephson). Paladore, Smith; Bireno, Henderson; Princess, Miss Younge.
"Who's the Dupe" (Mrs. Cowley). Gradus, King; Doyley, Parsons; Elizabeth, Mrs. Brereton.

### 1778-9.—*Covent Garden.*

"Berthred" (Anon). Buthred, Wroughton; Rena, Mrs. Hartley.
"Touchstone, or Harlequin Traveller" (a Speaking Pantomime). Harlequin, Lee Lewes.
"Calypso" (Masque, by Cumberland). Telemachus, Mrs. Kennedy; Calypso, Miss Brown.
"Fatal Falsehood" (Hannah More). Rivers, Lewis; Julia, Mrs. Hartley.

### 1779-80.—*Drury Lane.*

"Critic" (Sheridan). Sir Fretful, Parsons; Puff, King; Tilburina, Miss Pope.
"Times" (Mrs. Griffith). Lady Mary Woodley, Mrs. Abington.
"Zoraida" (Hodson). Zoraida, Mrs. Yates.

### 1779-80.—*Covent Garden.*

"Mirror, or Harlequin Everywhere" (Burletta-Pantomime, by Dibdin). Harlequin, Bates.
"Widow of Delphi" (Cumberland).
"Deaf Lover" (Pilon). Meadows, Lee Lewes.
"Belle's Stratagem" (Mrs. Cowley). Doricourt, Lewis; Laetitia Hardy, Miss Younge.

### 1780-81.—*Drury Lane.*

"Generous Impostor" (O'Beirne, afterwards Bishop of Meath). Sir Harry Glenville, Palmer; Mrs. Courtly, Mrs. Baddeley.
"Lord of the Manor" (Burgoyne). Trumore, Vernon; Moll Flagon, Suett.
"Royal Suppliants" (Dr. Delap). Acamas, Smith; Dejanira, Mrs. Crawford.
"Dissipation" (Andrews). Lord Rentless, Palmer; Lady Rentless, Mrs. Abington.

1780–81.—*Covent Garden.*

"Tom Thumb" (Fielding's piece turned into an opera, by O'Hara). Tom, Edwin; Arthur, Quick; Dolabella, Miss Catley.

"Siege of Sinope" (Mrs. Brooke). Pharnaces, Henderson; Thamyris, Mrs. Yates.

"Man of the World" (Macklin). Sir Pertinax, Macklin; Egerton, Lewis; Lady Rodolpha Lumbercourt, Miss Younge.

1781–2.—*Drury Lane.*

"Fair Circassian" (Pratt,—Courtney Melmoth). Omar, Bensley; Hamet, Smith; Fair Circassian, Miss Farren.

1781–2.—*Covent Garden.*

"Duplicity" (Holcroft). Sir Harry Portland, Lewis; Melissa, Mrs. Inchbald.

"Count of Narbonne" (Jephson). Count, Wroughton; Countess, Miss Younge.

"Which is the Man" (Mrs. Cowley). Lord Sparkle, Lee Lewes; Fitzherbert, Henderson; Lady Bell Bloomer, Miss Younge.

"Walloons" (Cumberland). Father Sullivan, Henderson.

1782–3.—*Drury Lane.*

"Fatal Interview" (Hull). Montague, Smith; Mrs. Montague, Mrs. Siddons.

"School for Vanity" (Pratt). Onslow, Brereton; Ophelia Wyndham, Miss Farren.

1782–3.—*Covent Garden.*

"Castle of Andalusia" (O'Keefe). Spado, Quick; Lorenzo, Signora Sestini.

"Philodamus" (T. Bentley). Philodamus, Henderson.

"Rosina" (Mrs. Brooke). Belville, Bannister; Rosina, Miss Harper.

"Mysterious Husband" (Cumberland). Lord Davenant, Henderson; Sir Edmund, Yates; Lady Davenant, Miss Younge.

"Bold Stroke for a Husband" (Mrs. Cowley). Julio, Lewis; Olivia, Mrs. Mattocks.

1783–4.—*Drury Lane.*

"Reparation" (Andrews). Lord Hectic, Dodd; Lady Betty Wormwood, Miss Pope.

"Lord Russell" (Rev. Dr. Stratford).

1783–4.—*Covent Garden.*

"Poor Soldier" (O'Keefe). Patrick, Mrs. Kennedy; Dermot, Johnstone; Bagatelle, Wewitzer; Norah, Mrs. Bannister.

"More Ways than One" (Mrs. Cowley). Bellair, Lewis; Arabella, Mrs. Stephen Kemble.

"Robin Hood" (Mac Nally). Robin, Bannister; Clorinda, Mrs. Martyr.

1784–5.—*Drury Lane.*

"The Carmelite" (Cumberland). Montgomerie, Kemble; St. Valori, Smith; Matilda, Mrs. Siddons.

"Natural Son" (Cumberland). Blushenly, Palmer; Lady Paragon, Miss Farren.

### 1784–5.—*Covent Garden.*

"Fontainebleau; or, Our Way in France" (O'Keefe). Lackland, Lewis.
"Follies of a Day" (Holcroft, from Beaumarchais). Figaro, Holcroft; Almaviva, Lewis; Susanna, Miss Younge.

### 1785–6.—*Drury Lane.*

"Heiress" (Burgoyne). Sir Clement Flint, King; Alscrip, Parsons; Lady Emily Gayville, Miss Farren.
"Captives" (Dr. Delap). Everallin, Kemble; Malvina, Mrs. Siddons.

### 1785–6.—*Covent Garden.*

"Omai." Grand spectacle, by O'Keefe.

### 1786–7.—*Drury Lane.*

"Richard Cœur de Lion" (Burgoyne). Richard, Kemble; Antonio, Miss Romanzini; Matilda, Mrs. Jordan; Lauretta, Mrs. Crouch.
"School for Greybeards" (Mrs. Cowley). Alexis and Gaspar (the Greybeards), King and Parsons; Seraphina, Miss Farren.
"Seduction" (Holcroft). Lord and Lady Morden, Kemble and Mrs. Siddons.
"Julia" (Jephson). Mentevole, Kemble; Julia, Mrs. Siddons.

### 1786–7.—*Covent Garden.*

"Richard Cœur de Lion" (Mac Nally). Blondel, Johnstone; Queen Berengaria, Mrs. Billington.
"He Would be a Soldier" (Pilon). Caleb, Edwin; Charlotte, Mrs. Pope.
"Eloisa" (Reynolds). St. Preux, Pope; Eloisa, Miss Brunton.
"Such Things Are" (Mrs. Inchbald). Elvirus, Holman; Lady Tremor, Mrs. Mattocks.

### 1787–8.—*Drury Lane.*

"New Peerage; or, Our Eyes may Deceive Us" (Hariett Lee). Lady Charlotte Courtley, Miss Farren.
"Fate of Sparta" (Mrs. Cowley). Cleombrotus, Kemble; Chelonice, Mrs. Siddons.
"Love in the East" (Cobb). Warnford, Kelly; Ormellina, Mrs. Crouch.
"The Regent" (B. Greathead). Manuel, Kemble; Dianora, Mrs. Siddons.

### 1787–8.—*Covent Garden.*

"The Farmer" (O'Keefe). Jemmy Jumps, Edwin; Molly Maybush, Mrs. Martyr.
"Ton; or, the Follies of Fashion" (Lady Wallace). Lord Bonton, Wewitzer; Lady Bonton, Mrs. Mattocks.
"Animal Magnetism" (Mrs. Inchbald). Doctor, Quick; Constance, Mrs. Wells.

### 1788–9.—*Drury Lane.*

"Impostors" (Cumberland). Lord James, Palmer; Eleanor, Mrs. Jordan.
"Mary, Queen of Scots" (Hon. John St. John). Norfolk, Kemble; Queen Mary, Mrs. Siddons; Queen Elizabeth, Mrs. Ward.
"False Appearances" (General Conway). Marquis, Kemble; Cœlla, Mrs. Kemble.

### 1788–9.—*Covent Garden.*

"Highland Reel" (O'Keefe). Shelty, Edwin; Moggy, Miss Fontenelle.

"Child of Nature" (Mrs. Inchbald). Almanza, Farren; Amanthis, Miss Brunton.
"The Toy, or Hampton Court" (O'Keefe). Alibi, Quick; Lady Jane, Miss Brunton.
"Dramatist" (Reynolds). Vapid, Lewis; Ennui, Edwin; Willoughby, Macready; Louisa Courtney, Miss Brunton.

### 1789-90.—*Drury Lane.*

"Marcella" (Hayley). Hernandez, Kemble; Marcella, Mrs. Powell.
"Haunted Tower" (Cobb). Lord William, Kelly; Lewis, Suett; Lady Elinor, Mrs. Crouch.
"Love in Many Masks" (Kemble, from Aphra Behn). Willmore, Kemble; Valeria, Mrs. Kemble; Helena, Mrs. Jordan.

### 1789-90.—*Covent Garden.*

"Marcella" (Hayley). Hernandez, Harley; Marcella, Mrs. Pope.
"Eudora" (Hayley). Raymond, Holman; Eudora, Mrs. Pope.
"Widow of Malabar" (Marianna Starke). Indamora, Miss Brunton.

### 1790-91.—*Drury Lane.*

"Better Late than Never" (Reynolds and Andrews). Saville, Kemble; Flurry, Dodd; Augusta, Mrs. Jordan.
"Siege of Belgrade" (Cobb). Seraskier, Kelly; Peter, Dignum; Katharine, Mrs. Crouch.

### 1790-91.—*Covent Garden.*

"School for Arrogance" (Holcroft). Sheepy, Munden; Lady Peckham, Mrs. Mattocks.
"Two Strings to Your Bow" (Jephson). Lazarillo, Munden; Ferdinand, Macready; Clara, Mrs. Harlowe.
"Woodman" (the Rev. Bate Dudley). Wilford, Incledon.
"Modern Antiques" (O'Keefe). Cockletop, Quick; Frank, Munden.
"Lorenzo" (Merry). Lorenzo, Holman; Zoriana, Miss Brunton (afterwards Mrs. Merry).
"Wild Oats" (O'Keefe). Rover, Lewis; Ephraim Smooth, Munden; Lady Amaranth, Mrs. Pope.

### 1791-2.—*Drury Lane Company at the King's Theatre, Haymarket.*

"Huniades" (Hannah Brand). Huniades, Kemble; Agmunda, by the authoress, her first appearance on any stage.
"Fugitive" (Richardson). Young Manley, Palmer; Lord Dartford, Dodd; Mrs. Larron, Miss Pope.
"Dido" (Hoare). Æneas, Mrs. Crouch; Dido, Madame Mara.

### 1791-2.—*Covent Garden.*

"Notoriety" (Reynolds). Nominal, Lewis; Sophia, Mrs. Wells.
"Road to Ruin" (Holcroft). Goldfinch, Lewis; Old Dornton, Munden; Sophia, Mrs. Merry.

"Irishman in London" (Macready). Murtoch Delaney, Johnstone; Collvoony, Macready; Cubba, Mrs. Fawcett.

1792-3.—*Drury Lane at Haymarket Opera; except on Tuesdays and Saturdays, then at the Haymarket Theatre.*

"The Prize" (Hoare). Lenitive, Bannister, jun.; Caroline, Signora Storace.
"Rival Sisters" (Murphy). Thescus, Palmer; Ariadne and Phædra, Mrs. Siddons and Mrs. Powell.
"False Colors" (Morris). Sir Paul Panick, King.

1792-3.—*Covent Garden.*

"Columbus" (Morton). Columbus, Pope; Cora, Mrs. Pope.
"Every One has his Fault" (Inchbald). Harmony, Munden; Lady E. Irwin, Mrs. Pope.

1793-4.—*Drury Lane, under Colman, at the Haymarket.*

"Sprigs of Laurel" (O'Keefe). Nipperkin, Munden.
"Mountaineers" (Colman). Octavian, Kemble; Floranthe, Mrs. Goodall (was first acted in the summer of 1793, before the company went to Drury Lane in September).
"Children in the Wood" (Morton). Walter, Bannister.
"Lodoiska" (Kemble). Loviuski, Palmer; Lodoiska, Mrs. Crouch.

1794.—*Drury Lane; in the new House built by Holland.*

"The Jew" (Cumberland). Sheva, Bannister, jun.; Eliza Ratcliffe, Miss Farren.

1794.—*Covent Garden.*

"Siege of Berwick" (Jerningham). Seaton, Pope; Ethelberta, Mrs. Pope.
"Love's Frailties" (Holcroft). Sir Gregory Oldwort, Quick.
"Travellers in Switzerland" (Bate Dudley). Dorimond, Johnstone; Sir Leinster M'Laughlin, Rock.
"Siege of Meaux" (Pye). St. Pol, Pope; Matilda, Mrs. Pope.

1794-5.—*Drury Lane.*

"Emilia Galotti" (from Lessing, by Thompson). Appiani, C. Kemble; Orsina, Mrs. Siddons.
"Wedding Day" (Mrs. Inchbald). Young Contest, C. Kemble; Sir Adam, King; Lady Contest, Mrs. Jordan.
"Wheel of Fortune" (Cumberland). Penruddock, Kemble; Henry Woodville, C. Kemble; Emily Tempest, Miss Farren.
"Adopted Child" (Birch). Michael, Bannister, jun.; Nell, Mrs. Bland.
"First Love" (Cumberland). Billy Bustler, Suett; Sabina Rosny, Mrs. Jordan.

1794-5.—*Covent Garden.*

"The Rage" (Reynolds). Darnley, Holman; Clara, Mrs. Mountain.
"Town before You" (Mrs. Cowley). Tippy, Lewis; Fancourt, Fawcett; Mrs. Fancourt, Mrs. Mattocks.

"Mysteries of the Castle" (Andrews and Reynolds). Hilario, Lewis.
"England Preserved" (Watson). Surrey, Holman.
"Life's Vagaries" (O'Keefe). George Burgess, Fawcett; L'Œillet, Farley; Augusta Woodbine, Miss Wallis.
"Deserted Daughter" (Holcroft). Mordant, Pope; Item, Quick; Joanna Mordant, Miss Wallis.
"Secret Tribunal" (Boaden). Herman, Holman; Ida, Miss Wallis.

### 1795–6.—*Drury Lane.*

"Man of Ten Thousand" (Holcroft). Dorrington, Kemble; Olivia, Miss Farren.
"Iron Chest" (Colman). Sir Edward Mortimer, Kemble; Judith, Miss De Camp.
"Almeyda" (Miss Lee). Alonzo, Kemble; Almeyda, Mrs. Siddons.
"Mahmoud" (Hoare). Mahmoud, Kemble.
"Vortigern" (Ireland, but acted as Shakspeare's). Vortigern, Kemble; Constantius, Bensley; Fool, King; Edmunda, Mrs. Powell; Flavia, Mrs. Jordan.

### 1795–6.—*Covent Garden.*

"Speculation" (Reynolds). Tanjore, Lewis; Lady Katharine Project, Mrs. Davenport.
"Days of Yore" (Morton). Voltimer, Pope; Adela, Mrs. Pope.
"Lock and Key" (Hoare). Brummagem, Munden; Fanny, Mrs. Martyr.

### 1796–7.—*Drury Lane.*

"Conspiracy" (Jephson). Sextus, Kemble; Vitellia, Mrs. Siddons.
"The Will" (Reynolds). Veritas, R. Palmer; Albina Mandeville, Mrs. Jordan.

### 1796–7.—*Covent Garden.*

"Abroad and at Home" (Holman). Harcourt, Incledon.
"Cure for the Heart Ache" (Morton). Young Rapid, Lewis; Bronze, Farley; Ellen Vortex, Mrs. Pope.
"Wives as they Were and Maids as they Are" (Inchbald). Bronzely, Lewis; Miss Dorillon, Miss Wallis.

### 1797–8.—*Drury Lane.*

"Cheap Living" (Reynolds). Sponge, John Bannister.
"Castle Spectre" (Lewis). Osmond, Barrymore; Percy, Kemble.
"Blue Beard" (Colman). Abomelique. Palmer; Fatima, Mrs. Crouch.
"Knave or not" (Holcroft). Monrose, Palmer; Susan, Mrs. Jordan.
"Stranger" (Kotzebue). Stranger, Kemble; Mrs. Haller, Mrs. Siddons.

### 1797-8.—*Covent Garden.*

"False Impressions" (Cumberland). Scud, Quick.
"Secrets worth Knowing" (Morton). Undermine, Munden.
"He's much to Blame" (Holcroft). Versatile, Lewis; Lady Jane, **Miss** Betterton (afterwards Mrs. Glover).
"Curiosity" (by the late King of Sweden.
"Blue Devils" (Colman the Younger). Megrim, Fawcett.

## LIST OF NEW PLAYS.

### 1798-9.—*Drury Lane.*

"Aurelio and Miranda" (Boaden). Aurelio, Kemble; Miranda, Mrs. Siddons.
"Secret" (Morris). Lizard, jun., John Bannister; Rosa, Mrs. Jordan.
"East Indian" (Lewis). Mortimer, Kemble; Zorayda, his daughter, Mrs. Jordan.
"Castle of Montval" (Whalley). Old Count, Kemble; Matilda, Mrs. Powell.
"First Faults" (Miss De Camp). Fallible, C. Kemble; Tulip, Miss Mellon.
"Pizarro" (Sheridan). Rolla, Kemble; Alonzo, C. Kemble; Cora, Mrs. Jordan; Elvira, Mrs. Siddons.

### 1798-9.—*Covent Garden.*

"Lovers' Vows" (Inchbald). Frederick, Pope; Amelia, Mrs. H. Johnston.
"Ramah Droog" (Cobb). Sidney, Incledon.
"Jew and the Doctor" (T. Dibdin). Abednego, Fawcett.
"Laugh When You Can" (Reynolds). Gossamer, Lewis.
"Votary of Wealth" (Holman). Leonard, Pope; Julia, Mrs. Pope.
"Five Thousand a Year" (T. Dibdin). Fervid, Lewis; Maria, Miss Betterton.
"Birthday" (T. Dibdin). Captain Bertram, Munden.
"Fortune's Frolic" (Allingham). Robin Roughead, Fawcett.

### 1799-1800.—*Drury Lane.*

"Adelaide" (Pye). Richard, Kemble; Adelaide, Mrs. Siddons.
"Of Age To-Morrow" (T. Dibdin). Frederick, John Bannister.
"De Montfort" (Joanna Baillie). De Montfort, Kemble; Jane, Mrs. Siddons.
"Indiscretion" (Hoare). Maxim, King; Julia, Mrs. Jordan.
"Antonio" (Godwin). Antonio, Kemble; Helena, Mrs. Siddons.

### 1799-1800.—*Covent Garden.*

"Management" (Reynolds). Mist, Fawcett; Mrs. Dazzle, Mrs. Davenport.
"Turnpike Gate" (Knight). Crack, Munden.
"Joanna" (Cumberland, from Kotzebue). Joanna, Mrs. Pope.
"Speed the Plough" (Morton). Bob Handy, Fawcett.
"Paul and Virginia" (Cobb;—music by Mazzinghi). Paul, Incledon; Virginia, Mrs. H. Johnston.

In the next chapter, we will examine something of the progress of the stage, as indicated by the above records.

## CHAPTER XII.

#### OF AUTHORS, AND PARTICULARLY OF CONDEMNED AUTHORS.

A GLANCE at the foregoing list will serve to show that from the retirement of Garrick to the close of the 18th century, tragic literature made no progress. It retrograded. It did not even reach the height of Fenton and Hughes, in whom Walpole discerned some faint sparkling of the merit of the older masters. After Shakspeare's time, "Theatric genius," says Walpole, "lay dormant;" but he adds, that "it waked with some bold and glorious, but irregular and often ridiculous flights, in Dryden; revived in Otway; maintained a placid, pleasing kind of dignity, in Rowe; and even shone in 'Jane Shore.' It trod in sublime and classic fetters in 'Cato;' but was void of nature, or the power of affecting the passions. In Southerne, it seemed a genuine ray of nature and Shakspeare, but falling on an age still more Hottentot, was stifled in those gross and barbarous productions, tragi-comedies. It turned to tuneful nonsense in the 'Mourning Bride,' grew stark mad in Lee; whose cloak, a little the worse for wear, fell on Young; yet in both was still a poet's cloak. It recovered its senses in Hughes and Fenton, who were afraid it should relapse, and accordingly kept it down with a timid, but amiable, hand; and then it languished."

And continued to languish; I cannot more fully show to what extent, than by remarking that the century which opened with Rowe concluded with Pye; both Poets Laureate, but of different qualities. "Tamerlane" and "Jane Shore" have not yet dropped from the list of acting plays; but who knows any thing more of "Adelaide" than that it was insipid, possessed not even a "tuneful nonsense," and was only distinguished for having made Mrs. Siddons and John Kemble appear almost as insipid as the play. Godwin's "Antonio," played in 1800, was as complete a failure as Pye's "Adelaide."

For the tragic poets who occupy the period beween Garrick's retirement and the coming of Pye and Godwin, a few words will suffice. Mason's "Caractacus" was a noble effort, but it produced less effect than D'Egville's ballet on the same subject in the succeeding century. Cumberland's "Battle of Hastings" was as near Shakspeare as Ireland's "Vortigern" was; and Home's "Alfred" died, three days old.

Jephson was, after all, the favorite playwright of Walpole, who says of his "Law of Lombardy," that it was even "too rich" in language! but then Jephson always improved the passages to which Walpole objected. Walpole gave orders for alterations in Jephson's plays, as he might for the repairs of a cabinet. Sometimes, his criticism is excellent; and at others, it involves a social illustration, as in that on the "Count of Narbonne." Raymond, in the last scene, says, "Show me thy wound; oh, hell! 'tis through her heart!" "This line," says Walpole, "is quite unnecessary, and infers an obedience in displaying her wound, which would be shocking; besides, as there is often a buffoon in an audience, at a new tragedy, it might be received dangerously. The word 'Jehovah!' will certainly not be suffered on the stage." Walpole praises Miss Younge's acting, and says, "the applause to one of her speeches lasted a minute, and recommenced twice before the play could go on." Jephson, however, wrote fair acting pieces, which is more than can be said for Bentley's "Philodamus," which, in spite of being pronounced by Gray, the best dramatic poem in the language, was hilariously laughed off the stage. It was at least original, which can hardly be said of any of Cumberland's plays, except the "Carmelite," a tragedy that terminates merrily! Cumberland was as much out of his line in tragedy as Reynolds, whose "Werter" and "Eloisa" brought him eight pounds!

"And very good pay too, sir!" said Macklin, "so go home and write two more tragedies, and if you gain £4 by each of them, why, young man! the author of Paradise Lost will be a fool to you!"

Hayley, of whom Walpole said, "That sot Boswell is a classic in comparison;" and Murphy, with undeniable powers, failed in their attempts at tragedy during this period. Boaden may be said to have been below the level of Pye himself. On the former's "Aurelio and Miranda" some criticism was made, before it was acted. The author was reading his play to the actors, when he remarked, that he knew nothing so terrible as having to read it before so critical an audience. "Oh, yes!" exclaimed Mrs. Powell, "there is something much more terrible." "What can that be?" asked Boaden, foolishly. "To be obliged to sit and hear it," was the reply of Lady Emma Hamilton's old fellow-servant.

But if tragedy languished miserably, comedy was vivacious and triumphant. This period gave us the "School for Scandal," perhaps the most faultless comedy of the whole century. It gave us Murphy's, "Know your own Mind;" the "Critic," that admirable offspring of the "Rehearsal;" Macklin's "Man of the World," the most muscular of comedies, which contrasts so forcibly with the sketchy sentimental, yet not nerveless comedies of Holcroft; General Burgoyne's "Heiress," which is not only superior to General Conway's "False Appearances" (a translation from a comedy by Boissy), but is, perhaps, the second best comedy of the period; Cumberland's "Jew" and "Wheel of Fortune;" Colman's seriocomic "Mountaineers," and the rattling "five-act farces" of Reynolds. At the head of all these, and of many others, stood Sheridan's immortal comedy. He may, as he said, have spoiled Vanbrugh's "Relapse," in converting it into the "Trip to Scarborough;" but the "School for Scandal" has been accepted as the best comedy of the English stage. In its dazzling brilliancy, the labor expended to effect it is all forgotten. Garrick took the greatest interest in its success, and when a flatterer remarked to him that its popularity would only be ephemeral, and that with Garrick himself the Atlas of the stage had departed, the latter calmly replied that, in Mr. Sheridan, his successor in the management, the stage had a Hercules equal to any labor it might require at his hands.

I turn, less to newspapers than to private contemporary sources, to see what was thought of this comedy on its first appearance. Walpole was present at the acting, and he says: "To my great astonishment, there were more parts performed admirably in the 'School for Scandal,' than I almost ever saw in any play. Mrs. Abington was equal to the first of her profession; Yates, Parsons,

Miss Pope and Palmer, all shone. It seemed a marvellous resurrection of the stage. Indeed, the play had as much merit as the actors. I have seen no comedy that comes near it, since the ' Provoked Husband.' " The chief characters were thus represented: Sir Peter, King; Sir Oliver, Yates; Backbite, Dodd; Charles Surface, Smith; Joseph Surface, Palmer; Crabtree, Parsons; Lady Teazle, Mrs. Abington; Mrs. Candour, Miss Pope; and Maria, by Miss P. Hopkins, daughter of the prompter,—soon to be the wife of Brereton, and subsequently that of John Kemble.

Walpole objected, that the comedy was too long, despite great wit and good situations; and that there were two or three bad scenes that might be easily omitted, and which, to his thinking, wanted truth of character. He does not specify the scenes, and he acknowledges that he had not read the play, and that he " sat too high to hear it well." When he had read it, he came to the conclusion that it was " rapid and lively, but far from containing the wit he had expected, on seeing it acted."

To Walpole, the " Heiress," by Burgoyne, was "the *genteelest* comedy" in the English language. Of Macklin's "Man of the World," the same writer says: " Boswell pretended to like it, which would almost make one suspect that he knows a dose of poison had already been administered; though, by the way, I hear there is little good in the piece, except the likeness of Sir Pertinax to twenty thousand Scots."

It was the great merit of nearly all these writers, that while they caricatured folly, they scourged vice; and not only showed society what it was, but instructed it in what it should be. Cumberland wrote his " Jew," expressly to create a feeling of sympathy for a despised people. Howard, the philanthropist, walked, under fictitious names, through more than one piece,—inculcating the duties of love and charity; and the too fashionable or foolish people of the day, by being rendered ridiculous, served to demonstrate, merrily, their own defects. In this application of dramatic literature, the ladies, whom I have not yet mentioned, were as busily engaged as the gentlemen.

If we glance at the ladies who wrote for the stage during the latter half of the last century, and some of them before, we shall find a marked contrast between them and their sisters of the preceding century. There is Hannah More, who introduces into "Percy" a sermon of which the first part denounces war, and the second draws a character of the Saviour! Of Mrs. Cowley, kinswoman to Gay—the unknown Anna Matilda who corresponded with Della Crusca (Merry), the fastidious Walpole unjustly declared that she was as freely spoken as Aphra Behn. She was the first lady who held an " At Home day," on which to receive her friends. She affected, like Congreve, to despise being an "author," and showed skill in shaping old characters into new, in comedies which still survive; as well as in defending herself against the acute people who had "a good nose for inuendo." In tragedy, she was not so successful; and she winced at the epigram of Parsons, on her "Fate of Sparta," which said:—

"Ingenious Cowley! while we viewed
Of Sparta's sons, the lot severe,
We caught the Spartan fortitude,
And saw their woes, without a tear."

Of Mrs. Griffith's plays, not one is now remembered; but the author and actress is remarkable for having published, as guides to young people, the correspondence of herself and husband, before marriage, under the title of *The Letters of Harry and Frances*; and if they describe all the love-making, the lady was not likely to have resembled the Platonic Wife, in her own play so called, who laments, throughout, that her husband will not be exactly what he was when he was her lover. An incident, connected with this play, will show how ungallant players could be to female poets, and how free they could be with their audience. In the third act, when Powell and Holland were on the stage, the hissing was universal; and at the end of it, the two actors thrust their heads out from behind the drop-curtain, and implored the house to damn the piece at once, and release them from having to utter any more nonsense!

The gentle Frances Brooke's novels are better than her dramas, —save the pretty musical farce, "Rosina," in which she has so cleverly secularized the scriptural story of Ruth and Boaz. Unlike Mrs. Brooke, Elizabeth Inchbald's plays are as good as her novels;—in both, the romantic daughter of a Suffolk farmer exhibited a skill and refinement, the latter of which she must have acquired after the period when, a wayward and beautiful girl of sixteen, she ran away from home, and manifested wonderful ability in framing stories of her own, to mislead the curious. After the death of her husband,—the "Garrick of Norwich,"— whose marriage with her was as romantically begun as it singularly ended, she took to writing for the stage, on which she was a respectable actress. In her plays, the virtues are set in action; and there is much elegance in her style. She was so successful, that a friend accused her of inculcating sedition in "Every One Has His Fault." Sometimes, her success was owing more to the actors than herself. King and Mrs. Jordan, as Sir Adam and Lady Contest, in the "Wedding Day," were such a pair as have never been *quite* approached by their successors.

Petulant Sophia Lee, daughter of a country actor, excelled all the foregoing ladies in one point,—the skill with which she mingled broad comedy with natural pathos,—as in her "Chapter of Accidents." The Lady Wallace was a thousand times more petulant than Miss Lee, without even a thousandth part of her ability. She resembled the female writers of the last century only in her vulgarity, and not in their poor wit. Then, there was Hannah Brand, schoolmistress, like Hannah More; poet, and actress, mad with much learning,—or with very little, of which she thought very much; and proud as an *artchangel*, as she pronounced the word! The great feat of imperious Miss Brand was in her "Huniades," which, on its failure, she altered, by leaving the whole part of Huniades out! She called the incomprehensible fragment "Agmunda," and heard it hissed (she playing the heroine), to her great disgust.

The century was within a year of its close, when Miss De Camp taught parents not to cross the first love of their children, in "First Faults." Then Joanna Baillie finished one and began another century, with her series of Plays of the Passions; none of which was intended for the stage, or succeeded when it was represented. The old Scots, who shuddered at "Douglas" being written by a minister, must have been stricken with awe at the idea of the daughter of the divinity professor at Glasglow composing three profane tragedies in a single year.

In the supplement to the last chapter, indications will be found of the progress of Opera on the English stage. Music and singing were not uncommonly introduced into our early plays, and they ranked among the chief attractions of our masques, down to the reign of Charles I. Under the Commonwealth, and in the reign of Charles II., we had pieces sung in recitative, till Locke awoke melodious echoes by his music for the operas of "Psyche," "Macbeth," and the "Tempest;" and Purcell excelled Lawes in vigor and in harmony, and composed music to the words of Dryden.

Our first English male stage-singers were simply actors, with good, but not musically-trained voices. Walker, the original Macheath, could "sing a good song," but he was a tragedian; and some of our songstresses might be similarly described. Mrs. Tofts, at the beginning of the eighteenth century, and Miss Campion, were trained vocalists. In Beard and Miss Brent—he, living to marry an earl's daughter, and realize a large fortune; *she*, to want bread, and (as Mrs. Pinto) to thank the older Fawcett for a shilling—Garrick found his most dangerous opponents. The "Beggars' Opera" and "Artaxerxes," mark epochs; and after Arne arose Linley, Jackson, Arnold, Dibdin, and Shield, as composers; and Leoni and Miss Browne—the former sweeter than Vernon, and the lady rich in expression, secured rare laurels for themselves and the "Duenna," in which opera they played the principal characters. Jackson's music in "The Lord of the Manor," brought Mrs. Crouch, then Miss Phillips, into notice; but it was not till Stephen Storace began his career, that concerted pieces and grand finales were introduced by him, and English opera rendered more complete. With his operas are most associated the names of Crouch, Kelley, and Braham—which last name, and that of Mrs. Billington, are the brightest in the operatic annals of the close of the eighteenth, and opening of the nineteenth century.

With operas and musical entertainments, the romantic drama greatly flourished for awhile. Indeed, the beautiful and hapless Mrs. Cargill made a romantic hero of Macheath; her tremor, when the bell sounded for execution, was a bit of natural tragedy which excited tears. But of real romantic drama, the most successful was the sensational "Castle Spectre," the merit of which was pointed out by a joke of Sheridan's. In a dispute with Lewis, the author, the latter offered, in support of his opinion, to bet all the money which that drama had brought into the treasury. "No," said Sheridan, "I'll not do that; but I don't mind betting all its worth!"

So few of the plays in the preceding list have survived even in memory, that there must necessarily have been much suffering among disappointed authors. But it was not merely those of this half century who incurred disappointment. I have incidentally mentioned some of these before. I may add one more sample of the condemned in Flœnoe, who was among the worst of the writers of the seventeenth century, and was also the most independent, or the most truculent, in denouncing his critics. When the managers rejected his "Demoiselles à la Mode," he printed the piece with a preface, in which he remarked that :—"For the acting this comedy, those who have the government of the stage, have their humor, and would be entreated; and I have mine, and won't entreat them; and were all dramatic writers of my mind, the Masters should wear their old plays threadbare ere they should have any new, till they better understood their own interest, and how to distinguish between good and bad."

But poets better skilled than this ex-Jesuit had to endure disappointment. Rowe ranks among the condemned (the hilarious condemned), by his failure in comedy. His idea was good. In the early part of the century, society was beset by the "Biters." These were the would-be jokers of the day, who, on hoaxing their friends, exclaimed "Bite!" and exposed the trick they had played. An instance is afforded in the *Spectator*, of a condemned felon, who sold his body to a surgeon, but who, on receiving the purchase-money, called out "Bite! I'm to be hung in chains!" Rowe took one of these humorists for the hero of his bustling three-act comedy or farce, entitled the "Biter." This part, Pinch, was played by Pack, at Lincoln's Inn Fields, in 1704; but that clever actor rattled through it in vain. The jokes fell lifeless, to the great disgust of Rowe, who was in the pit. As the audience would not, or could not laugh, but rather yawned or hissed, the author set them the example he would have them follow, and at every jest he led the way with an explosion of laughter, which must have become the more lugubrious on every repetition. A good man struggling against evil destiny is said to be a sublime spectacle to gods and men; but a dramatic author, known to half the audience, upholding his own piece, and striving to rescue it from ruin by a convulsive hilarity, must have been a sight as astonishing to his foes as to his friends. The poor fellow laughed vehemently; but the house could not be tempted to sympathize with him, and the "Biter" was condemned under the applause and laughter of its hysterical author.

Aaron Hill took his failures more calmly. The public of 1710, at Drury Lane, would not tolerate his "Elfrid." Aaron shared the public opinion, and devoted *twenty years* to rewriting his tragedy, which was subsequently produced under the title of "Athelwold." Mrs. Centlivre was not equally patient with *her* public; from whom, a month earlier, she withdrew in pique her coolly-received comedy, "The Man's Bewitched." Elkanah Settle was so systematically visited with damnation, that he was at last compelled to bring out his plays under fictitious names, and during the long vacation, lest when the town was full, some enemy should discover him. Pope was as sensitive as Settle, if the story be true that he was one of the authors of "Three Hours after Marriage," and that the cool reception of this piece caused him to express dislike for the players. Dennis, however, was perhaps the most irritable of his race. When his adaptation of "Coriolanus" ("The Invader of his Country") failed, in 1719, to draw £100 to the house, and was consequently shelved by the management, Dennis thundered against the insolence, incapacity, and disloyalty of Cibber and his colleagues, and invoked against them the vengeance of the Duke of Newcastle, the Lord Chamberlain! Theobald took another course; and when the pit hissed his pieces, he abused the "little critics," in a preface, scorned their "ill-nature," and appealed to "better judges."

Gay, considering his dramatic failures in tragedy, found more consolation than most damned authors. The public of 1724 had no sympathy for his "Captives;" which, despite Booth, Wilks, and Mrs. Oldfield, soon disappeared from the stage. To console the author, the Princess of Wales requested him to read this play in presence of herself and little court. On being ushered into the august company, Gay, nervous from long waiting, tragedy in hand, bashful and blundering, fell over a stool, thereby threw down a screen, and set his illustrious audience in a comical sort of confusion, which, notwithstanding the kindness of the princess, marred the self-possession of the poet. The piece, however, went off more merrily at Leicester House than it had done at Drury Lane.

More touching than this was the way in which the aged Southerne, in 1726, took the condemnation of his "Money, the Mistress," at Lincoln's Inn Fields. The audience refused the request made in the prologue to protect the man who had filled their mother's eyes with tears. They had no particular reverence for "the last of Charles's bards;" nor especial regard for "great Otway's peer and greater Dryden's friend." The audience hissed mercilessly. The old man was standing at a wing with Rich, who asked him, if " he heard what they were doing." " No, sir," said Southerne, calmly, "I am very deaf!" So quietly did he see fall from his gray head, the wreath " for half a century with honor worn."

But "Money" was not more unequivocally damned on the first night than was the "Provoked Husband," in 1728, at Drury Lane. The difference was that the last piece suffered shipwreck, on political grounds, but survived the storm. All the Jacobites in town united to condemn a play, by the author of the "Nonjuror," with Vanbrugh for colleague. Cibber played Sir Francis Wronghead, in the face of the hurricane, and never forgot his part, though he gave up all as lost when, in the fourth act, the play was brought to a "stand-still," by the fierce antagonism of the house. Nevertheless, Colley persevered, and the comedy went on to the end. The critics acknowledged or boasted that it had been a miserable failure, but Cibber would not confess himself beaten. The "Provoked Husband" ran for eight-and-twenty successive nights, and on the last of those nights drew £140, " which happened," says the naturally-exulting Cibber, " to be more than in fifty years before could be said of any play whatsoever."

Gay read his tragedy, after it had been consigned to the limbo of such pieces, to a court circle ; Tracy read his heavy "Periander" before it was damned at Lincoln's Inn Fields, in 1731, to a circle of friends, who were regaled on the occasion with a magnifi cent supper. Dr. Ridley spoke on behalf of himself and brother critics, and assured the author that they had been exceedingly well pleased with the entertainment provided; he alluded particularly, he said, to the supper. This was held for wit, but it was not so neat, so happy, or so friendly as Carl Vernet's reply to the author of the *Maison à Vendre*. As the curtain fell, Carl remarked, "J'ai cru voir une Maison à Vendre, et je ne vois qu'une pièce à louer!"

Fielding took disapprobation with infinite indifference. In 1743, his "Wedding Day" was produced at Drury Lane, with Garrick as Millamour, and Macklin as Stedfast. Garrick had asked the author to suppress a scene which, he thought, would imperil the piece. Fielding refused. "If the scene is not a good one," said he, "let 'em find it out." This scene *did* excite violent hissing; and Garrick left the stage for the green-room, as violently disturbed. "There," says Murphy, "the author was indulging his genius, and solacing himself with a bottle of champagne. He had, at this time, drank pretty plentifully; and cocking his eye at the actor, while streams of tobacco trickled down from the corner of his mouth, 'What's the matter, Garrick?' said he; 'what are they hissing now?' 'Why the scene I begged you to retrench. I knew it wouldn't do; and they have so frightened me, that I shall not be able to collect myself the whole night.' 'Oh! d—— 'em!' replies the author, 'they *have* found it out, have they?'"

Fielding suffered as severely as most authors at the hands of the critics, but he was bold enough to publish one unlucky play, not "as it was acted," but "as it was damned at the Theatre Royal." He accounted, however, for such failures, in himself and others, through Fustian, his tragic poet, in a Pasquin." "One man," says Fustian, "hissses out of resentment to the author; a second, out of dislike to the house; a third, out of dislike to the actor; a fourth, out of dislike to the play; a fifth, for the joke's sake; a sixth, to keep the rest in company;—enemies abuse him; friends give him up; the play is damned; and the author goes to the devil." Fielding might have given another illustration,—such as that of the Frenchman who clapped and hissed at the same moment, and explained his apparent inconsistency, by stating that he had received a free ticket from the author, and that he clapped out of gratitude to the donor, but that he hissed for the satisfaction of his own conscience. Again, there was one French critic who took a more singular way still of expressing his opinion. In the tragedy of "Anthony and Cleopatra," a mechanical asp was introduced, which hissed as "dusky Egypt" took it up to apply to her bosom. The Parisian critic, on hearing the sound, arose and said to the pit—"Gentlemen, I am of the same opinion as the asp!"

Fielding published his play, "as it was damned," but he did not add, "as it deserved to be." He was less candid than Bernard Saurin, a French dramatist of the last century. Saurin's comedy, the "Trois Rivaux," was pitilessly hissed. The author printed it, not to shame the critics, but to confess the justice of their verdict. "Authors who have been humiliated," he says, "are not always the more humble on that account. Self-love supports itself." After enumerating many instances, he adds: "There are few unlucky playwrights who do not look beyond their piece for the cause of an effect which their play alone has produced. After wearying the public by their insipidity, they disgust it by their pride, displayed in some haughty preface to their drama. Perhaps there is a refinement of self-love in what I am myself now doing, when I candidly confess, that my comedy of the 'Three Rivals' thoroughly merited its fate."

Less reasonable than Saurin was Anthony Brown, the Templar, who produced his "Fatal Retirement," at Drury Lane, in 1739. This conversational tragedy, in which nobody is excited much above the level of every-day talk, fell at the first representation. Anthony Brown attributed the failure to Quin, who, after selecting one part, chose another, and finally threw up both. This conduct, according to Brown, rendered the other players indifferent, and brought on a catastrophe, which the condemned poet, of course, held to be unmerited. Accordingly, down went Templars and the Templars' friends, night after night, to hiss the offending Quin. He was commanded to make an apology, and he did so in his characteristic way. Addressing the audience, he said, blandly, that he had read "Fatal Retirement," at the author's request, and, under like impulse, had given him his sincere opinion of the tragedy, namely, that it was the very worst he had ever read, and that he could not possibly take a part in it. The audience were amused at the apparent frankness of this communication, and the Templars, allowing Anthony Brown to be non-suited, satisfied their indignation by visiting it upon poor Parson Miller, who had been so ungallant to Mistress Yarrow and her daughter. The "Hospital for Fools" was not brought out in Miller's name, but the Templar champions of the fair knew it to be his, and hissed it from the stage accordingly, despite the acting of Yates, Woodward, and Mrs. Clive, and that part of the audience who would fain have listened, if the noisy Templars would only have allowed them. Out of Miller's fiasco, Garrick subsequently made a success, and on the "Hospital for Fools" founded his "Lethe," in which he was famous in the character of Lord Chalkstone.

There is one anonymous author who exhibited a strange humor in his protest against the condemnation of his tragedy, the plot of which had been pronounced improbable. "You (critics)," says the dolorous author, "harp eternally on my improbabilities. You deal rigorously with inferior dramatists, on the score of their delinquencies as to the probable; but when the same fault is found in some great master, like Shakspeare, oh! then you give the word probability quite a liberal and kindly latitude of interpretation. And is not improbability as great a sin in the richest as it is in the poorest dramatic genius?" Campbell's just reply is, "No: we forgive the fault, in proportion as it is redeemed by wit and genius."

This author, so angry at being damned, should not have ventured his plays on the stage. He would have done well to imitate Thomas Powell, who wrote dramas, but did not wish the public to know it. So fearful of condemnation was he, that when a friend, who thought well of a tragedy he had written, called "Edgar," on the same subject as Ravenscroft's and Rymer's, offered to present it to Garrick, in order to its being acted,—"No, no!" exclaimed sensitive Powell, "by no means would I wish even to be known as an author, attackable by all." The mere pleasure of writing was enough for him. He fancied his triumphs; and they were thus never marred by hiss from the pit, or howl from adverse critic.

Some have taken their fate swaggeringly, with a protestation that the public were not so enlightened as they might be. Others have whistled, some have sung, a few have reasoned over it, one or two have acknowledged the condemnation; not one, except Bentley, has confessed that it was just. When the best scenes in the "Good-natured Man" were bringing down hisses and imperilling the comedy, Goldsmith fell into a tremor, from which the bare success of the play could not relieve him. But he concealed his torture, and went to the club and talked loud and sang his favorite songs, but neither eat nor drank, though he affected to do both. He sate out the whole of the company save Johnson, and when the two were alone, the disappointed author burst into tears, and swore, something irreverently, that he would never write again. Johnson behaved like a true man, for he comforted Goldsmith, and never betrayed his friend's weakness. *That*, of course, Goldsmith was sure to do for himself. Long after, when they were dining with Percy, at the chaplain's table at St. James's, Goldsmith referred to the dreadful night, the hisses, his sufferings, and his feigned extravagance. Johnson listened in astonishment. "I thought it had all been a secret between you and me, Doctor," said he, "and I am sure I would not have said any thing about it for the world."

Some poets thought the players had the better time of the two; but if poets incurred one peril, the players of this period incurred another. For instance, in 1777, the Edinburgh company going to Aberdeen by sea, were snapped up by an American privateer, and carried off captives to Nantz. How they were ransomed, I am unable to show.

Walpole may be registered, if not among the damned, yet among the discontented authors of this half century. Chute might be pleased, and even Gray approve; but Garrick seems to have had small esteem for Horace as a dramatic poet. Hence was Garrick, in Walpole's eyes, but a poor writer of prologues and epilogues, a worse writer of farces, and a patron of fools who wrote bad comedies, which they allowed Garrick to make worthless; but yet worthy of the town which had a taste for them! Walpole wished to see his "Mysterious Mother" acted, although he well knew that the story, and the inefficient way in which he had treated it, would have insured its failure. Indisposed to be numbered among the condemned, he ascribed his reluctance to venture, to two causes:

Mrs. Pritchard was about to retire, and she alone could have played his Countess; "nor am I disposed," he says, "to expose myself to the impertinences of that jackanapes, Garrick, who lets nothing appear but his own wretched stuff, or that of creatures still duller, who suffer him to alter their pieces as he pleases." In this strain Walpole was never weary of writing. Of Garrick's "Cymon" the disappointed Horace was especially jealous, and he sneered at its pleasing "the mob in the boxes as well as the footman's gallery," which privileged locality was not yet abolished in 1772. Garrick might be the best actor, but, said Walpole, he is "the worst author in the world!"

I have noticed the mirthful dénoûement of Cumberland's tragedy, the "Carmelite." Such dénoûements were approved by some part of the French public.

When the "Gamester" was adapted to the French stage, under the title of "Beverley, a tragedy of Private Life," the adapter was the Saurin, of whom I have spoken, and his attempt excited the critics, and divided the town. The poisoning fascinated some, and revolted others. One French poet protested against the "horrible" in tragedy, and exclaimed :—

> "Laissons à nos voisins ces excès sanguinaires,
> Malheur aux nations que le sang divertie,
> Ces exemples outrés, ces farces mortuaires
> Ne satisfont ni l'âme ni l'esprit.
> Les Français ne sont point des tigres, des feroces
> Qu'on ne peut amouvoir que par des traits atroces."

The ladies united with the poet, and Saurin found himself compelled to give two fifth acts; and, as the piece was attractive, the public were informed whether the dénoûement on that particular night would be deathless or otherwise! In the former case, as Beverley was about to take the poison, his wife, friend, and old servant, rushed in just in time to save him, and, in common phrase, to assure him that things were "made comfortable," in spite of his follies, his weakness, and rascality. Grimm jokes over plots admitting of double dénoûements, and alludes to the Norman vicar of Montchauvet, who wrote a tragedy on the subject of Belshazzar. The vicar thought that dramatic catastrophes depended on how the poet started. In his tragedy every thing turned upon whether Belshazzar should sup or not, in the fifth act. If he does not sup, there can be no hand on the wall, and so "good-night" to the piece. Accordingly, the poet says, in the first act, that the king will sup; in the second, that he will not; in the third, that he will; in the fourth, that he will not; and, consequently, in the fifth, that he must, and will. Had the vicar intended otherwise, he would have begun, he says, in different order!

Ducis adapted Shakspeare's "Othello" to the French stage, for which he furnished two versions. In the first, he killed Desdemona according to tradition. At this, ladies fainted away, and gentlemen protestingly vociferated. Ducis altered the catastrophe, whereat Paris became divided into two parties, who supported the happy or the tragic conclusion, as their feelings prompted them. Talma played the Moor; and, bred as he had been in the shadow and the sunlight of the English stage, he was disgusted with the liberty taken with Shakspeare. One night, when the piece was to end as merrily as a comedy, and the last act was about to begin, Ducis heard Talma muttering at the wing, "I will kill her. The pit will not suffer it, I am sure; well, I will make them endure, and enjoy it. She shall be killed!" Ducis tremblingly acquiesced, and Talma restored the old catastrophe. There was some opposition, and a little fainting on the part of the susceptible, but, in presence of the marvellous talent of the actor, all antagonism gave way; and Talma, with reasonable pride, notified to his friends on the English stage the successful effort he had made in support of the integrity of the Shakspeare catastrophe.

Some authors have altogether refused to despair of the success of their piece, however adverse or indifferent the audience may have been. Take, as a sample, the case of Joseph Mitchell, the Scottish stonemason, but "University-bred." Towards the middle of the last century, the public sat, night after night, quite incapable of comprehending the mysteries and allusions of his "Highland Fair, or the Union of the Clans." At length, on the fourth night, the audience took to laughing at the nonsense served up to them, and as the last act proceeded, the louder did the hilarity become. Poor Mitchell took it all for approval, and going up to Wilks, with an air of triumph, he exclaimed, "De'il o' my saul, sare, they begin to taak the humor at last!"

Hoole, another of the stage-damned, was less self-deluding. When his "Cleonice" was about to be played, a publisher gave him a liberal sum for the copyright, Hoole's reputation, as a poetical translator from the Italian, being then very great. The play, however, was condemned, and Hoole was the first to acknowledge the unwelcome truth. He, accordingly, returned a portion of the sum he had received, to the publisher. He had intended, he said, that the tragedy should be equally profitable to both, and now that it had failed, he would not allow the chief loss to fall on him who had bought the copyright. The watchmaker's son was a gentleman.

Hoole was as indifferent to condemnation as the French dramatist, Hardy, with less greed for money than influenced the latter, who, however, was moved by a proper sense of the value of labor. This French author, Hardy, who died about the year 1630, saw his plays damned with as much indifference as he wrote them. He composed between six and eight hundred, published forty of them, and did not see one live a fortnight. A couple of thousand lines a day were nothing to this ready dramatist, who furnished the players for whom he composed, with a new drama every third day. And it was a day when French dramas were full of incident. We hear of princesses who are married in the first act; the particular heroine is mother of a son in the second, whose education occupies the third; in the fourth he is a warrior and a lover; and in the fifth he marries a nymph who was not in existence when the play began. Hardy was the best of these inferior poets, and was original in this; he was the first who introduced the custom of getting paid for his pieces, a thing unknown till then, and which the poets, his successors, have not failed, says a French writer, "to observe very regularly ever since."

Mrs. Siddons's Bath friend, Dr. Whalley, was not so indifferent to the success of his muse as Monsieur Hardy; but he ranks among damned authors, who have accepted condemnation or neglect with a joke. His "Castle of Montval" was yawned at rather than hissed; but as it was acted beyond the third night, the doctor went down to Mr. Peake, the treasurer, to know what benefit might have accrued to him. It amounted to nothing. "I have been," said the author, an old picquet-player, to an inquiring friend, "I have been piqued and re-piqued;" and therewith he went quietly back to Bath, where he lived upon a private fortune, and the rich stipend from an unwholesome Lincolnshire living, which a kind-hearted bishop had given him, on condition that he never resided on it!

The tragedy of the other friend of Mrs. Siddons, Mr. Greathead (the "Regent"), was not much, if any, more successful, than Dr. Whalley's; but the author was so satisfied with his escape, that he gave a supper—that famous banquet, which was followed by a drinking bout at the Brown Bear, in Bow Street, at which a subordinate actor, named Phillimore, was sufficiently tipsy to have courage to fight his lord and master, John Kemble; who was elevated enough to defend himself, and generous enough to forget the affair next morning.

Sheridan kept his self-possession under merrier control than this. His "Rivals" was at first a failure. Cumberland, the most sensitive author in the world, under condemnation, declared that he could not laugh at Sheridan's comedy. "That is ungrateful of him," said Sheridan, to whom the comment was reported by a particular friend—"for I have laughed at a tragedy of his from beginning to end!" But this not having been said in Cumberland's hearing, was less severe than a remark made by Lord Shelburne, who could say the most provoking things, and yet appear quite unconscious of their being so. In the House of Lords he referred to the authorship of Lord Carlisle. "The noble lord," said he, "has written a comedy." "No, no!" interrupted Lord Carlisle, "a tragedy! a tragedy?" "Oh! I beg pardon," resumed Lord Shelburne, "I thought it was a comedy!" The piece thus adjudged of was the "Father's Revenge," an adaptation from Boccaccio, of "Tancred and Sigismunda," never played, and seldom read.

Cumberland, who bore his own reverses with impatience, and was ever resolute in blaming the lack of taste on the part of the public, rather than ready to acknowledge his own shortcomings, endured the triumphs of his fellow-dramatists with little equanimity. During the first run of the "School for Scandal," he was present, with his children, in a stage-box, sitting behind them. Each time they laughed at what was going on, on the stage, he pinched them playfully, and asked them at what they were laughing. "There is nothing to laugh at, my angels," he was heard to say: and if the juvenile critics laughed on, he less playfully bade them be silent —the "little dunces!"

The dramatists whom he "adapted," declined to be involved in his reverses. After his "Joanna," an adaptation from Kotzebue, had been damned, the German author took care to record in the public papers that the passages hissed by the English public were not his, but additions made by Cumberland. Sir Fretful found consolation. "If I did not succeed," says this frequently damned author, "in entertaining the audience, I continued to amuse myself. . . . I never disgraced my colors by abandoning *legitimate comedy*, to whose service I am sworn, and in whose defence I have kept the field for nearly half a century—till at last I have survived all true national taste, and lived to see buffoonery, spectacle, and puerility so effectually triumph, that now to be repulsed from the stage is to be recommended to the closet; and to be applauded by the theatre is little less than a passport to the puppet-show."· This spirit of self-satisfaction, and depreciation of the public taste, was nothing new. The author or adapter of "Richard II." (Nahum Tate), finding his piece prohibited by authority, published it with a self-congratulatory preface; but he had already done more in the epilogue; mindful of past reverses, and anticipatory of present condemnation, he made Mrs. Cook say:—

> "And ere of you, my sparks, my leave I take,
> For your unkindness past these prayers I make—
> Into such dulness may your poets tire,
> Till they shall write such plays as you admire!"

This was thoroughly in the old spirit of Flecknoe; but of samples of the spirit of "damn-ed authors," having given enough, let us pass among the audiences of the last half of the eighteenth century, whose "censure," in the old signification of the term, was challenged by the playwrights.

## CHAPTER XIII.

THE AUDIENCES OF THE LAST HALF OF THE EIGHTEENTH CENTURY.

In the first half of the above century, if a quiet man in the pit ventured on making a remark to his neighbor, who happened to be a "nose-puller," and who disagreed with the remark, the speaker's nose was sure to be painfully wrung by the "puller." In the same period, those very nose-pullers sat quietly, merely grimacing, when the great people in the boxes found it convenient to spit into the pit! But sometimes, the house, pit and all, was full of great people. Thus, on the night of the 7th March, 1751, Drury presented a strange appearance. The theatre had been hired by some noble amateurs, who acted the tragedy of "Othello," thus cast in the principal characters: Othello, Sir Francis Delaval; Iago, by John, subsequently (1786) Lord Delaval; Cassio, E. Delaval; Roderigo, Captain Stephens; Desdemona, Mrs. Quon (sister of Sir Francis, and later, the wife of Lord Mexborough); Emilia, Mrs. Stephens. Macklin superintended the rehearsals, and Walpole was present; for he says of the amateurs, in his characteristic way: "They really acted so well, that it is astonishing they should not have had sense enough not to act at all! . . . . . The chief were a family of Delavals, the eldest of which was married by one Foote, a player, to Lady Nassau Poulett, who had kept the latter. The rage was so great to see this performance, that the House of Commons adjourned at three o'clock on purpose. The footman's gallery was strung with blue ribbons. What a wise people! what an august senate! Yet my Lord Granville once told the prince, I forget on occasion of what folly: 'Sir, indeed your royal highness is in the wrong to act thus; the English are a grave nation.'"

The prince, and other members of the royal family were present in the stage box on this occasion; and the presence of blue ribbons, in place of livery tags, in the footman's gallery, was owing to the circumstance that tickets were issued numerously enough to completely fill the house, but without indicating to what part of the house the bearers would be admitted. The first who arrived took the best places; and tardy peers, knights of the garter, their wives and ladies, were content to occupy the gallery, for once, rather than have no place at all. Such an audience was never seen there before, and has never been seen there since.

At this time swords were still worn, and evil results followed, to others, as well as to the wearers. On the night of Saturday, September 21, 1751, as the "Way of the World" was being played at Drury, a quarrel, and then a fight with swords took place, between two gallants in the box-lobby. From some cries which arose, the audience thought the house was on fire, and fearful confusion, with fierce struggling, and terrible injury, ensued. Many women attempted in their terror to drop from the gallery to the pit. This was not so frightful as it might at present seem, for in those days the front of the lower gallery came down to the roof of the lower boxes. The occupants were a recognized power in the house, often appealed to, and were of very great intelligence and respectability, in one especially favorite locality,—the Old Haymarket, as long as the house lasted. Professional men, and poets, and merchants and their wives, sat there to see, hear, and enjoy, whose grand-daughters now sail into stalls, unconscious that there is a gallery in the house, and ignorant that they are of a race who once condescended to sit in it.

In those days royalty's presence formed a great attraction at the theatre; and royalty enjoyed a "row" as heartily as the most riotous there.

When Garrick, in 1754, found that he could not fill Drury Lane,—notwithstanding the ability of his company of actors, unless he played himself, and that his own strength was not equal to the task of playing without intermission,—he brought forward a magnificent ballet-pantomime, called the "Chinese Festival." It was composed by Noverre,—who had treated of his art,—dancing, as a branch of philosophy! As many competent English dancers as could be found, were engaged: and there was a supplementary, but prominent and able body of foreign dancers. Little would have been thought of this, but for the circumstance, that when the gorgeous show was set before the public, in the autumn of 1754, war had recently broken out between England and France. Thereupon, John Bull was aroused in a double sense,—his patriotism would not allow of his tolerating the enemy on the English stage; and his sense of religious propriety, not otherwise very remarkable at that time, was shocked at the idea of his condescending to be amused by Papists.

His offended sense was further irritated by the circumstance, that George II., by his presence on the first night, seemed to sanction favoritism of the enemy and the hostile church. Aggravated by that presence, which they did not at all respect, the pit heaved into a perfect storm, which raged the more as the old King sat and enjoyed,—nay, laughing at the tempest! The Brunswick dynasty was included within the aim of the hisses and execrations which prevailed. Had Garrick followed Lacy's counsel, he would have withdrawn the piece; but Davy was reluctant to lose his outlay, striving to save which, he lost hundreds more. As the "spectacle" was repeated, so was the insurrection against it; but the "quality" interfering,—as they deemed it the *ton* to uphold what great Brunswick approved,—a new element of bitterness was superadded. The boxes pronounced pit and galleries "vulgar;" and these powers waged war the more intensely, because of the arrogance of the boxes, whose occupants were assailed with epithets as unsavory as any flung at the dancers. Then ensued strange scenes and encounters. Gentlemen in the boxes drew their swords, leaped down into the pit, pricked about them in behalf of "gentility," and got terribly mauled for their pains. The galleries looked on, shouting approbation, and indiscriminately pelting both parties. Not so the fair, who occupied the boxes. They, on seeing the champions of propriety and of themselves, being menaced or overpowered in the pit, pointed the offenders out to the less eager beaux who tarried in their vicinity, and who, for their very honor's sake, felt themselves compelled to out with their bodkins, drop into the surging pit, and lay about them, stoutly or faintly, according to their constitutions. The stronger arms of the plebeians carried the day; and when these had smitten their aristocratic opponents, they celebrated their victory with the accustomed Vandalism. They broke up benches, tore down hangings, smashed mirrors, crashed the harpsichords (always the first of the victims in the orchestra); and finally, charging on to the stage, cut and slashed the scenery in all directions. Some evidence of the improved civilization of the audiences of this half of the century is afforded by the circumstance, that no one suggested that the house should be set on fire. But the pious and patriotic rioters rushed out to Mr. Garrick's house in Southampton street (now Eastey's hotel), and broke every window they could reach with missile, from basement to garret. The hired soldiery could not protect him; nor on their bayonets could he prop up the "Chinese Festival," wooden shoes and popery. This affair cost him a sum of money, the loss of which made his heart ache for many a day.

On our side of the Channel, royal personages have been more amusingly rude than the inferior folk. A good instance of this presents itself to my memory, in the person of the young King of Denmark, who married the sister of George III., and who frequently visited the theatres in London, in 1768. At the play of the "Provoked Husband," it was observed that he applauded every passage in which matrimony was derided; which was commented on as an uncivil proceeding, as his wife was an English princess.

This wayward lad offended audience and actors on another occasion, in quite a different way. In October, he commanded the edifying tragedy of "Jane Shore," during the performance of which he fell fast asleep, and remained so, to the amusement of the audience and the annoyance of Mrs. Bellamy, who played Alicia. That haughty and hapless beauty was not likely to let the wearied King sleep on; and accordingly, having to pronounce the words, "Oh thou false lord!" she approached the royal box, and uttered them expressly in such a piercing tone, that the King awoke in sudden amazement, but with perception enough to enable him to protest, that he would not be married to a woman with such a voice though she had the whole world for a dowry. Two nights later he went to see "Zara," Garrick being the Lusignan; and it is to his credit, that he sat through that soporific sadness without winking.

The greatest excitement prevailed among the audience when the King went to see Garrick act Ranger, in the "Suspicious Husband." The pit was so crowded and so hot, that every man (and there were few or no women there) took off his coat and sat in his shirt or waistcoat sleeves, in presence of the King. The various hues formed a queer sight; but many of the men fainted. At the thunder of the cheers which greeted his coming, Denmark looked frightened, but bowed repeatedly; and when, at Garrick's appearance, the roar of applause was renewed, his majesty appropriated it to himself, and again bowed to all sides of the house, while Ranger waited to congratulate himself on "having got safe to the Temple."

There was little indecorum in Mrs. Bellamy's act of rousing the sleepy King of Denmark with a scream, but greater, and what would now seem gross and unpardonable liberties, were taken by the actors, with their patron George III. For instance, in the "Siege of Calais," there is a scene between two carpenters who erect the scaffold for the execution of the patriots. Parsons played chief carpenter, in which character it was put down for him to say, "So, the King is coming! an the King like not my scaffold, I am no true man." George III. and family were present, one night, at the Haymarket, when this piece was played by command, and Parsons gave this unseemly turn to the set phrase. Advancing close to the royal box, he exclaimed: "An the King were here, and did not admire my scaffold, I would say, D—n him! he has no taste!" At this sally the King laughed louder and longer than even the hilarious audience!

Sir Robert Walpole was readier to take offence than King George. He could smile at the innuendoes of the " Beggars' Opera ;" but when he was deeply interested in the success of his Excise Bill, and an actor sneeringly alluded to it, in his presence, the minister went behind the scenes, and asked if the words uttered were in the part. It was confessed they were not; and thereupon Sir Robert raised his cane, and gave the offending player a sound thrashing.

In Parson's case, monarch and audience alike, knew that no offence was intended, in detection of which loyalty rendered the audience over-acute; as in the case when Jack Bannister got into disgrace with the house. "God Save the King" was being sung, and Jack, dressed for Lenitive in the " Prize," stood among an undistinguished group of choristers at the back of the stage. Gentlemen in the boxes called upon him vociferously to come into the front rank and sing so as to be heard. There was great disapprobation, in which the press joined, and poor Jack, as loyal a Briton as any in those days, had to explain, that being dressed in an extravagant costume, he had kept in the back ground, out of respect, as his caricatured garb seemed to him to be out of keeping with the words of the national anthem, which, to his thinking, were as something sacred.

Indeed, the loyalty of the actors to "King and Country" could not be doubted. When the Emperor of the French was collecting a host for the invasion of this country, the actors were among the first to enrol themselves as volunteers; and it was not an unusual thing to find the theatre closed, on account of the unavoidable absence of the principal performers, summoned to drill, or other military service then rigidly enforced.

On the other hand, there were, what was then called, disloyal factions among the audiences, and these drove "Venice Preserved" from the stage, for a time, by the furious applause which they gave to passages in favor of Liberty, and which applause was supposed to indicate hostility to the British Constitution!

Yet many of these factious people, who did not dislike the King because they loved liberty, were delighted to mark the unrestrained enjoyment of the royal family at the theatre. If George III. roared at the oft-repeated tricks of the clown, little Queen Charlotte shook with silent laughter at the intelligible action of the great comic performers. Once, when Foote, caricaturing an over-dressed lady, with a head-tire a yard in height, and nearly that in breadth, accidentally let fall the whole scaffolding of finery, and stood bare-polled upon the stage, the Queen's laughter was then audible through the house. Perhaps it was all the higher as she herself wore a modest and becoming adornment for the head. Indeed, she was proud only of her beautiful arms, and these the plain-featured lady contrived to display to the lieges assembled, with a dexterity worthy of the most finished coquette.

There was great homeliness, so to speak, in this intercourse between royal and lay folk, in those days, and much familiarity. The young Princes were often behind the scenes. On one of these occasions, the "sailor-prince," the Duke of Clarence, saw Bannister approach, dressed for Ben, in "Love for Love." The actor wore a colored kerchief round his neck. "That will never do for a man-of-war's man," said the Prince; who, forthwith, ordered a black kerchief to be sent for, which, putting round the pseudo-sailor's neck, he tied the ends into the nautical slip-knot, and pronounced the thing complete.

The royal patronage and presence did not always give rise to hilarity. Tragedy sometimes attended it. I can remember nothing more painful in its way than a scene, at the Haymarket, on the third of February, 1794. The King and Queen had commanded three pieces, by Prince Hoare; "My Grandmother," "No Song, No Supper," and the "Prize." Fifteen lives were lost that night in the precipitate plunge down the old pit-stairs, as the little green doors were opened to the loyal and eager crowd. Whether those who rushed over the fallen bodies were conscious of the extent of the catastrophe, cannot be determined; but the royal family were kept in ignorance of it, from their arrival till the moment they were about to depart. While they had been laughing to the utmost, many a tear had been flowing for the dead, many a groan uttered by the wounded who had struggled so frightfully to share in the joyousness of that evening, and the King's own two heralds, York and Somerset, were lying crushed to death among the slain.

On another occasion, tragic enough in the character of a chief incident, the conduct of the simple-minded King rose to the dignity of heroism. I allude to the night of the eleventh of May, 1800, at Drury Lane, when George III. had commanded Cibber's comedy, "She Would and She Would not." He had preceded the other members of the royal family, and was standing alone at the front of the box, when Hatfield fired a pistol at him from below. The excitement, the dragging of the assassin over the orchestra, the shouts of the audience, the fear that other would-be regicides might be there, moved everybody but the King, who calmly kept his position, and, as usual, looked round the house through his monocular opera-glass. The Marquis of Salisbury, very much disconcerted and alarmed, if not for himself, at least for the King, urged the latter to withdraw. "Sir," said George III.,

Vol. II.—8

"you discompose me as well as yourself; I shall not stir one step." He was a right brave man in this act and observation; and while the comedy was got through confusedly, the avenues to the stage crowded by people eager to see the assailant, the audience breaking spasmodically into cries in behalf of the King, and the Queen and Princesses in tears throughout the evening, George III. alone was calm, cheerful, self-possessed, and bravely undemonstrative.

Before we leave these august personages, let us take one glance as they sit among the audience, "in state."

When their Majesties, with the Prince of Wales, the Princess Royal, and the Princess Augusta, went thus, *in state*, on October 8, 1783, to see Mrs. Siddons play Isabella, there was much quaint grandeur employed to do them honor. The sovereign and his wife sat under a dome covered with crimson velvet and gold; the heir to the throne sat under another of blue velvet and silver; and the young ladies under a third of blue satin and silver fringe. My readers may desire to know how royalty was attired when it went to the play in state some fourscore years ago. There was some singularity about it. George III. wore "a plain suit of Quaker-colored clothes with gold buttons. The Queen a white satin robe, with a head-dress which was ornamented by a great number of diamonds. The Princess Royal was dressed in a white and blue figured silk, and Princess Augusta in a rose-colored and white silk of the same pattern as her sister's, having both their head-dresses richly ornamented with diamonds. His Royal Highness the Prince of Wales had a suit of dark-blue Geneva velvet, richly trimmed with gold lace." The handsome young fellow, as he was then, must have looked superbly, and in strong contrast with his sire,—King in Quaker-colored suit, and Prince in blue Genoa velvet.

George III. was not always lucky in his Thursday-night commands, and people laughed, when, after the solemn funeral of his uncle, the Duke of Cumberland, he ordered "Much Ado about Nothing" to be played in his presence. For Shakspeare, he had less regard than his father. Prince Frederick once suggested that the whole of Shakspeare's plays should be represented, under his patronage,—at the rate of a play a week, but difficulties supervened, and the suggestion made no progress.

Let us turn from these royal to less noble folk. We find, on a July night of 1761, Mr. Walpole at Drury Lane, to witness the performance of Bentley's " Wishes." He has left a pleasant sketch of the audience-side of the house, whither he went " actually feeling for Mr. Bentley, and full of the emotions he must be suffering." But,—" what do you think in a house crowded was the first thing I saw? Mr. and Madame Bentley perched up in the front boxes, and acting audience at his own play! No, all the impudence of false patriotism never came up to it! Did one ever near of an author who had courage to see his own first night in public! I don't believe Fielding or Foote himself ever did. And this was the modest, bashful, Mr. Bentley, that died at the thought of being known for an author, even by his own acquaintance. In the stage-box was Lady Bute, Lord Halifax, and Lord Melcombe. I must say the two last entertained the audience as much as the play. Lord Halifax was prompter, and called out to the actor every minute to speak louder. The other went backwards and forwards behind the scenes, fetched the actors into the box, and was busier than Harlequin. The *curious* prologue was not spoken, the whole very ill acted. It turned out just what I remembered it; the good parts extremely good, the rest very flat and vulgar; the genteel dialogue, I believe, might be written by Mrs. Hannah. The audience were extremely fair; the first act they bore with patience, though it promised very ill; the second is admirable, and was much applauded; so was the third; the fourth woful; the beginning of the fifth it seemed expiring, but was revived by a delightful burlesque of the ancient chorus, which was followed by two dismal scenes, at which people yawned, but were awakened on a sudden, by Harlequin's being drawn up to a gibbet, nobody knew why or wherefore,—at last they were suffered to finish the play, but nobody attended to the conclusion. Modesty and his lady sat all the while with the utmost indifference. I suppose Lord Melcombe had fallen asleep before they came to this scene." The piece was condemned, and the author was the first to recognize the fitness of such a fate. His nephew, Cumberland, sat on one side of him, and when Harlequin was hanged in the sight of the audience, as the fulfilment of the last of the " Three Wishes," Bentley whispered into his complacent kinsman's ear: " If they don't damn this, they deserve to be damned themselves!" The piece lingered for a few nights, and an unsuccessful attempt was made to revive it in 1782. So ended the (not first) experiment of introducing a witty-speaking Harlequin, in place of the dumb hero of pantomime.

At the period when this play was first acted, Garrick and his fellows labored under a serious disadvantage, when attempting to give full effect to stage illusions,—I allude to the crowding of the stage by a privileged part of the public. In spite of this, Garrick could render perfect and seemingly real, on the same evening, the frantic sorrows of old Lear, and the youthful joyousness of Master Johnny, in the "School Boy." In Dublin, there was often more annoyance than what resulted from mere crowding. Garrick was once playing Lear there, to the Cordelia of Mrs. Woffington, when one Irish gentleman, who was present, actually advanced, put his arm round Cordelia's waist, and thus held her, while she answered with loving words to her father's reproaches. Our sparks never went so far as this, in face of the public, but their intrusion annoyed the great actor. Such annoyance was not felt by his colleagues, and when Garrick resolved, once and for ever, in 1762, to keep the public from the stage, there was an outcry on the part of the players, who declared that, on benefit nights, when seats and boxes, at advanced prices, were erected on the stage, they should lose the most munificent of their patrons, if these were prohibited from coming behind the curtain. A compromise followed, and Garrick agreed to compensate for driving a part of the audience from the stage, by enlarging the house, and thus affording more room, and the old advantages on benefit nights. Thus, one evil was followed by another, for the larger houses were less favorable to the actor and less profitable to managers,—but stage spectacle became more splendid and effective than ever.

At this time amateur-acting was a fashionable pastime, and it had princely countenance. The Blake Delavals led the taste in this respect at their neat little theatre in Downing street. The Duke of York, who had distinguished himself early at the Leicester House theatricals, which Quin, I believe, superintended, was a very efficient actor, and he especially merited praise for the grace and spirit with which he played Lothario to the Calista of Lady

Stanhope, a Delaval by birth. Admission to these performances was not easily obtained. Walpole did not lack curiosity, but he would not solicit for a ticket, lest he should be refused. "I did not choose," he says, in his comic-jesuitical way, "to have such a silly matter to take ill!"

English and French audiences essentially differed in one pleasant feature, at this time. In France it was not the custom for young unmarried ladies to appear at the great theatres, especially the Opera. As soon as they were married they appeared at the latter in full bridal array, and the plaudits of the house indicated to them the measure of their success. With us, it was otherwise. Ladies, before marriage, appeared at the Opera more frequently than at church; and with much the same feelings regarding both. "I remember," says Lady M. W. Montague, writing to her daughter, Lady Bute, " to have dressed for St. James's Chapel with the same thoughts your daughters will have at the Opera."

At the latter house, one of the most conspicuous young ladies of her day, was Miss Chudleigh, afterwards Duchess of Kingston. She was constantly challenging the attention of the house. On one occasion, when a chorus-singer happened to fall on his face in a fit, Miss Chudleigh drew more notice than sympathy to herself, by pretending to fall into hysterics, and accompanying the pretence with a succession of shrieks and wild laughter. Walpole characteristically ridicules this affectation : " As if she had never seen a man fall on his face before!"

But ordinary confusion was as nothing, compared with that made on benefit nights, when audiences stood, or were seated in a "building on the stage." When Quin returned to play Falstaff for Ryan's benefit, the impatience of the house was great to behold their old favorite; but he was several minutes forcing his way to the front, through the dense crowd which impeded his path. As for Mrs. Cibber, Wilkinson had seen her as Juliet, lying on an old couch, in the tomb of the Capulets, all solitary, with a couple of hundred of the audience surrounding her. This occurred only on benefit nights, but even Garrick was unable to abolish it altogether.

It was really high time for this reformation, seeing that on one occasion, when Holland was acting Hamlet, for his benefit, and all

Chiswick (his father's *bakery* still exists close to the churchyard) was there to support their fellow-villager, a young girl, seeing him drop his hat, the three-corned cock, which Hamlet still wore, she ran, picked it up, and clapped it on his head, wrong side before, in such a way that gave the Dane a look of tipsiness; but see the respect of audiences for Shakspeare: they refrained from laughing, till Hamlet and the Ghost were off the stage, and then gave way to peal on peal of unextinguishable hilarity.

The author of a "Letter to Mr. Garrick," whom the writer treats with very scant courtesy, remarks, in contrasting the French and English audiences of his time, that it was then usual in France, for the audience of a new and well-approved tragedy, to summon the author before them, that he might personally receive the tribute of public approbation due to his talents. "Nothing like this," he says, "ever happened in England!" "And I may say, never will!" is the comment of the author of a rejoinder to the above letter, who adds:—"I know not how far a French audience may carry their complaisance, but were I in the author's case, I should be unwilling to trust to the civility of an English pit or gallery. We know it is the privilege of an English audience to indulge in a riot, upon any pretence. Benches have been torn up, and even swords drawn, upon slighter occasions than the damning of a play. Suppose, therefore, upon your principle, that every play that is offered should be received, and suppose that some one of them should happen to be damned, might not an English audience, on this occasion, call for the author, not to partake of their applause, indeed, but to receive the tokens of their displeasure. Maugre the good opinion which I have received of my own talents, I would not run the hazard of having my play acted upon these terms; for I think it less tremendous, and much safer, to bear at distance, the groans and cat-calls of ill-disposed critics, than to stand the brunt against half-eaten apples and sour oranges from the two galleries." These calls, however, are now common enough; but the French were before us in adopting the fashion.

Truculent as were the fine gentlemen in our theatres, in the days when swords were worn, they were less pugnacious than Irish audiences in their wrath. Mossop found this, when he was manager at Cork, in 1769. On one night of the season the house was unusually thin, but especially in the pit, where sat one little Major, determined to see all, though he sat alone. Mossop, unwilling to play at a loss, and to save his having to pay the actors whose salaries were regulated by the number of days on which they performed, came forward, announced that there would be no play, and intimated that all the admission money would be returned. The little Major insisted that the play should proceed. Mossop remonstrated, but kept to his purpose. The Major drew his sword and continued to insist. Mossop gently put his hand to *his*, and declined to act. In a couple of leaps the Major was on the stage, where the soldier and the player's swords were speedily crossed, and the two men fighting as fiercely as for some dear and noble purpose in peril. The actors and the audience seem to have enjoyed the spectacle; at least no attempt was made to part the combatants till the Major had run his sword through the fleshy part of Mossop's thigh, and Mossop had more slightly wounded the Major in the arm. Both sides claimed a victory; for the manager, unable to act, closed the theatre; and the soldier, too much hurt to be immediately removed, remained *in* the house, as he had declared his intention to do.

Since that period the manners of most Irish audiences have *unfortunately* improved, because the old fun and humor have departed with the exercise of the old license. Not that the old license was not frequently of a somewhat uncivilized nature, as when the Irish footmen in attendance upon masters and mistresses within, being angered by the withdrawal of some privilege, flung their lighted torches into the house, and nearly succeeded in burning both theatre and audience. Sometimes the license had an aspect of rough gallantry. When an actress was more than ordinarily pretty, it was the custom of ardent officers and gentlemen to insist upon escorting the lady home, after the play. An incident of this sort once put John Kemble's life in peril. The father of Miss Phillips (afterwards Mrs. Crouch) being, through illness, unable to attend his daughter, procured for her the guardianship of Kemble, who was but too happy to afford it. After the play, Miss Phillips's dressing-room door was beset by a crowd of adorers, sword in hand, and hearts burning beneath their waistcoats, sworn to see her home, whether she would or no. The lady was too alarmed to leave her room; but her deputed and faithful Squire urged her to do so, and as she appeared, he gave her his arm, announced the commission he held from the young lady's father, and declared that he would resent any affront offered to her, or to him. Therewith he moved forwards, with his charge under determined escort, and the riotous champions gave way, in good-natured admiration of his resolute courage. It was the more resolute, as the gentleman is said to have then entertained a tender regard for the lady; though, as with that for Mrs. Inchbald, it was all in vain.

Mr. Maguire, Mayor of Cork, and M. P. for Dungarvon, has recently stigmatized the Cork Theatre as being a locality which has preserved all the ferocity, and lost all the accompanying fun of the olden time. But even a Cork audience, in the last century, could be shocked. The Rev. C. B. Gibson, in his *History of the County and City of Cork*, tells us of a tailor there who was hanged for robbery, but who was restored to life by an actor named Glover, who probably was in his debt, and dreaded the summary demands of executors. The process of restoration was long and difficult; after it had been accomplished, the tailor arose, went forth, and got drunk, in which state he went to the theatre in the evening, told his story, exhibited the mark of the rope, and tendered very tipsy acknowledgments to the actor, for the service rendered. The audience did not at all relish this part of the evening's entertainment. At present, the Cork Gallery seems to be as vulgar and witless as that of the Sheldonian Theatre at Oxford, when filled with under-graduates. The liberty of English audiences has never been dealt with so harshly as that of audiences in continental theatres. In 1772, a theatrical riot took place in the Copenhagen Theatre. In a burlesque piece, a critic, who had dealt severely with the author, was quite as severely satirized, and a fierce tumult ensued. To prevent its recurrence, hissing and all equivalent marks of disapprobation were magisterially prohibited. This prohibition was long in force, and it is still maintained in continental theatres, when crowned heads are present. On these occasions the audience neither applaud nor hiss, but leave al demonstrations of approval or censure to the illustrious visitors, as if they alone were endowed, for the nonce, with critical acumen.

Charles Fox wound up the idler part of his early life by joining in private theatricals. Before he seriously commenced his career as a public man, in 1774, he played Horatio, in the "Fair Penitent," to the Lothario of his lively friend, Fitzpatrick, at Winterslow House, near Salisbury, the seat of the Hon. Stephen Fox. In the after-piece, "High Life Below Stairs," Fox played Sir Harry's Servant, with immense spirit; and after the curtain fell the house was burnt to the ground.

On the 10th of January, two days later, the Duke of Gloucester and his Duchess, formerly Lady Waldegrave, were at Covent Garden, "for the first time, in ceremony." The Duchess was confounded with the excessive applause; turned pale, colored, and won by her modesty, confusion, and beauty, the acclamations which the audience were willing to spare her, on acount of the apparent condition of her health. The marriage of this pair had offended the King. The piece selected by them was "Jane Shore," as illustrative, perhaps, of the evils of *dishonorable* connections between princes and ladies of lower degree. Two nights after this visit of ceremony, the King and Queen went in state to Drury Lane, and saw the "School for Wives." It is only to be wondered at that numerous applicable passages in both plays were not noticed by the applause or murmurs of the audience.

Walpole gives a pretty picture of the audience side of Drury Lane, on the 25th of May, 1780, on which night Lady Craven's comedy, the "Miniature Picture," which had been once privately played at her own house, was acted for the first time in public. "The chief singularity was that she went to it herself the second night 'in *form*,' sat in the middle of the front row of the stage-box, much dressed, with a profusion of white bugles and plumes, to receive the public homage due to her sex and loveliness. The Duchess of Richmond, Lady Harcourt, Lady Edgecumbe, Lady Aylesbury, Mrs. Damer, Lord Craven, General Conway, Colonel O'Hara, Mr. Lennox, and I were with her. It was amusing to see a young woman entirely possess herself; but there is such an integrity and frankness in the consciousness of her own beauty and talents, that she speaks of them with a *naïveté*, as if she had no property in them, but only wore them as the gift of the gods. Lord Craven, on the contrary, was quite agitated by his fondness for her, and with impatience at the bad performance of the actors, which was wretched indeed; yet the address of the plot, which is the chief merit of the piece, and some lively pencilling, carried it off very well, though Parsons murdered the Scotch Lord (Macgrinnon), and Mrs. Robinson, who is supposed to be the favorite of the Prince of Wales, thought on nothing but her own charms, or him. There was a very good, though endless, prologue, written by Sheridan, and spoken in perfection by King, which was encored (an entire novelty) the first night; and an epilogue that I liked still better, and which was full as well delivered by Mrs. Abington, written by Mr. Jekyll."

The prologue was called for a second time, at the conclusion of the play, which was acted after the "Winter's Tale." King had long before left the house, but though it was past midnight, the audience waited till he was sent for from his own residence, whence he returned to speak the address!

"The audience," adds Walpole, "though very civil, missed a very fair opportunity of being gallant; for in one of those *logues*, I forget which, the noble authoress was mentioned, and they did not applaud as they ought to have done exceedingly, when she condescended to avow her pretty child, and was there looking so very pretty. I could not help thinking to myself, how many deaths Lady Harcourt would have suffered rather than encounter such an exhibition; yet Lady Craven's exhibition had nothing displeasing—it was only the case that conscious pre-eminence bestows on sovereigns, whether their empire consists in power or beauty. It was the ascendant of Millamant, of Lady Betty Modish, and Indamore; and it was tempered by her infinite good nature, which made her make excuses for the actors, instead of being provoked at them."

Nineteen years later, Lady Craven, then Margravine of Anspach, having with unprecedented kindness and liberality, lent Mr. Fawcett the manuscript of her magnificent and interesting opera, the "Princess of Georgia," that actor announced it for his benefit, April 19th, 1799, with an assurance that "nothing should be wanting on his part to render it as acceptable to the public as it was to the nobility who had the pleasure of seeing it at Brandenburgh House Theatre." On this occasion, however, the house was not so splendidly attended as when the "Miniature Picture" was represented, and in spite of the melody of Incledon, the grimaces of Munden, the humor of Fawcett, the grace of Henry Johnston, and the energy of his wife, the " Princess of Georgia" was heard of no more.

There is one circumstance which made a striking difference between the aspects of the French and English pit. One of the popular grievances which the French Revolution did not redress, was the appearance of an armed guard, with fixed bayonets, within the theatre. When the curtain rises, the menacing figures withdraw a little; but they are at hand. In the last century they remained throughout the performance, and they kept the pit in a purely passive condition, whatever might be its displeasure, disgust, or discomfort. Under the gleam of the bayonet, a spectator no more dared to laugh too loudly at a comedy, than to sob too demonstratively at a tragedy. But Gaul and Frank were not always to be restrained, and they would hiss heartily at times. Ah " Il est bien des sifflets mais nous avons la garde !" A too prominent dissentient was sure to be seized by the sentinel, who escorted him to the captain of the guard, who judged him militarily, and, after procuring the signature of the commissary of police, a pure matter of form, sent the offender, for the night, to prison.

With this restraint, it is not wonderful that the French audiences were coerced into brutality, and that they readily took offence, were it only to show their manhood. With us it was different. The whole house laughed aloud, or smiled contemptuously at sarcasms fired at them from prologue or epilogue, or by implication in the play. It is singular, too, that so late as 1782, though French audiences *would* express an opinion, the actors themselves cared little for its being unfavorable, and careless players grew accustomed to be hissed, without being the more careful for it. To remedy this, Mercier proposed the appointment of a writer who should watch the theatres, and register the insults inflicted on the public by incompetent or indifferent actors, and by incapable poets. It was a proposition, in fact, for the establishment of a theatrical critic, whose judgments were to be recorded in the journals. There was public criticism of all other arts, but up to this time the art of acting was exempt from the censure of the

French journals. So, at least, says Mercier, who seems, however, to have forgotten that when the Abbé Raynal conducted the *Mercure* some thirty years previously, the merits of actors *were* occasionally discussed.

French sentinels grew careless, or French individuals waxed bolder. Our own gallery was once famous for the presence of a trunkmaker, whose loud applause or shrill censure used to settle the destiny of authors. The house followed according as the trunkmaker howled or hammered. I know nothing in French audiences to compare with this, except the notorions Swiss in the days of towering feathers and broad head-dresses—a double fashion, which he succeeded in suppressing. When seated in the back row of a box, unable to see the stage for the fashionable impediments in front, it was his custom to produce a pair of shears, and cut away all the obstructions between him and the delights for which he had paid, but could not enjoy. It was probably only a demonstration of destruction which he made, but the result was effectual. At first the ladies made way for him to come to the front; but ultimately they took down their feathers, and narrowed their head-gear, and the Swiss, shorn of his grievance, was soon forgotten.

This intruder must have often marred the efforts of the best actor; but I remember a case in which the best actor of his day was entirely discountenanced by the quietest and most attentive auditor in the house. John Kemble was playing Mark Anthony, in Dublin, when his eye happened to fall on a sedate old gentleman, who was eagerly listening to him through an ear-trumpet. The sight first caused the actor to smile, and that at an inappropriate moment, for he was surrounded by his wife, Octavia (Mrs. Inchbald), and her children, the play being Dryden's "All for Love," and the situation affecting. The more John Kemble endeavored to suppress his inclination to smile, the less he was able to control himself; as his agitation increased, the ear-trumpet was directed towards him more pertinaciously; seeing which, the actor broke forth into a peal of laughter, and rushed in confusion from the stage. The audience had discovered the cause, and laughed with him; while the deaf gentleman, unconscious of his own part in the performance, and marking the hilarious faces around him, dropped his trumpet with the vexed air of a man who had lost a point, and could not account for it.

Then, if there were infirm, so were there sentimental, authors. In the *Morning Post*, of September 27, 1776, we are told that— " A gentleman, said to be a captain in the army, was so very much agitated on Miss Brown's appearance on Wednesday night, that it was imagined it would be necessary to convey him out of the house; but a sudden burst of tears relieved him, and he sat out the farce with tolerable calmness and composure. The gentleman is said to have entertained a passion for that lady last winter, and meant to have asked her hand as a man of honor, but— !" There were other curiosities in front, besides this sentimental captain. The famous Lady Hamilton drew large audiences to Drury Lane towards the close of the century, when it was announced that the performance would be honored by the attendance of herself and her husband, Sir William, our minister to the Neapolitan court. The house gazed upon the beauty, and the beauty was deeply interested in the acting of Mrs. Powell, who, in her turn, was as deeply interested in my lady. Between the two women a connection existed which was little suspected by the audience. The ambassador's wife and the tragedy queen had first met under very different circumstances, in the house of Dr. Budd, in Blackfriars, where Jane Powell filled the office of housemaid, and Emma Harte, as she was then called, was employed as under-maid in the nursery.

At this period, I do not know that our galleries at least were more civilized than they were in earlier days,—that is, our provincial galleries: that of Liverpool, for instance,—as the obese, little, low comedian, Hollingsworth, once experienced. He was looking at the house through the aperture in the curtain, when the twinkle of his eye being detected by a ruffian aloft, the latter, running a penknife through an apple, hurled it, perhaps at random, but so fatally true, that the point of the knife struck the unoffending actor so close to the eye, that for some time his sight was despaired of. The gallery patrons of the drama, in London, were as rude, but less cruel, in their ruffianism. An orange, flung at a lady in court-dress, seems to have been a favorite missile for a favorite pastime. I meet with one of these ruffians in presence of a magistrate, who solemnly assures him, that if he is ever guilty of a similar outrage, he will be taken on to the stage and compelled to ask pardon of the house;—an honor, at which the fellow would, probably, have been exceedingly gratified.

We have a sample of the coolness of an Irish debutant and the patience of an audience of the last century; the first, in the person of Dexter, whom Garrick, on the secession of Barry from his company, brought over, with Ross and Mossop, from Dublin. Dexter, on the night of his first appearance, in Oronooko, was comfortably seated in the pit, where he remained chatting with his friends and supporters until the "second music" commenced. This music, in the old days, was ordinarily played half an hour before the curtain rose. This was a long period for an audience to be kept further waiting; but it was a short period wherein a tragedian might prepare and deck himself for a sort of solemn ordeal. The *début* proved successful; and Garrick generously expressed great admiration and hopefulness of the young actor, who, nevertheless, soon fell out of estimation of the audience, as might have been expected, from the cool and careless proceeding of his first night, when he walked out of a crowded pit to hastily dress himself for an arduous part.

This was a sort of liberty which a French pit would not have tolerated. It bore, however, with other freedoms. When it laughed, as the children were brought in, in "Inez de Castro," Madame Duclos, who was the weeping Inez, turned suddenly round, and exclaimed, "Fools! it's the most touching part of the piece!" and then resumed weeping. Again: Du Fresne, acting Sévère, in "Polyeucte," speaking low as he was confiding a perilous secret to a friend, was interrupted by cries of "louder! louder!" "And you, sirs, not so loud!" cried the calmly-angry actor, to a pit which took the rebuke meekly;—as meekly as our public took the verdict of Foote, who says, in his *Treatise on the Passions*,— "There are twelve thousand play-goers in London; but not the four-and-twentieth part of them can judge correctly of the merits of play or players."

Then, considering the measure of respect which actors used to profess that they entertained for audiences, the liberties which the former occasionally took with the latter was remarkable. When Mrs. Griffiths's "Wife in the Right" was coldly received, she laid the blame on Shuter (Governor Andrews), who had neglected to attend rehearsal. On a succeeding night, accordingly, the audience hissed, as soon as he appeared. He defended himself, by asserting that illness had kept him from rehearsal; "but, gentlemen," said he, " if there is any one here who wants to know if I had been drunk three days before, I acknowledge that I had, and beg pardon for that." The audience forgave the rude actor, and condemned the play.

Again : a few years subsequently, at York, Mrs. Montagu was cast for the Queen, in Hull's romantic play, " Henry II." She was a great favorite; and she claimed the more agreeable part of Rosamond, which had been taken by Mrs. Hudson,—the play being acted for her benefit. Mrs. Montagu refused to study the part of Queen Eleanor; and under the plea of illness preventing study, she sent an actor forward to state that she would read the part. Mrs. Hudson's friends insisted on Mrs. Montagu appearing, to explain her own case; and then the imperious lady swept on to the stage, with the saucy exclamation, " Who's afraid?" and the equally saucy intimation, that she *would* read the part, for she had not had time to learn it. This excited the wrath of the house; and some one cried out, that the audience would rather hear it read by the cook-wench at the next ale-house, than by her. Then, dame Montagu, as she was called, fired by the remark, and by cries forbidding her to read and commanding her to act, looked scornfully at the pit, flung the book which she held into the centre of the crowd, and with a "There!—curse you all!" swept off the stage, amid the mingled hisses and laughter of the house. But she was not permitted to act again.

Covent Garden audiences were more patient with saucy actresses; and they could even bear with Mrs. Lesingham, the handsome and too intimate friend of Harris, the proprietor, coming on to speak a prologue, in which she was so imperfect, that a man stood close to her with a copy, to prompt her in the words. For less disrespect than this, the same audience had demanded the dismissal of an actor, and condemned him to penury. Macklin suffered twice in this way, from the capricious but cruel judgment of the house; and having here mentioned his name, I will proceed to notice the career of a man who belongs to so many eras.

## CHAPTER XIV.

#### CHARLES MACKLIN.

A LITTLE child, about the last year of the reign of William III., —a boy who is said to have been born, *Anno Domini*, 1690, was taken to Derry, to kiss the hand of, and wish a happy new year to, the old head of his family, Mr. M'Laughlin. This ceremony was kept up in the family circle, because the M'Laughlins were held to be of royal descent, and the Mr. M'Laughlin in question to be the representative of some line of ancient kings of Ireland!

In the summer of 1797, an old actor is dying out in Tavistock Row, Covent Garden. Hull and Munden, and Davies and Ledger, and friends on and off the stage, occasionally look in and talk of old times with that ancient man, whose memory, however, is weaker than his frame. He has been an eccentric but rare player in his day. He had acted with contemporaries of Betterton; had seen, or co-operated with, every celebrity of the stage since; and did not withdraw from that stage till after Braham, who was among us but as yesterday, had sung his first song on it. He gave counsel to old Charles Matthews, and he may have seen little Edmund Kean being carried in a woman's arms from the neighborhood of Leicester Square to Drury Lane Theatre, where the pale little fellow had to act an imp in a pantomime. The old man, carried, in the summer last named, to his grave in the corner of St. Paul's, Covent Garden, was the child who had done homage to a traditional king of Ireland, so many years before. If Macklin (as Charles M'Laughlin came to call himself) was born at the date above given, the incidents of his life connect him with very remote periods. He was born two months before King William gained the Battle of the Boyne; and he lived to hear of Captain Nelson's prowess, to read of the departure to India of that Lieutenant-Colonel Wellesley, whose career of martial glory culminated at

Waterloo, and to have seen, perhaps, a smart young lad, just then in his teens, the Hon. Henry Temple,—now Viscount Palmerston and Prime Minister of England! Five sovereigns and five-and-twenty administrations, from Godolphin to Pitt, succeeded each other, while Charles Macklin was thus progressing on his journey of life.

Charles Macklin represents contradiction, sarcasm, irritability, restlessness. It all came of a double source,—his descent and the line of characters which he most affected. His father was a stern Presbyterian farmer, in Ulster; his mother a rigid Roman Catholic. At the siege of Derry, three of his uncles were among the besiegers, and three among the besieged; and he had another,—a Roman Catholic priest, who undertook to educate him, but who consigned the mission to Nature. I have somewhere read that at five-and-thirty, Macklin could not read, perfectly; but *that* is a fable; or at eight or nine he could hardly have played Monimia, in private theatricals at the house of the good Ulster lady, who looked after him more carefully than the priest, and more tenderly than Nature.

In after years, Quin said of Macklin, that he had—not *lines* in his face, but *cordage;* and again, on seeing Macklin dressed and painted for Shylock, Quin remarked that if ever Heaven had written villain on a brow it was on that fellow's! One can hardly fancy that the gentle Monimia could ever have found a representative in one who came to be thus spoken of; but he is said to have succeeded in this respect, perfectly, and in voice, feature, and action, to have counterfeited that most interesting of orphans with great success.

It was a fatal success, in one sense. It inspired the boy with a desire to act on a wider stage. It created in him a disgust for the vocation to which he was destined,—that of a saddler,—from which he ran away before he was apprentice enough to sew a buckle on a girth; and the lad made off for the natural attraction of all Irish lads,—Dublin. His ambition could both soar and stoop; and he entered Trinity College as a badge-man, or porter, which illustrious place and humble office he quitted in 1710.

Except that he turned stroller, and suffered the sharp pangs which strollers feel,—and enjoyed the roving life led by players on the tramp, little is here known of him. He seems to have served some five years to this rough and rollicking apprenticeship, and then to have succeeded in being allowed to appear at Lincoln's Inn Fields, in 1725, as Alcander, in "Œdipus." His manner of speaking was found too "familiar," that is, too *natural*. He had none, he said, of the hoity-toity, sing-song delivery then in vogue; and Rich recommended him to *go to grass again;* and accordingly to green fields and strolling he returned.

I suppose some manager had his eye on Macklin at Southwark Fair, in 1730, for he passed thence immediately to Lincoln's Inn Fields. He played small parts, noticed in another page, and was probably thankful to get them, not improving his cast till he went to Drury Lane, in 1733, when he played the elder Cibber's line of characters, and in 1735, created Snip, in the farce of the "Merry Cobbler," and came thereby in peril of his life. One evening, a fellow-actor, Hallam, grandfather of merry Mrs. Mattocks, took from Macklin's dressing-room, a wig, which the latter wore in the farce. The players were in the "scene-room," some of them seated on the settle in front of the fire, when a quarrel broke out between Hallam and Macklin, which was carried on so loudly that the actors then concluding the first piece were disturbed by it. Hallam, at length, surrendered the "property," but after doing so, used words of such offence, that Macklin, equally unguarded in language, and more unguarded in action, struck at him with his cane, in order to thrust him from the room. Unhappily, the cane penetrated through Hallam's eye, to the brain, and killed him. Macklin's deep concern could not save him from standing at the bar of the Old Bailey, on a charge of murder. The jury returned him guilty of manslaughter, without malice aforethought, and the contrite actor was permitted to return to his duty.

Among the friends he possessed was Mrs. Booth, widow of Barton Booth, in whose house was domiciled as companion, a certain Grace Purvor, who could dance almost as well as Santlow herself, and had otherwise great attractions. Colley Cibber loved to look in at Mrs. Booth's, to listen to Grace's well-told stories; Macklin went thither to tell his own to Grace, and John, Duke of Argyle, flitted about the same lady, for purposes of his own, which he had the honesty to give up, when Macklin informed him of the honorable interest he took in the friend of Mrs. Booth. Macklin married Grace, and the latter proved excellent both as wife and actress,—of her qualities in the latter respect I have already spoken.

For some years, Macklin himself failed to reap the distinction he coveted. The attainment was made, however, in 1741, when he induced Fleetwood to revive Shakspeare's "Merchant of Venice," with Macklin for Shylock.

There was a whisper that he was about to play the Jew, as a serious character. His comrades laughed, and the manager was nervous. The rehearsals told them nothing, for there Macklin did little more than walk through the part, lest the manager should prohibit the playing of the piece, if the nature of the reform Macklin was about to introduce should make him fearful of consequences. In some such dress as that we now see worn by Shylock, Macklin, on the night of the 15th of February, 1741, walked down the stage, and looking through the eyelet-hole in the curtain, saw the two ever-formidable front-rows of the pit occupied by the most highly-dreaded critics of the period. The house was also densely crowded. He turned from his survey calm and content, remarking, "Good! I shall be tried to-night by a Special Jury!"

There was little applause, to Macklin's disappointment, on his entrance, yet people were pleased at the aspect of a Jew whom Rembrandt might have painted. The opening scene was spoken in familiar, but earnest accents. Not a hand yet gave token of approbation, but there occasionally reached Macklin's ears, from the two solemn rows of judge and jury in the pit, the sounds of a "Good!" and "Very good!" "Very well, indeed!"—and he passed off more gratified by this than by the slight general applause intended for encouragement.

As the play proceeded, so did his triumph grow. In the scene with Tubal, which Doggett in Lansdowne's version had made so comic, he shook the hearts, and not the sides of the audience There was deep emotion in that critical pit. The sympathies of the house went all for Shylock; and at last, a storm of acclamation, a very hurricane of approval, roared pleasantly over Macklin. So far all was well; but the trial scene had yet to come.

It came; and there the triumph culminated. The actor was not loud, nor grotesque; but Shylock was natural, calmly confident, and so terribly malignant, that when he whetted his knife, to cut the forfeit from that bankrupt there, a shudder went round the house, and the profound silence following, told Macklin that he held his audience by the heart-strings, and that his hearers must have already acknowledged the truth of his interpretation of Shakspeare's Jew. When the act-drop fell, then the pent-up feelings found vent, and Old Drury shook again with the tumult of applause. The critics went off to the coffee-house in a state of pleasurable excitement. As for the other actors, Quin (Antonio) must have felt the master-mind of that night. Mrs. Pritchard (Nerissa), excellent judge as she was, must have enjoyed the terrible grandeur of that trial-scene: and even Kitty Clive (Portia) could not have dared, on that night, to do what she ordinarily made Portia do, in the disguise of young Bellario; namely, mimic the peculiarities of some leading lawyer of the day. And Macklin? —Macklin remarked, as he stood among his fellows, all of whom were, I hope, congratulatory, "I am not worth fifty pounds in the world; nevertheless, on this night am I Charles the Great!"

That Pope was in the house on the third night, and that he pronounced Macklin to be the Jew that Shakspeare drew, is not improbable; but the statement that Macklin, soon after, dined with Pope and Bolingbroke at Battersea is manifestly untrue, for the latter was then living in retirement, at Fontainbleau. It could not have been in such company, at this period, that Pope asked the actor, why he dressed Shylock in a red hat, and that Macklin replied, it was because he had read in an old history that the Jews in Venice were obliged, by law, to wear a hat of that decided color;—which was true.

Macklin was proud and impetuous, and often lost engagements, by offending; and regained them by publicly apologizing. He was an actor well established in favor, when, in the season of 1745-6, he made his first appearance as an author in an *apropos* tragedy for the '45 era, "Henry VII., or the Popish Impostor." The anachronism in the title is only to be matched by the violations done to chronology and propriety in the play,—a crude work, six weeks in the doing. It settles, however, in some degree, the time when Macklin left the Church of Rome for that of England. It must have been prior to the period in which he wrote the above-named piece. After it took place, he used to describe himself "as staunch a Protestant as the Archbishop of Canterbury, and on the same principles;"—a compliment, I suppose, to John Potter!

After playing during four seasons at Drury Lane, Macklin spent, from 1748 to 1750, in Dublin, where he and his wife were to receive £800 a year. He delighted the public, and helped to ruin the manager, Sheridan, who was unable to fulfil his engagement, and got involved in a lawsuit. From 1750 to 1754, Macklin was at Covent Garden, where one of his most extraordinary parts was Mercutio, to Barry's Romeo!—a part for which he was utterly unfit, but which he held to be one of his best!—not inferior to Woodward's! His view of the rival Romeos, too, had something original in it. Barry, he said, in the garden scene, came on with a lordly swagger, and talked so loud that the servants ought to have come out and tossed him in a blanket; but Garrick sneaked into the garden, like a thief in the night. And at this critical comment the latter did not feel flattered.

In 1754 Macklin introduced his daughter, with a prologue, and withdrew himself from the stage, to appear in a new character, that of master of a tavern, where dinners might be had at 4s. a head, including any sort of wine the guest might choose to ask for! The house was under the Piazza, in Covent Garden; and Mr. Macklin's "Great Room in Hart Street" subsequently became George Robins's auction-room. I do not like to contemplate Macklin in this character, bringing in the first dish, the napkin over his arm, at the head of an array of waiters, who robbed him daily; that done, he steps backwards to the side-board, bows, and then directs all proceedings by signs. The cloth drawn, he advances to the head of the table, makes another servile bow, fastens the bell-rope to the chair, and hoping he has made everything agreeable retires!

The lectures on the drama and ancient art, and the debates which followed, in his Great Room, the "British Inquisition," were not in much better taste. The wits of the town found excellent sport in interrupting the debaters, and few were more active in this way than Foote. "Do you know what I am going to say?" asked Macklin. "No," said Foote, "*do you?*" On the 25th of January, 1755, Charles Macklin was in the list of what the *Gentleman's*

*Magazine* used to politely call the "B——ts," as failing in the character of vintner, coffee-man, and chapman. His examination only showed that he had failed in prudence. He had been an excellent father, and on his daughter's education alone he had expended £1,200.

He remained disengaged till December 12th, 1759, when he appeared at Drury Lane, as Shylock, and Sir Archy Macsarcasm, in "Love à la Mode," a piece of his own. From the profits received on each night of its being acted, Macklin stipulated that he should have a share during life. The arrangement was advantageous to him, although this little piece was not at first successful. After a season at Drury, he passed the next at the Garden, and in 1763 reappeared in Dublin, at Smock Alley, then at Crow Street and Capel Street, under rival managers, Mossop, Sheridan, or Barry, and with more profit to himself than to them. In 1773 he returned to Covent Garden, where he made an attempt at Macbeth, which brought on that famous theatrical "row" which Macklin laid to the enmity of Reddish and Sparks, and of which I have spoken, under that year. With intervals of rest, Macklin continued to play, without increase of fame, till 1780, when he produced his original play, the "Man of the World," and created, at the age, probably, of ninety years, Sir Pertinax Macsycophant, one of the most arduous characters in a great actor's repertory. The Lord Chamberlain licensed this admirable piece with great reluctance, for though the satire was general, it was severe, and susceptible of unpleasant and particular application. Shylock, Sir Pertinax, and Sir Archy, were often played by the old actor, whose memory did not begin to fail till 1788, when it first tripped, as he was struggling to play Shylock. The aged actor tottered to the lights, talked of the inexplicable terror of mind which had come over him, and asked for indulgence to so aged a servant; and then he went on, now brilliantly, now all uncertain and confused. He was to play the same character for his benefit, on May 7th, 1789, and went into the green room dressed for the part. Whether he was then in his 90th or his 100th year, the effort was a great one; and, anticipating it might fail, the manager had requested Ryder, an actor of merit, who had been a great favorite and a luckless manager in Ireland, to be ready to supply Macklin's place.

The older performer seeing good Miss Pope, in the green room, asked her if she was to play that night. "To be sure I am, dear sir," she said; "you see I am dressed for Portia." Macklin looked vacantly at her, and, in an imbecile tone of voice, remarked, "I had forgotten; who plays Shylock?" "Who? why you, sir; you are dressed for it!" The aged representative of the Jew was affected; he put his hand to his forehead, and in a pathetic tone deplored his waning memory; and then went on the stage; spoke, or tried to speak, two or three speeches, struggled with himself, made one or two fruitless efforts to get clear, and then paused, collected his thoughts, and in a few mournful words, acknowledged his inability, asked their pardon, and, under the farewell applause of the house, was led off the stage, forever.

As an actor, he was without trick; his enunciation was clear, in every syllable. Taken as a whole, he probably excelled every actor who has ever played Shylock, say his biographers; but I remember Edmund Kean, and make that exception. He was not a great tragedian, nor a good light comedian, but in comedy and farce, where rough energy is required, and in parts resembling Shylock, in their earnest malignity, he was paramount. He was also an excellent teacher, very impatient with mediocrity, but very careful with the intelligent. Easily moved to anger, his pupils and, indeed, many others stood in awe of him; but he was honorable, generous, and humane; convivial, frank, and not more free in his style than his contemporaries; but naturally irascible, and naturally forgiving. Eccentricity was second nature to him, and seems to have been so with other men of his blood. His nephew and godson, the Rev. Charles Macklin, held an incumbency in Ireland which he lost because he would indulge in a particular sort of Church discipline. At the close of his sermon he used to administer the benediction, and the bag-pipes. With the first he dismissed the congregation, and, taking up the second, he blew his people out with a lusty voluntary.

When Macklin left the stage, his second wife, the widow of a Dublin hosier, and a worthy woman, looked their fortune in the ace. It consisted of £60 in ready money, and an annuity of £10. Friends were ready, but the proud old actor was not made to be wounded in his pride; he was made, in a measure, to help himself. His two pieces, "Love à la Mode," and the "Man of the World," were published by subscription. With nearly £1,600 realized thereby, an annuity was purchased of £200 for Macklin's life, and £75 for his wife, in case of her survival. And this annuity he enjoyed till the 11th of July, 1797, when the descendants of the royal M'Laughlins died, after a theatrical life, not reckoning the strolling period, of sixty-four years.

If Macklin was really of the old school, that school taught what was truth and nature. His acting was essentially manly, there was nothing of trick about it. His delivery was more level than modern speaking, but certainly more weighty, direct, and emphatic. His features were rigid, his eye cold and colorless; yet the earnestness of his manner, and sterling sense of his address, produced an effect in Shylock that has remained, with one exception, unrivalled.

Boaden thought Cooke's Sir Pertinax noisy, compared with Macklin's. "He talked of *booing*, but it was evident he took a credit for suppleness that was not in him. Macklin could inveigle as well as subdue; and modulated his voice almost to his last year, with amazing skill."

In his earlier days, Macklin was an acute inquirer into meaning; and always rendered his conceptions with force and beauty. In reading Milton's lines,

> "Of man's first disobedience and the fruit
> Of that FOR-BID-DEN tree—whose mortal taste
> Brought DEATH into the world, and ALL our woe."

the first word in capitals was uttered with an awful regret, the suitable forerunners, says Boaden, "to the great amiss" which follows.

Macklin's chief objection to Garrick was directed against his reckless abundance of action and gesture; all trick, start, and ingenious attitude, were to him subjects of scorn. He finely derided the Hamlets who were violently horrified and surprised, instead of solemnly awed, on first seeing the Ghost. "Recollect, sir," he would say, "Hamlet came there to see his father's spirit."

Kirkham gives us a picture of Macklin, in his old age, which is illustrative of the man, and his antagonism to Quin. The scene is at the Rainbow Coffee-House, King Street, Covent Garden, in 1787, where some one of the company had asked him if he had ever quarrelled with Quin. "Yes, sir," was the answer. "I was very low in the theatre, as an actor, when the surly fellow was the despot of the place. But, sir, I had—had a lift, sir. Yes; I was to play the—the—the boy with the red breeches;—you know who I mean, sir;—he, whose mother is always going to law;—you know who I mean!" "*Jerry Blackacre*, I suppose, sir?" "Aye, sir,—*Jerry*. Well, sir, I began to be a little known to the public; and egad, I began to make them laugh. I was called the *Wild Irishman*, sir; and was thought to have some fun in me; and I made them laugh heartily at the boy, sir,—in Jerry.

"When I came off the stage, the surly fellow who played the scolding Captain in the play; Captain—Captain—you know who I mean!" "*Manly*, I believe, sir?" "Aye, sir,—the same *Manly*. Well, sir, the surly fellow began to scold me; told me I was at my tricks, and that there was no having a chaste scene for me. Everybody, nay, egad, the manager himself, was afraid of him. I was afraid of the fellow, too; but not much. Well, sir, I told him I did not mean to disturb *him* by my acting, but to *show off a little myself*. Well, sir, in the other scenes I did the same, and made the audience laugh incontinently;—and he scolded me again, sir. I made the same apology; but the surly fellow would not be appeased. Again, sir, however, I did the same; and when I returned to the green-room, he abused me like a pickpocket, and said I must leave off my *d——d tricks*. I told him I could not play otherwise. He said I *could*, and I *should*. Upon which, sir, egad, I said to him flatly,—'you lie.' He was chewing an apple at this moment; and spitting the contents into his hand, he threw them in my face." "Indeed!" "It is a fact, sir! Well, sir, I went up to him directly (for I was a great *boxing cull* in those days), and pushed him down into a chair, and pummelled his face d——bly."

"You did right, sir."

"He strove to resist, but he was no match for me; and I made his face swell so with the blows, that he could hardly speak. When he attempted to go on with his part, sir, he mumbled so, that the audience began to hiss. Upon which, he went forward and told them, sir, that something unpleasant had happened, and that he was really very ill. But, sir, the moment I went to strike him, there were many noblemen in the green-room, full dressed, with their swords and large wigs (for the green-room was a sort of state-room then, sir). Well, they were all alarmed, and jumped upon the benches, waiting in silent amazement till the affair was over.

"At the end of the play, sir, he told me I must give him satisfaction; and that when he changed his dress, he would wait for me at the Obelisk, in Covent Garden. I told him I would be with him;—but, sir, when he was gone, I recollected that I was to play in the pantomime (for I was a great pantomimic boy in those days). So, sir, I said to myself, 'D—— the fellow; let him wait; I won't go to him till my business is all over; let him fume and fret, and be hanged!' Well, sir, Mr. Fleetwood, the manager, who was one of the best men in the world,—all kindness, all mildness, and graciousness and affability,—had heard of the affair; and as Quin was his great actor, and in favor with the town, he told me I had had revenge enough; and that I should not meet the surly fellow that night; but that he would make the matter up, somehow or other.

"Well, sir, Mr. Fleetwood ordered me a good supper, and some wine, and made me sleep at his house all night, to prevent any meeting. Well, sir, in the morning he told me, that I must, for *his sake*, make a little apology to him for what I had done. And so, sir, I, to oblige Mr. Fleetwood (for I loved the man), did, sir, make some apology to him; and the matter dropped."

Macklin's character has been described in exactly opposite colors, according to the bias of the friend or foe who affords the description. He is angel or fiend, rough or tender, monster, honest man or knave,—and so forth; but he was, of course, neither so bad as his foes nor so bright as his friends made him out to be. One thing is certain, that his judgment and his execution were excellent. In a very few tragic parts, he acted well; in comedy and farce, where villany and humor were combined, he was admirable and original. Of characters which he played originally (and those were few), he rendered none celebrated, except Sir Archy, Sir Pertinax, and Murrough O'Doherty, in pieces of which he was the author. His other principal characters were Iago, Sir Francis Wronghead, Trappanti, Lovegold, Scrub, Peachem, Polonius, and some others in pieces now not familiar to us.

That Macklin was a "hard actor" there is no doubt; Churchill, who allows him no excellence, says he was affected, constrained, "dealt in half-formed sounds," violated nature, and that his features, which seemed to disdain each other,—

> "At variance set, inflexible, and coarse,
> Ne'er know the workings of united force,
> Ne'er kindly soften to each other's aid,
> Nor show the mingled pow'rs of light and shade."

But "Cits and grave divines his praise proclaimed," and Macklin had a large number of admiring friends. In his private life, he had to bear many sorrows, and he bore them generally well, but one, in particular, with the silent anguish of a father who sees his son sinking fast to destruction, and glorying in the way which he is going.

Ten years before Macklin died, he lost his daughter. Miss Macklin was a pretty and modest person; respectable alike on and off the stage; artificially trained, but yet highly accomplished. Macklin had every reason to be proud of her, for everybody loved her for her gentleness and goodness. As a child, in 1742, she had played childish parts, and since 1750, those of the highest walk in tragedy and comedy, but against competition which was too strong for her. She was the original Irene, in "Barbarossa," and Clarissa, in "Lionel and Clarissa," and was very fond of acting parts in which the lady had to assume male attire. This fondness was the cause, in some measure, of her death; it led to her buckling her garter so tightly that a dangerous tumor formed in the inner part of the leg, near the knee. I do not fancy that Miss Macklin had ever heard of Mary of Burgundy, who suffered from a similar infirmity, but the actress was like the Duchess in this,—from motives of delicacy she would not allow a leg which she had liberally exhibited on the stage, to be examined by her own doctor. Ultimately, a severe operation became necessary. Miss Macklin bore it with courage, but it compelled her to leave the stage, and her strength gradually failing, she died in 1787, at the age of forty-eight, and I wish she had left some portion of her fortune to her celebrated but impoverished father.

Miss Macklin reminds me of Miss Barsanti, the original Lydia Languish, whose course on the London stage dates from 1777. The peculiarity of Miss Barsanti,—a clever imitator of English and Italian singers,—was the opposite of that which distinguished Miss Macklin. She had registered a vow that she would never assume male attire; nevertheless, she was once cast for Signor Arionelli, in the "Son-in-Law," a part originally played by Bannister. This was after her retirement from London, and when she was Mrs. Lisley,—playing in Dublin. The time of the play is 1779, but the actress, who might have worn a great-coat, if she had been so minded, assumed—for a music-master of that period, in London, the oriental costume of a pre-Christian, or of no, period, worn by Arbaces, in *Artaxerxes!*

Miss Barsanti was an honest woman who, on becoming Mrs. Lisley, wished to assume her husband's name, but that gentleman's family forbade what they had no right to prohibit. Her second husband's family was less particular, and in theatrical biographies, she is the Mrs. Daly, the wife of the active Irish manager, of that name; who is forever memorable as being the *only* Irish manager who ever realized a fortune, and took it with him into retirement.

There remain to be noticed, before we pass to the Siddons period, several actresses, of higher importance than the above ladies, as well as actors, whose claims are only second to those of Macklin.

## CHAPTER XV.

A BEVY OF LADIES ;—BUT CHIEFLY, MRS. BELLAMY, MISS FARREN, MRS. ABINGTON, AND "PERDITA."

A DOZEN more of ladies, all of desert, and some of extraordinary merit, passed away from the stage during the latter portion of the last century. Mrs. Green, Hippisley's daughter, and Governor Hippisley's sister,—the original Mrs. Malaprop, and, but for Mrs. Clive, the first of petulant Abigails, finished, in 1779, a public career which began in 1730. In the same year, but after a brief service of about eight years, Mason's Elfrida and Evelina, the voluptuous Mrs. Hartley, in her thirtieth year, went into a retirement which she enjoyed till 1824. She was "the most perfect beauty that was ever seen,"—more perfect than "the Carrara," who was "the prettiest creature upon earth." Her beauty, however, was of feature, lacking expression, and though an impassioned, she was not an intelligent actress, unless her plunging her stage-wooers into mad love for her be a proof of it. No wonder, had Smith only not been married, that he grew temporarily insane about this young, graceful, and fair creature.

Then, from the London stage, at least, fell Mrs. Baddeley, at the end of the season, 1780–81. She was a pretty actress with a good voice, and so little love for Mr. Baddeley and so much for George Garrick, that a duel came of it. The parties went out, to Hyde Park, on a November morning of 1770. Baddeley was stirred up to fight Davy's brother, by a Jewish friend, who, being an admirer of the lady, wanted her husband to shoot her lover! The two pale combatants fired anywhere but at each other, and then the lady rushed in, crying " Spare him !" without indicating the individual ! Whereupon, husband and friend took the fair one, each by a hand, and went to dinner; and the married couple soon after played together in " It's well it's no worse !"

But worse did come, and separation, and exposure, and *Memoirs* to brighten Mrs. Baddeley, which, like those of Mrs. Pilkington, only blackened her the more. She passed to country engagements, charming audiences for a while with her Polly, Rosetta, Clarissa, and Imogen, till laudanum, cognac, paralysis, and small sustenance, made an end of her when she had lost every thing she could value, save her beauty.

The third departure was of as mad a creature as she, Miss Catley—the Irish songstress, all smiles and dimples, and roguish beauty; who loved, like Nell Gwyn, to loll about in the boxes, and call to authors that she was glad their play was damned; and to ladies, to stand up that she might look at them, and to display the fashion of her dress, which those ladies eagerly copied. Her "Tyburn top," which she wore in Macheath, set the mode for the hair for many a day; and to be *Catley-fied* was to be decked out becomingly.

A more illustrious pair next left the stage more free to Mrs. Siddons, or her coming rendered it less tenable to them; namely, Mrs. Yates, and George Anne Bellamy—the former appearing for the last time for the benefit of the latter. More than thirty years before, as Mrs. Graham, young, fat, and weak-voiced, she failed in Dublin. In 1753–4, she made almost as unsatisfactory a début at Drury Lane, in a new part, Marcia, in "Virginia," in which she only showed promise. Richard Yates then married and instructed her, and she rapidly improved, but could not compete with Mrs. Cibber, till that lady's illness caused Mandane (" Orphan of China") to be given to Mrs. Yates, who, by her careful acting, at once acquired a first-rate reputation. In the classical heroines of the dull old classical tragedies of the last century, she was wonderfully effective, and her Medea was so peculiarly her own, that Mrs. Siddons herself never disturbed the public memory of it, by acting the part.

When Mrs. Cibber died in 1765, Mrs. Yates succeeded to the whole of her inheritance, some of which was a burden too much for her; but she kept her position, with Mrs. Barry (Crawford) for a rival, till Mrs. Siddons promised at Bath to come and dispossess both. Mrs. Yates recited beautifully, was always dignified, but seems to have wanted variety of expression. With a haughty mien, and a powerful voice, she was well suited to the strong-minded heroines of tragedy; but the more tender ladies, Desdemona or Monimia, she could not compass. To the pride and violence of Calista she was equal, but in pathos she was wanting. Her comedy was as poor as that of Mrs. Siddons; her Jane Shore as good; her Medea so sublime as to be unapproachable. I suspect she was a little haughty; for impudent Weston says in his will: "To Mrs. Yates I leave all my humility!"

In one character of comedy she is said, indeed, to have excelled —Violante, in the "Wonder," to the playfulness, loving, bickering, pouting, and reconciliations, in which her "queen-like majesty" does not seem to have been exactly suitable. Her *scorn* was never equalled but by Mrs. Siddons, and it would be difficult to determine which lady had the most lofty majesty. In passion, Mrs. Yates swept the stage as with a tempest; yet she was always under control. For instance, in Lady Constance, after wildly screaming—

"I will not keep this form upon my head,
When there is much disorder in my wit"—

she did not cast to the ground the thin cap which surmounted her head-dress, but quietly took it from her head, and placed it on the right side of the circumference of her hoop! Mrs. Yates died in 1787.

George Anne Bellamy is unfortunate in having a story, which honest women seldom have. That pleasant place, Mount Sion, at Tunbridge Wells, was the property of her mother, a Quaker farmer's daughter, named Seal, who, on *her* mother falling into distress, was taken by Mrs. Gregory, the sister of the Duke of Marlborough, to be educated.

Miss Seal was placed in an academy in Queen's Square, Westminster, so dull a locality, that the rascally Lord Tyrawley had no difficulty in persuading her to run away from it in his company, and to his apartments, in Somerset House. When my lord wanted a little change, he left Miss Seal with her infant son, and crossed to Ireland to make an offer to the daughter of the Earl of Blessington. She was ugly, he said, but had money; and when he got possession of both, he would leave the first, and bring the latter with renewed love, to share with Miss Seal.

The lady was so particularly touched by this letter, that she sent it, with others, to the earl, who, rendered angry thereat, forbade his daughter to marry my lord, but found they were married already. Tyrawley hoped thus to secure Lady Mary Stewart's fortune ; but discovering she had none at her disposal, he naturally felt he had been deceived, and turned his wife off to her relations. Having gone through this amount of villany, King George thought he was qualified to represent him at Lisbon, and thither Lord Tyrawley proceeded accordingly.

He would have taken Miss Seal with him, but she preferred to go on the stage. Ultimately she *did* consent to go ; and was received with open arms ; but she was so annoyed by the discovery of a swarthy rival, that she listened to the wooing of a Captain Bellamy, married him, and presented him with a daughter with such promptitude. that the modest captain ran away from so clever a woman and never saw her afterwards.

Lord Tyrawley, proud of the implied compliment, acknowledged the little George Anne Bellamy, born on St. George's day, 1773, as his daughter. He exhibited the greatest care in her education. He kept her at a Boulogne convent from her fifth to her eighth year, and then brought her up at his house at Bexley, amid noble young scamps, whose society was quite as useful to her as if she had been at a "finishing" school.

Lord Tyrawley having perfected himself in the further study of demi-rippism, went as the representative of England to Russia, leaving an allowance for his daughter, which so warmed up her mother's affections for her, that George Anne was induced to live with her, and George Anne's mother hoped that her annuity would do so too ; but my lord having different ideas, stopped the annuity, and did not care to recover his daughter.

The two women were destitute ; but the younger one was very youthful, was rarely beautiful, had certain gifts, and, of course, the managers heard of her. She had played Miss Prue for Bridgewater's benefit, in 1742, and gave promise. In 1744, Rich heard her recite, and announced her for Monimia. Quin was angry at having to play Chamont to "such a child;" but the little thing manifested such tenderness and ability, that he confessed she was charming. Lord Byron thought so too, and carried her off in his coach to a house at the corner of North Audley Street, which looked over the dull Oxford Road to the desolate fields beyond. Much scandal ensued; amid which Miss Bellamy's half-brother appeared, shook his sister as a pert baggage, and sorely mauled my lord; but Lord Byron lived to murder Mr. Chaworth in a duel, to be found guilty of slaughtering the poor man, and consequently, being a peer, to be discharged on paying his fees!

Then Miss Bellamy went among some Quaker relations who had never previously seen her, and charmed them so by her soft, and winning and simple Quakerish ways, that they would have made an idol of her, if Friends ever made an idol of any thing, but lucre and themselves. A discovery that she was an actress brought this phase of her life to an end, and it was followed by a triumphant season on the Dublin stage, from 1745 to 1747, where she made such a sensation, reigned so like a queen, and was altogether so irresistible and rich, that Lord Tyrawley's family acknowledged her. My lord himself became reconciled to her, through old Quin, and would have spent her income for her after she was re-engaged at Covent Garden, in 1748, if she would only have married his friend, Mr. Crump. Rather than do that, she let a Mr. Metham carry her off from Covent Garden, dressed as she was to play Lady Fanciful, to live with, quarrel with, and refuse to wed with him.

What with the loves, caprices, charms, extravagances, and sufferings of Mrs. Bellamy, she excited the wonder, admiration, pity, and contempt of the town, for thirty years. The Mr. Metham, she might have married, she would not,—Calcraft and Digges, whom she would have, and the last of whom she thought she *had* married, she could not, for both had wives living. To say that she was a siren who lured men to destruction, is to say little, for she went down to ruin with each victim; but she rose from the wreck more exquisitely seductive and terribly fascinating than ever, to find a new prey whom she might ensnare and betray.

Meanwhile she kept a position on the stage, in the very front rank, disputing pre-eminence with the best there, and achieving it in some things; for this perilous charmer was unequalled in her day for the expression of unbounded and rapturous love. Her looks glowing with the passion to which she gave expression, doubled the effect; and whether she gazed at a lover or rested her head on the bosom of her lord, nothing more tender or subduing was ever seen, save in Mrs. Cibber. She was so beautiful, had eyes of such soft and loving blue, was so extraordinarily fair, and was altogether so irresistible a sorceress, that Mrs. Bellamy was universally loved as a charming creature, and admired as an excellent actress; and when she played some poor lady distraught through affection, the stoutest hearts under embroidered or broadcloth waistcoats crumbled away, often into inconceivable mountains of gold-dust.

She laughed, and scattered as fast as they piled it, and in the gorgeous extravagance of her life began to lose her powers as an actress. She had once almost shared the throne assumed by Mrs. Cibber, but she wanted the sustained zeal and anxious study of that lady, and cared not, as Mrs. Cibber did, for one quiet abiding home, by whomsoever shared, but sighed for change, had it, and suffered for it. When her powers began to decay, her admirers of all schools deplored the fact. In tragedy, natural as she was in feeling, she belonged to the old days of intoned cadences; and the old and the rising school mourned over her, yet both were compelled to avow that only in the ecstacy of love was Mrs. Bellamy equal to the Cibber, and in that, Mrs. Cibber, when acting with Barry, in the younger days of both, was often George Anne's superior.

From reigning it like a queen on and off the stage,—imperious and lovely, and betraying everywhere,—to the figure of a poor, bailiff-persecuted, famishing wretch, stealing down the muddy steps of old Westminster Bridge to drown herself in the Thames, how wide are the extremes! But in both positions we find the original Volumnia of Thomson, the Erixine of Dr. Young, and the Cleone, to whom Dodsley owed the success of his heart-rending tragedy. To the last, she was as unfortunate as she had been reckless. Two old lovers, one of whom was Woodward, bequeathed legacies to her, which she never received. Those sums seemed as life to her; but, in the days of her pride and her power, and wicked but transcendent beauty, she would have scorned them as mere pin-money; and so she grew acquainted with gaunt misery, till some friends, weary, perhaps, of sustaining the burden she imposed upon them, induced the managers to give her a farewell benefit, in 1784, on which occasion Mrs. Yates returned to the stage to play for her the Duchess in "Braganza." More than forty years before, the brilliant little sylph, Miss Bellamy, had floated on to the same Covent Garden stage, confident in both intellectual and material charms. Now, the middle-aged woman, still older through fierce impatience at her fall, through want, hopelessness, every thing but remorse, had not nerve enough to go on and utter a few words of farewell. These were spoken for her by Miss Farren, before the curtain, which ascended at the words—

"But see, oppressed with gratitude and tears,
To pay her duteous tribute, she appears;"

and discovered the once beautiful and happy siren, a terrified, old-looking woman, lying, powerless to rise, in an arm-chair. But the whole house—some out of respect for the erst charmer, others out of curiosity to behold a woman of such fame, on and off the stage—rose to greet her. George Anne, urged by Miss Catley, bent forward, murmured a few indistinct words, and, falling back again, the curtain descended, for the last time, between the public and the Fallen Angel of the stage.

Half a dozen minor lights are extinguished before we come to a name, a desert, and a fortune, more brilliant and lasting than that of George Anne Bellamy,—the name, merit, and fortunes of Miss Farren. Mrs. Wilson, the original Betty Hint, in the "Man of the World," is not now remembered either for her genius or her errors. Mrs. Belfille made but one appearance on the London stage as Belinda, in "All in the Wrong." She wanted animation and humor, but was distinguished for the splendor of her stage wardrobe, which was all her own. She joined Whitlock and Austin's company in the north. Whitlock married Mrs. Siddons's sister Elizabeth, and took her to America, where her acting drew rather the admiration than the tears of the Indians. Mrs. Belfille and Mrs. Whitlock were together in the company named above. On the back of one of the bills I find a MS. note made by Austin, in which he says that Mrs. Belfille was an elegant actress, very fashionable, and genteel in dress and manner; and, he adds, "Mrs. Whitlock could not keep her temper while Mrs. Belfille was with me, in Newcastle, Chester, &c."

A year later, in 1789, the charming Bacchante, Mrs. Barresford, Goldsmith's Miss Richland and Miss Hardcastle, and Sheridan's Julia, in the "Rivals," left the London stage for Edinburgh, where, says Jackson, "her Lady Racket will be remembered as long as one of her audience remains alive."

Pretty-Mrs. Wells, famous for her imitations, now disappears. She was O'Keefe's Cowslip. She was the Jewish gentleman, Mr. Sumbell's, wife, which he denied; and she so far rivalled Mrs. Siddons, that, in "Isabella," as it was the fashion for the house to shriek when the actress shrieked, so, when Mrs. Wells shrieked, her friends shrieked louder than those of Mrs. Siddons, and, *therefore*, thought Cowslip was the greater tragedian of the two. Then, the first of the Miss Bruntons, the Louisa Courtney of Reynold's "Dramatist," finished her seventh and last season, in London, in 1792, as the wife of Della Cruscan Merry. She began as an expected rival of Mrs. Siddons, but London did not confirm the testimony of Bath. Three other actresses passed away before Miss Farren: mad Hannah Brand, who was a sort of female Mossop; Mrs. Esten (who tried to disturb Mrs. Siddons, Mrs. Jordan, and Miss Farren, but who, failing, settled in the north, and very much disturbed the heart and the purse of the Duke of Hamilton), and Mrs. Webb, the original Mrs. Cheshire to the above Cowslip; than whom, actress of more weight never made the boards groan, and who turned her corpulence to account by playing Falstaff.

The first glimpse to be caught of Miss Farren is as picturesque as can well be imagined. Her father, once a Cork surgeon, but now manager of a strolling company, is in the lock-up of the town of Salisbury; he fell into durance through an unconscious infringement of the borough law. The story is told, at length, in my *Knights and their Days*. On a wintry morning, a little girl carries him a bowl of hot milk, for breakfast, and she is helped over the ice to the lock-up window, by a sympathizing lad. The nymph is Miss Farren, afterwards Countess of Derby; the boy is the very happy beginning of Chief-Justice Burroughs.

This incident occurred in 1769. Three years later, Elizabeth was playing Columbine at Wakefield. She could sing as well as she could dance, gracefully; and, out of very love for the beautiful girl, Younger brought her out, at Liverpool, where her maternal grandfather had been a brewer of repute and good fortune, and where his grand-daughter proved such a Rosetta, that more than half the young fellows were more deeply in love with her than the paternal Younger himself.

After five years' training, the now radiant girl, glowing with beauty and intelligence, first charmed a London audience, on June the 9th, 1777, by appearing at the Haymarket, as Miss Hardcastle; Edwin making his appearance on the same night, as Old Hardcastle. In that first year of London probation, her Miss Hardcastle was a great success; the town was ecstatic at that and her Maria, in the "Citizen," was rapt at her Rosetta, rendered hilarious by her Miss Tittup, and rarely charmed by her playfulness and dignity, as Rosara (Rosina), in the "Barber of Seville." Of this character, she was the original representative. Colman omitted the scene in which the Count was disguised as a tipsy dragoon, on the ground of its being injurious to morality! The same Colman thought the fool, in " Lear," too gross for a London audience!

In the following year, the success of her Lady Townly transferred her to Drury Lane, where she divided the principal parts with Miss Walpole, Miss P. Hopkins (Mrs. Kemble, subsequently), and Perdita Robinson; and not one of the four was twenty years of age.

Her Lady Townly was no new triumph. She had produced such an effect in it at Liverpool, where, after her father's death, Younger had engaged the whole family, that, on the strength of the promise of fortune to come, tradesmen offered them unlimited credit.

For about a score of years she maintained a pre-eminence which she did not, however, attain all at once, or without a struggle; her most powerful and graceful opponent being Mrs. Abington. Her early days had been of such stern and humble aspect, such a strolling and starving with her stage-mad and improvident father, that an anonymous biographer says of her: "The early parts of the history of many eminent ladies on the stage must be extremely disagreeable to them, in the recital; and to none, we apprehend, more than to Miss Farren, who, from the lowest histrionic sphere, has raised herself to the most elevated."

During the years above-named, she played principally at Drury Lane and the Haymarket, and chiefly the parts of fine ladies, for which she seemed born; though she attempted tragedy, now and then; and assumed low comedy characters, occasionally; but her natural elegance, her tall and delicate figure, her beautiful expression, her superbly modulated voice, her clear and refined pronunciation, made of her fine lady a perfect charm; not merely the Lady Betty Modish, and similar personages, but the sentimental Indianas and Cecilias.

Walpole says emphatically of Miss Farren, that in his estimation, she was the most perfect actress he had ever seen. Adolphus praises "the irresistible graces of her address and manner, the polished beauties of her action and gait, and all the indescribale little charms which give fascination to the woman of birth and fashion," as among the excellencies which secured a triumph for Burgoyne's " Heiress." In that play she acted Lady Emily Gayville.

Among her original characters were Rosara (Rosina), in the "Barber of Seville; Cecilia, in "Chapter of Accidents;" Sophia, in "Lord of the Manor;" Lady Emily Gayville, in the "Heiress;" Eliza Ratcliffe, in the "Jew;" and Emily Tempest, in the "Wheel of Fortune." In the "Heiress" Adolphus again says of her:— "Whether high and honorable sentiments, burning and virtuous sensibility, sincere and uncontrollable affection; animated, though sportive reprehension; elegant persiflage, or arch and pointed satire were the aim of the author, Miss Farren amply filled out his thought, and by her exquisite representation, made it, even when faint and feeble in itself, striking and forcible." In fewer words, she had feeling, judgment, grace, and discretion.

It was when playing Rosara that her life became in danger, by her long gauze mantilla taking fire from the side-lights. She was not aware of her peril, till Bannister (Almaviva) had quietly thrown his Spanish cloak around her, and had put out the flames with his hands.

During her stage career she was the manageress of the private theatricals at the Duke of Richmond's,—those most exclusive of dramatic entertainments. She moved, as it is called, in the best society, where she was Queen "amang them a'." Charles James Fox is said to have been more or less seriously attached to her; but long before she withdrew from the stage it was said, and was printed, that when "*one* certain event should happen, a Countess's coronet would fall on her brow."

And thereby hangs a tale that has something in it extremely unpleasant, for this one event, waited for during a score of years, was the death of the Countess of Derby, the only daughter of the Duke of Hamilton.

To the Duchess of Leinster, who knew something of Miss Farren's family in Ireland, the actress was indebted for introductions to Lady Ailesbury, Mrs. Damer, and others, through whom Miss Farren became acquainted with the Earl of Derby, who was himself a clever actor, in private theatricals. A Platonic affection, at least, was soon established. Walpole writing, in 1791, to the Miss Berrys, says: "I have had no letter from you these ten days, though the east wind has been as constant as Lord Derby," not to his wife, whom he had married in 1774, but to Miss Farren, who first came to London three years later.

On the 14th of March, 1797, the long-tarrying Countess departed this life; on the 8th of April following, Miss Farren took final leave of the stage, in Lady Teazle. After the play, Wroughton led her forward, and spoke a few farewell words for her, at the end of which she gracefully curtseyed to all parts of the house; and that once little girl who carried milk to her father in the Round House, went home, and was married to the Earl, on the May Day of the year in which he had lost his first wife! Six weeks 'twixt death and bridal! and yet we hear that Miss Farren's greatest charm consisted in her "delicate, genuine, impressive sensibility, which reached the heart by a process no less certain than that by which her other powers effected their impression on their fancy and judgment."

At all events, Miss Farren never acted so hastily, nor Stanley so uncourteously to the memory of a dead lady, as on this occasion, and it was not one for which youthful widowers might find an apology, for the erst strolling actress was considerably past thirty, and her swain within five years of the age at which Sir Peter Teazle married "my lady."

Of the three children of this union, only one survived, Mary, born in 1801, and married, twenty years afterwards, to the Earl of Wilton. Through her, the blood of an actress once more mingles with that of the peerage; with the same result, perhaps, as followed the match of Winnifred, the dairymaid, with the head of the Bickerstaffes.

No marriage of an English actress with a man of title ever had such results as that which followed the union of Fleury's beautiful sister with the gallant Viscount Clairval de Passy. When the match was proposed, the parents of the lady were in a fever of delight that their daughter should be a viscountess. Doubtless, she became so in law and fact; but instead of taking place as such with the Viscount, *he* laid by his title, and out of love for his wife and her profession, turned actor himself! The happy pair played together with success, and when you meet with the names of Monsieur and Madame Sainville in the annals of the French stage, you are reading of that very romantic pair,—the happy Viscount and Viscountess Clairval de Passy.

In 1796, after more than a quarter of a century of service, Mrs. Pope, once Garrick's favorite, Miss Younge, withdrew to die, and leave her younger husband to take a less accomplished actress for his second wife. But the loss which the stage felt as severely as it did that of Miss Farren, was, in 1798, in the person of a lady, with whom we first become acquainted as a vivacious and intelligent little girl selling flowers in St. James's Park. She is known as "Nosegay Fan." Her father, a soldier in the Guards, mends shoes, when off duty, in Windmill Street, Haymarket, and her brother waters the horses of the Hampstead stage, at the corner of Hanway Yard. Who would suppose that this little Fanny Barton, who sells moss-roses would one day set the fashions to all the fine ladies in the three kingdoms; that Horace Walpole would welcome her more warmly to Strawberry Hill than an ordinary princess, and that "Nosegay Fan" would be the original and never-equalled Lady Teazle?

Humble, however, as the position of the flower-girl is, there is good blood in her very blue veins. She comes of the Bartons of Derbyshire, and not longer ago than the accession of King William, sons of that family held honorable office in the church, the army, and in government offices. Fanny Barton ran on errands for a French milliner, and occasionally encountered Baddeley, when the latter was apprenticed to a confectioner, and was not dreaming of the Twelfth Cake he was to bequeath to the actors of Drury Lane. Then ensued some passages in her life that remind one of the training and experiences of Nell Gwyn. The fascinating Fanny, in one way or another, made her way in the world, and, for the sake of smile, lovers courted ruin. This excessively brilliant, though not edifying, career did not last long. Among the many friends she had acquired was that prince of scamps and Bardolphs, Theophilus Cibber, who had just procured a license to open the theatre in the Haymarket. He had marked the capabilities of the "vivacious" Fanny, and he tempted her to appear under his management, as *Miranda*, in the "Busy Body," to his Marplot. This was on the 21st of August, 1755, when the debutante was only seventeen years of age. She immediately excited attention as an actress of extraordinary promise; and, in the short summer season, she exhibited her versatility by playing Miss Jenny, in the "Provoked Husband;" Desdemona, Sylvia, in the "Recruiting Officer," and finally enchanted her audience as Prince Prettyman, in the "Rehearsal."

From the Haymarket this clever girl went to Bath and fascinated King, the manager; thence to Richmond, where Laccy, the manager there, fell equally in love with her, and engaged her for Drury Lane (1756–7), where, however, the presence, success, and claims of Miss Pritchard, Miss Macklin, and Mrs. Clive, kept her out of the line of characters for which she was especially qualified. She was, moreover, ill-educated, and she forthwith placed herself under tuition. Fanny took for music-master, Mr. Abington, who, of course, became desperately in love with her, and married his pupil. The young couple established a splendid home in the then fashionable quarter, St. Martin's Lane; but soon after, the convenient Apollo disappears, and even the musical dictionaries fail to tell us of the being and whereabout of a man whose wife made his name famous.

After four seasons at Drury, she went on a triumphant career to Dublin. There she acquired all she had hitherto lacked, and when, in the season of 1765–66, she reappeared at Drury Lane, as Cherry, upon terms granted by Garrick, which were no longer considered extravagant, so conspicuous was her talent, the play-going world was in a fever of delight. Her career, from 1755 to 1798, lasted forty-three years; and though, like Betterton, Time touched her person, it never weakened her talent. Critics praise her elegant form, her graceful address, the animation and expression of her looks, her quick intelligence, her perfect taste. Expression served her more than beauty, and her voice, once hardly better than Peg Woffington's, became perfectly musical by her power of modulation. Every word was pronounced with a clearness that made her audible in the remotest parts of the theatre, and this was a charm of itself in such parts as Beatrice, and Lady Teazle, where "every word stabbed," as King was wont to remark. In short, she was one of the most natural, easy, impressive, and enchanting actresses that ever appeared on the stage. Reynolds took her for his Comic Muse, and it is worth a pilgrimage to Knowle Park to look on that wonderful impersonation, and realize something of the grace and perfection of Mrs. Abington. In 1771, Walpole wrote to her, "I do impartial justice to your merit, and fairly allow it not only equal to any actress I have seen, but believe the present age will not be in the wrong if they hereafter prefer it to those they may live to see." On one occasion, he describes her, in Lady Teazle, as "equal to the first of her profession." She "seemed the very person," an "admiration of Mrs. Abington's genius made him long desire the honor of her acquaintance." He goes to sup with her, hoping "that Mrs. Clive will not hear of it;" and he throws Strawberry open to her, and as many friends as she chooses to bring with her. When the fever of his enthusiasm had somewhat abated, and he remembered the "Nosegay Fan" of early days, his admiration was more discriminating. Mrs. Abington, then, "can never go beyond Lady Teazle, which is a second-rate character, and that rank of women are always aping women of fashion without arriving at the style." Out of the line of the affected fine lady, says Lady G. Spencer, "Mrs. Abington should never go. In that she succeeds, because it is not unnatural to her." This criticism is just, for Lady Teazle is a *parvenu*. The country-bred girl apes successfully enough the woman of fashion, but in her early home, as we are told, she wore a plain linen gown, a bunch of keys at her side, her hair combed smooth over a roll; and her apartment was hung round with fruits in worsted, of her own working. Her girlish occupation was to inspect the dairy, superintend the poultry, make extracts from the family receipt-book, comb her aunt Deborah's lap-dog, draw patterns for ruffles, play Pope Joan with the curate, read a sermon aloud, and strum her fox-hunting father to sleep at the spinnet. This "fine lady," by accident and not by birth, Mrs. Abington could play admirably; better than she could Lady Modish, who was a lady by birth and education. But even in the latter character she is described as having been the accomplished and well-bred woman of fashion. Her intercourse with ladies of rank, an intimacy which made her somewhat vain, was of use to her in such impersonations; but she was not received so unreservedly as Mrs. Oldfield, for many remembered her early wild course, and saw no compensation for it in the later and better regulated life. She turned such schooling as she could obtain in drawing-rooms to the best account; but Mrs. Oldfield, in the University of Fashion, took first-class honors.

Coquettes, chamber-maids, hoydens, country girls, and the women of the Lady Teazle, Lady Fanciful, and Lady Racket cast, she played without fear of a rival. Her chamber-maids seem to have been over-dressed, and this superfluity attended some of her other characters, in which she was as much beplumed as the helmet in the *Castle of Otranto*. For more than a quarter of a century, her Widow of Belmour, in the "Way to Keep Him," was a never-failing delight to the public. Murphy says, that her graces of action gave to this part brilliancy, and even novelty, every time she repeated it. She was the original representative of thirty characters, among which we find,—Lady Bab, in "High Life Below Stairs;" Betty, in the "Clandestine Marriage;" Charlotte, in the "Hypocrite;" Charlotte Rusport in the "West Indian;" Roxalana, in the "Sultan;" Miss Hoyden in the "Trip to Scarborough;" and her crowning triumph, Lady Teazle.

Like other clever players, she committed a fault,—her's was in acting Scrub, for a wager,—at her benefit, in 1786. Genest says, "In point of profit, it no doubt answered; but she is said to have disgraced herself in Scrub, and to have acted the part with her hair dressed for Lady Racket," which she played in the after-piece. Her portrait, as Scrub, with her hair thus dressed, gives her an absurd appearance. She figured in the private theatricals at Brandenburgh House, of the Margravine of Anspach. In one of the plays represented,—the "Provoked Wife,"—the piece was cut down, in order that no female character should have equal prominence with that of Lady Brute, played by the Margravine herself; but Mrs. Abington asserted her professional right, and played her once-famous scene of Lady Fanciful, straight through, to the united delight of herself and audience.

In her later years she lost her old grace and fine figure; and she, who had snatched the mantle from Kitty Clive, found it taken from her, in her turn, by the gentle, yet all-conquering Miss Farren, whom, however, she survived on the stage. From 1798 to 1815, Mrs. Abington lived in retirement, active only in works of charity; and when she died in the latter year, few remembered in the deceased wealthy lady, the vivacious "Nosegay Fan" of three quarters of a century before.

There remains to be noticed one who, in the annals of the stage, appears like a brief but charming episode,—a fair promise, hastily made and not realized; an actress of whom Garrick augured well, and whom he gave to the stage, from which she was snatched by a prince. Miss Darby was a native of Bristol, and a pupil of Hannah More. She was the heiress of a fair fortune, which her philanthropic father dissipated, in attempts to civilize the Esquimaux Indians. Having thereby beggared his wife and child, the man, with a heart for all mankind, but not for his home, left the latter; and the mother then was supported by what Miss Darby could earn as a governess. What she could then spare, she devoted to acquiring "the usual accomplishments." Among the latter, was dancing; and her master (a Covent Garden ballet-master) introduced her to Garrick. After some training, she recited Cordelia, like a pretty and clever child, as she was; and then disappeared.

She was not sixteen when she married Mr. Robinson,—a young man of good fortune, apprenticed to the law. The happy couple ran through their fortune in splendid haste, and Mrs. Robinson spent more than a year with him in prison. Misery drove her again to Garrick, who, though now withdrawn from the stage, rehearsed Romeo to her Juliet; and sat in the orchestra on the night of the 10th of December, 1776, when she played the latter part to the Romeo of Brereton. She was then only eighteen; and her success was all that could be expected from her talent and beauty, and a voice which reminded Garrick of his darling, Mrs. Cibber. Thus commenced the brief stage career which ended in May, 1780, with the "Winter's Tale," and her own farce, the "Miniature Picture," on which occasion, she played Perdita and Eliza Camply.

In the interval, she had played the tender or proudly loving ladies in tragedy, and the refined and sprightly nymphs in comedy; and she was the original Amanda, in the "Trip to Scarborough." Since Mrs. Woffington and the first blush of Mrs. Bellamy, such peculiar grace and charms had not been seen on the stage. The critics extolled both, the fine gentlemen besieged her with billets-doux, and the artists protested that they had never beheld better taste than hers in costume.

On the 3d of December, 1779, their Majesties' servants played, by command, at Drury Lane, the "Winter's Tale," for the sixth time. Gentleman Smith was Leontes; Bensley, Polixenes; Brereton, Florizel; Miss Farren, Hermione; and Mrs. Robinson, Perdita.

The King, Queen, and royal family were in their box, when Perdita entered the green room, dressed more exquisitely and looking more bewitching than ever. "You will make a conquest of the Prince, to-night," said Smith, laughingly; "I never saw you look so handsome as you do now!" He was a true prophet. The Prince was subdued by her beauty, and subsequently wrote letters to her, which were signed "Florizel," and were carried by no less noble a go-between than William Anne Capel, Earl of Essex; but others ascribe this messengership of love to his son, Viscount Malden, who subsequently married Miss Stephens, the vocalist, and present dowager countess.

The messenger of love wooed her for the Prince, while he adored her himself,—at least he said so. He gave her the Prince's portrait, and a heart,—not in precious metal, but in paper,—a symbol of the worth and tenacity of the Prince's. On this token was a double motto, in French, for the air of the thing: "Je ne change qu'en mourant;" and in English, for the emphasis of it: "Unalterable to my Perdita through life."

This young creature's husband was living in profligacy on her salary, which he received at the treasury; and she was wooed by a young Prince, with a magic of wooing which, she said, she should never forget. The first step she made towards the latter was, by meeting him in a boat, moored off Kew. The second, was by meeting him by moonlight, in Kew gardens. But then, the "Bishop of Osnaburgh" was present! And the lady herself was a furbelowed Egeria to a powdered Numa. "During many months of confidential correspondence," she says, "I always offered his royal highness the best advice in my power."

Deathless was to be the young Prince's love, and his munificence was to be equal to his truth. In proof of the latter, he gave her a bond for £20,000, to be paid to her on his coming of age. In a few months he attained his majority, refused to pay the money, and made no secret to the lady of his deathless love having altogether died out. He passed her in the park, affecting not to know her; and the spirited young woman, who had given up a lucrative profession for his sake, flung a remark at him, in her indignation, that ought to have made him blush, had he been to that manner born. However, she was not altogether abandoned. The patriotic Whig statesman, Charles Fox, obtained for the Prince's cast-off favorite an annuity of £300,—out of the pockets of a tax-paying people!

Perdita would fain have returned to the stage, but her friends dissuaded her. No one could tell how a moral people would receive the abandoned of "Florizel!" So, restless, she dwelt, now here, now there; now in France, where Marie Antoinette gave a purse, knitted by her luckless fingers to "la belle Anglaise;" now in Brighton, where also resided, in the brightest of her beauty, and the highest of her splendor, Mrs. Fitzherbert;—the married Polly and the royal Macheath's neglected Lucy.

Perdita was not idle; she wrote poems and novels: the former, tender in sentiment and expression; the latter, not without power and good sense. She had undertaken to supply the *Morning Post* with poetry, when she died, after cruel suffering, in the last year of the last century (1800); and she herself the last of the pupils of David Garrick.

There was good in this hapless creature. Throughout life, she was the loving and helping child of her mother; the loving and helping mother of her child, for both of whom she labored ungrudgingly, to the last. Hannah More, herself, would not harshly construe the conduct of her pupil. "I make the greatest allowance for inexperience and novel passions," was the comment of Horace Walpole. "Poor Perdita!" said Mrs. Siddons, "I pity her from my very heart!"

She fell into bad hands,—beginning with those of her father. In her husband's, she was still less cared for, though she spent nearly a year with him in a sponging-house, to leave which she was importuned by worthless peers and equally worthless commoners,—from ancient dukes down to young city merchants. There was a public admiration for her which scarcely any other actress so practically experienced. Thus, on the night in 1776, when the "Trip to Scarborough" was undergoing temporary but loud condemnation, Mrs. Yates, yielding to the storm, suddenly withdrew, and left Mrs. Robinson, as Amanda, standing alone on the stage, where she was so bewildered by the continued hissing, that the Duke of Cumberland stood up in his box, requested her not to be alarmed, and cheered her by calling out, "It is not you, but the piece, they are hissing."

She gave rather the promise than the actuality of a fine actress; she had good taste, and manifested it in an attention to costume, when propriety therein was not much cared for. She describes the outward presentment of her Statira ("Alexander the Great"), by saying: "My dress was white and blue, made after the Persian costume; and, though it was then singular on the stage, I wore neither a hoop nor powder. My feet were bound with sandals, richly ornamented; and the whole dress was picturesque and characteristic."

Between this period and the time when she lay stricken by paralysis, the interval was not long; and then the forsaken creature, if vanity abided with her, was obliged to content herself with reminiscences of the past,—when she was the Laura Maria of Della Crusca, and when Merry declared that future poets and ages would join, "to pour in Laura's praise, their melodies divine." During that same time, Peter Pindar called her—"*The* nymph of my heart;" Burgoyne pronounced her "perfect as woman and artist;" Tickle proclaimed her, "the British Sappho;" John Taylor hailed her, " Pensive songstress;" Boaden recorded her, " mentally perfect;" the Hon. John St. John asserted that " Nature had formed her, queen of song;" Kerr Porter saluted her in thundering heroics; and two theatrical parsons, Will Tasker and Paul Columbine, flung heaps of flowers at her feet, with the zeal of heathen priests before an incarnation of Flora.

And so passes by this vision of fair last-century women, to make way for a group of actors of the Garrick school,—standing a little apart from whom is John Henderson,—whom the town was willing to take for David's successor.

## CHAPTER XVI.

A GROUP OF GENTLEMEN.

THE players of the Garrick period and the years immediately succeeding it, followed in due time their great master. Of these, Samuel Reddish was a player of that great epoch, who, for some especial parts, stood in the foremost rank. We first hear of him in the season of 1761-2, strengthening Mossop's company in Smock Alley, Dublin, by his performance of Etan, in the "Orphan of China." Of his origin, no one knows more than what he published of himself in the Irish papers,—that he was "a gentleman of easy fortune." This description was turned against him by his old enemy, Macklin, on one occasion, when Reddish, in a part he was acting, threw away an elegantly bound book, which he was supposed to have been reading. Macklin's comment was, that, however unnatural in the character he was representing, it was quite consistent in Mr. Reddish himself, who, "you know, has advertised himself as a gentleman of easy fortune."

In September, 1767, Reddish first appeared in London, at Drury Lane, as Lord Townly, to Mrs. Abington's "My Lady." A few nights after, he played Posthumus to the Imogen of Mrs. Baddeley. It was in this last character that he took his melancholy leave of the stage at Covent Garden, shaken in mind and memory, —on the 3d of May, 1779; Mrs. Bulkley was then the Imogen. His career in London was but of twelve years, and it might have been longer and more brilliant but for that *fast* life which consumed him,—and for one illustration of which, when he was rendered incapable of acting, he made humble apology on the succeeding evening.

Within those dozen years, Sam Reddish played an infinite variety of characters, from tragedy to farce. Among those he originated were Darnley ("Hypocrite"), Young Fashion ("Trip to Scarborough"), and Philotas ("Grecian Daughter"). As an actor his voice and figure were highly esteemed in Dublin, but the latter was not considered so striking, in London. I gather from his critics, that Reddish was easy and spirited; that he spoke well in mere declamatory parts, but for want of feeling and variety in the play of his features, failed in parts of passion. His most attractive character was Edgar, in "King Lear;" Posthumus stood next; he thought Romeo was one of his happiest impersonations, but the public preferred his Macduff and Shylock. As Alonzo ("Revenge"), he made a favorable impression; his Castalio, Lothario, and Orlando, were indifferent, and his Alexander bad. Reddish was, however, an impulsive actor, often feeling more than the immobility of his features would permit him to show; and he endeavored to make up for it by violence and impetuosity of action. He was once acting Castalio, when the part of his brother Polydore was played by Smith. In the last act of the "Orphan," Polydore gives his brother the lie, calls him "coward!" adds "villain!" and at length so exasperates Castalio that the latter, drawing his sword, exclaims, "This to thy heart, then, though my mother bore thee!" and before Smith was well ready for the fight, Reddish thrust his sword into him and stretched him bleeding on the stage. The next words Castalio should have uttered were, "What have I done? My sword is in thy breast!" but the poor fellow could only exclaim, "My sword *was* in thy breast!" and the play came to an end. Smith, however, did not die (as in the play) with a "How my head swims! 'tis very dark! good night!" He recovered of his wounds, and lived to die again.

When Churchill said, "With transient gleam of grace Hart sweeps along," he was praising the lady whom Reddish married soon after he came to London, and who lost the "transient gleam" in ungracefully growing fat. His second wife was a woman of very different quality,—a respectable, but impoverished, widow in Mary-le-bone, named Canning, whose first husband had, in 1767, published a translation of the first book of Cardinal Polignac's *Anti-Lucretius*. The widow Canning's son, George, subsequently became prime minister of England, "for giving birth to whom," says Genest, "she was in due time rewarded with a handsome pension," which she enjoyed as Mrs. Hunn, down to 1827. Reddish, I suppose, met with her on the stage at Drury Lane, where the lady made her first public appearance (6th of November, 1773) in "Jane Shore," Reddish playing her husband; while Garrick acted Hastings, at the request of several ladies of rank who patronized Mrs. Canning. She repeated Jane Shore, and subsequently played Perdita to the Florizel of "gentle" Cautherley,—who was said to be a natural son, certainly a well-trained pupil, of Garrick. Her next part was Mrs. Beverley to Garrick's Beverley; her fourth Octavia (in "All for Love") to the Antony of Reddish, whose wife she became, or at least is said to have become, at an unlucky season. As early as the year 1773, Reddish exhibited one symptom of the malady which compelled him, ultimately, to retire, namely the want of memory, which indicates weakness of the brain. In March of that year, he played Alonzo, in Home's tragedy so called; he was the original representative of the part. Although Alonzo is the hero, he does not appear till the play is half over, and when the piece came to nearly that point on the particular night, Reddish was missing; a riot ensued, and his part was read by one of the Aikens. Just before the curtain fell, the truant appeared, declaring that he had only just remembered that it was not an oratorio night. His comrades believed him, and for fear the public should be less credulous, he ran from the theatre to Bow Street Office, and there, in presence of Sir Sampson Wright, made oath to the same effect. The affidavit was published the next day, and he thereto adds, "that this unhappy mistake may not be misconstrued into a wilful neglect of his duty, he most humbly begs pardon of the public for the disappointment." The public forgave him, and received him kindly on his next appearance. His wife, who was a favorite in the provinces, was ultimately hissed from the stage of Old Drury.

Gradually, his memory grew more disturbed, till it could no longer be at all relied on. During the season 1777–8, he was incapable of acting, and was supported by the fund. In the following season, he essayed Hamlet, but it was almost as painful as the Ophelia of poor, mad, Susan Mountfort. Later in the season, in May, 1779, the managers gave him a benefit, when "Cymbeline" was acted, and Reddish was announced for Posthumus. An hour or two before the play began, he called at a friend's house, vacant, restless, and wandering. Some one congratulated him on being well enough to play. "Aye, sir! and I shall astonish you in the garden scene!" He thought he was to act Romeo. He could neither be persuaded nor convinced to the contrary, for a long time, and then only to fall into the old delusion. "Am I to play Posthumus? I'm sorry for it, but what must be, must be!" and then he walked to the theatre, his friend accompanying him, and pitying the poor fellow, who went on rehearsing Romeo, by the way. He was so impressed by his false idea, that his colleagues of the green room, who had vainly striven to keep him to Posthumus, saw him go to the wing, with the expectation on their part that he would look for Benvolio's cue, "Good morrow, cousin!" and would be prepared to answer, "Is the day so young?" With that expectation, they pushed him on the stage, —where the old situation wrought a temporary cure in him. To the welcoming applause he returned a bow of modest respect and by the time the Queen had uttered the words—

"'Twere good
You leaned unto his sentence with what patience
Your wisdom may inform you,"—

his eye had lighted up, and he answered with calm dignity—

"Please your highness,
I will from hence to-day,"

and went through the scene with more than his usual ability. But he had no sooner passed the wing than the old delusion returned; he was all Romeo, waiting for and longing to begin the garden-scene with—

"Soft! what light from yonder window breaks?
It is the East, and Juliet is the sun!"

And many were the fears that at his second going on, he would be disturbed. He stood dreamingly waiting at the side, but when Philotas had exclaimed. "Here comes the Briton! Let him be so entertained amongst you as suits with gentlemen of your know ing, to strangers of his quality;"—Reddish was Posthumus again, and to the remark of the Frenchman, "Sir, we have known together in Orleans," he replied in the clear, level, tone which distinguished him,—"Since when I have been debtor to you for courtesies, which I will be ever to pay and yet pay still." Thenceforward, his mind became healthy, and he played to the close with a burst of inspiration and talent, such as he had not shown, even in his best days.

His mind, however, was healthy only for the night; fitful seasons there were in which he tried to act in the country; but he soon became diseased again, and, shut up in a mad-house, poor Reddish might be seen on visitors' days at St. Luke's, a sad and humiliating spectacle, herding among the lunatics in that once popular place of cruel exhibition. Two old feelings survived the otherwise complete wreck,—his love of good living, and his dislike of inferior company. He drank greedily his draught of milk, out of a wooden bowl, but the "gentleman of easy fortune" complained bitterly of his forced association with the low people who thronged the gallery. Poor Reddish! he was moved to better air, improved diet, and less plebeian society, —in the Asylum at York. The outside world had been by him long forgotten, and he forgotten by the world, when he happily died there, not one hour too soon, in the last month of the year 1785. Little more than eight years later his step-son, George Canning, made his maiden-speech in the Commons, as Tory member for Newport, and *failed;* but like noble actors in another house, he gained ultimate success, by turning his experience to advantage.

About the same time disappeared from the London stage, Ross, who, like Barton Booth, was a Westminster boy, and the son of a gentleman. Less fortunate than Booth, his father discarded him, for going on the stage. Ross, the actor, had for school-fellow Churchill, the poet; John Nicoll, then being master; and Booth had for condiscipulus the poet Rowe, under the famous mastership of Busby. Like Booth, Ross first tried his fortune on the Dublin stage in 1749, when he came to London to be of the school of Garrick, as Booth came, to be a follower of Betterton. Both men had pleasing and powerful voices and fine figures, but

Ross's countenance lacked expression. Ross, like Booth, played Young Bevil with great ability, and, as the Ghost of Banquo, produced almost as much effect as Booth in the Ghost of Hamlet's father. Here, however, all parallel ends. Wanting Booth's industry, Ross never raised himself to Booth's level; he originated very few characters, wasted his powers, grew fat and indolent, and lost, what Barry kept to the last,—

"A voice as musically clear
As ever pour'd, perhaps, upon the ear."

With a passion for the stage, and every qualification but industry, he marred his prospects by letting "mere chance conduct him every night," till the town wearied of him. He had been at Drury Lane, from 1751, when he first appeared as Young Bevil, to 1757; and at Covent Garden, where he commenced with Hamlet, from that year to 1768, when he became manager of the new theatre in the Canongate, Edinburgh.

In Edinburgh, Ross is remembered, however, as the founder of the legal stage. That is, he was the patentee of the first theatre that had the sanction of the law. When the new town of Edinburgh was projected, in 1767, care was taken for the lawful establishment of the Scottish stage, and Ross built that pleasant house which, till 1859, occupied the site, where now stands the New Post-Office. It says something for Ross's prudence, despite his defects, that he had saved £7,000 which he expended on the construction and completion of this house. It was opened in December, 1769. "Strange," says Mr. Robert Chambers, "to recall the circumstances of its opening. No Princes Street then, for the belles and beaux—no new town whatever, only one or two houses building at wide intervals. The North Bridge unfinished and broken down; ladies and gentlemen obliged to come to these mimic scenes through Leith Wynd, and other and still narrower alleys." Thence came failure; and Ross let the house to Foote, and subsequently to Digges, "a spendthrift gentleman of good connections," for £500 a year.

At the end of four years, Ross was back at Covent Garden; but he had ceased to attract, and he ultimately fell into distress (the Edinburgh Theatre failing to be profitable to him), from which he was relieved by receiving annually from an anonymous donor the sum of £60. It was by mere accident that Ross discovered the gallant seaman, Barrington, to be his munificent friend; but what connection existed between the two men, I am not aware.

Such is the record of a player who entirely threw his chance away by his neglect. Possessing power, he wanted will, and was always looking to others for help; and, indeed, he often got it. He played George Barnwell with such effect that dissipated and felonious apprentices were turned from their evil ways; and young men given to philandering with Milwoods and to thoughts of killing their uncles, were frightened into a better state of things. One who was thus rescued used to send, anonymously, ten guineas yearly to Ross, with a suitable acknowledgment on his benefit night. "You have done more good by your acting," said Dr. Barrowby to him, "than many a person by his preaching." The fact is, that Ross's Barnwell was a sermon which went home to the bosoms of the Athenians.

The next to disappear from our group is Yates (1736–1782), the only actor of his day who had a just notion how to play Shakspeare's fools; he was ever natural, but frequently imperfect; in low comedy, not to be surpassed; but in fine gentlemen, he "looked like Tom Errand in Beau Clincher's clothes." Philip, in "High Life Below Stairs," Sir Bashful Constant, Major Oakley, and Sir Oliver Surface, were among his original characters. His forte was old men; but in stolid clowns, he was inimitable. Yates did not act so well off the stage as on, for he declined to subscribe to the theatrical fund, on the ground that he was not likely ever to need its assistance!

Next passes from the stage to private life, Gentleman Smith, son of a city grocer, and one of the few players who have been pupils at Eton. Cambridge, he left in some disgrace, to avoid being compelled to leave. In 1753, as the pupil of Barry, he first appeared as Theodosius. In 1786 he retired, after playing his original character, Charles Surface. Meanwhile, he had earned the honorable addition to his name. If the stage had no, greater clown and old man than Yates, it had no more perfect gentleman than Smith; who besides Charles Surface, originally represented (in London) Glenalvon, Mason's Athelwold, and Edwin. In gay comedy lay his strength, but he was the most refined of light tragedians, and played Richard with effect even in Garrick's days. His qualifications for both comedy and tragedy were without a single drawback, save a monotony of voice, the enunciation of which, in other respects, was perfect. His Falconbridge was not surpassed till Charles Kemble made the part his own.

Smith made two remarkable marriages. His first was with a daughter of that Viscount Hinchinbroke, who did not live to succeed his father, the third Earl of Sandwich. This lady was the young widow of a Courtenay of Devon, and her union with an actor was described as a disgrace to her family. Smith offered to withdraw from the stage, if the family would secure to him an annuity equal to his salary; but this was refused, and the player continued his vocation, in order that he might make suitable provision for his wife. The union was dissolved by her death in 1762.

Smith was indefatigable in his profession, and proud of his own position in it, congratulating himself on never having had to act in a farce, or sink through a trap. On his retirement, he married a widow with a fortune ample enough, when added to his own, to enable him to live like a country gentleman at Bury St. Edmund's, whence he came in 1798, to play Charles Surface, at sixty-six, with some fat, and legs a little shaky, but with youthful spirit, for the farewell benefit of King.

Then there is Tate Wilkinson, whose reverend father of the Savoy Chapel, Garrick had contributed to transport, by informing against him for illegally performing the ceremony of marriage. Garrick, in return, helped forward the son—an *exotic*, as he said, rather than an actor; but as an imitator never equalled, for he represented not only the voice and manner of other persons, but could put on their features, even those of beautiful women! He played in tragedy and comedy well; but only when he mimicked some other actor throughout the piece. He used also to reproduce Foote's imitations of the older actors, and I remember Matthews's imitations of the imitations of Wilkinson. He had been long connected with York, and very little with London, if at all, at the period of Smith's retirement. Wilkinson, who has added to the literature of the drama, is further to be remembered for having prohibited his York actors from soliciting, bill in hand—the latter ready to grasp the usual fee of half a crown—patronage for their benefits; a custom which, I think, did not survive 1784, though Wilkinson lived till 1805.

From 1765 to 1790—beginning at Dublin, and ending at Covent Garden—indicates the career of poor Edwin. He was execrable when he began, in Sir Philip Modelove; but two years of practice in Dublin, and nine in Bath, fashioned him into a perfect actor for the metropolis. When a stage-struck youth there, and vexing his friends, and about to lose his clerkship in the Pension Office, Ned Shuter used to say to him, "You'll be a great actor when I am laid low." The town, at first, did not relish his humor; but, at last, relished it so much, that they allowed him any liberty. He might go out of his part, and make appeals to them, or forget his words through "the drink, dear Hamlet"—his pardon was sure to follow. When young, he played old men; when old, young; and to his humor and ability O'Keefe owed such obligation, that it was said whenever Edwin died, O'Keefe would be d——d!

His fault was his remembrance of the audience. He was always playing *to* them, not *with* his fellows; but it was so exquisitely done, that the audience least of all objected. "He was sure of applause, whether he had to utter the humor of Shakspeare, the wit of Congreve or Sheridan, or merely to sing 'Tag-rag-merry-derry;'" says Adolphus. Henderson pronounced his by-play as unequalled. In Sir Hugh Evans, when preparing for the duel, Henderson had seen him, we are told, for many minutes together, keep the house in an ecstasy of merriment, without uttering a single word. Edwin was the original Lingo, Darby, Peeping Tom, Sheepface, Ennui ("Dramatist"), and a hundred other light parts, in which he wore that peculiar smile, which had not passed away when his comrades, in October, 1790, looked on his shrouded face before they escorted him to the grave.

The two Aikens, belonging to the last century, demand no further notice than that one brother was distinguished as "Tyrant Aiken;" the other for having fought a bloodless duel with John

Kemble, on some stage-management dispute, in which Bannister acted as second to both parties.

West Digges, proud of the blood of the Sackvilles, not less than of being Home's original Norval, and of being called the "gentleman actor," was a player, who, like Brereton, was always struggling to reach the highest eminence, only to fall short of it. Digges died of paralysis, and Garrick's pupil, Brereton, of madness.

Lee Lewes, a sort of counterfeit Woodward, also struggled and failed, though not without merits, either in Harlequin or Flutter, of which latter he was the original representative. His self-estimation could not maintain him before a London audience, and he travelled to India, in search of others which cared even less for him; and, after all, came back to read, lecture, live straitly, and die.

In contrast with this erst deputy-postman, passes grave and dignified Bensley, whom not even the idea that he was poisoned, could induce to forget his identity with his part. Sensitive in other respects, this scholarly actor, with a glare in his eye, a prominence in his gait, and a peculiar tone in his voice, earnestly implored Bannister to omit him from his imitations in Dick ("Apprentice").

Bensley's great part was Eustace de St. Pierre, in Colman's "Siege of Calais," in which he was remarkable for his mingling of churlish humor with the most tender sympathy. His career extended from 1765 to 1795; and there was no actor with so many natural defects who so ably surmounted them. His Pierre, his Ghost (in "Hamlet"), his Iago, Clytus, and Malvolio were excellent.

The ex-lieutenant Bensley may be said to have made his first appearance in the drama, in Richmond Park, where he unconsciously had the park-keeper for his admiring audience. The part was Pierre, for some instructions in which he was indebted to Colman, and which he used to rehearse in the park at early morn, with the "six tubs," or trees, planted on Queen Caroline's Mount, for scene and senate. The park-keeper, who had often seen him wending that way, full of thought, once lay hidden near, and watched his proceedings. Bensley was rehearsing the scene before his judges, and the listener must have been sorely puzzled, as he heard allusions made to chains and conquests, and the centre tub addressed as a "great duke," who, "shrunk, trembling, in his palace;" and references to the Duchess Adriatic, in terms that must have perplexed his judgment. He simply set the poor gentleman down as mad, and left him to teach the loose Venetians "the task of honor, and the way to greatness," without farther molestation.

About the same time that Bensley left the stage to become barrack-master at Knightsbridge, Moody retired from the public scene. Lady Morgan, when contrasting her father with Moody, does great injustice to the latter. She cites Cumberland as saying to Mr. Owenson, after seeing the latter play Cumberland's Major O'Flaherty:—"Mr. Owenson, I am the first author who has brought an Irish gentleman on the stage, and you are the first who ever played it *like* a gentleman." Moody was the original Major; and Lady Morgan remarks, that he "knew as much of Ireland as he did of New Zealand. English audiences, however," she adds, "were satisfied, for they had not yet got beyond the conventional delineation of Teague and Father Foigard, types of Irish savagery and Catholic Jesuitism. Cumberland and Sheridan both thanked my father for redeeming their creations from caricature." Hereby does Moody suffer retribution. The best actor of Irishmen of his time, he was ashamed of being taken for one. His name was Cochrane; he was a native of Cork, where he had been apprenticed to his father, a hairdresser; but he chose to call himself Moody, and to declare that he was not born in Cork, but somewhere near Clare Market. Foolish ambition! Taking him at his word, Sydney Owenson rejoins that he knew as much of Ireland, as he did of New Zealand! Nevertheless, Moody knew a good deal of Ireland, and something, at least, of Jamaica, to which island he ran away from his own, and played the leading tragic characters there for several years. He made no effect at Covent Garden, till he was cast for Captain O'Cutter, in Colman's "Jealous Wife"—an Irish gentleman before Cumberland's Major O'Flaherty. His fine humor and correct judgment gained for him the universal applause. Hitherto all stage Irishmen had been funny ruffians. Churchill has recorded the merit of Moody:—

"Long, from a nation ever hardly used,
At random censured, wantonly abused,
Have Britons drawn their sport, with partial view
Form'd general notions from the rascal few;
Condemn'd a people as for vices known,
Which from their country banish'd, seek our own.
At length, howe'er, the slavish chain is broke,
And sense, awaken'd, scorns her ancient yoke ;
Taught by thee, Moody, we now learn to raise
Mirth from their foibles, from their virtue, praise."

The *Dramatic Censor* speaks of Moody as the best Teague the stage ever knew, but the crown of his reputation was set by his representation of Major O'Flaherty, for which he reaped as golden a harvest of fame as the author did by his piece. Indeed, he was the first who brought the stage Irishman into repute, and rendered the character one of a distinct line whereby a performer might acquire reputation. The Thespian Dictionary says of Owenson, for whose sake Lady Morgan disparaged Moody, "he chiefly supported Irish characters, in which he was a favorite, particularly with the galleries; but his representation of them (as it was in the country itself) was *high colored*, and would therefore have been too *coarse* for an English audience. He has now (1802) quitted the stage for business, which is still in the *public* line."

More careful Moody combined stage *and* business. Like many of his profession, he had his suburban villa; and in his garden by the side of Barnes Common, he not only raised vegetables, but carted them, and carried them thence to market. The original Lord Burleigh selling cabbages!

Moody, however, could very well support the dignity of his character as man and actor. In the Half-Price Riots of 1763, he supported Garrick. Moody stood between him and the angry audience with a good humor which so exasperated the latter, that they insisted on his begging pardon on his knees, a humiliation to which he refused to submit, though the refusal might drive him from his profession. Honest John Moody, however, kept his own, and had no rival till Johnstone appeared in 1784, without any idea of rivalry, for the latter began his career as an operatic singer. Moody created Sir Callaghan O'Brallaghan, in "Love à la Mode;" Captain O'Cutter, in the "Jealous Wife;" the Irishman, in the

"Register Office;" Major O'Flaherty, in the "West Indian;" Sir Patrick O'Neale, in the "Irish Widow," and other Irish characters of less note. His range of character beyond this was indefinite, for he played Iago and Sir Tunbelly Clumsey; Henry VIII. and Dogberry; Shylock, Peachem, and a hundred other opposites, between the years 1759 and 1796. Towards the end of that period, he grew torpid with good luck. His Sir Lucius was without humor and his Major lacked spirit, but Johnstone was at hand to supply a place from which Moody retired a few years too late.

In 1796, another of the players, who dated from the Garrick days, passed away from the stage,—and from life; I mean little Dodd. Like Moody and the Kembles, he had a sire who was connected with hair-dressing, but who gave his boy a very excellent education. At a London school, he played Davus, in the "Andria," to such purpose, that at sixteen, he was off to Sheffield, where he commenced his histrionic course as Roderigo, in "Othello." He served the hard apprenticeship of itinerancy, and then so distinguished himself on the Bath stage, by his comic acting,—although he had been engaged for general business, that Garrick beckoned him up to London, and by consigning to him the part of Faddle, in the "Foundling," showed that he took perfect measure of his ability. From that year 1765 to 1796, Dodd was the darling of the public, in his peculiar line. For fops of the old school, or old men who would pass for young fops, for simpletons and cunning knaves, for wearing a now obsolete modish costume, for "the nice conduct of a clouded cane," for carrying a china snuff-box, and, above all, for his unsurpassable style of taking a pinch, Dodd was really a wonderful actor. He wore his sword, cocked or carried his hat, displayed his ruffle, and moved about in a poising, tottering, sort of way, which was all his own, and always perfect. His Abel Drugger stood next to Weston's, if not to Garrick's,—but Garrick said Weston's was the finest the stage had ever seen; and his Sir Andrew Aguecheek was as truly Shaksperian as the author could have desired. Master Slender, Master Stephen, Watty Cockney, were among the parts which were said to die with him; and in his original characters of Lord Foppington ("Trip to Scarborough"), Sir Benjamin Backbite, Dangle, Le Nippe, and Adam Winterton, ("Iron Chest"), he has never been "touched," probably, by the most able of his successors. Of Dodd dying, no one dreamt till it was done. I can only think of him as going forward on the tips of his toes, mincingly, hat in one hand, cane in the other, a smile on his face, and with a bow to the Summoner, sinking contentedly back on a convenient sofa,—one little sigh perhaps of weariness, and little, fresh, cheery, gentleman-like Dodd is gone, sir!

That he once loved Mrs. Bulkeley, the Miss Wilford of earlier days, does not surprise me; for had the fiercest of the stage-hating Presbyterians in Edinburgh, where her Lady Racket was talked off by old men, at the beginning of this century, with their hand on their heart and over their waistcoat-pocket,—had one of the severer stock only seen her, he would have loved her too. Dodd and Mrs. Bulkeley went into housekeeping together, like Booth and Susan Mountfort, but the nymph was faithless, and there was a scandal, and a separation. The public condemned the lady, as she one night learned by their hissing, but the saucy beauty stepped unabashed to the front, and told her censurers that if she failed in her duty or powers as an actress, they were right in their reproof; 'but,' she added, with an air of Woffington about her, "as for my private affairs, I beg to be excused!" The audience condoned the erring beauty; they could not be angry with a Lady Grace of peculiar elegance; and the original Miss Hardcastle, and Julia in the "Rivals," was allowed to have her pretty way unreproved. She was on the London stage from 1764 to 1789, and at the time of her death had been known for two years as Mrs. Barresford.

About the same time as Bentley, Moody, and Dodd, the stage of the last century lost Baddeley. He is said to have been a confectioner, to have even acted as cook to Foote, and to have travelled in some humble capacity abroad, where he learned French, and the way to play French valets and similar characters. Baddeley was the original Canton ("Clandestine Marriage"), and Moses ("School for Scandal"), and he was dressed for this part when, in 1794, he was taken ill, and shortly after expired.

Baddeley, before dying, thought of his old comrades, and of his successors, in his own good-natured way. He bequeathed his cottage at Moulsey to the Drury Lane Fund, desiring that four poor comedians, not disinclined to live sociably together, might therein have a joint home. There was ample accommodation for such a company, in four bed-chambers, and two sitting-rooms. He assigned to them a little bit of acting also;—that they might not appear dependents, he bequeathed a trifle to each, which each was to give away in charity, with an air of its being his own! Mindful, too, of their ease, habits, and sentiments, he left funds for the building of a "smoking summer-house," out of wood from Old Drury, and in sight of the temple to Shakspeare in Garrick's garden at Hampton. In remembrance of his own old vocation as a pastry-cook, and in token of love for brothers and sisters of his later calling, he left £100 Three per Cents for the purchase of a Twelfth Cake and wine, to be partaken of annually, "forever," by the company of Drury Lane, in green room assembled.

Kelly says, the trustees of the Theatrical Fund sold Baddeley's house at Moulsey. Adolphus thinks that the deviser infringed the statute of mortmain, and that the property, for want of heirs, escheated to the crown. Strange, that of property left by players for the use of players, the poor actors should be cheated, at Moulsey as elsewhere.

Baddeley is said to have challenged Foote to a duel with swords, as he did George Garrick to one with pistols:—"Here's a pretty fellow!" cried Foote; "I allowed him to take my spit from the rack and stick it by his side, and now he wants to stick me with it!" Baddeley is reported to have been cook, not only to Foote, but to Lord North.

A greater artist than Baddeley left the stage soon after him, in 1795, after three and thirty years of service; namely, Parsons, the original Crabtree, and Sir Fretful Plagiary, Sir Christopher Curry, Snarl to Edwin's Sheepface; and Lope Tocho, in the "Mountaineers."

Parsons was a Kentish man, who might have been an apothecary, or an excellent artist, but that he preferred the stage. He was a merry, honest fellow, who kept the house in a roar by his looks as well as words, and loved to make the actors laugh, who were on the stage with him, by some droll remark, uttered in an undertone.

His forte lay in old men, his picture of whom, in all their characteristics, passions, infirmities, cunning, or imbecility, was perfect.

When Sir Sampson Legend says to Foresight, "Look up, old stargazer! Now is he poring on the ground for a crooked pin, or an old horse-nail, with the head towards him!" we are told "there could not be a finer illustration of the character which Congreve meant to represent, than Parsons showed at that time in his face and attitude." He was finely discriminating, too. His Skirmish in the "Deserter" presented, says Adolphus, "a shrewd, quick-witted fellow, whose original powers were merged, but not absolutely drowned, in drink." In his own estimation, Corbaccio was his best played character; but, said he, generously, "All the merit I have in it I owe to Shuter."

The last character he acted was Elbow, on the 30th of December, 1794, when Kemble revived "Measure for Measure;" but asthma had then reduced him to a shadow, and he had to yield the part to Waldron. He died soon after, and then ensued a singular domestic incident. His second wife was Dorothy Stewart, niece to the Earl of Galloway, whom he had married after the lively young lady had run away from a convent at Lille. Of this marriage there was a little son, who had for tutor a reverend young clergyman; and this tutor Dorothy Parsons married, four days after her husband's decease. So that she had two husbands in the house; one dead and the other living! The first had left her a fortune. The second spent it, and left herself and son destitute.

The town had not an old comic actor it esteemed more highly, except, perhaps, Palmer. The early life of John Palmer was full of disappointment; the latter end of trials; the middle, of some follies; but nothing more. When he was in hopes of employment in the theatre, he had been told to go for a soldier. Garrick would not have him; Foote pronounced his tragedy bad; but thought his comedy would do. He "strolled," struggled, starved; and then was engaged first by Garrick, then by Foote, to do any thing he was told to do, at a salary which barely found him in bread. Again he went to the country; married, or was married by a lady of expectations, which came to nothing, as she had mated with an actor.

When again in London, Palmer was too frightened at Barry, to play Iago to his Othello; Garrick eventually engaged him, but ridiculed his alleged powers of study; on which point, however, Davy soon changed his mind. Palmer slowly made his way, but it was very nearly stopped for ever, by Mrs. Barry, in the "Grecian Daughter," stabbing him (Dionysius), with a real dagger. He subsequently built and opened the Royalty Theatre, in Wellclose Square, but was compelled to close it, by the patentees. From the difficulties in which this involved him, he never relieved himself, and his life became a struggle between bailiffs eager to catch him, and Palmer eager to escape from bailiffs. Sometimes, he passed a week together in the theatre; at others he was carried out of it in some mysterious bit of theatrical property. From 1761 to 1798 he was on the London stage, one of the best general actors it ever had, except in singing parts and old men, and some tragic characters. His fine figure, nevertheless, was always a help to him. His Young Wilding was pronounced "perfect;" and among the best of his characters were Face, Captain Flash, Dick, Stukely, Sir Toby Belch, Captain Absolute, Young Fashion, Joseph Surface, Prince of Wales, Sneer, Don John, Volpone, Sir Frederick Fashion, Henry VIII., Father Philip, Villeroy, Brush, &c. Among those he originated were Joseph Surface, Count Almaviva, Sneer, Lord Gayville, Cohenberg, Sydenham, and Dick Dowlas.

He was often careless, and would go on the stage very imperfect, trusting to his wits, his impudence, and the "usual indulgence" of the audience. On one occasion he delivered a prologue, without knowing a line of it. The prompter was beneath a toilet table, and to Palmer standing near, he gave line for line, which Palmer repeated, with abounding smile and action to make up for dropped words. On another occasion, this actor took advantage of an uproar in front, to seem to deliver a prologue of which he knew nothing. He moved his lips, extended his arms, touched his heart, and said nothing. Suddenly came a lull, and then Palmer looked reproachfully, as if the noise had embarrassed him; whereupon one half of the house stormed at the other, for not keeping silence, and under cover of the storm, Palmer seemed to conclude the prologue, and made a grateful bow, as if pleased with the fact of having been enabled to perform a pleasant task.

After playing Father Philip and Comus, at Drury Lane on the 19th of June, 1798, Palmer proceeded to Liverpool. He had finished at Drury as radiant with gayety, on the stage, as if his heart were not breaking. Death had taken from his family circle his wife and the most dearly loved of his sons. Sorrow for those who had departed, and anxiety for the remaining children who depended on him, affected him deeply, and despite all effort, even when acting, he could not keep the dead or the living for a moment out of his memory. At length the night came when he was to repeat the character of the "Stranger," and then there was no simulation in his mournful aspect. He had got through his part to the middle of the opening scene of the fourth act. He had answered, "I love her still," to the query of Baron Steinfort (Whitfield) respecting his wife; and then to the question as to his children, he gave the reply, "I left them at a small town hard by;" but the words, falteringly uttered, had scarcely passed his lips, when he fell, dead, at Whitfield's feet!

The sensation which this caused was most painful; and it was not allayed by those pious persons who saw in this sudden death an especial judgment launched by Heaven on the head of a man who exercised an unrighteous calling. To support their theory, they invented the story that Palmer was stricken after uttering the quotation, in the first scene of the third act, "there is another and a better world!" These words suited the inferences they wished to draw. They did not agree with the facts; but it was the old story, "so much the worse for the facts!" The lie yet lives.

Poor Palmer! One cannot help having a kindly feeling for "Plausible Jack." Can you not see him coming up to Sheridan, when reconciliation had followed quarrel, with his head bent blandly forward, his eyes turned up, his hand on his heart, and a phrase after the manner, if not of the very matter of Joseph Surface, of which he was the original representative? "If you could but see my heart, Mr. Sheridan!" and Sheridan's pleasantly remonstrating remark, "Why, Jack, you forget I wrote it!"

And then he was so modest. "Plausible, am I?" he once asked, "you really rate me too highly. The utmost I ever did in that way was, on once being arrested by a bailiff, when I persuaded the fellow to bail me!"

After many of these actors had commenced their career, and long before some of them concluded it, a great player came, charmed, and departed, leaving a name and a reputation which render him worthy of a chapter to himself. I allude to Henderson.

## CHAPTER XVII.

### JOHN HENDERSON.

In the bill of the Bath Theatre for October the 6th, 1772, the part of Hamlet is announced to be performed "by a young gentleman." On the 21st of the month, we read, "Richard III., by Mr. Courtney, the young gentleman who acted Hamlet." Mr. Courtney repeated those characters, and subsequently played Benedick, Macbeth, Bobadil, Bayes, Don Felix, and Essex; and on the 26th of December, having thus felt his way and become satisfied of his safety, we have "Henry IV.," with "Hotspur by Mr. Henderson."

After being anonymous and pseudonymous, he added, under his last and proper designation, the following characters to those he had previously acted: Fribble, Lear, and Hastings, Alonzo, and Alzuma; and Mr. Henderson was an established Bath favorite.

At this time, Henderson was five-and-twenty years of age. Descended from Scottish Presbyterians and English Quakers, with a father who was an Irish factor, Henderson is the sole celebrity of the street in which he was born, in March, 1747, Goldsmith Street, Cheapside. The father died too soon for his two sons to remember him in after life; but the boys had an excellent mother, who unconsciously trained one of her sons to the stage, by making him familiar with the beauties of Shakspeare.

Having succeeded so far in art as to obtain a prize when he was Fournier's pupil, for a drawing exhibited at the Society of Arts; and having been as reluctant as Spranger Barry to be bound apprentice to a silversmith, Henderson longed to win honor by the sock and buskin. This desire was probably fostered by the sight of Garrick in the shop of Mr. Becket the bookseller, a friend of Henderson's. Garrick seldom went to coffee-houses, and never to taverns, but at Becket's shop he held a little court, and Henderson sighed to be as great as he.

The weakly-voiced lad, with no marked presence, and a consumptive look, could obtain audience or favor from no one; least of all, from Roscius. He went up to remote Islington, and, in the long room of an inn there, delivered Garrick's *Ode on the Shakspeare Jubilee*. After this, and, perhaps, in consequence, Garrick received him, heard him recite, shook his head at a voice which was more woolly than silvery, and, after some counsel, procured for him an engagement at Bath, and at a trifling salary.

For five seasons he was a rising, improving, and the cherished actor at Bath. But his fame did not influence the London managers. At length, *exeunt* Garrick, Barry, Woodward, and Foote; and Colman, lacking novelty, at the Haymarket, invites, somewhat unwillingly, young Henderson from Bath. He appeared at the Little Theatre in 1777, and, in a little more than a month of acting nights, put £4,500 into the manager's pocket. He played Shylock, Hamlet, Leon, Falstaff (in "Henry IV.," and in the "Merry Wives"), Richard III., Don John, and Bayes.

In this first season he played three of his greatest parts—Shylock, Hamlet, and Falstaff. The first was selected for his *début*, contrary to his own inclination. Macklin's Shylock was the Shylock of all playgoers; but the difference between it and Henderson's attracted attention and audiences. Old Macklin himself praised his young rival's conception of the part with energetic liberality. "And yet, sir," said Henderson, "I have never had the advantage of seeing you in the character." "It is not necessary to tell me that, sir," said Macklin, with no conceited modesty. "I knew you had not, or you would have played it differently." Garrick also saw Henderson in the part, and remarked that Tubal was very creditably played indeed! It is said that Henderson, after delighting Garrick, when breakfasting with him in 1772, by imitations of Barry, Woodward, Love (whose single character of note was Falstaff), and some others, offended him by a close imitation of Garrick himself. Colman is reported to have been equally offended by an imitation of himself, at his own table, by Henderson, who did not, as Foote would have done, watch his host, and mimic him at other tables. Henderson seems to have been so little willing to offend, that in playing Bayes, he omitted the imitations of contemporary performers, by which all other actors of the parts had been wont to reap rich harvests of applause.

Macklin said of him that the young man had learned a great deal; but what remained for him was to unlearn much of it, in order that he might learn to be an actor. In this oracular manner there was more kindness than Henderson met with from Foote, previous to his first season in London, and of which Genest has compiled this account:—

"Henderson, accompanied by two friends, waited on Foote, and was received with great civility. Foote's imagination was so lively, his conceptions were so rapid as well as so exuberant, that by a torrent of wit, humor, pleasantry, and satire, he kept the company for a considerable time in convulsions of laughter; however, Henderson's friends thought it, at last, time to stop the current of Foote's vivacities, by informing him of the reason of their visit, and Henderson was permitted to begin a speech in 'Hamlet;' but before he could finish it, Foote continually interrupted him by some unlucky joke or droll thought. . . . . At the conclusion Henderson was, without interruption, allowed to speak Garrick's prologue on his return from the continent. This being no caricature, but a fair representation of Garrick's manner, did not make any impression on Foote; however, he paid the speaker a compliment on the goodness of his ear—dinner was now announced, and when Henderson took his leave, Foote whispered one of the company, *he would not do.*

"Henderson once requested Palmer 'not to bring him forward in too many parts;' observing that it must be for the manager's interest, as well as his own credit, to have him studied in the parts he was to appear in: he added, 'to learn words, indeed, is no great labor, and to pour them out no very difficult matter; it is done on our stage almost every night, but with what success I leave you to judge—*the generality of performers think it enough to learn the words ;* and thence all that vile uniformity which disgraces the theatre.' " This was rather proud criticism, as it referred to his early Bath colleagues; but Henderson's standard of propriety would not allow him to speak otherwise.

In his second character in London, Hamlet, he came into more direct contrast with Garrick, whose greatest idolaters found heavy fault in Henderson's young Dane for flinging away his uncle's picture,—subsequent to the famous speech in which he compares the portraits of his father and uncle. On the following night, he retained the picture in his hand, and the same party ridiculed him, on the ground that if he was right the first night, he must necessarily have been wrong on the second! He was said, too, not to have managed his hat properly on first seeing the Ghost; and similar carpings were made against the new actor, only to hear whose words, "the fair Ophelia!" people went, as to the most exquisite music. But what was that to the Garrick faction who pronounced him disqualified, because in the closet scene he did not, in his agitation, upset the chair. "Mr. Garrick, sir, always overthrew the chair."

During his short, but brilliant and honorable career, he orinated no new character that may be found in any acting play of the present day. I think he was the first actor who, with Sheridan, gave public readings. They filled Freemason's Hall, and their own pockets, by their talents in this way, and Henderson could as easily excite tears by his pathos, as he could stir laughter by a droll way of reciting Johnny Gilpin, which gave wild impetus to the sale of that picturesque narrative.

His own temperament, however, was naturally grave, derived from that mother whose occasional melancholy was nearly allied to insanity. Yet he was not without humor, or he could not have played Falstaff with a success only inferior to Quin, nor have founded the Shandean Club in Maiden Lane, nor have written so quaint a pastoral love-song as his Damon and Phyllis. In acting Æsop, he delivered the fables with great significance. The chief characteristic of the part lay in its grim splenetic humor, such as he himself showed when he, the high-spirited pupil of Fournier, had to drive his master, when he gave drawing-lessons, and to clean the horse and chaise after reaching home again!

He loved praise, honestly owned his love, and worked hard to win public favor. When he was cast for a new character, he read the entire play, learned his own part, read the play again, and troubled himself no more about it, although a fortnight might elapse between the last rehearsal and the first performance. Previous to which latter occasion, it was his custom to dine well, and sit at his wine till summoned to rise and go forth. A Garrick-worshipper told him he was wrong. Mr. Garrick, on such occasions, shut himself up for the day, and dined lightly. Henderson was the last of the school of Garrick, and once imitated his master in his diet. The result was a cold and vapid performance of Bireno, in the "Law of Lombardy;" and Henderson registered a vow, to be original and dine generously on like occasions, in future.

Henderson was, in every respect, a gentleman; his social position was as good as that of any gentleman of his time. In Dublin, as in London, he was a welcome guest in the best society, even in that for which the stage had few attractions. Personally, he had natural obstacles to surmount. He was short, not gracefully moulded, lacked intelligent expression of the eye, and had a voice too weak for rage, and not silvery soft enough for love. But he had clear judgment, quick feeling, ready comprehension, and accurate elocution. Cumberland names Shylock, Falstaff, and Sir Giles, as his best characters, but there were portions of others in which he could not be excelled; "in the variety of Shakspeare's soliloquies, where more is meant than meets the ear, he had no equal," and this is high praise, for the difficulty of the task is work for a genius.

Never strong, his poor health failed him early, and on the 8th of November, 1785, he acted for the last time. The part was Horatius, in the "Roman Father." In less than three weeks, and at the early age of thirty-eight, troops of friends escorted the body of the man they had esteemed, to Westminster Abbey,—one more addition to the silent company of the great of all degrees and qualities, from actors to kings. Professionally, Henderson did not die prematurely. Kemble had already been two years at Drury Lane, and the new school of acting was supplanting the old.

Let me add a word of Henderson's brother. He, too, belonged to art, and promised to be a great engraver, but consumption struck him down early. He was residing, for his health, on the sunny side of a house in then fashionable Hampstead, when death came suddenly upon him. Among the company in the same house was the most beautiful and gayest of gay women,—Kitty Fisher. But, she was true woman, too, and hearing of a lonely stranger menaced with death, she went straightway to tend him, and Henderson's brother died in Kitty's arms.

His readings were attended frequently by Mrs. Siddons and John Kemble  his voice was so flexible that his tones conveyed every phase of meaning. Even his way of reading the words: "They order this matter, said I. better in France," had a world of significance in it, not to be found when uttered by others; and the letter of Mrs. Ford to Falstaff, when he read it on the stage, shook the house with such laughter as was seldom heard, save indeed when he imitated Garrick and Dr. Johnson, the former reciting his ode, and the latter interrupting him by critical objections. I do not wonder that both Munden and John Kemble, who, all their lives, had a longing to play Falstaff, abandoned the idea when they remembered Henderson's excellence.

At the period of Henderson's death, his early prophecy had been fulfilled, with regard to Mrs. Siddons;—to whose career we will now direct our notice.

## CHAPTER XVIII.

### SARAH SIDDONS.

ON the 13th of June, 1755, when Garrick and Mrs. Cibber, Yates and Mrs. Pritchard, Woodward and Mrs. Clive, were the leaders in the Drury Lane company,—while Barry and Mrs. Bellamy, Ryan and Mrs. Woffington, were among the "chiefs" of Covent Garden, Sarah Kemble was born, the first of twelve children, at a public-house in Brecon, in which town, exactly a score of years later, was born her youngest brother, Charles.

By both parents she belonged to the stage. Her mother's maiden name was Ward. This lady's father had been a respectable actor under Betterton, and was a strolling manager when the hairdresser of the company, a handsome fellow, poor of course, and a Roman Catholic, eloped with and married the manager's daughter. His name was Roger Kemble. He was an actor too; love, at first, had helped to make him a very bad one. Fanny Furnaval, of the Canterbury company, drilled him into the worst Captain Plume that ever danced over the stage; but Mrs. Roger Kemble, a woman who illustrated the truth that beauty is of every age, used in her later days to look at the grand old man, and assert that he was the only gentleman-like Falstaff she had ever seen.

Mr. and Mrs. Kemble were "itinerants" when the first child of their marriage was born,—a child who made her *début* on the London stage long before her father;—the latter playing, and playing very well, the Miller of Mansfield, at the Haymarket, in 1788, for the benefit of the wife of his second son, Stephen. When Roger carried off Miss Ward, her father with difficulty forgave her, —and only on the ground that she had, at all events, obeyed his injunction,—not to marry an actor. "He will never be that," said the old player, of the Betterton era. With which remark, his discontent was exhausted.

Her grandsire acted under Betterton, and Booth; her parents

had played with Quin ;—she herself fulfilling a professional career which commenced with Garrick, and ended with her performing Lady Randolph to Mr. Macready's Glenalvon ;—when I add to this record that she saw the brilliant but checkered course of Edmund Kean to nearly its close, and witnessed the *début* of Miss Fanny Kemble,—the whole history of the stage since the Restoration seems resumed therein.

Roger Kemble's itinerant company, as his children were born, received them as members. They played,—Sarah, John, Stephen, Elizabeth, almost as soon as they could speak. Sarah's first audience compassionately hissed her, as too young to be listened to; but she won their applause by reciting a fable. At thirteen, she played in the great room of the King's Head, Worcester,—among other parts, Ariel, in the "Tempest," her father, mother, sister Elizabeth, and brother John, acting in the same piece. For the next four or five years, there was much of itinerant life, till we find her at Wolverhampton, in 1773, acting in a wide range of characters, from Lee's heroines to Rosetta, in "Love in a Village." In the latter case, the young Meadows was a Mr. Siddons, who had acted Hippolito in Dryden's "Tempest," when she played Ariel. In her father's company she was always the first and greatest. She played all that the accomplished daughter of a manager chose to play, among her father's strollers,—and she attracted admirers both before and behind the curtain. The Earl of Coventry and sundry squires were among the former. Among the latter was that poor player, an ex-apprentice from Birmingham, named Siddons, between whom and Sarah Kemble, there was true love, for which, however, there was lacking parental sanction. The country audiences sympathized with the young people, and applauded the lover, who introduced his sad story into a comic song, on his benefit night. As he left the stage, the stately manageress received him at the wing, and there greeted him with a ringing box of the ears.

This led to the secession of both actors from the company. Mr. Siddons went,—the world before him where to choose; Sarah Kemble,—to the family of Mr. Greathead, of Guy's Cliff, Warwick shire. "She hired herself," says the *Secret History of the Green Room*, published in the very zenith of her fame,—" as lady's maid to Mrs. Greathead, at £10 per annum." "Her station," says Campbell, " was humble, but not servile, and her *principal* employment was to read to the elder Mr. Greathead." She probably fulfilled the double duty,—no disparagement at a time when the maids of ladies were often decayed ladies themselves.

Old Roger Kemble is said to have been very unwilling that any of his children should follow that profession, in exercising which he had wandered far, suffered much, and profited sparingly. The unwillingness was natural, but he seems to have put it in practice when too late;—after he had allowed his attractive young people to enjoy some of the perilous delights of the stage. There are bills extant which show that some of them, at least, were playing in his company, when they were of tender years. When Sarah Kemble went to Guy's Cliff, it was with no idea of permanently leaving the stage; and if it be true, as alleged in the series of dramatic biographies, published by Symonds at the beginning of the present century, that Roger Kemble apprenticed his daughter Elizabeth to a mantau-maker in Leominster, and Frances to a milliner in Worcester, he narrowly missed marring their good fortunes. A similar vocation could not keep Anne Oldfield from the stage, and though Elizabeth and Frances Kemble were not actresses of extraordinary merit, they had not to regret that they abandoned the vocations chosen for them by their parents, for that which was followed by their parents, themselves.

From Guy's Cliff, Sarah Kemble was ultimately taken by her persevering wooer, to whom her father reluctantly gave her, at Trinity Church Coventry, on the 6th of November, 1773. The bride was in her nineteenth year. The married couple continued but for a brief period in the Kemble company. A month after the marriage, the name of " Mrs. Siddons," was, for the first time, in the playbill, at Worcester, to Charlotte Rusport, in the " West Indian," and Leonora, in the " Padlock." Shortly after, Roger Kemble saw Mr. and Mrs. Siddons depart for Chamberlain and Crump's company, in Cheltenham. Here Mrs. Siddons at once took her place. Her Belvidera excited universal admiration. Lord Ailesbury, the cousin of the Pretender's wife, the Countess of Albany, mentioned her to Garrick; and Lord Dungarvon's daughter, Miss Boyle, directed her wardrobe, lent her many of her own dresses, and helped to make others for her with her own hands.

The Cheltenham "propertys" were of the poorest; but there were some that even the Honorable Miss Boyle could not supply. Thus, for the male disguise of the Widow Brady, Mrs. Siddons found, on the night of performance, that no provision had been made; but we are told that a gentleman in the boxes lent her his coat, while he stood at the side-scenes, with a petticoat over his shoulders, and ready to receive his property when done with!

Garrick, on Lord Ailesbury's report, sent King down to see this actress of promise, and on King's warrant, engaged her for Drury Lane, at £5 per week. Others say that it was on the warrant of Parson Bates, of the *Morning Post*, who greatly praised her Rosalind.

Her first appearance was on the 29th of December, 1775, as Portia, "by a young lady," to King's Shylock. On January 2d, 1776, she repeated Portia, "by Mrs. Siddons." On the 18th, she played Epicœne, but the part was subsequently assigned to another. On the 2d of February, she acted Julia, in a new and poor farce, the "Blackamoor washed White," and on the 15th, Emily, in Mrs. Cowley's new comedy, the "Runaway," which part she had to surrender to Mrs. King. She was not more fortunate in Maria, her third original character, in "Love's Metamorphoses;" nor in a subsequent part, that of Mrs. Strictland to Garrick's Ranger, did she excite any further remark save that it was played in a pathetic manner. Her second appearance with Garrick was as Lady Anne to his Richard, which she repeated twice, the last time on June 5, in presence of the royal family. Five nights later, Garrick took his farewell of the stage, and Mrs. Siddons's engagement was at an end.

In Belvidera, for which she had been praised by King, she was not permitted to appear. Bates had commended her Rosalind, but she had to see it played by Miss Younge. Even Miss Hopkins, who became her sister-in-law, had better parts than she; and there was Mrs. Yates keeping Calista and Isabella, and Mrs. King playing Lady Macbeth, and Mrs. Canning (mother of the future statesman) allowed on the benefit of Reddish, whom she married, to play Monimia. Mrs. Siddons concluded that the other actresses who plagued Garrick's life out, hated her, because Garrick was polite and even kind to her. Sheridan alleged, as a reason for not re-engaging her, that Garrick did not recognize in her a first-rate actress (which she was far from being at that time). Woodfall thought her sensible, but too weak for London. "You are all fools!" said buxom Mrs. Abington.

The fragile, timid, faltering actress acquired strength in the country. Henderson, himself rising to excellence, acted with, and spoke well of, her. York pronounced her perfect, and Bath took her with the warrant, and retained her, its most cherished tragic actress, object of public applause and private esteem, till the year 1782. It was here, in truth, that the great actress was perfected, and *that* amid as many matronly as professional duties. On leaving the Bath stage, she pointed to her children as so many reasons for the step; and therewith went up, with no faint heart, this time, to the metropolis. "She is an actress," said Henderson, "who has never had an equal, and will never have a superior." "My good reception in London," writes Mrs. Siddons, "I cannot but partially attribute to the enthusiastic accounts of me which the amiable Duchess of Devonshire had brought thither, and spread before my arrival." Poor Henderson!

With broken voice, the old nervousness, and a world of fears, she rehearsed Isabella, in Southerne's tragedy. When the night of the 10th of October, 1782, arrived, she dressed with a desperate tranquillity, and many sighs, and then faced the public, her son Henry, then eight years of age, holding her by the hand, and her father, Roger, looking on with a dismay that was soon converted into delight. Smith played Biron, and Palmer, Villeroy,—but Siddons alone was heeded on that night, in which she gave herself up so thoroughly to the requirements of the part, that her young son, who had often rehearsed with her, was so overcome by the reality of the dying scene, that he burst into tears. "I never heard," she writes, "such peals of applause in all my life. I thought they would not have suffered Mr. Packer to end the play."

With the echoes of the shouting audience ringing in her ears, she went home solemnly and silently. "My father, my husband, and myself," she says, "sat down to a frugal, neat supper, in a silence uninterrupted, except by acclamations of gladness from

Mr. Siddons." With succeeding nights, the triumph went on increasing. The management gave her Garrick's dressing-room, and gentlemen learned in the law presented her with a purse of a hundred guineas.

After the tender Isabella came the heroic loveliness of Euphrasia, with Bensley for Evander, her success in which shook the laurels on the brows of Mrs. Yates, and the widow of Spranger Barry. Having given new life to Murphy's dull lines in a play which, nevertheless, does not lack incident, she appeared as Jane Shore to Smith's Hastings, and with such effect that not only were sobs and shrieks heard from the ladies, but men wept like children, and "fainting fits," says Campbell, "were long and frequent in the house."

To the Lothario of Palmer and Horatio of Bensley, Mrs. Siddons next played Calista, in another of Rowe's tragedies, the "Fair Penitent,"—that impersonation of pride, anguish, anger, shame, and sorrow, and with undiminished success. But in Belvidera (to the Jaffier of Brereton, and Pierre of Bensley), she seems to have surpassed all she had hitherto accomplished over the minds and feelings of the audience, whom she fairly electrified. Her Belvidera, with its honest, passionate, overwhelming love and truth, was well contrasted with her scorn and magnificence of demeanor in Zara. The whole season was one of triumph,—the only dark spot in which was the failure of Hull's "Fatal Interview," in which she played Mrs. Montague, but with so little effect, where, indeed, no opportunity was given her of creating any, as to injure for a moment a prestige, which grew all bright again by her performance of Calista.

It is singular that she liked her part in Hull's play—"a new tragedy, in prose," she writes; "a most affecting play, in which I have a part that I like very much;" but she adds, from her house, 149, Strand, "the 'Fatal Interview' has been played three times, and is quite done with. It was the dullest of all representations."

Of Mrs. Crawford (Barry), the new actress entertained some small fears, which are not too generously expressed in a letter to Dr. Whalley. "I should suppose she has a very good fortune, and I should be vastly obliged if she would go and live very comfortably upon it . . . let her retire as soon as she pleases!" At this time, when her second benefit brought her nearly £700, her ideas of supreme bliss were limited to a cottage in the country, and a capital of £10,000.

Her success brought her many an enemy, the most virulent and unmanly of whom was an anonymous paragraph-writer in the newspapers, who slandered her daily, and for a brief moment excited against her the ill-will of the public. "He loaded her with opprobrium," says an anonymous contemporary, "for not alleviating the distresses of her (alleged) sister," Mrs. Curtis, a vicious woman, who, according to the quaintly circumstantial writer, "would not conform to modesty, though offered a genteel annuity on that condition." Mrs. Curtis read lectures at Dr. Graham's Temple of Health, and the wayward woman attempted to poison herself in Westminster Abbey. The enemies of Mrs. Siddons somehow connected her with both circumstances, as they subsequently did with that of old Roger Kemble applying, humbly, for relief from some charitable fund, in the hands of a banker. Probably the ex-hairdresser was proud, and may have preferred to apply for aid to a fund which he had helped to sustain than to take it from his children. The story is detailed by Genest, who seems inclined to place some faith in it!

Ireland eagerly invited the new actress, and she crossed from Holyhead to Dublin in a storm, which she looked on or endured with a "pleasing terror." Landing in the middle of a wet night in June, no tavern even would then receive a woman and a stranger, and it was with difficulty that her companion, Brereton, a promising Irish actor, whom she had instructed in Jaffier, procured accommodation for her, in the house where he himself lodged. She played with equal success at Cork as at Dublin, particularly in Zara. From the former place she writes to Dr. Whalley:—"I have sat to a young man in this place who has made a small full length of me in Isabella, upon the first entrance of Biron . . . he has succeeded to admiration. I think it more like me than any I have ever yet seen." Who was this unnamed artist? Where is this young Isabella?

Mrs. Siddons returned to England, richer by £1,000 by her Irish summer excursion, and with an antipathy against the people, which could only be momentary in the daughter of a lady born in Clonmel. Her season of 1783-4 at Drury, was doubly marked; she played two Shaksperian characters; Isabella, in "Measure for Measure," to Smith's Duke; and Constance, in "King John,"—to the King of her own brother, John Kemble. The first was a greater success than the second; but Constance became ultimately one of the most perfect of her portraitures.

To see her Isabella, in the "Fatal Marriage," the whole royal family went in quaint state. To her brother's Beverley, she played the wife, in a way which affected the actors as much as it did the audience. In the Countess of Salisbury, one of Mrs. Crawford's great parts, and Sigismunda, she comparatively failed; but she achieved a double triumph in Lady Randolph. It will be remembered how she had desired the retreat of Mrs. Crawford. The old actress had been famous for her performance of Lady Randolph, which she played on her reappearance at Covent Garden in November, 1783. Her oldest admirers (some critics excepted) confessed that her powers were shaken. A month afterwards Mrs. Siddons played the same character, for her benefit, to the Young Norval of Brereton, when the old actress succumbed at once, by comparison; but it is doubtful if Mrs. Siddons excelled her, if the comparison be confined to the period when each actress was in youth, strength, and beauty. "Mrs. Siddons," says Campbell, "omitted Mrs. Crawford's scream, in the far famed question, "Was he alive?" In 1801, the year when Mrs. Crawford was laid by the side of her husband, Barry, in Westminster Abbey, Mr. Simons, says Genest, "in a small party at Bath, went through the scene between Old Norval and Lady Randolph,—his imitation of Mrs. Crawford was most perfect, particularly in 'Was he alive?' Mrs. Piozzi, who was present, said to him,—'Do not do that before Mrs. Siddons; she would not be pleased.'"

The King shed tears, however, at her acting; and the Queen, turning her back to the stage, styled it in her broken English "too *disagreeable*;" but she appointed Mrs. Siddons preceptress in English reading to the Princesses, without any emolument, and kept her standing in stiff and stately dress, including a hoop, which Mrs. Siddons especially detested, till she was ready to faint! The King, too, praised her correct emphasis, mimicked the false ones of other actors, and set her above "Garrick on one point, that of repose, whereas, he said, Garrick could never stand still. He was a great fidget."

The Countesses entrapped her into parties where crowds of well-bred people stood on the chairs to stare at her. One invalid Scotch lady, whose doctor had forbidden her going to the theatre, went unintroduced to Mrs. Siddons's residence, then in Gower Street, and calmly sat down, gazed at her for some minutes, and then walked silently away. Sir Joshua Reynolds painted his name on the *hem of her garment*, in his portrait of her as the Tragic Muse, and Dr. Johnson kissed her hand, and called her "My dear Madam," on his own staircase. Statesmen were glad, when she played, to sit among the fiddlers; and the fine gentlemen of the day, including him of "Wales," visited her in her dressing-room, after the play, "to make their bows." And then she rode home in "her own carriage!"

Edinburgh was impatient to see her, but slow in making up its mind about her. One supreme effort alone, in Lady Randolph, elicited from a generous critic in the pit, the comment, uttered aloud, "That's nae bad;" after that sanction the house shook with applause. Glasgow, not to be behind-hand, gave her not only applause but a service of plate. In Dublin, where, probably, her expressed dislike of the Irish people had been reported, there was great opposition to her. Her engagements stood in the way of charitable benefits, and no sacrifices she made to further the latter, whether for societies or individuals, were allowed to her credit. I think, too, that the Irish actors little relished her stage arrangements made for proper effect, and Irish managers were not delighted with her terms of half the receipts; altogether, Mrs. Siddons returned to London in saddened temper. In Dublin she had raised a storm; in Edinburgh, where crowds of unwashed people were crammed nightly to see her, in an unventilated theatre, a fever, such as used to be in crowded jails, broke out and spread over the city. As once in the case of Garrick, so now with the great actress; it was called the *Siddons fever*, as if she were responsible for it!

The anecdote of "That's nae bad!" then, is not to be quoted to the disadvantage of Scottish audiences. The Edinburgh people, moreover, had been told that Mrs. Siddons was unwilling to be interrupted by applause, which, however, was not true; as she herself alleged that the more applause the less fatigue, as she had more breathing time. Indeed, the Edinburgh enthusiasm anent the great actress surpassed all such manifestations elsewhere. Fancy the General Assembly of the Kirk being obliged to arrange their meetings with reference to Mrs. Siddons's acting, as the younger members followed the artist, as Bossuet used to follow contemporary actors, to study elocution. People, during her first engagement of three weeks, assembled in crowds, hours before the doors were opened, sometimes as early as noon. As soon as admission was given, there ensued a fierce struggle which disregarded even the points of bayonets, whose bearers were called in to quell disorder; and, as soon as the play was over, and the doors were closed, porters and servants took up a position, standing, lying, sleeping, but all ready to secure places on the opening of the box-office on the following day. On one occasion there were applications for 2,557 places, of which the house numbered but 630; and when, at night, the struggle was renewed for these, the loss of property, in costume and its attendant luxuries of jewellery and the like, was enormous.

One night, as Mrs. Siddons was playing Isabella, and had uttered the words by which she used to pierce all hearts, words uttered on discovering her first husband, in whose absence she had remarried, "Oh, my Biron! my Biron!" a young Aberdeenshire heiress, Miss Gordon of Gight, sent forth a scream as wild as that of Isabella, and, taking up the words in a hysterical frenzy, was carried out, still uttering them. Next year this impressible lady was wooed and won by a Byron, the honorable John of that name, by whom she became the mother of one more famous than the rest, Lord Byron, the "lord of himself, that heritage of woe." Lady Gray, of Gask, told my friend, Mr. Robert Chambers, that she "never could forget those ominous sounds of "Oh, my Biron!"

Notwithstanding all this success, I find contemporary critics expressing an opinion that she played too frequently. "If she hopes," says one, "to have the gratification of being followed by crowds, she should never perform more than once a week, or twelve times in a season." The arithmetical computation seems defective; but it is singular that Mrs. Delancy made a similar remark with respect to Garrick.

Mrs. Siddons was, however, equal to more fatigue than some of her admirers would have had her undergo. I find it recorded, with admiration, in a paper three-quarters of a century old, that in four days she had achieved the (then) incredible task of acting in three theatres, so wide apart as London, Reading, and Bath!

Walpole thus speaks of her in Isabella:—" I have seen Mrs. Siddons; she pleased me beyond my expectation, but not up to the admiration of the *ton*, two or three of whom were in the same box with me, particularly Mr. Boothby, who, as if to disclaim the stoic apathy of Mr. Meadows in "Cecilia," was all bravissimo. Mr. Crawfurd, too, asked me if I did not think her the best actress I ever saw? I said, 'by no means; we old folks were apt to be prejudiced in favor of our first impressions.' She is a good figure, handsome enough, though neither nose nor chin according to the Greek standard, beyond which both advance a good deal. Her hair is either red, or she has no objection to its being thought so, and had used red powder. Her voice is clear and good; but I thought she did not vary its modulations enough, nor ever approach enough to the familiar; but this may come when more habituated to the awe of the audience of the capital. Her action is proper, but with little variety; when without motion her arms are not genteel. Thus, you see, madame, all my objections are very trifling; but what I really wanted, but did not find, was originality, which announces genius, and without which I am never intrinsically pleased. All Mrs. Siddons did, good sense or good instruction might give. I dare to say that were I one-and-twenty, I should have thought her marvellous; but, alas! I remember Mrs. Porter and the Dumesnil; and remember every action of the former in the very same part." Subsequently, he says:—" I cannot think Mrs. Siddons the greatest prodigy that ever appeared, nor go to see her act the same part every week, and cry my eyes out every time; were I five-and-twenty, I suppose I should weep myself blind, for she is a fine actress, and fashion would make me think a brilliant what now seems to me only a very good rose-diamond."

That Mrs. Siddons abandoned the reddish brown powder then in fashion, we shall see in the chapter on costume. Meanwhile, let us keep to her career on the London stage. On her return thither from Ireland, she found the town possessed by reports of her pride, arrogance, and lack of kindness to her poorer colleagues. A cabal interrupted her performance during several nights; but even when she triumphed over it, by proving the injustice of her accusers, she did not entirely recover her peace of mind. She felt that she had chosen a humiliating vocation. There were, however, bright moments in it. In Franklin's absurd tragedy—the "Earl of Warwick," her superb Margaret of Anjou caused the playgoers who had applauded Mrs. Yates, to acknowledge, that great as the original representative was, a greater had arisen in Mrs. Siddons. But when the latter played Zara, the supremacy of Mrs. Cibber was only divided. In Cumberland's "Carmelite," in which she played Matilda to the Montgomerie of Kemble, she produced little effect. The great actress had no such poets as the great Mrs. Barry had, to fit her with parts; and, lacking such, fell back upon the old. Her Camiola, in Massinger's "Maid of Honor," was, however, only a passing success.

She made ample amends for all by her triumph in Lady Macbeth, in 1785. With this character her name and fame are always most closely associated. Walpole himself could hardly have questioned the grand originality of her conception of the part. Mrs. Siddons imagined the heroine of this most tragic of tragedies to be a delicate blonde, who ruled by her intellect, and subdued by her beauty, but with whom no one feeling of common general nature was congenial; a woman prompt for wickedness, but swiftly possessed by remorse; one who is horror-stricken for herself and for the precious husband, who, more robust and less sensitive, plunges deeper into crime, and is less moved by any sense of compassion or sorrow.

From this night, Mrs. Pritchard, the Lady Macbeth of past days, was unseated from her throne in the hearts of many old admirers. Mrs. Siddons certainly never had a superior in this part, the night of her first success in which formed an epoch in dramatic history. Sheridan, the manager, had dreaded a fiasco, for no other reason than that in the sleep-walking scene Mrs. Siddons would not carry the candlestick about with her! Mrs. Pritchard had always done so, and any omission in this respect—so he thought—would be treated by the audience as a mark of disrespect to the memory and to the observances of the older actress. The audience were too enthralled by the younger player to think of such stage trifles. Mason, the poet, hated Mrs. Siddons for surpassing his idol, Pritchard, and friends abstained from pronouncing her name in his presence. She subdued him, of course, and they played duets together at Lord Harcourt's; but she could make nothing of the old poet's Elfrida, played to the Athelwold of Smith—and Mrs. Pritchard was never displaced from the shrine she occupied in his memory.

Lord Harcourt's judgment of Mrs. Siddons, in Lady Macbeth, is thus expressed:—"To say that Mrs. Siddons, in one word, is superior to Mrs. Pritchard in Lady Macbeth, would be talking nonsense, because I don't think that it is possible; but, on the other hand, I will not say with those *impartial* judges, Mr. Whitehead and Miss Fauquier, that she does not play near as well. But there are others too, and in the parts for Mrs. Siddons, that are of this opinion; that she has much more expression of countenance, and can assume parts with a spirit, cannot be denied; but that she wants the dignity, and above all, the unequalled compass and melody of Mrs. Pritchard. I thought her wonderful and very fine in the rest of that scene. She throws a degree of proud and filial tenderness into this speech, 'Had he not resembled,' &c., which is new, and of great effect. Her 'Are you a man!' in the banquet scene, I thought inferior to Mrs. Pritchard's; and for the parts spoken at a great distance her voice wanted power. Her countenance, aided by a studious and judicious choice of head-dress, was a true picture of a mind diseased in the sleeping scene, and made one shudder; and the effect, as a picture, was better in that than it had ever been with the taper, because it allows of variety in the actress of washing her hands; but the sigh was not so horrid, nor was the voice so sleepy, nor yet quite so articulate as Mrs. Pritchard's."

This is a less summary criticism than that of the Calais landlady, on whom Mrs. Siddons had made an impression. "She looks like a Frenchwoman; *but* it will be a long time before she gets the grace and dignity of a Frenchwoman!"

If Walpole may be trusted, Mrs. Siddons's ideas of Lady Macbeth had not always been identical. I find this in a pretty picture painted by Walpole, in 1783 :—"Mrs. Siddons continues to be the mode, and to be modest and sensible. She declines great dinners, and says the business and cares of her family take her whole time. When Lord Carlisle carried her the tribute money from Brookes's, he said she was not *maniérée* enough. - - I suppose she was grateful,' said my niece, Lady Maria. Mrs. Siddons was desired to play Medea and Lady Macbeth. 'No,' she replied, 'she did not look on them as female characters.'"

At that time she had not made up her mind to attempt a part in which Mrs. Pritchard had been unrivalled. As far as Medea was concerned, Mrs. Siddons left the laurels of Mrs. Yates unshaken, and declined to play that supremely tragic part. One of her chief desires was that Walpole should see her in Portia, in which she had failed; Walpole preferred witnessing her Athenais. In the passionate scenes of so poor a play as "Percy," Walpole greatly admired her; but he found her voice hollow and defective in cool declamation.

Of course, there were various individuals who were said to be —who affected to be—or who really were in love with the great actress. Among these was Brereton, son of the major of that name, and who was a poor actor till rehearsing Jaffier to Mrs. Siddons's Belvidera she inspired him, as Malibran did Templeton into something like excellence. Mrs. Siddons having thus effected for him what Garrick had failed to do, Brereton was exceedingly grateful, and his good-natured friends not only conduced to Mrs. Brereton's peace of mind, by reporting that he was in love with the great actress, but when "a malady not easily accounted for," as the theatrical biographies call the insanity which impeded his performances with Mrs. Siddons in Dublin, compelled him to leave the stage, the madness was set down to over much regard for, and a little difference with "a great tragic actress, of whom he is said to be very fond." To this matter Mrs. Siddons doubtless alludes in a curious letter to Dr. Whalley, dated March 13, 1785. "I have been very unhappy; now 'tis over, I will venture to tell you so, that you may not lose the dues of rejoicing. Envy, malice, detraction, all the fiends of hell have compassed me round about to destroy me; 'but blessed be God who hath given me the victory,' &c. I have been charged with almost every thing bad, except incontinence; and it is attributed to me as thinking a woman may be guilty of every crime, provided she retain her chastity. God help them, and forgive them; they know but little of me."

Poor Brereton died in confinement, in 1787; and if his wife had ever been rendered unhappy by the report of his love for Mrs. Siddons, his widow was rendered happy by the love of Mrs. Siddons's brother for herself; and Mrs. Brereton, the lively Priscilla Hopkins of the old days when her father was prompter, became Mrs. John Kemble. Meanwhile, at other adorers of her own, Mrs. Siddons only laughed. "If you should meet a Mr. Seton," she writes to Dr. Whalley, "who lived in Leicester Square, you must not be surprised to hear him boast of being very well with my sister and myself, for since I have been here I have heard the old fright has been giving it out in town. You will find him rather an unlikely person to be so great a favorite with women." But her Desdemona certainly increased the number of her lovers, old and young. The character is in such strong contrast with that of Lady Macbeth, that the public were not prepared for the new and more delicate fascination. "You have no idea," she writes, "how the innocence and playful simplicity of my Desdemona have laid hold on the hearts of the people. I am very much flattered by this, as nobody has ever done any thing with that character before."

Nevertheless, the sense of humiliation does not seem to have left her. She announces the marriage of her sister Elizabeth with Mr. Whitelock, a "worthy man," though an actor; but that of another sister, Frances, has a more jubilant tone in the proclaiming: "Yes, my sister is married, and I have lost one of the sweetest companions in the world. She has married a most re-respectable man, though of small fortune; and I *thank God, that she is off the stage.*" This was Mrs. Twiss. Of another sister, we only remember her as the old-fashioned novelist, "Anne" (Hutton) "of Swansea."

Of theatrical gossip Mrs. Siddons's letters do not contain much, but it is generally epigrammatic: "Miss Younge," she writes to

Dr. Whalley, "is married to Mr. Pope, a very boy, and the only one she will have by her marriage." In 1786, she says, "We have a great comic actress now, called Mrs. Jordan. She has a vast deal of merit, but, in my mind, is not perfection." What Mrs. Siddons had acquired already by the stage, we learn from her own words: "I have at last, my friend, attained the ten thousand pounds which I set my heart upon, and am now perfectly at ease with respect to fortune." From lodgings, at 149, Strand, she had gone to a house of her own, in Gower Street, Bedford Square, "the back of it is most effectually in the country, and delightfully pleasant." There, in then suburban Gower Street, was established a happy and flourishing household, the master of which had friends who borrowed four hundred pounds at a time, and the mistress others to whom she lent smaller sums, and who thought her exceedingly ungrateful when she asked, as she did without scruple, for her money.

Mrs. Jordan, "to my mind, is not perfection," wrote Mrs. Siddons, but the former was more perfect than the latter in Rosalind, which Mrs. Siddons played for her benefit, in April, 1785, to the Orlando of Brereton; King played Touchstone; Palmer, Jacques. Mrs. Siddons dressed the character ill, as the disguised Rosalind; her costume was severely handled by the critics. As Miss Seward magniloquently put it, "the scrupulous prudery of decency produced an ambiguous vestment, that seemed neither male nor female." The character was "totally without archness," said Young; "how *could* such a countenance be arch?" Campbell, like Walpole, says, that in comedy she gathered no laurels. Miss Farren and Mrs. Jordan excelled her there; and her Mrs. Lovemore, in the "Way to Keep Him," must be reckoned amongst her failures. That some of her heroines, in dull and defunct tragedies, rank only next to failures, must be laid to the account of the poets. Throughout the kingdom she was recognized as Queen of Tragedy. In Scotland, a sensitive man in the Glasgow gallery exclaimed, "She's a fallen angel!" and Edinburgh fish-wives looked with interest on the lady who had "gar them greet, yestreen!"

"I am going to undertake your adored Hermione this winter," writes Mrs. Siddons to Dr. Whalley. "You know I was always afraid of her, and I am not a bit more bold than I was.' This timidity was not justified; her Hermione, indeed, was not equal to that of a later actress, Rachel, but it had grand points. The simple words, "Why, *Pyrrhus!*" when Orestes (Smith) asked her whom she would have him murder, thrilled the remotest auditor by their emphasis. But she could thrill actors as well as auditors; playing Ophelia for her second benefit, 1786, in the mad scene, she spoke some words in so strange a manner, as she touched the arm of the Queen, that the memory of so practised a player as Mrs. Hopkins was disturbed, and she stood awed and silent.

Though Ophelia was not a triumph,—nor the Lady in "Comus," nor Cleone, to which nobody went on the second night, for the strange reason, that Mrs. Siddons was too affecting!—her position was unassailably established. Mrs. Jordan she put out of all competition with her in certain parts, by playing Imogen; for which she asked of the artist Hamilton to sketch for her "a boy's dress to conceal the person as much as possible."

Whether she desired to set aside Mrs. Jordan altogether as a rival in comedy, is doubtful; but she certainly continued to try comic parts, but the laugh excited was not hearty; her Lady Townly had no airiness; her smiles are spoken of as glorious condescensions; when Bannister was asked if her comic acting had ever pleased him, he "shook his head, and remarked," says Campbell, "that the burthen of her inspiration was too heavy for comedy," in which, according to Colman, she was only "a frisking Gog." Miss Baillie, on the other hand, insists that but for unfair discouragement she would have been a great comic actress. In private life, she had great relish for humor, and told laughable stories in her slow way, as well as read scenes in comedy with great effect. And yet Katherine, with its passionate expression, was as little thought of as Rosalind. One would have thought this character would have fitted her; her own judgment as to what suited her is not satisfactorily exhibited in her preference of Tate's Cordelia and of Dryden's Cleopatra to those of Shakspeare. But she distrusted her own judgment in some things. "Mr. Siddons," she remarks to Dr. Whalley, "is a much better judge of the conduct of a tragedy than myself."

This remark occurs in a letter written in September, 1787, under perplexing circumstances. Young Mr. Greathead, of Guy's Cliff, was the author of a tragedy, the "Regent," the heroine in which he designed for her acting. She liked neither the play nor her own part in it; but how could she disoblige the present head of a family where she had found an asylum, when love had disturbed the tenor of her life. Therefore, she wrote this letter to her friend Dr. Whalley, who did *not* burn it, as he ought to have done:—"September 1, 1787.—Mrs. Piozzi may be an excellent judge of a poem possibly, but it is certain that she is not of a tragedy, if she has really an opinion of this. It certainly has some beautiful poetry, but it strikes me that the plot is very lame, and the characters very, very ill-sustained in general, but more particularly the lady, for whom the author had me in his eye. This woman is one of those monsters (I think them) of perfection, who is an angel before her time, and is so entirely resigned to the will of heaven, that (to a very mortal like myself) she appears to be the most provoking piece of still life one ever had the misfortune to meet. Her struggles and conflicts are so weakly expressed, that we conclude they do not cost her much pain, and she is so pious that we are satisfied she looks upon her afflictions as so many convoys to heaven, and wish her there, or anywhere else but in the tragedy. . . Mr. G. says that it would give him too great trouble to alter it, so that he seems determined to endeavor to bring it on the stage, provided I will undertake this milksop lady. . . . Mr. Siddons says it will not do at all for the stage in its present state, for the poetry seems to be all its merit; and if it is to be stripped of that—which it must be, for all the people in it forget their feelings to talk metaphor instead of passion—what is there to support it? I wish, for his own sake, poor young man, that he would publish it as it is. . . .

"Your truly affectionate S. Siddons."

The event justified her sentiments, and the "Regent" did not live. She continued, however, to reap her harvests of laurels, gathering them most profusely by her acting in that Queen Katherine, which had been recommended to her by Dr. Johnson. We continue to associate her name with this part, in which she was more queenly and dignified, I suspect, than Katherine herself; certainly more imposing, if it be true that by simply saying, "You were the Duke's Confessor, and lost your office on the complaint of the tenants," she put the surveyor, to whom the words were addressed, into such perspiring agony, that as he came off, crushed by her earnestness, he declared he would not for the world meet her black eyes on the stage again!

I doubt, however, if the poor fellow could afford to give up his engagement; and I know that some of these "affectations" are assumed by inferior actors. I have heard of a lady so audibly affected, as she stood at the wing, by the acting of her manager, then on the stage, that she was invited to his room to partake of cake and wine. But Mrs. Siddons undoubtedly possessed power above all other actresses, of attracting and subduing. In the procession scene, in her brother's barbarous mutilation of Shakspeare's Coriolanus, which he played so inimitably, her dumb show, as Volumnia, triumphing in the triumph of her son, attracted every eye, touched every heart, and caused the pageant itself to be as nothing, except as she used it for her purpose. It is strange that one so gifted should have ventured, at four-and-thirty, to act Juliet, who

"Even or odd, of all days in the year,
Come Lammas-eve at night, shall be fourteen!"

and to Lammas-eve it wanted " a fortnight and odd days."

But authors, of course, make as many mistakes as actresses. When the King, in Miss Burney's tragedy, "Edwy and Elgiva," cried "bring in the Bishop," the audience, thinking of the pleasant mixture so called, broke into laughter, which was only exceeded by that which broke forth when Mrs. Siddons died, under a hedge, and on a superb couch! I do not believe, with Genest, that anybody ever laughed at her dying Zara; but when in "Edward and Eleanora," the two babes were brought in, in imperial frocks and long coating, and were handed into the bed of their dying mother, the audience did break forth into loud hilarity. Indeed, babies in arms were stumbling blocks to Mrs. Siddons's dignity. At a later period than that above mentioned, when acting in Sotheby's "Julian and Agnes," she had to make her exit, carrying an infant. The exit was made precipitately, and in the doing of it she so violently struck the passive baby's head against a door-post as to discover that the said head was made of wood. The audience laughed again, and Agnes, Countess of Tortona, all taken aback as she was, laughed heartily, too. Once also, when Mrs. Siddons was playing Agnes in Lillo's "Fatal Curiosity," and the flesh of the audience crept at her suggestion of murdering the stranger, who is her son,—as the scene proceeded towards the murder, one gentleman in the pit laughed aloud; he would have been roughly treated by the audience, but for the discovery that he was in hysterics, at her acting.

At other times, the actress was overcome by herself. In the pretended fainting scene of Arpasia, in "Tamerlane," after the wild cry "Love! Death! Moneses!" Mrs. Siddons fell back violently, clutching her drapery, and her dress all disordered,—a swoon in earnest, which caused a rush, from the pit and boxes, of part of the excited and sympathizing audience. The agitation of the actress was almost perilous to her life!

There were occasions, however, on which that audience refused to be sympathetic. When she and her brother acted in Jephson's dull "Conspiracy," we are told that they "acted to vacancy: the hollow sound of their voices was the most dreary thing in the world." This was among the least of her troubles; at the moment of her greatest exertions, family cares and sorrows pressed on her. Mr. Siddons's speculations alarmed her prudent mind. Mr. Sheridan's money, when he held the purse at Drury Lane, flowed but slowly and intermittently into her banker's coffers; and if this, or even illness, drove her into temporary retirement, she had enemies who reported that her brain was not as well as it might be.

At the beginning of the present century Mrs. Siddons more than once expressed a desire "to be at rest." The labors of her life, and the troubles of it, too, were equal in magnitude to her triumphs. Could she but realize £300 a year above that she had already acquired for her family by her sole and brilliant exertions, she would begin to be "lazy, saucy, and happy." Nevertheless, when the period of 1812 arrived, and she had determined on retirement, she was less bold of spirit. It was like taking the first step of the ladder, she said, which led to the next world. Once she was in peril of taking that first step less agreeably. While standing as the statue in the "Winter's Tale," the flowing white drapery of her dress caught fire from behind, but it was extinguished by the courage and prudence of a poor scene-shifter, before she knew the whole of her danger. He saved her life; and she not only rewarded him liberally, but saved his son, a deserter from the army, from the horrible punishment which was then inflicted on such offenders.

She upheld the dignity of her vocation, by refusing to act with the "young Roscius," while to act inferior parts in the same piece with her, actresses of reputation esteemed it an honor. Miss Pope, on having the part of Lucy, in "George Barnwell," sent to her, returned it with some anger; but when she was told that Mrs. Siddons was about to play Milwood to Charles Kemble's Barnwell, Miss Pope resumed the character with eagerness. On the stage, and even in the green room, she seldom departed from the humor of the part she sustained on that particular evening; but she had no sooner concluded it than she was herself again. Miss Seward records with particular delight, after seeing the great actress in Beatrice, at Birmingham, that Mrs. Siddons having made a courtesy generally to the house, made one in particular, with an especial smile of benignity to Miss Seward and her friends in the stage-box.

She began and ended her London theatrical life with Shakspeare —commencing in 1775 with Portia, and terminating in June, 1812, with Lady Macbeth. Some few subsequent appearances, indeed, there were. When her son, Henry Siddons, was the somewhat unlucky proprietor of the Edinburgh Theatre, he thought that if his mother and uncle would but play for him, in the same pieces, on the same night, he should retrieve his fortunes. He wrote separately to both, and received respective answers. That from Mrs. Siddons intimated that she would act for half the receipts and a free benefit. The reply from John Kemble expressed his readiness to act,—for a free benefit and half the receipts! Henry Siddons, much perplexed, had to look elsewhere for less expensive aid. After his death, and subsequent to his mother's farewell to the London Stage, she played several nights, in Edinburgh, *gratis*, for the benefit of his family;—and critics saw no other change in her, than that she looked older.  Her "last" appearance in public was in June, 1819, when she played Lady Randolph for the benefit of Charles Kemble.  The Shakspearian characters for which she enjoyed the greatest fame, are Lady Macbeth and Queen Katherine; and these were included in the readings which she continued to give during a few years.  These last were especially relished by Queen Charlotte and her family;—the guerdon for many of which, including Othello, read aloud at Windsor one Sunday evening, was a gold chain with a cross of many-colored jewels.

Her beauty, personal and mental, she retained to the last,—the former only slightly touched by time.  *That* was marked, in the Gallery of the Louvre, even amid the finest examples of mortal and godlike beauty from the hands of Greek sculptors.  Her sense of the beautiful was also fresh to the last.  Standing rapt at the sublimity of the scenery in the neighborhood of Penmanmawr, she heard a lady remark, "This awful scenery makes me feel as if I were only a worm, or a grain of dust, on the face of the earth!" Mrs. Siddons turned round and said: "*I* feel very differently."

She had the misery to outlive all her children, except her daughter Cecilia, but in successive visitations she was so well-tempered as to create the means of consolation, and in modelling statuary, often found at least temporary relief from sorrow.  Hannah More as heartily applauded her in private life as the warmest of her admirers ever did in public; and in truth her religion was cheerful, and her rule of life honest.  She was not only a great artist, but a thorough English lady, a true, honest, exquisite woman;—one of the bravest and most willing of the noble army of workers.  Proud, she may have been, and justly so.  Simple she was, and simple-minded, in many respects.  The *viola amœna* was her favorite flower; and, from the purple borders of her garden in spring time up at then secluded Westbourne,—her managing handmaid acquired the name of Miss Heartsease.

Those who knew her best have recorded her beauty and her grace, her noble carriage, divine elocution, and solemn earnestness; her grandeur and her pathos, her correct judgment, her identification of whatever she assumed, and her abnegation of self.  Erskine studied her cadences and intonations, and avowed that he owed his best displays to the harmony of her periods and pronunciation

According to Campbell, she increased the heart's capacity for tender, intense, and lofty feelings, and seemed something above humanity, in presence of which, humanity was moved, exalted, or depressed, according as she willed. Her countenance was the interpreter of her mind, and that mind was of the loftiest, never stooping to trickery, but depending on nature to produce effect.

She may have borne her professional habits into private life, and "stabbed the potatoes," or awed a draper's assistant by asking, "Will it wash?" but there was no affectation in this;—as she said, still in her tragic way, "Witness truth, I did not wish to be tragical!"

I have alluded to the apparent lack of judgment in her assuming, at thirty-four, the character of Juliet, a girl not yet fourteen. Miss Weston, however, writes:—"a finer performance was never seen. she contrived to make her appearance light, youthful, and airy, beyond imagination, and more beautiful than any thing one ever saw. Her figure, she tells me, was very well fitted by previous indisposition."

In carrying into private life her stately stage manner, Mrs. Siddons undesignedly imitated Clairon, the "Queen of Carthage," as the French called her, from her marvellous acting as Dido. "If," said Clairon, "I am only a vulgar and ordinary woman during twenty hours of the day, I shall continue to be a vulgar and ordinary woman, whatever efforts I may make, in Agrippina or Semiramis, during the other four."

There remains but to be said that this "lofty-minded actress," as Young called Mrs. Siddons, died on the 8th of June, 1831,—leaving a name in theatrical history, second to none, and deep regret that the honored owner of it had departed from among the living. Of the latter was the elder brother, who owed much of his greatness to her, and who is noticed in the next chapter.

## CHAPTER XIX.

### JOHN KEMBLE.

On the 1st of February, 1757, John Philip Kemble was born, at Prescot, in Lancashire. His father's itinerant life not only led to his appearance on the stage, when a child, but to his being placed at school, at Worcester, whence he passed through Sedgley to Douay, where he was remarkable for his elocution. He had for college fellow, Miller, or Milner, as he chose to call himself,—and who, when a Roman Catholic prelate, used to affirm that, in point of elocution, he was considered equal to Kemble!

In 1776, the year in which Garrick retired, Kemble may be said to have made his first public appearance as an actor, at Wolverhampton, and Boaden thinks he was too good for his audience. In various northern towns he endured a stern probation, and made sundry mistakes. He played Plume, Ranger, and Archer, which were totally unsuited to him; and he was actually laughed at in tragedy,—by some persons of distinction in the boxes, at York. He resented this with such dignity, that the York fine people, who could not understand the latter feeling, insisted on an apology; and when the rest of the house declared he should make none, he thanked them with such a weight of heavy argument to show they and he were right, that those bewildered Yorkists demanded of him to beg pardon immediately.

Subsequently, John Kemble published fugitive poems, which he was afterwards glad to burn; wrote a tragedy, "Belisarius," and a comedy, the "Female Officer;" composed a Latin ode, *Ad Somnium*, and a Latin epitaph for his dead comrade, Inchbald; laid the foundations of friendship with the Percys; gave lectures on oratory; and, at twenty-three, made an attempt to improve Shakspeare's "Comedy of Errors," by turning it into a farce, called "Oh, it's impossible!" the chief point in which was that the audience should be as puzzled about the two Dromios, of whom he made a couple of niggers, as their masters themselves.

If, at York, the admirers of the now forgotten Cummins contended that he was superior to Kemble, so in Ireland those who remembered their old favorite Barry, were slow to admit Kemble's equality. But, though he nearly made shipwreck of his fame by playing comedy, he rose in Irish estimation by his acting in tragedy; and he won all hearts by his finished performance of Jephson's "Count of Narbonne," in which he represented the Count, to the Adelaide of Miss Francis—the Mrs. Jordan of later years. Jephson was an Irishman, and Dublin was grateful to the actor who helped him to a triumph. Black Rock, I dare say, is to this day proud of the author.

On the 30th of September, 1783, John Kemble first appeared in London, at Drury Lane, as Hamlet. The fierceness and variety of the criticism denote that a new and a great actor had come before the critics. His novel readings were severally commented on—some of them were admirable, but bold. The utmost one critic could urge was that the player was "too scrupulously graceful;" and objection was fairly made to his pronouncing the word "lisp," to Ophelia, as "*lithp*." Boaden calls this "a refinement;" but he is forced to allow that it was "below the actor."

Just previous to this successful *début* at Drury Lane, John Kemble's brother Stephen had very moderately succeeded in Othello, at Covent Garden, where the management had secured the *big*, instead of the *great*, Mr. Kemble. Just subsequent to the former first appearance, two sisters of these players, Elizabeth and Frances Kemble (afterwards Mrs. Whitelock and Mrs. Twiss), made an attempt to share in a theatrical and family glory, in which, however, they had no abiding part. These ladies passed away, and left that glory to be divided by John Kemble, and his sister, Mrs. Siddons. But some time elapsed before the latter were permitted to play in the same piece. Smith had possession of parts of which custom forbade his being deprived; and it was not till each had played singly in various stock pieces, that they came together in "King John," and subsequently in the "Gamester." Previous to Kemble's undertaking the former character, the old actor, Sheridan, read the part to him as Sheridan was used to play it; but grandly as the King was played, the Constance in the hands of Mrs. Siddons was the magic by which the audience was most potentially moved. It was the same in the "Gamester;" the sufferings of Mrs. Beverley touched all hearts; but the instability, selfishness, cowardice, and maudlin of the wretched husband, excited both contempt and execration—but that was precisely what the author, as well as the actor, intended.

This union of genius was not, however, permanent; when Mrs. Siddons played Lady Macbeth, Smith acted, with graceful indifference, the Thane; and it was not till March, 1785, that brother and sister appeared together in another play, and then in "Othello"—the Moor and Desdemona being assigned to them. Neither player was ever identified with the character respectively acted; but what could even John Kemble do, who performed the Moor in the uniform of a British general of the actor's own time? He made a more certain flight by selecting "Macbeth" for his benefit, and playing the chief part to his sister's Lady; but it was only for one night. The Thane belonged by prescriptive right to Smith, and as long as he remained a member of the company, the original Charles Surface was entitled to one of the sublimest parts in all the range of tragedy. Even when Mrs. Siddons selected the "Merchant of Venice" for her benefit, and played Portia, Shylock fell, as by right, to King, and John Kemble had to be content with Bassanio!

He had his revenge; not in playing the insipid heroes of the new tragedies, which were then more or less in fashion, but in acting Lear to his sister's Cordelia, on occasion of her benefit, in January, 1788. The greatest admirers of Garrick confessed that Kemble's Lear was nearly equal to that of their idol; but Boaden records that he never played it so grandly and so touchingly as on that night.

Kemble is said to have been so much attached to Miss Phillips (afterwards Mrs. Crouch), that he was exceedingly moved on reading the epitaph on her tomb, by Boaden. He is reported also to have been tenderly affected by Mrs. Inchbald—for he composed a Latin epitaph for the tomb of her defunct husband. I find further mentioned "a young lady of family and fortune at York," whose cruel brother interfered menacingly in the matter, and also that "the daughter of a noble lord, once high in office, was strongly attached to him, and that the father bought off the match with £3,000. It is certain that Mrs. Siddons was highly offended at the alliance (subsequently with Mrs. Brereton)—perhaps she looked with anxious hope to a consanguinity with the noble house of G———." So sneers old legend, and here follows truth.

The lady he *did* marry was a very excellent lady indeed. Her own parents had fought their way well through life, for Mr. Hopkins was a strolling player when he married the daughter of a Somersetshire Boniface; but the bridegroom became Prompter, and Mrs. Hopkins a respectable actress at Drury Lane. One of their daughters, Priscilla, subsequently belonged to the company, when young Brereton persuaded her to take his name, and share his fortunes. Whether excess of admiration for Mrs. Siddons, with whom he frequently acted, drove Brereton mad or not, his widow kept her senses under cool control, and about a year after the death of her first husband, one of Garrick's ineffective pupils, she said to Mrs. Hopkins, "My dear mother, I cannot guess what Mr. Kemble means: he passed me just now, going up to his dressing-room, and chucking me under the chin, said, 'Ha, Pop! I shouldn't wonder if you were soon to hear something very much to your advantage!' What could he mean?" "Mean!" the sensible mother answered—Adolphus so styles her—"why he means to propose marriage; and if he does, I advise you not to refuse him."

The wedding was dramatic enough. Mrs. Hopkins, her daughter, Jack Bannister and his wife, walked from Jack's house in Frith Street, to John's in Caroline Street, Bedford Square, to breakfast with the bridegroom, who did not seem to expect them. Thence, on a December morning, 1787, in two hackney coaches, the party went to church, and were married by "the well-known Parson Este." The bride—no dinner having been thought of by any one else—dined early, the bridegroom late, at the Bannisters'; at whose house Kemble remained with Mrs. Bannister, or rather taking his wine without her, while Mr. Bannister and Mrs. Kemble went to Drury Lane, where they had to act in the "West Indian." The lady's former name was in the bill. On her return to Frith

Street, Kemble took his good wife home, and the next acting day, Monday, Lady Anne was acted by Mrs. Kemble to the Richard of Mr. Smith. On the 14th, man and wife played together, Sir Giles and his daughter Margaret; the delicate audience seizing on a marked passage in the play, and laughing as they applauded, to indicate they knew all about it. Sir Giles remained grave and self-possessed.

Subsequently, Kemble attained the management of Drury Lane, succeeding King, who had been merely the servant of the proprietors, in 1788–9. He could now play what parts he chose,—and his first character was Lord Townly; his second, Macbeth. In the first, he was only second to Barry; in Macbeth, from the weakness of his voice, he failed to rise to an equality with Garrick. Leon followed, with some state; Sciolto, in which he rendered the stern paternal principle sublime; Mirabel, in which he was to be altogether distanced by his brother, Charles; and Romeo, in which he never approached the height of Barry. On his first revival of "Henry VIII.," he left Bensley in possession of his old part, Wolsey, and for the sake, it is said, of giving a "duteous and intelligent observance" to his sister in the heavier scenes, doubled the parts of Cromwell and Griffith, in his own person. His great Wolsey triumph was a glory of a later time; so was the triumph of his Coriolanus, not yet matured; but in which he was not only never surpassed, but never equalled. His first season as manager was a decided success, as regards the acting of himself and sister, and also the novelties produced.

His second was marked by some revivals, such as "Henry V." and the "Tempest," and adaptations of the "False Friend" of Vanbrugh, and the "Rover" of Aphra Behn. In the first piece, in which Kemble played the King better than he did his other Kings, Richard and John, he made a fine point in starting up from prayer and expression of penitence, at the sound of the trumpet. In lighter pieces he was less successful. His Don John, the Libertine, was as far beyond his powers as were the songs of Cœur de Lion, in Burgoyne's pretty recasting of Sedaine. How he cared to attempt such a feat as the last is inexplicable,— but did not droll little Quick, George III.'s favorite actor, and almost personal friend, once play the Hunchback Richard? and did not Kemble play Charles Surface? and also take as a compliment Sheridan's assurance that he had "entirely *executed* his design?"

Nevertheless, fortune attended the Kemble management, although George III.'s especial patronage was bestowed on the rival house. It had its perils, and once brought him to a *duello* with James Aikin, a spirited actor, who had caused the destruction of the Edinburgh Theatre, through his refusal to beg pardon of the audience on his knees. His only offence was in having succeeded a favorite, but discharged actor, named Stayley. In this duel, fought in Marylebone Fields, with Jack Bannister as sole second to both combatants, Aikin's fire was not returned by his manager, and the adversaries were soon reconciled.

With a short interval, John Kemble was manager of Drury Lane till 1801. In the following year he went abroad, the affairs of Drury having fallen into confusion; and in 1803, having purchased a sixth share of Covent Garden, he succeeded Lewis in the management of that theatre, and remained there till his retirement in 1817, at the close of the season in which Mr. Macready made his first appearance in London, as Orestes; and Lucius Junius Booth, as Richard, flashed promise for a moment and straightway died out.

With Kemble's departure from Drury Lane closes the first part of his career. He had begun it with £5 per week, and ended it with a weekly salary strangely reckoned, of £56 14s. He had borne himself well throughout. He had a lofty scorn of anonymous assailants; was solemn enough in his manners not to give a guinea, for drink, to the theatrical guard, without stupendous phrases; but he could stoop to "knuckle down" at marbles with young players on the highway; and to utter jokes to them with a Cervantic sort of gravity.

He addressed noisy and unappreciative audiences with such neat satire that they thought he was apologizing, when he was really exposing their stupidity. I do not know if he were generous in criticism of his fellow-actors; he said of Cooke's Sir Pertinax, that comedy had nothing like it. This has been called "liberal;" but it looks to me satirical; and he certainly never praised Cooke's tragedy. The utmost, indeed, he ever said of

Kean was, that "the gentleman was terribly in earnest." On the other hand, his own worshippers nearly choked him with incense. Boaden may not have been far wrong when he said that Kemble was at the head of the Academics, but he certainly was so, in describing Cooke as merely at the head of the vulgar; and he approached blasphemy when he tells us that Kemble's features and figure as the Monk in "Aurelio and Miranda" reminded him, and could only be compared with, those of ONE, to name WHOM would be irreverent!

Kemble's secret of success lay in his indefatigable assiduity. In studying the part of the Stranger he neglected, for weeks, that for which he was particularly distinguished,—neatness of costume. Whatever the part he had to play, he acted it as if it were the most important in the piece; and, like Betterton, Booth, Quin, Barry, and Garrick, he made his impersonation of the Ghost as distinct a piece of art as Hamlet, when that character fell to him, in its turn. Even in Earl Percy, in the "Castle Spectre," an inferior character, he took such pains as nearly to break his neck, and in the scene of the attempted escape, fell back, from the high window to which he had climbed, to the sofa below, from which he had painfully ascended, with the agility and precision of a harlequin.

Rolla would have seemed to me unworthy of him, but that I remember Pitt, on seeing him in that character, said, "There is the noblest actor I ever beheld!" Sheridan had almost despaired of Kemble's success in Rolla; but Kemble felt that everything was in his favor, and gave all his own admiration to his sister, who, in Elvira, rendered so picturesque "a soldier's trull."

I have heard eye-witnesses describe his Octavian, not as a heart-rending, but a heart-dissolving display, the feelings of the spectators being all expressed by tears; and yet he could win a laugh from the same spectators in Young Marlow, and shake their very hearts again in that mournful Penruddock, his finest effort in comedy; but in comedy full of tragic echoes. Next to Penruddock, Boaden classes his Manly, for perfection; I have heard that parts of his Lord Townly surpassed them both. There the dignity and gravity were of a quality quite natural to him.

In Henry V. he was so much the King that an Earl, Guilford,

wrote an essay, by way of eulogy on it; and his Hotspur had but one fault, that of being incorrectly dressed. In Roman parts, and in the Roman costume, he seemed native and to the manner born. His Coriolanus and Hamlet are the characters the most associated with his name. Nevertheless, I do not discern any great respect, on Kemble's part, for Shakspeare, in his revival of Coriolanus or of any other of the plays of the national poet. The revival of Coriolanus was a mixture of Thomson and Shakspeare's tragedies, with five of the best scenes in the latter omitted, and what was judicious in the former, marred. I cannot help thinking that Kemble had only that sort of regard for Shakspeare which people have for the picturesque, who tear away ivy from a church-tower in order to white-wash its walls.

Then, again, in that matter of Ireland's forgery of "Vortigern," as Shakspeare's, it is not clear what opinion Kemble held of it previous to the night of its performance. Mrs. Siddons declined to play Edmunda; but Kemble's consenting, or rather resolving, to play the principal character in the tragedy, would seem to indicate that, at the best, he had no opinion, and was willing to leave the verdict to be pronounced by the public. I take from a communication to *Notes and Queries*, by an eye-witness, an account of what took place on the eventful night when an alleged new piece, by William Shakspeare, was presented to the judgment of a public tribunal:

"The representation of Ireland's tragedy took place on Saturday, April 2, 1796. Being one of those who were fortunate in gaining admittance and a seat on the second row in the pit, I am anxious, while my life is spared, to state what I saw and heard on this memorable occasion. The crowd and the rush for admittance were almost unprecedented. I do not think that twenty females were in the pit, such was the eagerness of gentlemen to gain admittance. Mr. Ireland's father, I remember, sat in the front box on the lower tier, with some friends around him. His son was behind the scenes. There was little or no disapprobation apparently shown by the audience until the commencement of the fifth act, when Mr. Kemble, it was probable, thought the deception had gone on long enough. Such, I think, was Ireland's own opinion; for in his *Confessions*, published in 1805, I find the following account of the disaproval of the audience, given by himself.

"'The conduct of Mr. Kemble was too obvious to the whole audience to need much comment. I must, however, remark, that the particular line on which Mr. Kemble laid such a peculiar stress was, in my humble opinion, the *watchword* agreed upon by the Malone faction for the general howl. The speech alluded to ran as follows; the line in italics being that so particularly noticed by Mr. Kemble :—

"'Time was, alas! I needed not this spur.
But here's a secret and a stinging thorn,
That wounds my troubled nerves. O Conscience! Conscience!
When thou didst cry, I strove to stop my mouth,
By boldly thrusting on thee dire Ambition:
Then did I think myself, indeed, a god!
But I was sore deceived; for as I passed,
And traversed in proud triumph the Basse-court,
There I saw death, clad in most hideous colors:
A sight it was, that did appal my soul;
Yea, curdled thick this mass of blood within me.
Full fifty breathless bodies struck my sight;
And some, with gaping mouths, did seem to mock me;
While others, smiling in cold death itself,
Scoffingly bade me look on that, which soon
Would wrench from off my brow this sacred crown,
And make me, too, a subject like themselves:
Subject! to whom? To thee, O Sovereign Death!
Who hast for thy domain this world immense:
Churchyards and charnel-houses are thy haunts,
And hospitals thy sumptuous palaces;
And, when thou wouldst be merry, thou dost choose
The gaudy chamber of a dying king.
O! then thou dost ope wide thy bony jaws,
And, with rude laughter and fantastic tricks,
Thou clapp'st thy rattling fingers to thy sides:
*And when this solemn mockery is o'er,*
With icy hand thou tak'st him by the feet,
And upward so; till thou dost reach the heart,
And wrap him in the cloak of 'lasting night.'

"No sooner was the above line uttered in the most sepulchral tone of voice possible, and accompanied with that peculiar emphasis which, on a subsequent occasion, so justly rendered Mr. Kemble the object of criticism (viz, on the first representation of

Mr. Colman's 'Iron Chest'), than the most discordant howl echoed from the pit that ever assailed the organs of hearing. After the lapse of ten minutes the clamor subsided, when Mr. Kemble, having again obtained a hearing, instead of proceeding with the speech at the ensuing line, very politely, and in order to amuse the audience still more, redelivered the very line above quoted with even more solemn grimace than he had in the first instance displayed."

During John Kemble's fourteen years' connection with Covent Garden, he created no new character that added to his fame, except, perhaps, Reuben Glenroy, in Morton's " Town and Country." His other original parts were in poor pieces, more or less forgotten. In old characters which he assumed for the first time during his proprietorship in Covent Garden, the most successful was Gloucester, in " Jane Shore," to which he gave a force and prominency which it had never previously received. His Prospero was a marvel of dignity and beautiful elocution, and his Brutus perfect in conception and execution. Of other parts his Pierre was good, but his Iago was below the level of more than one fellow-actor; his Eustace de St. Pierre was, perhaps, as fine as Bensley's, but his Valentine, in the " Two Gentlemen of Verona," could have been better played, even then, by his brother Charles.

In judgment, he sometimes erred as Garrick did. He peremptorily rejected Tobin's " Honeymoon," which, with Elliston as the Duke Aranza and Miss Duncan as Juliana, became one of the most popular comedies of the day. He acknowledged his mistake; and he was as ready to acknowledge the sources of some of his best inspirations. His Wolsey, for instance, was one of his finest parts, but he confessed that his idea of the Cardinal was taken from West Digges. He was sensitive enough as to public criticism, and when about to try Charles Surface, he wrote to Topham, " I hope you will have the goodness to *give orders to your people* to speak favorably of the Charles, as more depends on that than you can possibly be aware of." The act was facetiously characterized as " Charles's Martyrdom," rather than " Charles's Restoration," and Kemble himself used to tell a story how, when offering to make reparation to a gentleman, for some offence, committed " after dinner," the gentleman answered that a promise on Mr. Kemble's part never to play Charles Surface again, would be considered ample satisfaction. Wine is said to have always made Kemble dull, but not offensive. Naturally dull he was not, though he was styled so by people who would have called Torrismond dull, because he said, " Nor can I think; or I am lost in thought!" Kemble was lively enough to make a good repartee, when occasion offered. He was once rehearsing the song in " Cœur de Lion,"— which he used to sing to the blaring accompaniment of French horns, that his voice might be the less audible,—when Shaw, the leader, exclaimed, " Mr. Kemble, Mr. Kemble, you really murder the time!" " Mr. Shaw," rejoined the actor, taking coolly a pinch of snuff, " it is better to murder Time than to be always beating him, as you are."

He bore misfortune manfully. When Covent Garden, Rich's old house, with the royal arms in the centre of the curtain, which had hung on the old curtain at Lincoln's Inn Fields, was burnt down after the performance of " Pizarro," on the night of the 19th of September, 1808, he was " not *much* moved," though, in the fire, perished a large amount of valuable property. Mrs. Kemble mourned over the supposed fact that they had to begin life again, but Kemble, after long silence, burst into a rhapsody over the ancient edifice, and straightway addressed himself to the rearing of that new building, which has since gone the way of most theatres. In the completion of that second playhouse on this spot, he was nobly aided by his patron, the Duke of Northumberland, who lent him £10,000, and at the dinner by which the opening was celebrated, sent the actor his bond, that he might, as a crowning effect, commit it to the flames. It was a princely act, and he who was thought worthy of being the object of it, must have been emphatically a gentleman.

In earlier days, Kemble was accustomed to be with the first of gentlemen. One of the finest of the few left makes some record of him. Walpole notices Kemble twice; and we find that he held him superior to Garrick in Benedick, and to Quin in Maskwell. In September, 1789, Walpole writes from Strawberry Hill to the Miss Berrys : " Kemble, and Lysons the clergyman, passed all Wednesday, here, with me. The former is melting the three parts of 'Henry VI.' into one piece. I doubt it will be difficult to make a tolerable play out of them." The only other notice is dated April, 1791; when the writer says to Miss Berry : " *A propos* to Catherine and Petruchio, I supped with their representatives, Kemble and Mrs. Siddons, t'other night, at Miss Farren's . . . ." at the bow-window house in Green Street, Grosvenor Square. " Mrs. Siddons is leaner, but looks well. She has played Jane Shore and Desdemona, and is to play in the ' Gamester,' all the parts she will act this year. Kemble, they say, shone in Othello."

Othello was one of Kemble's effective, yet not his most successful character; but his figure was well formed for it. He bore drapery with infinite grace, and expressed every feeling well, by voice, feature, and glance of the eye—though in the first, as with his brother Charles, lay his chief defect. It wanted strength. We are accustomed, perhaps, to associate him most with Hamlet, and old playgoers have told me of a grand delivery of the soliloquies; a mingled romance and philosophy in the whole character; an eloquent by-play, a sweet reverence for his father, a remembrance of the *prince*, with whatever companion he might be for the moment, of a beautiful filial affection for his mother, and of one more tender which he could *not* conceal, for Ophelia. When Kemble first appeared in Hamlet, the town could not say that Henderson was excelled, but many confessed that he was equalled. That confession stirred no ill-blood between them. " I never had an opportunity," said Kemble, later, " to study any actor better than myself, except Mr. Henderson."

Of the grandeur and sublimity of the passion-tossed Orestes he gave so complete a picture, that it was said—by that single character alone he might have reaped immortal fame.

On the other hand, his Biron was only a respectable performance; his Macbeth on a level with his Othello; his Richard and Sir Giles very inferior to Cooke's, still more so to those of Edmund Kean; and in comedy, generally, he was a very poor actor indeed, except in parts where he had to exercise dignity, express pathos, or pronounce a sentiment of moral tendency.

" Whene'er he tries the airy or the gay,
   Judgment, not genius, marks the cold essay."

The judgment was not always sensibly exercised, for Kemble was undoubtedly

"For meaning too precise inclined to pore,
And labor for a point unknown before."

I think, in the old Roman habit he was most at his ease; there, art, I am told, seemed less, nature more. In this respect he was exactly the reverse of Garrick, who could no more have competed with him in delineating the noble aim of the stern Coriolanus, than Kemble could have striven successfully against Garrick's Richard, or Abel Drugger.

And yet all the characters originally played by him, and successfully established on the stage, are of a romantic and not a classical cast. The prating patriot Rolla, the stricken, murmuring, lost Octavian, by which he sprung as many fountains of tears as his sister in the most heart-rending of her tragic parts; his chivalrous Cœur de Lion, his unapproachable Penruddock, his Percy ("Castle Spectre"), his Stranger, his De l'Epée, his Reuben Glenroy (the colloquial dialogue of which character, however, was always a burden to him), and his De Montfort, are all romantic parts, to many of which he has given permanent life; while more classical parts for which he seemed more fitted, and in plays of equal merit at least, such as Cleombrotus ("Fate of Sparta"), Huniades (which, certainly, is not *romantic*),—his Pirithous, and his Sextus ("Conspiracy"), are all forgotten. That his sympathies were classical, may in some sort be accepted from the fact, that he began his public life in 1776 (the year of Garrick's farewell), at Wolverhampton, with Theodosius, and closed it, at Covent Garden, in 1817, with Coriolanus. That Kemble's own departure from the stage did not, as was once expected, prove its destruction, is to be gathered from the circumstance that while his farewell performances were in progress, Sheil's tragedy of the "Apostate" was produced at the same theatre, with a cast including the names of Young, Macready, C. Kemble, and Miss O'Neill!—and Kean was then filling Drury Lane with his Richard, Shylock, and Sir Giles.

Kemble's nearest approach to a *fiasco* was on his playing Sir

Edward Mortimer. The "Iron Chest" had been ill rehearsed, and Kemble himself was in such a suffering condition on the first night that he was taking opium pills as the curtain was rising. The piece failed, till Elliston essayed the principal part; and, on its failure, Colman published the most insulting of prefaces to the play, in which he remarked that "Frogs in a marsh, flies in a bottle, wind in a crevice, a preacher in a field, the drone of a bagpipe, all—all yielded to the inimitable and soporific monotony of Mr. Kemble!"

In one class of character Kemble was pre-eminent. He was "the noblest Roman of them all." His name is closely associated with Coriolanus, and next with Cato. He was not a "general" actor, like some of his predecessors, yet he excelled in parts which Garrick declined to touch. A contemporary says of him, "He is not a Garrick in Richard, a Macklin in Shylock, a Barry in Othello, or a Mossop in Zanga," and adds, that "there is more *art* than *nature* in his performance; but let it be observed that our best actors have always found *stage trick* a necessary practice, and Mr. Kemble's *methodical* powers are so peculiar to himself, that every imitator (for there have been some who have endeavored to copy his manners) has been ridiculous in the attempt." Nevertheless, there was a Kemble school, the last of whose members is Mr. Cooper, who made his first appearance in London, at the Haymarket, in 1811, and has not yet, after more than half a century of service, formally retired from the stage. Not the least merit of actors formed on the Kemble model, was distinct enunciation; and this alone, in our large theatres, was a great boon to a listening audience.

As a dramatic author, Kemble has achieved no great reputation; he was, for the most part, only an adapter or a translator, but in both he manifested taste and ability, save when he tampered with Shakspeare. His solemn farewell, on the 23d of June, 1817, in Coriolanus, was made not too soon; his great powers had begun, after more than forty years' assiduous service, to fail, and he becomingly wished, "like the great Roman i' the Capitol," that he might adjust his mantle ere he fell. The memory of that night lives in the heart of many a survivor, and it lived in that of its hero till he calmly died, after less than six years of retirement, at

Lausanne, in February, 1823. The old student of Douay never formally withdrew from the Church, of which his father once destined him to be a priest, but he remained a true Catholic Christian, with a Protestant pastor for friend and counsellor, who was at his side, with a nearer and dearer friend, when the supreme moment was at hand. Such was the man. As an actor, he lacked the versatility and perfection of Garrick and Barry; and, says Leigh Hunt, "injured what he made you feel, by the want of feeling himself."

Of John Kemble's brothers, Stephen and Charles, the former was the less celebrated, but he was not without merit. The fame of his sister induced him to leave a chemist's, or an apothecary's counter for the stage, as, later in life, the reputation of the eldest brother tempted Charles Kemble to abandon an appointment in the Post-Office, in order to try his fortune as a player. In these respective trials, Stephen was less fortunate than Charles. Born in 1758, on the night his mother played Anne Boleyn, he was by seventeen years the elder of the latter. His theatrical life commenced in Dublin, after an itinerant training; but there John extinguished Stephen; and when, in 1783, he appeared at Covent Garden, as Othello, to the Desdemona of Miss Satchell, afterwards his wife, whatever impression he may have made, Stephen was speedily swept from public favor by the greater merit of John. After subsequently playing old men, at the Haymarket, Stephen opened a house in Edinburgh, against Mrs. Esten at the established theatre. The opposition led to, in some sense, a dignified strife. The Duke of Hamilton loved Mrs. Esten, and the Duke of Northumberland was a friend to the Kembles. In the law proceedings which followed, each Duke gave material support to his favorite, and here was the old feud of Douglas and Percy again raging in the north!

Ultimately Stephen left Edinburgh with no great amount of luck to boast of, and, after a wandering life, appeared, in 1803, at Drury Lane, as Falstaff, after the delivery by Bannister of a heavy set of jocular verses, making allusion to his obesity, which enabled him to act Falstaff without stuffing! He did not act it ill; but Henderson had not yet faded from the memory of play-goers, and Stephen Kemble could not attain higher rank than a place among the best of the second class of actors. Again he disappeared from the metropolis, but returned, and played a few of the parts to which he was suited, rather by his size than his merits; and in 1818, at Drury Lane, where he assumed the office of manager, opened the season by introducing his son Henry, from Bath, as Romeo. In 1819 he played Orozembo; and "therewith an end." The theatre was then let to Elliston; Henry Kemble sank from Drury to the Coburg, and Stephen withdrawing to a private life, not altogether ill provided, died in 1822.

In that last year his younger brother Charles had attained,—had perhaps rather passed,—the zenith of a reputation of which his early attempts gave no promise whatever. Hard work alone made a player of him. He could not have been a post-office clerk long after he left the Roman Catholic College at Douay, for he was but seventeen when he first acted, at Sheffield, in 1792,—Orlando, in "As You Like It." He began with Shakspeare, and he ended with him; his farewell being in Benedick, at Covent Garden, in 1836. On both occasions he played the part of a lover, and at the end of forty years he probably played it with more grace, tenderness, ardor, and spirit, than when he began.

There was much judgment in selecting Malcolm for his first appearance in London on the 21st of April, 1794, on the opening of New Drury Lane Theatre, the house built by Holland, and burnt in 1809,—to the Macbeth and Lady Macbeth of John Kemble and Mrs. Siddons. He had little in his favor but good intentions. He was awkward in action, weak in voice, and ungraceful in deportment. All these defects he corrected, except the weakness of voice, which he never got over. It did not arise from the asthmatic cough which so often distressed his brother, but from simple debility of the organ, and this weakness always marred parts in which he was called upon for the expression of energetic passion.

Gradually, Charles Kemble became one of the most graceful and refined of actors. He was enabled to seize on a domain of comedy which his brother and sister could never enter with safety to their fame. In his hands, secondary parts soon assumed a more than ordinary importance from the finish with which he acted them. His Laertes was as carefully played as Hamlet, and there was no other Cassio but his while he lived, nor any Falconbridge, then or since, that could compare with his; and in Macduff, Charles Kemble had no rival. Rae's Edgar was considered one of that gentleman's most effective parts, but Charles Kemble may be said to have superseded him in it. In the tender or witty lover, the heroic soldier, and the rake, who is nevertheless a gentleman, he was the most distinguished player of his time. Of all the characters he originated, that of Guido, in Barry Cornwall's "Mirandola," was, perhaps, his most successful essay; it was certainly among the most popular of his performances during the run of that play. I find his Jaffier, indeed, praised as being superior to that of any contemporary; but whatever be the character he represented, I also find critics occasionally complaining of a certain languor, and now and then a partial loss of voice, after it had been much exercised, which interfered with the completeness of the representation. Sheridan always thought well of him, particularly after his performance of Alonzo, in "Pizarro;" the grateful author used to address him as "My Alonzo!"

Charles Kemble's Hamlet was as fine in conception but inferior in execution to his brother's. Such, at least, as I am credibly informed, was the judgment delivered by Mrs. Siddons. That it was finely conceived, yet weaker in every point than Young's, I can well remember. In tragic parts there was a certain measured, however musical enunciation, of which Charles Kemble never got rid, and in the play of the features, the actor, and not the man represented, was ever present. This was particularly the case in Hamlet, in which his assumed seriousness rendered his long face so much longer in appearance than ordinary, that in the rebuke to his mother his eyebrows seemed to go up into his hair, and his chin down into his waistcoat.

That his voice ill fitted him for passionate, tragic heroes they will recollect who can recall to mind his Pierre and that of Young! Charles Kemble looked the part to perfection, and dressed it with the taste of a gentleman and an artist. Nothing could be finer, more gallant, more easy and graceful, than his entry; but he had scarcely got through "How fares the honest partner of my heart?" than the *pipe* raised a smile; it was so unlike the full, round, hearty, resonant tone in which Young put the query, and indeed played the part.

Nor was Charles Kemble invariably successful in all the comic parts he assumed. His Falstaff I would willingly forget. It was a mistake. When Ward, as the Prince, exclaimed "Peace, chewet, peace!" the command seemed very well timed. But his Mercutio! In that he walked, spoke, looked, fought, and died like a gentleman. Some of his predecessors dressed and acted as if this kinsman to the Prince and friend to Romeo had been a low-bred, yet humorous fellow, cousin to the lacqueys, Abraham and Peter; but Charles Kemble was as truly Shakspeare's Mercutio as ever Macklin was Shakspeare's Jew. In comedy of another degree; in Young Mirabel, for instance, in the "Inconstant," he was unequalled by any living actor. Indeed, his spirits here sometimes overcame his judgment; as in the last scene, when he is saved by the arrival of the "Red Burgundy," he leaped into the air like a man who is shot, and snapping his fingers, danced about the stage in a very ecstasy of delirium, too great, I thought, for a brave young fellow extricated from an awful scrape. But, whatever may be the worth of such thought, it is certain that in his Mirabel the delighted audience saw no fault; and who ever did in his Benedick?

Happy in his successes, he was thrice happy in his pretty and accomplished wife. Maria Theresa Decamp was one year his junior; and, like himself, was born in the purple. Miss De Camp's real name is said to have been De Fleury. She was a Viennese by birth. Her family belonged to the ballet and the orchestra, and she herself, at six years of age, was dancing Cupid in Noverre's ballets at the London Opera House; and, ultimately, was a leading, very young lady in those at the Circus, now the Royal Surrey. From the sawdust of the Transpontine Theatre she was transferred, on the recommendation of the Prince of Wales, it is said, to figure in similar pieces at Colman's house in the Haymarket.

She was reserved, however, for better things than this: but Miss De Camp was not to attain them without study; she had to learn English—to speak and to read it; music, and other accomplishments. By a genius all this may be speedily effected; and Miss De Camp, in the season of 1786-7, appeared at Drury Lane as Julia, in "Richard Cœur de Lion," her future brother-in-law playing the King. At this time she was scarcely in her teens; but she was full of such promise, that she bade adieu for ever to bal'et and the sawdust of the Royal Circus, and henceforth, and for upwards of thirty years, belonged to the regular drama. A score of years was to elapse before she was to change her name; but long previously she had made that first name distinguished in theatrical annals. She had exhibited unusual merit in singing and acting Macheath to the Polly of Charles Bannister, and the Lucy of Johnstone; and she created characters with which her name is closely associated in the memory of play-goers or play-readers. She was the original Floranthe in the "Mountaineers," Judith in the "Iron Chest," Irene in "Bluebeard," Maria in "Of Age to-Morrow," Theodore in "Deaf and Dumb," Lady Julia in "Personation," Annette in "Youth, Love, and Folly," Variella in the "Weathercock," and Morgiana in the "Forty Thieves."

And while the glory she derived from this last performance was still at its brightest, Miss De Camp in 1806 married Mr. Charles Kemble—some rather tempestuous wooing, for so tender and gallant a stage-lover—but for which he rendered public apology, not impeding the match. In the year of her marriage Mrs. C. Kemble joined the Covent Garden Company, and on making her appearance as Maria in the "Citizen," she was congratulated, on the part of the audience, by three distinct rounds of applause. Between this period, and 1819, when she withdrew from the stage, she created two parts in which she has had no successor, Edmund in the "Blind Boy," and Lady Elizabeth Freelove in "A Day after the Wedding;" and, in the last year of her acting, Madge Wildfire in the "Heart of Mid Lothian."

Ten years later, Mrs. Charles Kemble returned to the stage, (October 5, 1829), to do for her daughter what Mrs. Pritchard, on a like occasion, had done for hers—namely, as Lady Capulet, introduce the young *débutante* as Juliet. This one service rendered, Mrs. Charles Kemble finally withdrew.

She had a pleasant voice; charming, but not powerful in her early days, as a vocalist. In sprightly parts, in genteel comedy, in all chambermaids, in melo-dramatic characters, especially where pantomimic action was needed, she was excellent. Genest, who must have known her well, remarks, that "no person understood the business of the stage better; no person had more industry; at one time she nearly lived in Drury Lane Theatre. The reason of her not being engaged after 1819, is said to have been that she wanted to play the young parts, for which her time of life, and her figure (for she had grown fat), had disqualified her; whereas had she been contented to have played Mrs. Oakley, Mrs. Candor, Flippante, and many other characters of importance, which were not unsuitable to her personal apearance, it would have been greatly to her own advantage, and the satisfaction of the public."

Charles remained on the stage till December, 1863, but he returned for a few nights, a year or two later, when he went through a series of his most celebrated parts, for the especial gratification of the Duchess of Kent and the Princess Victoria, and for the gratification of the public generally. Occasionally he reappeared as a "Reader," in which vocation, his refined taste, his judgment, and his graceful, though not powerful elocution, were manifest to the last.

Mr. and Mrs. Charles Kemble added something to our dramatic literature; the lady's contribution to which, "A Day after the Wedding," still affords entertainment whenever it is performed. Her other piece, "First Faults," is now forgotten. Charles Kemble's additions to the literature of the stage, comprise the "Point of Honor," "Plot and Counterplot," and the "Wanderer;" the first two being translations from the French, and the third from the German.

In his later days Charles Kemble was afflicted with deafness, so complete that he could not hear the pealing thunder, but could fancy it was in the air; for, as he once remarked amid the crash, "I feel it in my knees!" It was, perhaps, this affliction which occasionally gave him that look of fixed melancholy which he occasionally wore. Of anecdotes of his later time, there are few known to me of any interest, except the following, which I cull from the *Athenæum*. It is in reference to his son, Mr. J. M. Kemble's Lectures at Cambridge, *On the History of the English Language*, which were unsuccessful. "After making a good deal to do about them," says the correspondent of the *Athenæum*, "he obtained the use of the Divinity School to lecture in, and it was pretty well crowded at the first lecture; but the lecture itself was such a sickener, and so unintelligible, that at the second, myself, and I think two others, formed the whole audience. The appearance was so absurdly ridiculous in the large room that Kemble gave notice, in announcing the day of his third lecture, that in future he should deliver them at his own private apartments. Meanwhile his father, Charles Kemble, the actor, came to see him, and on the day fixed for the third lecture, nobody was there to hear him but his said father and I; upon which, when we had waited in vain nearly an hour for an increase of audience, I moved, and his father seconded the proposal, that instead of inflicting the lecture upon us two, the lecturer should send in to Trinity College buttery, as it was then the hour it was open, and procure a quantity of ale and cheese, for the excellence of both which Trinity College was celebrated, and with the aid of these we passed the afternoon. Such was the end of Kemble's lectures."

Rogers has left in his *Table-Talk* some record of the Kembles, which, as coming from an eye and ear witness, may find admission here. From this we learn that Mrs. Siddons, to whom he had been telling an anecdote showing that, when Lawrence gained a medal at the Society of Arts, his brothers and sisters were jealous of him—remarked: "Alas! after *I* became celebrated, none of my sisters loved me as they did before!" And then, when a grand public dinner was given to John Kemble on his quitting the stage, the great actress said to the poet, "Well, perhaps in the next world women will be more valued than they are in this." "She alluded," says Rogers, "to the comparatively little sensation which had been produced by her own retirement from the boards; and doubtless she was a far, far greater performer than John Kemble."

When young, she had superseded Mrs. Crawford (Barry), then in her old age, and she rejoiced in being rid of so able a rival; but when other competitors crossed her own path, Mrs. Siddons rather unfairly remarked that the public were fond of setting up new idols, in order to mortify their old favorites. She had herself, she said, been three times threatened with eclipse: first, by means of Miss Brunton (afterwards Lady Craven); next, by means of Miss Smith (Mrs. Bartley); and lastly, by means of Miss O'Neill— "nevertheless," she is reported to have said, "I am not yet extinguished." She then stood, however, with regard to Miss O'Neill, exactly as Mrs. Crawford (Barry) had stood with respect to herself—the younger actress carried away the hearts, the older lived respected in the memories of the audience. But over audiences, Mrs. Siddons had, in her day, deservedly reigned supreme; and that should have been enough of greatness achieved by one whom Combes remembered to have seen, "when a very young woman, standing by the side of her father's stage, and knocking a pair of snuffers against a candlestick, to imitate the sound of a windmill, during the representation of some harlequinade."

When she had departed from the scene of her glory, the remembrance of that glory did not suffice her. When Rogers was sitting with her, of an afternoon, she would say, "Oh! dear! this is the time I used to be thinking of going to the theatre; first came the pleasure of dressing for my part; and then the pleasure of acting it; but that is all over now." This was not vanity, but the natural wail of an active spirit forced to be at rest. There was less dignity in the retirement of John Kemble, if what Rogers tells us be true, that "when Kemble was living at Lausanne, he was jealous of Mont Blanc; and he disliked to hear people always asking, 'How does Mont Blanc look this morning?'"

The two greatest rivalries that John Kemble had to endure before the final one, in which Kean triumphed, emanated from two very different persons—George Frederick Cooke and Master Betty. The success of both, marks periods in stage history, and demands brief notice here.

## CHAPTER XX.

### GEORGE FREDERICK COOKE.

ABOUT the time when Garrick was reluctantly bidding farewell to his home on the stage, at Drury Lane—a hopeful youth, of twenty years of age,—born no one can well tell where, but, it is said, in a barrack,—of an English sergeant and a Scottish mother, was making his first grasp at the dramatic laurel, in the little town of Brentford.

With the exception of a passing appearance at the Haymarket, for a benefit, in 1778, as Castalio,—when London was recognizing in Henderson, the true successor of Garrick, the town knew nothing of this ambitious youth for more than twenty years;—then he came to Covent Garden to dethrone John Kemble; and he disquieted that actor for a while. In ten years more, his English race was done; and while Kemble was beginning the splendid evening of his career, Cooke passed over to America, prematurely ending his course, in disgrace and ruin, and occupying a grave which a civilized Yankee speedily dishonored.

If Cooke was an Irishman, it was by accident. He was certainly educated in England; and he early acquired, by reading Otway and seeing Vanbrugh, a taste for the drama. In school theatricals, he made his Horatio outshine the Hamlet of the night; and his Lucia,—though the boy cried at having to play a part in petticoats,—won more applause than his schoolfellow's Cato. Schooltime over, the wayward boy went to sea, and came back with small liking for the vocation; turned to "business," only to turn from it in disgust; inherited some property, and swiftly spent it; and then we find him in that inn-yard at Brentford, enrolled among strollers, and playing Dumont in "Jane Shore," to the great delight of the upper servants from Kew, Gunnersbury, and parts adjacent, sent thither to represent their masters, who had not the "particular desire" to see the play, for which the bills gave them credit.

The murmur of London approval, awarded to his Castalio, was the delicious magic which drew him forever within the charmed circle of the actors, and George Frederick passed through all the heavy trials through which most of the vocation have to pass. He strolled through villages, thence to provincial towns, and I think when, in 1786, he played Baldwin to the Isabella of Mrs. Siddons, that lady must have been compelled, perhaps was willing, to confess, that there was a dramatic genius who, at least, approached the excellence of her brother.

From York, after much more probation, Cooke went over to Dublin, where he acted well, drank hard, and lost himself, in one of his wild fits, by enlisting. Fancy the proud and maddened George Frederick doing barrack scullery-work, and worse!—he who had played the Moor in presence of a vice-regal court! If his friends had not purchased his discharge, Miss Campion would certainly soon have heard that her Othello had hanged himself. The genius who would not be a soldier, though born in a barrack, found an asylum in the Manchester theatre; and subsequently Dublin welcomed him back to its well-trod stage. There, he and John Kemble met for the first time.

John took the lead, George Frederick played,—I can hardly call them secondary parts, for Booth had acted some of them to Betterton, Garrick to Sheridan, and one great performer to another,—such parts, in fact, as Ghost to Kemble's Hamlet, Henry to his Richard, Edmund to his Lear, and a similar disposition of characters. What Kemble then thought of his acting, I cannot say, but he complained of being disturbed by Mr. Cooke's tipsily defective memory. George Frederick was stirred to anger and prophecy. "I won't have your faults fathered upon me," he cried, "and hark ye, Black Jack,—hang me if I don't make you tremble in your pumps one day yet."

He kept his word. On the 31st of October, 1801, he acted Richard, at Covent Garden, to the Henry of Murray, the Richmond of Pope, the Queen of Miss Chapman, and the Lady Anne of Mrs. Litchfield;—and Kemble was present to see how Cooke would realize his promise. Kemble had played Richard himself that season at Drury Lane, to the Richmond of his brother Charles,—Henry, Wroughton; Queen, Mrs. Powell; Lady Anne, Miss Biggs. I fancy he was satisfied that in the new and well-trained actor there was a dangerous rival. Kemble acted Shylock and one or two other characters against him. They stood opposed in some degree as Quin and Garrick were, at Covent Garden and Drury Lane, in 1742-3. In that season, Garrick played Richard eleven times. In Cooke's first season at the Garden, he acted the same part double the number of times. Shylock, Iago, and Kitely, he acted each ten times. Macbeth, seven; Sir Giles Overreach, five; the Stranger, twice; and Sir Archy Macsarcasm, several times.

Of his first reception in Richard, Cooke speaks,—as being flattering, encouraging, indulgent, and warm, throughout the play and at the conclusion. Cooke was not blinded by this triumphant season. Long after he said, when referring to having played with and also against John Kemble: "He is an *actor*. He is my superior, though they did not think so in London. I acknowledge it!" Having made Black Jack "tremble in his pumps," Cooke honestly acknowledged, in homely phrase, that he could not stand in Kemble's shoes.

Kemble, however, was not superior to Cooke in all his range of characters. In the very first season of their opposition, after an obstinate struggle, Kemble gave up Richard; but in Macbeth, he remained unapproachable by Cooke, who, in his turn, set all competition at defiance, in his Iago, in which, says Dunlap, " the quickness of his action, and the strong natural expression of feeling, which were so peculiarly his own, identified him with the character." In Kitely, his remembrance of Garrick confessedly served him well. In Sir Giles, he excelled Kemble; but the Stranger was speedily given up by Cooke, and it remained one of his rival's glories to the last.

Cooke's general success, the position he had attained, and the prospect before him, steadied his mind, strengthened his good purposes, made him master of himself under a healthy stimulus, careful of his reputation, and strict in performing his duties. I record this, as his previous biographers have registered the character. Consequently, on the night he was announced to appear, to open his second season of anticipated triumph,—September 14th, 1801, —as Richard, a crowded audience had collected about the doors, to welcome him, as early as four o'clock. At that hour no one could tell where he was, and a bill was issued, stating that it was apprehended some accident had happened to Mr. Cooke; and the play was changed to "Lovers' Vows." In five weeks, the truant turned up, played magnificently, and was forgiven.

During his truant time, young Henry Siddons made his first appearance at Covent Garden. He played Herman in a dull new comedy, "Integrity," and Hamlet; but the charter-house student would have done better if he had accepted the vocation to which his mother would have called him,—the Church. Henry Siddons acted Alonzo to Cooke's Zanga, Hotspur to Cooke's Falstaff, and Ford to the other's Sir John, in the "Merry Wives." Cooke's criticism on his own performance was, that having acted all the Falstaffs, he had never been able to please himself, or to come up to his own ideas in any of them. His great failure was Hamlet, in which even young Siddons excelled him, but a triumph which compensated for any such failures, and for numerous offences given to the audience,—made victims of his "sudden indispositions,"— was found in Sir Pertinax, in which, even by those who remembered Macklin, he was held to have fully equalled the great and venerable original.

In the season of 1802, Cooke's indispositions became more frequently sudden, and lasted longer. On the days of his acting nights, his manager was accustomed to entertain him, supervise his supply of liquor, and carry him to the theatre; but George Frederick often escaped, and could not be traced. In many old characters, he sustained his high reputation, but his Hamlet and Cato only added to that of Kemble. Perhaps, his Peregrine, in "John Bull," of which he was the original representative, would have been a more finished performance but for—not the actor, but the author's indiscretion. "We got 'John Bull' from Colman," said Cooke to Dunlap, "act by act, as he wanted money, but the last act did not come, and Harris refused to make any further advances. At last, necessity drove Colman to make a finish, and he wrote the fifth act, in one night, on separate pieces of paper. As he filled one piece after the other, he threw them on the floor,

Vol. II.—13

and, finishing his liquor, went to bed. Harris, who impatiently expected the dénoûment of the play, according to promise, sent Fawcett to Colman, who found him in bed. By his direction, Fawcett picked up the scraps, and brought them to the theatre."

In the season of 1803–4, when Kemble became part proprietor and acting manager at Covent Garden, he played in several pieces with Cooke. They were thus brought into direct contrast. Kemble acted Richmond to Cooke's Richard; Old Norval to his Glenalvon; Rolla to his Pizarro; Beverley to his Stukely: Horatio to his Sciolto,—Charles Kemble playing Lothario, and Mrs. Siddons Calista,—such a cast as the "Fair Penitent" had not had for many years! John Kemble further played Jaffier to Cooke's Pierre; Antonio to his Shylock; the Duke, in "Measure for Measure," to his Angelo; Macbeth, with George Frederick for Macduff; Henry IV. to Cooke's Falstaff; Othello to his Iago; King John, with Cooke as Hubert, and Charles Kemble as Falconbridge; Mrs. Siddons being, of course, the Constance; Kemble also played Ford to Cooke's Falstaff, and Hamlet to Cooke's Ghost; and, in a subsequent season, Posthumus to his Iachimo, with some other parts, which must have recalled the old excitement of the times of Garrick and Quin, but that audiences were going mad about Master Betty, to the Rolla of which little and, no doubt, clever gentleman, George Frederick, needy and careless, was compelled to play Pizarro!

For a few seasons more he kept his ground with difficulty. He did not play many parts well, it has been said, but those he did play well, he played better than anybody else. But dissipation marred his vast powers even in these; and recklessness reduced this genius to penury. After receiving £400 in bank-notes, the proceeds of a benefit at Manchester, in one of his summer tours, he thrust the whole into the fire, in order to put himself on a level to fight a man, in a pothouse row, who had said that Cooke provoked him to battle, only because he was a rich man and the other poor!

It is not surprising that prison locks kept such a man from his duties in the playhouse; but the public always welcomed the prodigal on his return. When he reappeared at Covent Garden, as Sir Pertinax, in March, 1808, after a long confinement, it was to "the greatest money-house, one excepted, ever known at that theatre. Never was a performer received in a more flattering or gratifying manner."

But he slipped back into bad habits, was often forgetful of his parts, and was sometimes speechless; yet he was generally able to keep up the Scottish dialect, if he could speak at all, and his part required it. Once, when playing Sir Archy Macsarcasm, he forgot his name, called himself *Sir Pertinax Macsycophant*, and was corrected by a purist in the gallery. Cooke looked up, and happily enough remarked, "*Eets aw ane blude!*"

He was hardly less happy, when, for some offence given by him, on the stage, at Liverpool, he was called on to offer an apology to the audience. Liverpool merchants had much fattened, then, by a fortunate pushing of the trade in human flesh. "Apology! from George Frederick Cooke!" he cried; "take it from this remark: There's not a brick in your infernal town which is not cemented by the blood of a slave!"

The American Cooper found him in the lowest of the slums of Liverpool, and tempted, or kidnapped, him to America, from whence this compound of genius and blackguard never returned. On one of his early appearances, in New York, he is said, being elated, to have refused to act till the orchestra had played "God save the King;" and then he insisted, with tipsy gravity, that the audience should be "upstanding." In seventeen nights following the 21st of November, 1810, when he first appeared in New York, as Richard, the treasury was the richer by twenty-five thousand five hundred and seventy-eight dollars. He felt, and expressed, however, such a contempt for the Yankee character, that New York soon deserted him, and Philadelphia paid him little or no homage. Once, he was informed, that Mr. Madison was coming from Washington, expressly to see him in a favorite character.

"Then, if he does, I'll be——if I play before him. What, I, George Frederick Cooke, who have acted before the Majesty of Britain, play before your Yankee President! No! I'll go forward to the audience, and I'll say,

"LADIES AND GENTLEMEN: The King of the Yankee-doodles has come to see me act; *me*, George Frederick Cooke, who have stood before my royal master, George III., and received his imperial approbation . . . . . . . . it is degradation enough to go on before rebels; but I'll not go on for the amusement of a king of rebels, the contemptible King of the Yankee-doodles!"

From among the "Yankee-doodles" Cooke found, however, a lady with the old dramatic name of Behn, who became his second wife; but his condition was little improved thereby. Dr. Francis, in his *Old New York*, gives the following picture of him at this time:

"After one of those catastrophes to which I have alluded, I paid him a visit at early afternoon, the better to secure his attendance at the theatre. He was seated at his table, with many decanters, all exhausted, save two or three appropriated for candlesticks, the lights in full blaze. He had not rested for some thirty hours or more. With much ado, aided by Price the manager, he was persuaded to enter the carriage waiting at the door to take him to the playhouse. It was a stormy night. He repaired to the green-room, and was soon ready. Price saw he was the worse from excess, but the public were not to be disappointed. 'Let him,' says the manager, 'only get before the lights and the receipts are secure.' Within the wonted time Cooke entered on his part, the Duke of Gloster. The public were unanimous in their decision, that he never performed with greater satisfaction. As he left the house he whispered, 'Have I not pleased the Yankee-doodles?' Hardly twenty-four hours after this memorable night, he scattered some 400 dollars among the needy and the solicitous, and took refreshment in a sound sleep. A striking peculiarity often marked the conduct of Cooke: he was the most indifferent of mortals to the results which might be attendant on his folly and his recklessness. When his society was solicited by the highest in literature and the arts, he might determine to while away a limited leisure among the illiterate and the vulgar, and yet none was so fastidious in the demands of courtesy. When the painter Stuart was engaged with the delineation of his noble features, he chose to select those hours for sleeping; yet the great artist triumphed and satisfied his liberal patron, Price. Stuart proved a match for him, by occasionally raising the lid of his eye. On the night of his benefit, the most memorable of his career in New York, with a house crowded to suffocation, he abused public confidence, and had nothing to say but that Cato had full right to take liberty with his senate."

In this strange being, there are two phases of character that are beyond ordinary singularity. The first was his "mental intoxication," of which he thus speaks in one of his journals: "To use a strange expression, I am sometimes in a kind of mental intoxication; some, I believe, would call it insanity. I believe it is allied to it. I then can imagine myself in strange situations and strange places. This humor, whatever it is, comes uninvited, but it is nevertheless easily dispelled,—at least, generally so. When it *cannot* be dispelled, it must, of course, become madness." Here was a decided perception of the way he might be going,—from physical, through mental, intoxication, to the madhouse!

His common sense is another phase in the character of this great actor, who manifested so little for his own profit. He was the guardian of female morals against the perils of contempoary literature! "In my humble opinion," he says, "a licenser is as necessary for a circulating library, as for dramatic productions intended for representation; especially when it is considered how young people, particularly girls, often procure, and sometimes in a secret manner, books of so evil a tendency, that not only their time is most shamefully wasted, but their morals and manners tainted and warped for the remainder of their lives. I am firmly of opinion, that many females owe the loss of reputation to the pernicious publications too often found in those dangerous seminaries."

Cooke may be said to have been dying, from the day he landed in the, United States. His vigorous constitution only slowly gave way. It was difficult for him to destroy that; for in occasional rests he gave it, when he sat down to write on religion, philosophy, ideas for improving society, and diatribes against drinking, in his diary, his constitution recovered all its vigor, and started refreshed for a new struggle against drunkenness and death. The former, however, gave it a mortal fall, in July, 1812, when Death grasped his victim, forever. Cooke was taken ill, while playing Sir Giles Overreach, at Boston, on the 31st of the above month. He went home irrecoverably stricken, met his fate with decency, and calmly breathed his last in the following September, in full possession of his mental faculties to the supreme moment.

He was buried in the "strangers' vault" of St. Paul's Church, New York, with much respectful ceremony, on the part of friends who admired his genius, and mutilated his body, as I shall presently show. Meanwhile, let me record here, that Cooke was of the middle size, strongly and stoutly built, with a face capable of every expression, and an eye which was as grand an interpreter of the poets, as the tongue. He was free from gesticulation and all trickery, but he lacked the grace and refinement of less accomplished actors. In soliloquies, he recognized no audience; and his hearers seemed to detect his thoughts by some other process than listening to his words.

Kemble excelled Cooke in nobleness of presence, but Cooke surpassed the other in power and compass of voice, which was, sometimes, as harsh as Kemble's; and indeed I may say *the* Kemble voice was invariably feeble. In statuesque parts, and in picturesque characters,—in the Roman Coriolanus, and in Hamlet the Dane,—Kemble's scholarly and artistic feeling gave him the precedence; but in Iago, and especially in Richard, Cooke has been adjudged very superior in voice, expression, and style; "his manner being more quick, abrupt, and impetuous, and his attitudes better, as having less the appearance of study." Off the stage, during the progress of a play, he did not, like Betterton, preserve the character he was acting; nor like Young, tell gay stories, and even sing gay songs; but he loved to have the strictest order and decorum,—he, the most drunken player that had glorified the stage, since the days of George Powell! Could he have carried into real life the scrupulousness which, at one time, he carried into the mimicry of it, he would have been a better actor and a better man.

When Edmund Kean was in America, Bishop Hobart gave permission for the removal of Cooke's body, from the "strangers' vault," to the public burial-ground of the parish, where Kean was about to erect a monument to the memory of his ill-fated predecessor. On that occasion, "tears fell from Kean's eyes in abundance," says Dr. Francis; but those eyes would have flashed lightning, had Kean been aware that there was a headless trunk

beneath the monument; and that, whoever may have been the savage who mutilated the body and stole the head,—that head was in the possession of Dr. Francis! To what purposes it has been turned, this gentlemen may tell in his own words :
"A theatrical benefit had been announced at the Park, and 'Hamlet,' the play. A subordinate of the theatre at a late hour hurried to my office, for a skull. I was compelled to loan the head of my old friend, George Frederick Cooke. 'Alas, poor Yorick!' It was returned in the morning; but on the ensuing evening, at a meeting of the Cooper Club, the circumstance becoming known to several of the members, and a general desire being expressed to investigate, phrenologically, the head of the great tragedian, the article was again released from its privacy, when Daniel Webster, Henry Wheaton, and many others who enriched the meeting of that night, applied the principles of craniological science to the interesting specimen before them . . . . Cooper felt as a coadjutor of Albinus, and Cooke enacted a great part that night." If Cooke could have spoken his great part, he would assuredly have added something strong to his comments on what he used to call the civilization of Yankee-doodle.

The monument, erected by Edmund Kean, consists of a pedestal, surmounted by an urn, with this inscription:—"Erected to the memory of George Frederick Cooke, by Edmund Kean, of the Theatre Royal, Drury Lane, 1821 ;" and, beneath, this not very choice, nor very accurate distich :

"Three kingdoms claim his birth.
Both hemispheres pronounce his worth!"

And below this superscription lies all that has not been stolen of what was mortal, of one among the greatest and the least of British Actors.

During his career, flourished and passed into private life a boy, who still survives, rich with the fortune rapidly acquired in those old play-going days,—Master Betty.

## CHAPTER XXI.

#### MASTER BETTY.

WILLIAM HENRY WEST BETTY was born at Shrewsbury, in 1791, —a Shropshire boy, but of Irish descent. His father, a man of independent means, taught him fencing and elocution, and was unreasonably surprised to find that a histrionic affection came of this double instruction.

"I shall certainly die, if I do not become an actor!" said the boy, when residing near Belfast, and after seeing Mrs. Siddons in the ungrateful part of Elvira, in " Pizarro." He was then ten years old; was a boy with a will and decision of character; and, in his twelfth year, he made his first appearance at Belfast, on the 11th of August, 1803, as Osmyn, in "Zara." The judgment of the Irish manager, Atkins, was that he was an "Infant Garrick."

Master Betty also played Douglas, Rolla, and Romeo; and he went up to Dublin, in November, with the testimony of the Belfast ladies that he was "a darling." In the Irish capital, he acted Douglas, Frederick, Prince Arthur, Romeo, Tancred, and Hamlet. As he is said to have learned and played the last part within three days, I have small respect for his precocious cleverness, and do not wonder that the Dublin wits showered epigrams upon him.

"The public are respectfully informed that no person coming from the theatre will be stopped till after eleven o'clock." Such was the curious announcement on the Irish play-bill which invited the public to go and see Master Betty, and advised them to get home early, if they would not be taken for traitors. Those days were the days of United Irishmen, when Ireland was divided into factions, and Dublin not quite at unity as to Master Betty's merits.

The majority, however, worshipped the idol, before which Cork, Waterford, Londonderry, and other cities, bowed the knee. The popular acclaim wafted him to Scotland. In Glasgow, there was one individual who was not mad, and would criticise; but in return for "a severe philippic" administered by him, the wretch "was compelled to leave the city!"

If he went to Edinburgh, he found more excess of dotage than he had left in Glasgow. It was not merely that duchesses and countesses caressed the boy, but there was Home himself, at the representation of his own "Douglas," blubbering in the boxes, and protesting that never till then had young Norval been acted as he had conceived it! And he had seen West Digges, the original, in Edinburgh; and Spranger Barry, the original, in London. Critics said the Infant Roscius excelled Kemble; and Lords of the Court of Session presented him with books, and gave him old men's blessings!

Birmingham next took him up, and the English town confirmed the verdicts of Ireland and Scotland. Miss Smith (afterwards Mrs. Bartley) played mother to him one night, and maid beloved the next; and at the close of a dozen performances, the Infant Roscius was celebrated by a Bromwicham poet as having crushed the pride of all his predecessors, and being "Cooke, Kemble, Holman, Garrick, all in one!"

"Theatrical coach to carry six insides, to see the young Roscius," was the placard on many a vehicle which carried an impatient public from Doncaster Races to Sheffield, where crowds of amateurs from London fought with the country-folk for admission to the theatre, and a poetic Templar, rather loose in his Italian, remarked in a long poem in his praise:

> "Would Sculpture form APOLLO BELVIDERE,
> She need not roam to France, the model's here!"

Liverpool, Chester, Manchester, Stockport, all caught the frenzy, and adored the boy,—to whom Charles Young played subordinate parts! Occasionally, Master Betty played twice in the same day, and netted about £500 a week! Royal dukes expressed their delight in him, grateful managers loaded him with silver cups, and John Kemble wrote to Mr. Betty *père*, to express the happiness he and Mr. Harris would have in welcoming the tenth Wonder to Covent Garden Theatre,—at £50 per night and half a clear benefit.

Accordingly, on Saturday, the 1st of December, 1804, at ten in the morning, gentlemen were "parading" under the Piazza. By two o'clock serried crowds possessed every avenue, and when the doors were opened, there was a rush which, ultimately, cost some persons their lives. "The pit was two-thirds filled from the boxes. Gentlemen who knew that there were no places untaken in the boxes, and who could not get up the pit avenues, paid for admission into the lower boxes, and poured from them into the pit, in twenties and thirties at a time." Contemporary accounts speak in detail of the terrible sufferings not only of women, but men. "The ladies in one or two boxes were occupied almost the whole night in fanning the gentlemen who were beneath them in the pit. . . Upwards of twenty gentlemen, who had fainted, were dragged up into the boxes. . . Several more raised their hands as if in the act of supplication for mercy and pity." As for the play, "Barbarossa," the sensible public would have none of it before the scene in the second act, in which Selim (Master Betty) first makes his appearance. When that arrived, he was not disturbed by the uproar of applause which welcomed him; and he answered the universal expectation. "Whenever he wished to produce a great effect he never failed." He was found to be "a perfect master." His whisper was "heard in every part of the house," says a newspaper critic; "there is something in it like the under-notes of the Kembles; but it has nothing sepulchral in it. . . The oldest actor is not equal to him, he never loses sight of the scene. . . His judgment seems to be extremely correct. . . Nature has endowed him with genius which we shall vainly attempt to find in any of the actors of the present day;"—after which last sweeping judgment comes the qualifying line, "If he be not even now the first, he is in the very first line; and he will soon leave every other actor of the present day, at an immeasurable distance behind him."

The critics evidently had small confidence in their own judgments, but princes led the applause; their Majesties were charmed with their new "servant;" royalty received him in its London palace, and to the Count d'Artois (future King of France) and an august party at Lady Percival's, the small-eyed and plump-faced boy shook his luxuriant auburn curls and acted Zaphna, in French.

The philosophers went as mad as the "quality" and critics. *Quid*

## MASTER BETTY.

*noster Roscius egit* was given by Cambridge University as the subject for Sir William Brown's prize-medal. Old "Gentleman Smith," the original Charles Surface, came up from Bury St. Edmunds, and presented him with a seal bearing the likeness of Garrick, and which Garrick, in his last illness, had charged him to keep only till he should "meet with a player who acted from NATURE and from FEELING." Having found such actor, Smith consigned to him the keeping of the precious relic.

Then, if the overtaxed boy fell ill, as he did more than once,—the public forgot the general social distress, the threats of invasion, war abroad, and sedition at home, and evinced such painful anxiety,—that bulletins were daily issued, as though the lad were king-regnant or heir-apparent.

Subsequently, Drury Lane and Covent Garden shared him between them. In twenty-three nights, at the former house, he drew above £17,000, and this double work so doubled his popularity, that on one night having to play Hamlet, the House of Commons, on a motion by Pitt, adjourned, and went down to the theatre to see him! This flattery from the whole Senate was capped by that of a single legislator; Charles Fox read Zanga to the little actor, and commented on Young's tragedy, with such effect, that the young gentleman never undertook the principal character.

Except John Kemble and Mrs. Siddons, there was scarcely an actor of celebrity who did not play in the same piece with him, including Suett and Joey Grimaldi, who were the Gravediggers to his Hamlet. At the close of the season he passed through the provinces, triumphant, and returned to Drury Lane in 1805, to find "garlick amid the flowers," and a strong sibilant opposition, which he, however, surmounted, and again played the usual round of tragic heroes, carrying heaps of gold away with him to the country, where he easily earned large additions to the heap.

But the London furor henceforth subsided. The provinces continued their allegiance for a year or two, but the metropolis no longer asked for, or thought of him. His last season was at Bath, in 1808; in the July of which year he entered Christ's College, Cambridge, as a Fellow Commoner; subsequently hunted in the vicinity of the Shropshire estate, purchased for him by his father, and became Captain Betty of the North Shropshire Yeomanry Cavalry.

So ended Master Betty! But, in 1812, his father being dead, Mr. Betty longed again for the incense of the lamps and the dear homage of applause, and he went through a course of provincial theatres, ending with a month at Covent Garden, with questionable success. His old admirers would have it that he was the English, as he had been the Infant, Roscius; but the treasury account told another tale, and Mr. Betty could only take rank as a respectable actor.

His name, however, was still a tower of strength beyond the metropolis; and, in county towns, the intelligent young man drew audiences still. In Edinburgh, Mr. Macready played Edward to Mr. Betty's Warwick, in which last character, after fitful appearances in the country, and acting for a single night now and then in London, as an additional attraction for a benefit, Mr. Betty took his final farewell of the stage, at Southampton, on August the 9th, 1824, being then but thirty-two years of age.

There can be no doubt of Master Betty having been the most "promising" young actor that ever delighted his contemporaries, and disappointed those who were to be so hereafter. His wonderful memory, his self-possession, his elegance of manner, his natural and feeling style of acting—all but his habit of dropping his *h's*, were parts of a promise of excellence. But his early audiences took these for a whole and complete performance. He was master of words but not of ideas, and in his boyhood was imperfectly educated. He could learn Hamlet in three or four days, and, no doubt, he played it prettily; but to play prettily and act masterly, are different things. Hamlet is no matter for a boy to handle. Betterton acted it for fifty years, and, to his own mind, had not thoroughly fathomed the profoundest depths of its philosophy even then. Master Betty commenced too early to learn by rote; and the habits he then formed never permitted him to study as well as learn, by heart. The feeling and the nature, for which he was once praised, were those of a boy; they kept by him, and they were found weak and nerveless in the man. But therewith he reaped a large fortune, and he has prudently kept that, too. May the old man long enjoy what the young boy, between natural abilities and the madness of "fashion," earned with happy facility.

There remains but one name more of exceeding greatness to be mentioned,—that of Edmund Kean ; but, ere we let our curtain fall on him, I have to notice something of the manners, customs, sayings, and doings of a past time, which differed greatly from that in which Kean was reared, flourished, and fell. Let us glance at that olden period before we summon him to occupy our final scene.

## CHAPTER XXII.

#### STAGE COSTUME AND STAGE TRICKS.

IN the journals of 1723, I find various complaints of the deficiencies in the theatrical wardrobe. The shabbiness of the regal robes is especially dwelt upon, though those were splendid enough which were worn by a leading actor. Duncan and Julius Cæsar, at the above date, had worn the same robes *for a century;* and it was suggested that monarchy was brought into contempt by poorly-clad representatives.

It is said of Betterton, in Hamlet, that when he first beheld his father's spirit, he turned as white as his own neckcloth. Betterton wore the laced kerchief then in fashion. There was a worse fashion in part of Garrick's time. That actor dressed the young Dane in a court suit of black,—coat, waistcoat, and knee-breeches, short wig with queue and bag, buckles in the shoes, ruffles at the wrists, and flowing ends of an ample cravat hanging over his chest. Then, Woodward as Mercutio! This young nobleman of Verona, kinsman to a prince, and friend to the love-sick Montagu, did not walk his native city capped, plumed, and bemantled, according to the period, but in the dress of a rakish squire of Woodward's own days. On the top of a jaunty peruke was cocked one of those three-cornered hats, popularly known as an "Egham, Staines, and Windsor," from the figure of the fingerpost on Hounslow Heath pointing to those three towns. The hat was profusely gold-laced at the borders. Round the neck of the Veronese gentleman was negligently wound a Steinkirk cravat of muslin with *point of Flanders* ends. The rest of the attire was that of a modern state coachman on a drawing-room day, save that the material was chiefly of velvet, and that Woodward wore high heels to his gold-buckled shoes. The waistcoat descended over the thighs; and into its pocket, Woodward thrust one hand, as, with a finger of the other knowingly laid to his nose, he began the famous lines, "Oh! then, I see Queen Mab hath been with you!"

Booth's dress for Cato was not more or less absurd than Betterton's in "Hamlet." The Cato of Queen Anne's days wore a flowered gown and an ample wig!

Garrick's Macbeth was a modern Scottish sergeant-major, his Romeo "a beau in a new birthday embroidery." His Richard, fancifully, but more correctly decked, is preserved to us in Hogarth's picture; but when the King was thus attired, all the other persons of the drama wore court suits, powdered wigs, bags, cocked hats, and drawing-room swords! And yet the grandeur of the performance seems to have been in no way marred. When we smile at these things, we should remember that all managers who allow our old comedies to be played in modern costume offend equally against good sense. I would have Ranger acted in a wig, as Garrick, and not in the dress of the actor's time, as Elliston played it. The chronology of costume is worthy of every manager's notice, however accustomed the eye may become to anachronisms, —as with the dress worn in 1806 by Matthews as Old Foresight, in "Love for Love," which was the very famous and fashionable suit, worn for many a season by the graceful Wilks in that most airy of his parts, the youthful rake and gentleman, Sir Harry Wildair.

In Macklin's Macbeth, there was nothing of antiquity about the costume, which was a semi-military uniform of no, or of several periods, with a masquerade look about a good portion of it. His Hamlet was a modern gentleman in a black suit, such as might have been seen any day in the Mall. John Kemble dressed the sad young Dane, whose father had just been murdered by Hamlet's worst enemy, one who stood between him and his inheritance, in a fancy suit defying chronology, a carefully curled and powdered wig, such as never sat on Scandinavian head, and a blaze of jewelled orders—on the breast of him who courted seclusion! Altogether, there were strange things done on the stage in those days, not the least, perhaps, were comic solo dances, or compound hornpipes of a score of "merry sailors," with Highland reels, danced *between the acts* of the most solemn of Shakspeare's tragedies!

Reddish played Hamlet in a bag-wig, which Whitfield, as

Laertes, once carried off on the point of his sword! Henderson, who acted the Dane so well, dressed him ill,—in a three-cornered cock and flap hat, like my uncle Toby! Why not? since Lewis as Hippolitus, attired that hapless young man, of the era of Neptune and sea-calves, in knee-breeches, a jaunty silk jacket, tight-fitting boots, and a little court bodkin on his thigh—the thigh of the son of Theseus!

As for the ladies, they were as careless on the subject as the men, whether it was Mrs. Pritchard in Lady Macbeth, or Miss Younge as Zara, or Mrs. Yates as Cleopatra, they were all decked alike, court skirts over huge hoops, and trains tucked up to the waist, with powdered hair surmounted by a forest of feathers. Mrs. Siddons, when she made her first appearance in 1775, in Portia, played the part in a salmon-colored sack and coat; and her Euphrasia, to judge from her portrait, more nearly resembled an English than a Grecian matron, in the costume. But she soon improved in taste, or was able to exercise her own without interference; and Sir Joshua approved of her innovation of appearing in her natural hair, without *marischal* powder—of a reddish-brown tint, then in fashion, and worn with abundance of pomatum in the tubular curls of the ladies' head-dresses. She braided her locks into a small compass, in accordance with the size and shape of the head; and when long stiff stays and hoop petticoats were universally worn by stage heroines, as well as ladies in general, Mrs. Siddons had the courage to appear in a dress far from ample, with a waist of the very shortest; and King George III. himself warned Mrs. Siddons against using white paint (*blanc d'Espagne*, I suppose) on her neck, as dangerous to health.

Mrs. Esten depended for effect almost entirely on her dresses, and a languishing manner. Her success, when she first appeared in Belvidera, was attributed to "the picturesque and elegant manner" in which she dressed the character. This lady was the daughter of Mrs. Bennett, the author of *Juvenile Indiscretions*, and could have afforded her mother with matter for a dozen more volumes, had not the older lady been indiscreet enough to possess abundant material in her own experiences.

I think that the custom of noblemen presenting their cast-off court-suits to great players (Betterton played Alexander the Great in one), went out before the middle of the last century. A better custom prevailed in France. Not only princes of the house of Bourbon, but noblemen at court, sent theatrical costumes to Lekain—according to the stage fashion of the period—but the actor never wore any other. There was as little variety in this actor's wardrobe as in the style of his acting, which was very circumscribed. With two or three tunics and a turban, one expression and a single attitude, he carried about with him "French tragedy."

In France, not only Hamlet, as once with us, but Orestes, wore powder! But in this there was nothing more absurd than was to be found in Quin's Chamont, a young Bohemian nobleman of a remote romantic era. At the age of sixty, Quin played this youthful lover " in a long, grizzly, half-powdered wig, hanging low down on each side the breast, and down the back; a heavy scarlet coat and waistcoat, trimmed with broad gold lace, black velvet breeches, a black silk neckcloth, black stockings, a pair of square-toed shoes, with an old-fashioned pair of stone buckles, and a pair of stiff, high-topped white gloves, with a broad, old scolloped hat. Were the youthful, fiery Chamont," adds the anonymous biographer, "to appear on the stage in such a dress now, the tragedy would cause more laughter than tears." Absurd as this must seem in Quin, it was not more absurd than the dress worn by Hale, an actor of Garrick's time, who playing Charles I. in Havard's tragedy, wore a full-bottomed wig of the reign of Queen Anne—of the lightest color, and flowing over back and shoulders; in short, a perfect "cataract peruke!" Hale always fancied himself fascinating in this head-piece, as Mrs. Hamilton thought herself irresistible in jewels, with which she used so to load her dark hair, that they were compared to glow-worms in a furze-bush.

That there *is* much in a wig beyond the head it covers is, however, certain. No actor ever had such a wonderful collection of them as Suett, or looked so comic in them; though his horrible depression, and his terrific and painful dreams, nearly drove him mad. Such importance was attached to these wigs, that when the entire collection was burnt in the fire that destroyed the Birmingham Theatre, a friendly writer expressed a hope, that "until Mr. Suett can replace them,—the public will make an allowance for the great drawback their loss must be upon his comic abilities."

In some theatres, one coat has served successive generations of actors. It was not so with the dress which Garrick wore when he first appeared at Goodman's Fields, as Richard. This fell into the keeping of a man named Carr, who, when a strolling manager, used to act in it—let the character he had to represent be what it might! Greater actors than Carr were as negligent with respect to costume. Gentleman Smith, for instance, I meet with, complaining of the shabbiness of his Richard III.'s hat, and asking if he cannot have that which Powell wore as King John!

The *Morning Chronicle* for November 14, 1783, after extolling Mrs. Crawford's Lady Randolph as a triumph of acting which no competitor could reach, assails the costumes. "Lord Randolph and Glenalvon were as fine as if they were designed for the soft service of Venus, and meant to be present in an Eastern ball-room; and yet the whole scene of the play lies in the hardy region of the North, &c., &c. Old Norval's dress," it is added, "had not the most distant semblance of the ordinary habit of a Scotch shepherd."

Of John Kemble's anachronisms in Hamlet, I may add to the record, that in that play, the period of which is before the Norman conquest, he wore the order of the Elephant, which was not instituted till the middle of the fifteenth century! In Hotspur, too, he always wore the order of the Garter, even after proof was laid before him that Young Harry Percy had never been a member of the order. Elliston imitated Kemble; but when he heard that Hotspur did not belong to that chivalrous fraternity, he took the garter from his knee, as he was one night at the wing, ready to go on.

Originally, Kemble even acted Hamlet with the order of the Garter beneath his knee! He also wore the ribbon and star, with a black velvet court-dress, diamond buckles, and his powdered hair dishevelled, in the mad-scene. The Vandyke dress, with black bugles, and dark, curled wig,—a dress which knew but little change till Mr. Fechter introduced a portrait-costume more appropriate, from Albert Durer,—was first worn by John Kemble during his own management of Drury Lane. In one respect, the latter actor was the exact reverse of Henderson, who was so careless in the matter of costume, that he once boasted of having played ten different characters, in one season, in the same dress! Lewis was nearly as negligent as Henderson. His Earl Percy, for instance, was a marvel of anachronism and indifference. The noble Northumbrian was attired in a light summer attire of no possible age, and suited to no possible people. His hair was flowing, but profusely powdered; and these pendent locks were prettily tied up in a cluster of light-blue streamers, which his airiness made flutter in the breeze. But those were days in which every thing was borne with and nothing questioned. The beautiful Mrs. Crouch, for example, acted one of the witches in "Macbeth," in a killing, fancy hat, her hair superbly powdered, rouge laid on with delicate effect, and her whole exquisite person enveloped in a cloud of point lace and fine linen.

In 1791, Bensley acted Mortimer in the Hon. Frank North's jumble of tragedy, comedy, and opera, at the Haymarket,—the "Kentish Barons." The date of the piece was of the period of Richard II., but the costume was of an earlier time; and the figure which solemn Bensley cut, when skating through a scene in shoes with the peaks so long that they were turned up and fastened to his girdle, must have been one provocative of fun! Other players have been as incorrect, and infinitely more absurd. Take, for example, Edmund Kean himself in Orestes. He had seen Talma in that part in Paris, and the excellence of the French actor fired Kean to attempt the same character. But Edmund imitated him neither in correctness of costume, nor in having the part correct, by heart. Kean played Orestes only in Bath and Edinburgh. His dress, and that of his faithful Pylades (Ward), at the first place, were covered with ribbons. Neither of the ancient heroes had seen such silk manufacture in his life; but both of the actors had frequently seen ribbons, and that was enough. Defective in costume, Kean was also deficient in memory. At Bath he stumbled through the character; at Edinburgh he improvised a good deal of it; and in the mad-scene, substituted fragments from any other mad character he had in his mind for the moment, particularly Sir Giles Overreach! All this flustered the Pyrrhus especially, and his embarrassment was so marked that the Edinburgh critics took care to tell him that he ought to have exercised more industry in mastering the words of his part, when he had to play with so great a master as Mr. Kean!

A taste for mere finery in costume was long prevalent; and I have seen Young's dress for Macbeth, and that for Hamlet, censured as "too finical." In the latter part, not contented with the order of the Elephant, he sometimes wore a thick golden cord round his waist, with heavy bullion tassels. In Coriolanus and Brutus, Young introduced the toga for the first time in a perfect form on the English stage. But it was found that a perfect toga was not always the most proper dress, and Talma's senatorial robes were adopted by Charles Young, who, taught to wear them by the great French player, instructed in his turn, the ever willing to learn Charles Kemble. The latter dressed Charles Surface in the costume of his own day. It looked well enough, no doubt; but *now*, in Deighton's portrait, its absurdity is striking.

In my younger days of play-going there was a certain action of the hand and wrist on the part, especially, of actresses playing chambermaids, and rather lively young ladies, which was a trick of Mrs. Abington's, and had become, perhaps still is, a tradition. O'Keefe says: "Mrs. Abington's manner was charmingly fascinating, and her speaking voice melodious. She had peculiar tricks in acting, one was turning her wrist, and seeming to stick a pin in the side of her waist. She was also very adroit in the exercise of her fan; and though equally capital in fine ladies and hoydens, was never seen in *low or vulgar characters!* On her benefit night the pit was always railed into the boxes; her acting shone brightest when doing Estifania to Brown's Copper Captain." This refers to the season of 1759–60, when she was in Dublin, and before she had received "the stamp of a London audience." Her Kitty in "High Life Below Stairs" created a sort of infatuation for her at the Smock Alley Theatre. Her name was, so to speak, on the public lip, "and in ten days her cap was so much the fashion, that there was not a milliner's shop but what was adorned with it, and 'ABINGTON' appeared in large letters to attract the passers-by." The men "toasted" and adored her, the women paid her the highest homage by imitating her style in dress and carriage.

With old costumes, the actors of by-gone days had quaint tricks and ideas,—as strange to us now as their dresses. I may class with the former one circumstance of Quin's Falstaff in his later days. After the fight, when Falstaff, somewhat wearied and disposed to moralize, used to seat himself on the stump of a tree and give way to philosophizing, Quin calmly sank down into a crimson velvet chair with gold claws and blue fringe, conveniently pitched on the field of battle!

There used to be an old stage-trick for effect, employed in "Venice Preserved." Pierre, railing at the conspirators in defence of Jaffier, addresses himself, among the rest, to a pale, lean, haggard fellow, who, in such a picture, should be kept in the shade. But in the old days this fellow—all exaggerated ghastliness and horror—used to stand forth and exhibit his caricature of fright and famine, by sundry actions, the applause for which was even less reasonably given than that to the Gravedigger, in "Hamlet," when he deliberately doffed some score of waistcoats before he took to digging.

Mossop, too, had his trick in tragedy, which was sometimes akin to pantomime. In Macbeth, when with his truncheon he smote that white-livered loon of a messenger, he invariably broke in two the symbol of authority, over the unlucky envoy's skull. People applauded the earnestness of the tragedian as thus displayed; but the fact was, that Mossop always carried a truncheon made to fly in two when dealt on a victim's head. The absurdity of the act never struck himself.

More unmeaning but much more costly; more pantomimic, and much more improbable, was Barry's great trick in Alexander. He never, indeed, tried it in London; and I cannot account for its toleration by so refined and critical an audience as that of Dublin a century ago. In the triumphal entry into Babylon he was drawn down the stage in his car by unarmed soldiers. When he alighted to address them, each man placed his hand on some portion of the chariot, the machinery of which broke up into war accoutrements; the wheels into bucklers, the axles into sheaves of spears, the body of the vehicle into swords, javelins, lances, standards, and so forth. All which likely work having been accomplished, and the soldiers having arranged themselves in battle array, Alexander addressed his easily provided army amid a hurricane of applause, and O'Keefe protests that it was not only beautiful, but that he "never saw any thing to equal it, for simplicity!" *Oh*, sancta Simplicitas!

And this "simplicity" reminds me of the three separate ways in which Cibber, John Kemble, and Young, used to suit, or not suit, the action to the word in a passage of Wolsey:

> "This candle burns not clear. 'Tis I must snuff it;
> Then, out it goes."

Cibber's trick, to gain applause, was to fairly snuff the candle out. John Kemble, taking this in the light of an accomplished fact, was wont to look as one offended by the stink. Young, finding nothing more to do, always crossed his arms at this passage, smiled, and *did* nothing.

O'Keefe remarks, that it is a method with an old stager, who knows the advantageous points of his art, "to stand back out of the level with the actor who is on with him, and thus he displays his own full figure and face to the audience; but when two knowing ones are on together, each plays the trick upon the other. I was much diverted," he adds, "with seeing Macklin and Sheridan, in Othello and Iago, at this work; both endeavoring to keep back; they at last got together, up against the back scene. Barry was too much impassioned to attend to such devices." Edmund Kean is said to have practised this trick, when playing with actors or actresses taller than himself; but in so doing he was only putting himself on an equality with his taller colleague. I remember when, in my boyish days, the actors of the Théâtre Français used to take me behind the scenes, observing that when Talma was seated on the stage by the side of Mademoiselle Duchesnois, the seat of his chair was gradually raised towards the back, like a driving-box, and this enabled him to appear as tall as that ugly and able lady.

Garrick, too, had his chair-trick, in "Hamlet." When the Ghost appeared between the young Dane and his mother, Garrick, starting from his chair, used always to overturn the latter,—which was differently constructed from that used by the Queen. The legs of the actor's chair were, in fact, tapered to a point, and placed so far under the seat, that it fell with a touch.

Dr. Burney seems to think, that the elocution of Garrick and Mrs. Cibber was but exquisite trickery, and that a notation of their tones for a sort of musical declamation would be a good practical lesson for inferior actors, "and would be the means of conveying it" (the notation) "to posterity, who will so frequently meet with their names and eulogiums in the history of the stage, and be curious to know in what manner they acquired such universal admiration."

Very young children on the stage are, sometimes, as difficult to manage as "sagacious dogs," and other animals. The tricks resorted to, in order to preserve propriety, are amusing. When Mrs. Siddons was selected to play Venus, in Garrick's revived "Jubilee" (for which she was sneeringly called "Garrick's Venus"), she had little Tom Dibdin for Cupid. They were seated in the front of the stage; and it was necessary that the son of the goddess should smile in his mother's face,—but Tom was too much cowed to take any liberty of that sort. Whereupon, Venus looked fondly on him and asked, in a stage whisper, if he loved sugar-plums?—and what sort? and wouldn't he like some of the best quality when the piece was over? At all which, Cupid's face expanded into wreathed smiles, and he gazed on Venus with a laughing admiration,—in mental anticipation of the sweets in the hereafter. In 1785, Mrs. Siddons was the Tragic Muse in the "Jubilee," in which the Venus was represented by Mrs. Crouch, who might have smitten with jealousy Anadyomene herself.

Some actors have made audiences merry by a mistake; others, by spontaneous wit. When Quin, in Coriolanus, bade his soldiers lower their *fasces* (in which he pronounced the *a* long), down went their faces in the lowest of bows,—and up went the laughing shout of the audience. A similar effect was once produced by Charles Kemble, by transposing unconsciously, two letters in the phrase, "Shall I lay perjury upon my soul?" and making of it, "Shall I lay surgery upon my poll? No, not for all Venice!" More intentionally did Lewis once raise a foolish laugh when playing with little Cherry, who, as Drugget, exclaimed, "He looks as if he were going to eat me!" "Eat you!" exclaimed Sir Charles Racket (Lewis,) and, out of his character, "I could swallow you; I needn't make two bites of a cherry!" On the other hand, one individual at least, raised fun, and made money out of his own deformity; namely Coffey, who was monstrously hunchbacked, and who, for his own benefit, acted Æsop! There was more method in a whim like this than in the madness of Cassans, a promising actor of the last century, who lost his chance on the stage by preferring to sing ballads in the streets, or acting as waiter at a tavern, both of which offices he undertook seriously and acted to perfection.

Off the stage, there were performers whose fame was extended, by the second skill of a brother-player, as was the case with Deighton, of Drury Lane, who (like Emery) was a clever painter, and was the first who exhibited slightly-caricatured likenesses of his colleagues,—enough to indicate some queer peculiarity, but not enough to give offence. These used to attract the public round his shop-window, in Charing Cross, till Deighton (or Dighton, as the Sadler's Wells bills used to record) had to make his *exit*. The "Hundred Guilder Print," by Rembrandt, was missing from the British Museum; and to that print access had been given by Beloe, the keeper of the prints, to Deighton. There was a scandal which sent the actor into exile, and cost the translator of Herodotus his place.

From an incident between actor and audience, the more gorgeously dressed than elegantly spoken Mrs. Hamilton acquired the name of *Tripe Hamilton*. She had been hissed by the pit, for refusing to play for Mrs. Bellamy's benefit; and she explained wherefore. The language of the poets she could learn quickly, and deliver with dignity; but her own was of that sort which sponsors are supposed to be bound to teach. Mrs. Hamilton said: "Gentlemen and ladies,—I suppose as how you hiss 'cause I didn't play for Mrs. Bellamy. Well, I wouldn't, 'cause she said as how my audience on my benefit night, were nothing but tripe people, and made the house smell!" Yet this woman *could* play Lady Graveairs admirably.

There was another actress of the last century who had great power and much grace in addressing an audience, namely, Mrs. Fitzhenry. She is better remembered in Dublin than here; but I notice her on account of a curious circumstance, when she finally left the stage, there. On that occasion, she not only thanked the audience for past indulgence, but asked for future favor,—not for herself,—but for Mr. John Kemble, who had played several characters with her, but without being appreciated! Mrs. Fitzhenry gave assurance that there was sterling stuff in that young man, and hoped he would be encouraged!

This reminds me of another benefit night in Dublin, that of Mrs. Melmoth, wife of Courtenay Melmoth, whose real name was Pratt. To fill the house, the actress gave out that she was about being converted to the Roman Catholic religion, and she went daily and ostentatiously to mass. The house, however, was but a poor one, and Mrs. Melmoth became thereby convinced that the Romish Church had not that efficacy she had hoped to find in it; and she remained in her original belief,—the chief point of which was, that Courtenay was by no means so wise as he looked, nor so great as he thought himself. I know of no other case of conversion on the part of an actress, except that of Mrs. Wells, who, being confined in the Fleet, met there with Mr. Sumbell, of the Hebrew faith, and, on her enlargement, which she physically did not need, declared that she had married him, and had turned Jewess. This she had, indeed, done, at a splendid barbarico-comic marriage ceremony; but the ancient people doubted its validity, and so did Mr. Sumbell.

There was an actor of the last century, named Wignell, who was so doubly-refined that he could not deliver an ordinary message, without trying to make blank verse of it. "Wignell," said Garrick, "why can't you say, 'Mr. Strickland, your coach is ready,' as an ordinary man would say it, and not with the declamatory pomp of Mr. Quin, or Mr. Booth, when playing tyrants!" "Sir,' said poor Wignell, "I thought in that passage, I *had* kept down the sentiment!" *That*, he never could do; his Doctor, in "Macbeth," was so wonderfully solemn, that his audience was always in fits of laughter at it.

If this was rather taking a liberty with an actor,—the actors often took liberties with the audience. Just after Mrs. Bland was confined, for the first time, her husband, in Arionelli ("Son-in-law"), had to say, "Marriage! oh, that is quite out of my way." The actor of Cranky immediately responded with a speech, for which he ought to have been fined,—to the effect,—if that were the case, what about the little incident at home! But Emery once went further than this, and, when acting the Sentinel, in "Pizarro," contrived to let Rolla and the whole house know that Mrs. Emery had increased the number of his family circle. This freedom would be found to have no "fun" in it now.

No one better supported the dignity of the profession than Charles Murray, a son of Sir John Murray, of Broughton, and originally intended for the medical profession. In his younger days, before he fell into the line of old men, at Covent Garden, he was playing at Wakefield, where he so spiritedly resented an insult flung at him as an actor, that the party he thereby offended made a public quarrel of it, and the town was divided into two factions. Murray refused to ask pardon on the stage, and on a night he was to play in the "Beaux' Stratagem," knowing the intentions of his enemy in front, he entered booted and spurred, and announced that, aware of the opposition, he was about to set out for Doncaster. Whereupon, his friends leaped from the boxes to the stage, declared he should not be driven from the theatre, and guarding the wings they compelled Murray, dressed or undressed, as he was, to go through his part, and to remain on the stage throughout the piece, lest he should profit by an *exit*, to make his escape.

On the other hand, poor Jack Owen, the "successor" of Henry Mossop, and the "real Zanga," as he used to call himself, was always able to defend his own cause. He was one night hissed while playing Polydore, in the "Orphan," when under the influence of the grape. He had just dismissed the Page, with "Run quickly, then, and prosperous be thy wishes," when his imperfect utterance raised a storm of hisses. But he turned the first words of the succeeding soliloquy to good account,—and advancing to the footlights, growled to the house, "Here I am alone and fit for mischief,"—putting himself in a fighting attitude, and moving the house to laughter by his new reading.

The discipline of preparation for the stage in the older days was greater than it is now. It included strolling, slaving at country theatres, a course of probation at Norwich, Bath, York, and such towns,—after which there was an assured trial for an ambitious player, at every fresh season in London. But ere this point was reached, there was much to be endured.

Blissett and Dimond, for instance, walked from London to Bath, with half-a-crown between them, and the former ever after kept the shoes in which he had done it, as a memento of his hard days. Some strolling managers have flourished much better than their actors. Smith, proprietor of the Margate Theatre, had been a hostler; Copeland, of the Dover Theatre, a groom. At the former house, it was customary for the company to parade in front in full dress, on a balcony, while the house was filling, or was not filling. The Birmingham company used to send round a bell-man or a drummer to announce and praise the coming performances, and Dick Yates is said to have filled one or other office more than once. To these managers, candidates came with an ignorance that was only to be exceeded by that of their employers. "How ought I to look when I see the Ghost?" said a sucking Hamlet to the Margate manager. "Look!" said the latter; "well; oh!—look? why, as much as to say, 'Confound it, here's a rig!'"

Humble enough were some of these houses. The old Margate was over a stable, whence came all sorts of unpleasant reminiscences. The Tunbridge Wells house was of such dimensions that the audience part was in Kent, the stage in Sussex, and between the two ran a ditch, which players in debt found convenient, when bailiffs were after them, as they speedily evaded jurisdiction by escaping into another county. It was here that the ubiquitous, yet stationary, Mrs. Baker, the proprietress, stood at three pay places and took money at all!

In matters of costume, affairs were in a primitive condition. In a garrison town, Cato and the senators were generally decked out in old regimentals, lent by the Fort-Major; and there and in ordinary towns, ladies who commanded plays, provided the wardrobe for the actresses. Benefits, however, were seldom so to those for whom they were technically "given." Tate Wilkinson himself once, at Maidstone, netted only two pieces of candle and eighteen pence. This theatre was so near the river that the tide overflowed the pit, and threatened to float away the house. I do not know that "Hamlet" was really ever played without the principal character, but it is recorded of Waldron, at Windsor, that his company acted the "Suspicious Husband" without a Mr. Strickland, and "She stoops to Conquer," without a Miss Hardcastle. Windsor, nevertheless, was patronized by the old King, who went thither in much less state than the Margravine of Anspach, to the little theatre in Newbury.

In the hurry, anxiety, and disappointments in which the old strollers lived, study was imperfect, and I have heard of a play acted almost entirely from the prompting supplied from a book, borrowed from one of the audience; the actors neither knowing the piece, nor having a copy to learn it from! That such a life should have any attraction may seem surprising, but Incledon left the musical band of a man-of-war to sing ballads, on country stages, and to get little more than bread to keep him in voice. Occasionally, the strollers played in very good company,—as at Plymouth, where Sir Charles Bampfylde would play Captain Brazen, or any other part, "by particular desire of Sir Charles," as the bills had it! The Plymouth house is the only house, except the old Dublin, in which performances took place before the roof was on! On one night, of Shuter's benefit, the gallery was so crowded that the beam visibly bent, and two uprights were placed under it, to prevent the people, who came to be amused, from being killed. It must have been a cheerful night, free from anxiety!

Between country actors and audiences, there was an easy freedom. Miller, of Birmingham, played Frenchmen well, and Hamlet abominably, for which last, he was hissed, and thereupon he told the audience that since they wouldn't have his Hamlet, they shouldn't have his Frenchman! Mrs. Charke records that one night, as she was playing Pyrrhus, she was called upon to deliver some speeches of Scrub, in which she had distinguished herself the night before. In like manner, when Incledon was singing the most pathetic ballad, his rude hearers would demand some coarse popular song, nor let him off till he had sung it!

"Oh! take more pity in thine eyes!" said a Portsmouth Richard to Lady Anne. "Would they were *battle-axe*," said Miss White (instead of "*basilisks*"), "to strike thee dead!" This, however, was probably only a slip. At all events, it was not so shocking as Brereton's first indications of his insanity when, at a country theatre, and playing with his wife (afterwards Mrs. Kemble), he made her dance a *minuet* with him, when she ought to have been weeping; and when she died in character, the poor fellow (a *star* in the country) would, if not watched, walk up to her and seriously bewail the sad condition of his darling wife.

Brereton, in his day, had seen as much misery while strolling, as Bensley,—a gentleman as well born as himself. The latter once tramping it with Robinson, they found that they had but a penny between them. They tossed as to who should have the mutton pie which it could purchase, and Bensley burst into tears while the winner devoured the prize. Their next dinner was purchased by their cutting off their hair, then worn long, and selling it. And this incident of the hair reminds me of Fox, the manager's son at Brighton, who, when hair-powder was worn by some and denounced by others, because of the tax upon it, appeared, in some fine gentleman's part, with his head half in powder, and half without. To allay the uproar that ensued, he explained that he did it to please both parties, and of course gratified neither. Some old strolling companies, on the tramp, walked very many hundreds of miles, during the year. Even the richer brethren of the craft sometimes suffered tribulation. As once happened with the Bath company, when their scenery, machinery, dresses, and "property" of every theatrical sort, were burnt in their caravans, as they were crossing Salisbury Plain.

I return again to the old houses, for a moment, to consider three subjects not yet touched upon,—the old rage for prologues and epilogues,—the "dedications" of plays, and the "benefits" of the actors.

## CHAPTER XXIII.

**PROLOGUE, EPILOGUE; DEDICATIONS AND BENEFITS.**

In looking over the poetical addresses made to audiences in former days, our regret is that such abundant illustration, as they give, of life in and out of the theatre, is rendered unavailable by a licentiousness which runs through every line. From those of Aphra Behn, and her contemporaries and immediate successors, filthy missiles, as it were, were flung at morals generally, and at the audience in particular. Nevertheless, and down to a later period, the British appetite for prologue and epilogue was for many years insatiable. The public, though often insulted in both, with that sort of license which belonged to the old jester, whose master, however, could as readily chastise as laugh at him, listened eagerly; and only with reluctance saw the time arrive when the play was considered safe enough to go on without the introduction. Even when old plays were revived, the audience expected the prologue to enjoy resuscitation also. So, when "Cato" was reproduced at Covent Garden, for Sheridan, and the play commenced without the famous introductory lines by Pope, there was a vociferous shout from the house of "Prologue! prologue!" That eccentric actor, Wignell, was then on the stage as Portius, and in his fantastically pompous way had pronounced the opening passage of his part—

"The dawn is overcast, the morning lowers,
And heavily, with clouds, brings on the day,"—

when he was interrupted by renewed vociferations for the prologue. Wignell would neither depart from his character, nor leave the house without satisfactory explanation; and accordingly, after the word "day," without changing feature or tone, he solemnly went on, with this interpolation:—

"(Ladies and gentlemen: there has not been
For years a prologue spoken to this play—).
The great, the important day, big with the fate
Of Cato and of Rome."

Sometimes the prologue, in preceding the piece, did so in mournful verse, "As undertaker walks before the hearse;" and in the case of tragedy, it was etiquette for the speaker to be attired in solemn black, generally a court suit. Occasionally, the prologue to an historical tragedy was a brief lecture for the enlightenment of an ignorant audience. At all times it was held to be a better means of instruction than that followed by French writers of tragedy, through confidants,—

> "Who might instruct the pit,
> By asking questions of the leading few,
> And hearing secrets, which before they knew."

Few men wrote more of them than Garrick, though in that to "Virginia" he says that—

> "Prologues, like compliments, are loss of time,
> 'Tis penning bows and making legs in rhyme.
> 'Tis cringing at the door, with simp'ring grin,
> When we should show the company within."

But he subsequently wrote in the epilogue to the "Fathers," that—

> "Prologues and epilogues—to speak the phrase—
> Which suits the warlike spirit of these days—
> Are cannons charged, or should be charged, with wit,
> Which, pointed well, each rising folly hit."

Garrick, however, only wrote according to the humor of the hour, for elsewhere he describes prologues as "the mere ghosts of wit;" and proposes their abolition. Their alleged falseness of promise he illustrates, in a "Prologue upon Prologues," spoken when none at all was needed, by a story :—

> "To turn the penny, once, a wit,
> Upon a curious fancy hit,
> Hung out a board on which he boasted,
> 'Dinner for threepence, boiled and roasted!'
> The hungry read, and in they trip
> With eager eye and smacking lip:
> 'Here bring this boiled and roasted, pray!'
> Enter potatoes, *dressed each way!*

>     All stared and rose, the house forsook,
>     Cursed the dinner, and kicked the cook."

It is a singular thing that authors had little or no control over the prologues or epilogues attached to their plays. In this respect, the manager acted as he pleased, licensed such sentiments as *he* approved of, and was irresponsible. Thus, the refined Dr. Young was insulted by an unclean epilogue attached to his " Brothers," which was played for the benefit of the Society for the Propagation of the Gospel; and Dr. Browne, one of the vainest of authors, was horrified by hearing Garrick, in the epilogue to " Barbarossa," make Woodward ask the public—referring to the doctor, to " Let the poor devil eat! allow him that!" Home, however, seems to have exercised, in some respect, his own judgment, when " Douglas" was played. That is, he refused to tag a satirical address to so solemn a tragedy; but another poet laughed at him, through Barry, who came on exclaiming:—

> " 'An epilogue I asked! but not one word
>     Our bard would write! He vows 'tis most absurd
>     With comic wit to contradict the strain
>     Of tragedy, and make your sorrows vain."

But Shenstone, in his epilogue to Dodsley's " Cleone," a few years later, followed a double course. After that tragedy of anguish, the address began with,

> " Well, ladies, so much for the tragic style—
>     And now the custom is—to make you smile."

Then came hints that had the absent husband Lefroy lived in modern times, his Cleone would have proved a different damsel to her depicted by the poet; but Shenstone adds, in his moral strain:—

> " 'Tis yours, ye fair, to bring those days again,
>     And form anew the hearts of thoughtless men.
>     Make beauty's lustre amiable as bright,
>     And give the soul, as well as sense, delight;
>     Reclaim from folly a fantastic age,
>     That scorns the press, the pulpit, and the stage."

This was a good attempt to raise the character of women b

pointing to a duty which they might perform; and a similar moral strain was adopted long after by Sheridan. In the epilogue to his "Rivals," spoken by Mrs. Bulkeley, he says:—

> "Our moral's plain, without more fuss,
> Man's social happiness all rests on us:
> Through all the drama, whether damned or not,
> Love gilds the scene, and women guide the plot."

Among the curiosities of prologues and epilogues, may be reckoned the boasts, promises, and little confidences, in those delivered on the occasion when "Cato" was played at Leicester House, by the children of Frederick, Prince of Wales, and some of the young nobility. The prologue, indeed (spoken by Prince George), afterwards George III., was not especially remarkable. It lauded the wisdom of men who declared that—

> "To speak with freedom, dignity and ease,
> To learn those arts which may hereafter please,"—

nothing was required, but that "youth in earliest age" should "Rehearse the poet's labors on the stage." As for patriotism, said Prince George,—"Know,—'twas the first great lesson I was taught!" And, of course, he gloried that he was "A boy, in England born, in England bred!" Artists, who may hereafter paint the scene, will do well to remember what pictures were suspended on the walls:

> "Before my eyes those heroes stand,
> Whom the great William brought to bless this land;—
> To guard, with pious care, that gen'rous plan
> Of power well bounded, which he first began."

The epilogue was spoken by Lady Augusta (as Prince Frederick called his daughter) and Prince Edward, afterwards Duke of York. It was mere doggerel; but Augusta flouted at the fine phrases of the prologue, and Edward,—intrusted with a sly hit at George's boast of being English born,—declared that George had—

> "Vouchsafed to mention
> His future gracious intention,
> In such heroic strains, that no man
> Will e'er deny his *soul a Roman*."

There was an allusion to the imperial sway the elder brother was to enjoy, and the obedience the younger was to observe; after which, the latter, addressing the little sister, to whom he had been a suitor (Juba) in the play, said—

> "But sister, now the play is over,
> I wish you'd get a better lover."

To which the already destined bride of Brunswick, and future mother of that Caroline, who was so luckless and unlovely a Queen of England, made reply, wherein we see something of the training for high duties, then adopted in high places:

> "Why,—not to underrate your merit,
> Others would court with different spirit;
> And I, perhaps, might like another
> A little better than a brother,—
> Could I have one of England's breeding.
> But 'tis a point they're all agreed on,
> That I must wed a foreigner,
> Across the seas,—the Lord knows where!"

Whereupon, Prince Edward congratulated himself on being "wedded to the nation;" and, alluding to his mimic command in the tragedy, he hoped that future times would see him "general in reality," adding,—

> "Indeed, I wish to serve this land;—
> It is my father's strict command,"

And so forth, in like strain, wherein great purpose took the guise of low impertinence.

This address is said to have been extremely well delivered. On the regular stage, Woodward and King were remarkable as prologue speakers. A biographer of the latter says: "As a prologue speaker, in the comic style, he is undoubtedly unapproachable. There is a happy distinction in his case, manner, familiarity, and acting those dramatic exordiums, so as to render them, in his possession, entertainments of the first kind. Indeed, the audience are so sensible of this, that they never omit calling for them on those nights the pieces are represented, with an avidity and impatience that strongly indicate their pleasure." From the earliest times, indeed, it was the ambition of an actor to be considered an efficient speaker of prologues. Wilks was never so angry as when the office was intrusted to another; Cibber never so proud, as when Dryden made selection of *him*.

If the audience were almost invariably insulted in these old addresses, individual patrons were grossly flattered by authors in the dedication of their plays. Mrs. Behn leads the way decently enough with her " good, sweet, honied, sugar-candied reader," prefixed to her " Rover;" but she speedily turns from abstract to actual personages, and then the address out-Herods Herod. Passing from her, to select another sample from the hundreds about me, I come to Dryden's horrible farce of " Amboyna," with its unsavory jokes, Bacchanalian chants, hymn from the Basia, and unspeakable atrocities. It is dedicated to the first Lord Clifford, of Chudleigh. This patron of the poet was the grandson of a Protestant clergyman, but he became a Romanist before the Restoration. He was one of the defamers of Clarendon. In the Commons, he was as bold as he had ever been in any of his volunteer actions at sea. Pepys speaks of him as " a very fine gentleman, and one much set by at court, for his activity in going to sea, and strictness everywhere, and stirring up and down." Evelyn alludes to him in unrestrained terms of admiration and affection; and as far as Lord Clifford's private character is concerned, he was worthy of such praise. But he betrayed his country's liberties; and he vehemently desired to establish Popery. Clifford was a magnificent Lord High Treasurer, and one of the Cabal. Dryden's dedication to him, of his anti-Dutch farcical tragedy, probably rests on Clifford's deeds in sea-fight against the Dutch. But here we have an English poet lauding to the skies an un-English peer, who is said to have avowed, that he would rather see our King dependent on the French monarch than on five hundred kings in Parliament. Dryden says, that despairing of " repaying his obligements" to my lord, he is driven to "receive only with a profound submission the effects of that virtue which is never to be comprehended but by admiration;" and he receives my lord's "favors as the Jews of old received their law,—with a mute wonder." Perhaps there is a little satire in this, as there seems to be in the reference to his lordship's doings at the Treasury, where "no man attended to be denied." "Had that treasure been your own," says Dryden, "your inclination to bounty must have ruined you!" Which sounds very much like complimenting a man for robbing his master in order to distribute charity.

In the dedication of his plays, Dryden twice approaches royalty,—legitimate royalty,—in the persons of James, Duke of York, and Mary of Modena, his Duchess. To the former, he dedicates his *Conquest of Granada;* and the poet runs mad in praising the Prince's valor. To the Duchess, he dedicates his *State of Innocence;* and the bard runs wild in lauding the Princess's beauty!

The Almanzor of the play is a faint image of James himself! whose youth of bright deeds left his manhood nothing to perform, but to outdo himself! He was an honor to England, when England was a reproach to itself!—" and when the fortunate usurper sent his arms to Flanders, many of that adverse party were vanquished by your fame, ere they tried your valor. The report of it drew over to your ensigns whole troops and companies of converted rebels, and made them forsake successful wickedness to follow an oppressed and exiled virtue!" Armies, beaten by the Duke, learned from him to conquer! When he was not present, the guardian angel of the nation was careless as to how inferior generals got bruised! If James and Charles were concerned more with one thing than with another, it was in watching over the honor of England! In the former, the poet had found his model for the extraordinarily heroic Almanzor. He adds, with a spice of satire, which is to be found in most of Dryden's dedications, that there is, to be sure, in Almanzor, "a roughness of character, impatience of injuries, and a confidence of himself, almost approaching to an arrogance!" "But these errors," says the crafty bard, "are incident only to great spirits!"

There is more of insanity and insolence in the adulation with which Dryden deluges the Duchess. Her beauty is a deity, her grandeur a guardian angel! Of her beauty, he *will* rave. "I would not, without extreme reluctance, resign the theme to any other hand!" He is proud that he cannot flatter, and then pelts her with flattery as with missiles. The Creator had placed her near the crown that her beauty might give lustre to it! There would have been no contest for the apple, had *she* been alive when the prize was to be awarded! As it is, he cannot describe her wondrous excellence. "Like those who have surveyed the moon by glasses, I can only talk of a new and shining world above us, but not relate the riches and the glories of the place!" So resplendent is she, that she makes men false to other ladies, and then scorns the homage of the traitors. And, having libelled the men, he defames the women, by saying: "Your conjugal virtues have deserved to be set as an example to a less degenerate, less tainted age. They approach so near to singularity in ours, that I can scarcely make a panegyric to your royal highness, without a Satyr on many others!" Finally, having outraged all propriety, he can still go further, by the addition of a little blasphemy; and her royal highness is informed by her most obedient, most humble and most devoted servant, John Dryden, that her "person is so admirable, it can scarce receive addition when it shall be glorified!" Therefore, the Duchess is to dwell forever in Elysium, in her mundane body, unchanged, "for your soul, which shines through it," says the vile adulator, "finds it of a substance so near her own, that she will be pleased to pass an age within it, and to be confined to such a palace." Such was the incense which the greatest living poet of his day expected even a shrewd princess like Mary of Modena to inhale!

Otway crawls at the feet of the King's concubine, the rapacious Duchess of Portsmouth, in his dedication of "Venice Preserved," and almost invites her to void her rheum upon his head. However generous the woman may have been to him, the man is abject. The play he presents is but as the poor apple offered by a clown to an emperor! "Next to Heaven," all his gratitude is due to her Grace! It was she who dragged him from the mire, and set him to bask in "those royal beams whose warmth is all I have, or hope, to live by." Then, after asserting his loyalty and his scorn of republicanism, the poet thus tumbles for the amusement of, or by way of homage to, this handsome and painted Jezebel:—
"Nature and fortune were certainly in league when you were born, and as the first took care to give you beauty enough to enslave the hearts of all the world, so the other resolved to do its merit justice that none but a monarch fit to rule that world should e'er

possess it; and in it he had an empire. The young prince you have given him, by his blooming virtues early declared the mighty stock he came from;" and so forth. That this prince, the first Duke of Richmond of the present line, will always aid the cause of the Stuarts and smite all rebels, is part prayer, part prophecy, on the side of the poet, who in this case was no Vates, for the Duke served as aide-de-camp to William in Flanders and died a Lord of the Bedchamber to King George I.

In course of time, as the little Duke grows to manhood, the poets keep him in view, and in their dedications oppress him with praise of his parents' qualities and his own. Southern is among the foremost and the most flattering of these eulogists. He dedicates his first venture, the "Loyal Brother" (1682), to the Duke. "Could my vanity," says the author, when dedications were paid for at a rate, varying from five to twenty guineas, "carry me to the hopes of succeeding in things of this kind, I am confident my surest way would be, to draw my characters from you, in whom the fairest images in nature are shown in little. Your royal father's Greatness, Majestic Awfulness, Wit, and Goodness, are promised all in you. Your mother's conquering beauty triumphs again in you. Nothing is wanting to crown our hopes, but time, to make you in England what Titus was in Rome,—the Delight of Mankind." The Russian admiral, Livsoski, claims that title now for the Czar,—the holy master of the Mouravieffs and De Bergs,— whose shedding of human blood is gratefully acknowledged by the new Titus,—athirst for vengeance.

Etherege, ordinarily so impudent, pretends, in dedicating his "Man of Mode" to the Duchess of York, that his patroness's virtues and perfections are things not to be treated of in humble prose, and that he will address himself to the sublime subject some day, in poetry! Wycherley presents his "Love in a Wood" (1672), to the Duchess of Cleveland, who had gone two successive nights to see it acted. It is his first attempt, he says, at dedication; and he cannot lie, like other dramatists, who wreathe garlands for their patron's brow only to enjoy the perfume of them, themselves! And then he sings a long song of praise for his guineas, or in whatever other way his guerdon may have come, in which he tells the lady, among other fine things, that she has that perfection of beauty which others of her sex only think they have; "that generosity in your actions which others of your quality have only in their promises, with a spirit, wit, and judgment which fit heroes for command, and which fail to make *her* proud." It is not to be supposed that Wycherley believed this, for when he dedicated his "Plain Dealer" (1674) "to my Lady B——," or Mother Bennet, the most infamous woman in London, he especially praises her for her modesty, in keeping away from the representation of his play, even on the first day,—a play which he pretends to believe ought not to be witnessed by modest people?

Congreve sometimes insinuates praise, at others, he flings it. In the dedication of his " Old Bachelor," to Lord Clifford (Lanesborough), afterwards Earl of Burlington, he says, " I cannot give your Lordship your due, without tacking a bill of my own privileges." His "Double Dealer" goes to Charles, Lord Montague, with an assurance that poetry is my Lord's mistress, and the mother by him of a "most beautiful issue." He addresses his "Love for Love" to the Earl of Dorset, and hails him as the undisputed monarch of poetry! Dorset, whose best claim to being considered a poet, rests on the song, "To all ye ladies now on land," of his being the author of which, there is no positive assurance!

In the eighteenth century a man was killed in the streets of Morpeth, for maintaining that the blood of the Dacres was as good as that of the Ogles. Of the excellence of the latter, Shadwell entertained very exalted ideas. In 1680 there was living, and in the same year died, the Earl of Ogle, to whom was contracted in her infancy the famous lady Elizabeth, sole heiress of the last of the Earls of Northumberland. Her subsequent contract with Tom Thynne led to the murder of the latter by Count Königsmark. In the year above-mentioned, Shadwell produced at Dorset Gardens, and published, his " Woman Captain," in dedicating which to the Earl of Ogle, the Marquis of Newcastle's son, Shadwell says, " one virtue of your Lordship's I am too much pleased with not to mention, which is, that in this age, when learning is grown contemptible to those who ought most to advance it, and Greek and Latin sense is despised, and French and English nonsense applauded, when the ancient nobility and gentry of England, who not long since were famous for their learning, have now sent into the world a certain kind of spurious brood of illiterate and degenerate youth, your Lordship dares love books, and labors to have learning."

This is fine testimony, and not flattery to one of the most promising young gentlemen of the day. His child-wife subsequently married the proudest of dukes, and Swift has immortalized the red-haired beauty as " the d—d Duchess of Somerset!"

In one of the greatest of moral writers,—the Rev. Dr. Young, we meet with one of the most fulsome of adulators. This divine dedicated his "Revenge" to his friend Philip, Duke of Wharton, the most profligate and unprincipled, but one of the most accomplished men of his age. Young assures us that his Grace leads a virtuous pastoral life, such as your town rakes know nothing of; that his is given to study, and that he is a perfect master of all history, as well as of many languages; that he is as well skilled in men as in books, and that he "can carry from his studies such a life into conversation, that wine seems only an interruption to it." The Duke has, we are told, "so sweet a disposition that no one ever wished his abilities less, but such as flattered themselves with the hope of shining when near him." The poet even makes the peer his *collaborateur* in the piece, and acknowledges that he not only "suggested the most beautiful incident, but made all possible provision for the success of the whole."

But although authors may have been ready enough to flatter their patrons, the appetite of the latter was sometimes stronger than could be met by the supply. Peter Motteux, of whom I have already spoken, had a patron of this quality, whose name was Heveningham, and who, having accepted the dedication of one of Peter's dramatic trifles, was so little satisfied with the copy which was sent to him for approval, that he wrote one to himself, subscribed it with Motteux's name, and sent it to the press! Unluckily, Heveningham had mentioned therein an incident which could have been known only to himself; and the epigrammatic wits found their account in the oversight.

There is something more touching in the dedication of "Merope" to Bolingbroke, by poor Aaron Hill, when " hard up," through speculation, indiscreet generosity, and a profuse hospitality, in which there was no discretion at all! Aaron felt his position, and was conscious of an end approaching, to which the sad poet thus alludes :—

> "Cover'd in Fortune's shade, I rest reclin'd,
> My griefs all silent and my joys resigned.
> With patient eye Life's ev'ning gleam survey,
> Nor shake th' out-hast'ning sands, nor bid them stay;
> Yet while from life my setting prospects fly,
> Fain would my mind's weak off'ring shun to die;
> Fain would their hope, some time through light explore,
> The *name's* kind passport, when the *man's* no more."

I fear Bolingbroke had few means to materially help the writer, beyond the dedication fee. Even the profits of the author's three nights brought to his family little more than a hundred and odd pounds.

Murphy and Fielding were the first dramatic poets who departed from the old beaten track. Murphy dedicated his "Zenobia," not to an earl, but to an actress,—Mrs. Barry, who had saved his tragedy by her glorious acting. This dedication is gracefully worded, and is a faithful testimony to the ability of a great artist. Unfortunately, flattery could creep into such homage as this. For fulsomeness of praise, Soane's dedication of the "Dwarf of Naples," to Edmund Kean; and Sheil's, of his "Adelaide," to Miss O'Neill, equal any similar offence of the olden time.

I could cite more, but will only add that, of all the writers of dedications, by far the most amusing is the man who wrote none! This ingenious person called himself Adam Moses Emanuel Cooke, but his sole Christian name was simply Thomas. He was a Northumbrian by birth, an Oxonian by education, and a beneficed clergyman who drove all his parishioners mad by his superstitious practices, his mystical enthusiasm, and his turn for unintelligible mysteries. He took all the loving promises to the Jews so much to heart as to believe that the more nearly he approached them in all their old observances, the more true he should be to the Christian dispensation. Accordingly, he practised them all, did not hesitate at the most painful and characteristic, and was very much astonished that other men declined to follow his example.

Cooke was mad, in this one matter, no doubt; but considering that episcopal patience bore with the theatre-haunting Rev. Dr. Dodd, I think Cooke's bishop treated him a little harshly by procuring his deprivation, and driving him out to starve.

To starvation, however, the poor man had reasonable objections; and to obviate such an end, he turned dramatic author, as if to justify those who called him mad. It was then that he showed that there was method in his madness. Having nothing, he denounced the rights of property. Possessing nothing he could throw in to the common lot, he preached communism. At Will's, or Tom's, or Button's, at the Grecian, or any other well-frequented coffee-house, the hungry author of two unrepresented and unrepresentable plays, who might have thanked Heaven that he was not worth a ducat, would coolly enter and seat himself at the first table which he saw ready furnished with the meal for which he longed, and thought not of paying. The rightful owner, if ignorant of the ways of Adam Moses Emanuel, would blandly smile at the absent man, think sighingly of the mighty labors which had brought him to such a pass, and quietly move off. If the gentleman whose chocolate, toast, and eggs, Cooke appropriated, knew of the mystic's ways, he would smilingly submit to them, and await the moment which should bring the *Gastronome sans argent* and mine host into collision.

However this might be, the breakfast concluded, Cooke returned thanks, rose, shook his faded suit of sables, and made, calmly satisfied, for the door. Between that and himself ever stood the landlord, or head-waiter, and then ensued a controversy, to hear which, old beaux, middle-aged bucks, and younger bloods crowded with more eagerness than would have marked their going to a sermon. Cooke's theory was not "base is the slave that pays," but that, payment lacking on his part, it would be base to deprive him of breakfast. To the simple and conclusive reasoning of the master, he opposed texts from the Talmud, maxims from the Rabbis, and a clincher from Moses, according to whose legislation even a thief was not to be punished, if his so-called offence originated in the natural necessity of satisfying his stomach. Of course, when the audience grew tired of the argument, they clubbed the amount required, and sent the cunning author rejoicingly on his way.

That way took him from the landlord, who was quite "agreeable" to have him for a customer,—he drew so many others—to the patron from whom Cooke hoped to extract sufficient whereon to dine, have his claret, and spin out his evening, like a gentleman. He was always about to publish one of, perhaps both, the mad plays he had written: "The King cannot Err," and the "Hermit Converted, or the Maid of Bath Married." Or he was on the point of giving to the public some treatise on mystical divinity. For suitable patrons he had as fine a scent as for breakfast. He selected them among wealthy old Creoles, or rich young lords just returned from the grand tour; or peers who would be glad to give a guinea to get rid of him; or baronets who would think the fun got out of him well worth the fee; or simple 'squires and gentlemen honestly ready to contribute to the support of literature and distressed authors.

With the guinea, for subscription, in his pocket, Cooke withdrew on that day, to call on the same or some other patron the next, for permission to dedicate his drama to one of whose virtues, talents, magnanimity, divine endowments, and the like, the town was giving hourly assurance. The fish thus tickled generally proved a gold-fish, and with a dedication fee of, at least, five guineas, Cooke disappeared as solemnly as the Ghost in "Hamlet."

Like that shadowy majesty of Denmark, our dramatic author was a "revenant." He always returned. A happy thought had struck him. A copper-plate engraving of his patron's shield of arms, at the head of the dedication, would magnify every party concerned, and especially him of whose house it was the blazon! There were little incidental expenses, no doubt; but what were they to one so munificent and so disposed to promote the best interests of learning! And, accordingly, Cooke withdrew, all the richer by ten guineas,—for the engraver!

When Cooke's goose ceased to lay golden eggs—when no other was to be found, and managers cruelly refused to have any thing to do with his dramas, the reverend gentleman let his beard grow, turned street preacher, and, as the Bearded Priest, railed against sin generally, and those connected with plays and players, in particular. That drama having been played out, Cooke became a peripatetic, traversing the three kingdoms on foot, and meeting more examples and incidents for the *History of a Vagabond* than ever entered into the experience or the imagination of Goldsmith. He contrived to fall into the way of scholars and universities,—and from these, whether they were in Oxford, Dublin, or Edinburgh, he never turned, hungry. It is hardly necessary to say that his eccentricities brought him, by the way, to "Bedlam," that hell upon earth, where men were driven fiendishly mad, who were only harmlessly so before. Cooke, recovering his liberty, never recovered method with his madness. The latter was intensified by an aggravation in its old mystic element, and this poor fellow, who is said to have realized more money in fees for dedications which he never wrote, to plays which were never acted, died, characteristically enough, according to report, of the consequences of following an example set in heathen days, by Atys, and in a Christian period by Origen,—without, however, having had the cause pleaded by the one, or the reason alleged by the other.

To conclude this chapter with a word on Benefits. These are of royal invention, and the first, already recorded, was awarded by King James to Elizabeth Barry,—a tribute to her genius. The fashion has not died out, but that of announcing them, as of yore, *has*. For example, the *Spectator* often put in a good word for George Powell. Sometimes there was an intimation that George, well qualified, but ever and anon careless, would distinguish himself, if the public would only patronize the "Conquest of Mexico," to be acted for his benefit. When, in April, 1712, he was, on a like occasion, to play Falstaff, in the first part of "Henry IV.," it was after this fashion that the *Spectator* did a good turn for its particular friend. " The haughty George Powell hopes all the good-natured part of the town will favor him whom they applauded in Alexander, Timon, Lear, and Orestes, with their company this night, when he hazards all his heroic glory in the humbler condition of honest Jack Falstaff."

It is pleasant, too, to observe that though actors lost their engagements and endured much privation in consequence, they were not forgotten. I frequently meet with announcements of benefits "for some distressed actors, lately of this house;"—and, occasionally, if circumstances rendered the benefit less productive than was expected, a second is gratuitously given to make up for the deficit. Again, "For the benefit of a gentleman who has written for the stage," shows a delicate feeling for a modest, or a damned, author. And as "for sufferers from fire," "wards in Middlesex Hospital," or "for the building of churches and chapels," or for "Lying-in Hospitals," the stage was never weary of lending itself to such good purposes of relief. It was not till May, 1766, that the profession began to think of doing something for itself, and I find a benefit announced "towards raising a fund for the relief of those who, from their infirmities, shall be obliged to retire from the stage." Garrick played Kitely on this occasion.

In 1719, Spiller advertised a performance at Lincoln's Inn Fields, "for the benefit of himself and creditors." The announcement, in the shape of a letter, is a curious document. "I think," says this one-eyed comedian, "I have found out what will please the multitude . . I have tolerable good luck, and tickets rise apace, which makes mankind very civil to me, for I get up every morning to a levee of at least a dozen people, who pay their compliments and ask the same question, 'When shall we be paid?' All I can say is, that wicked good company has brought me into this imitation of grandeur. I loved my friend and my jest too well to grow rich: in short, wit," says the comedian, sporting with his own infirmity, "is my blind side." Theophilus Cibber was often as candid, sometimes more impertinent. In May, 1722, he announces "Richard III." for his benefit, "for the entertainment of those who will come." He sometimes advertised his benefit as being for himself and creditors conjointly, and in April, 1746, we find him,—a comedian of the first rank, thus appealing to the consideration of the public: "As I have, in justice to my creditors, assigned over so much of my salary as reduces the remainder to a very small pittance, I very much depend on the indulgence and encouragement of the town at my benefit, whose favors shall be gratefully remembered, by their very humble servant, Theophilus Cibber." Such an announcement would sound curiously in these days, but it was, perhaps, exceeded in singularity by Lillo's advertisement, in 1740, of the performance, on the third, or author's night, of his "Elmeric," "for the benefit of my poor relations." The frankness of the avowal and the liberality suggested are social traits worth preserving.

One of the observances which *beneficiaires* were expected to follow, has long gone out of usage,—namely, that of personally calling on those whose patronage was hoped for. Apologies for the omission are very common. In 1723, Bickerstaffe announces the "Mourning Bride" and "State Coach," with this appendix to his bill:—"N. B. Bickerstaffe being confined to his bed by his sameness, and his wife lying now dead, has nobody to wait on the quality and his friends, for him; but hopes they'll favor him with their appearance."

Again, Bullock in 1739, advertises the "Spanish Friar," with himself as Dominic. The once lively fellow thus pleads *his* excuse:—"Bullock hopes his great age, upwards of threescore years and twelve, will plead his excuse that he cannot pay his duty to his acquaintance and friends, whose good nature may engage them to assist him in his decline of life, in order to make the remainder of his days easy and comfortable to him. In his younger days he had the pleasure and happiness of entertaining the town; and Sir Richard Steele, in his *Tatler*, has been pleased to perpetuate his memory in honoring him with a memorial there. As this is the last time he may possibly beg the favor of the town, he hopes to receive their indulgence, which, for the few remaining days, shall be gratefully acknowledged by him."

In like half friendly, half humble, style, and with something, too, of the same reflective element, Chapman of Covent Garden, about to play Modely, in the "Country Lasses," adds the apologetic "N. B." to his advertisement:—"I, being in danger of losing one of my eyes, am advised to keep it from the air, therefore stir not out to attend my business at the theatre,—on this melancholy occasion, I hope my friends will be so indulgent as to send for tickets to my house, the corner of Bow Street, Covent Garden, which favor will be gratefully acknowledged by their obedient humble servant, Thomas Chapman." Chapman was only under misfortune; he was not like the younger Cibber, who was as extravagant and as deeply in debt in 1740 as in 1722. At the foot of the advertisement for his benefit in the first-named year are some singular but not altogether unsatisfactory words;—whereby his creditors are requested to meet and receive a fourth dividend of his salary! His creditors were interested in all his benefits.

In the following year, at the Goodman's Fields Theatre, Blakes and Miss Hippisley had a joint benefit, which was curiously announced as "for the entertainment of several of the ancient and honorable society of Free and Accepted Masons." The pieces were the "Miser," and "Lethe," Blakes playing Clerimont and the Frenchman, and Miss Hippisley, Lappet and Miss Lucy. The patronizing brethren met at the Fleece Tavern, and walked processionally and "cloathed," to that part of the pit which was especially railed in for them.

When Woodward advertised his benefit in 1745, at Covent Garden, on which occasion he played Sir Amorous la Foole, in the "Silent Woman," and Harlequin, in the "Rape of Proserpine," he made no especial appeal to the public. But Merchant Tailors did not forget their old school-fellow, and a letter in the *General Advertiser* called upon Merchant Tailors, generally, to rally round their condiscipulus, for,—"The original design of forming ourselves into a society was, as I take it, to serve and promote the interest of our school-fellows," &c.

The benefits of the greater actors, however profitable to themselves, must have afforded but few pleasant stage illusions to the public. On these occasions, the stage itself was converted into an amphitheatre, or was built round with boxes for the convenience of ladies, while the pit,—if necessary, was turned into ground tiers of boxes,—at increased prices. Remembering how fierce the spirit and unscrupulous the actions of that pit could be, when offended, the patience with which it endured being turned out was especially remarkable. The public of that day seems to have been treated with alternate contempt and servility. When Yates took his benefit at Goodman's Fields, he advertised the impossibility of his calling personally on theatrical patrons in the neighborhood, on the ground that he had got into such a strange part of the town, he could not find his way about the streets.

Sometimes an appeal was made to the compassion of the public, as by generally hilarious Hippisley, who, about to play Scrub for his benefit, at Covent Garden, in 1747, announces in the *General Advertiser*, "he is so far recovered from his late illness, that though considerably altered in his physiognomy, and lowered in spirits, he persuades himself a crowded house on Thursday next, at the 'Stratagem,' for his benefit, will create a smile on his countenance, raise his spirits, and make him appear as much a Scrub as ever."

In the same year there was an ambitious young actor at Goodman's Fields, named Goodfellow, who played Hamlet and Fribble, two of Garrick's best characters, for his benefit; for taking which he gave the singular reason, that " my friends having expressed a great dislike to my being on the stage, I have resolved upon taking this benefit to enable me to return to my former employment." The public accordingly patronized him in order to get rid of him, and the young fellow was so grateful that he remained on the stage!

These examples are cited as they occur to me, and I will not add to them; but rather turn away, to mark some eminent actors flitting from the stage, and some samples of the public opinion connected with it, before the coming of Edmund Kean.

## CHAPTER XXIV.

### OLD STAGERS DEPARTING.

OF the old actors who entered on the nineteenth century, King was the first to depart. He is remembered now, chiefly, as the original representative of Sir Peter Teazle, Lord Ogleby, Puff, and Dr. Cantwell. He began his London career at the age of eighteen in 1748, on Drury Lane stage, as the Herald in "King Lear,' and made such progress, that in the next year Whitehead selected him to play Valerius in his "Roman Father." By 1756 he was an established favorite, and he remained on the London stage, with hard summer work during the holidays, till the 24th of May, 1802, when he took his leave in Sir Peter, to the Lady Teazle of Mrs. Jordan. At the end of upwards of half a century he withdrew, to linger four years more, a man of straitened means—one whom fondness for "play" would not at first allow to grow rich: nor, after that was accomplished, to remain so. I have noticed a few of his principal original characters; of others, his Touchstone has not been equalled, nor his Ranger, save by Garrick and Elliston. He was a conscientious actor, and a prime favorite during the greater part of his career—but the once rapid, clear, arch, easy, versatile Tom King, remained on the stage somewhat too long.

Suett was to "low," what King was to "genteel," comedy; and the stage lost Dicky in 1805, in which year he died. Dicky Suett was the successor, but not the equal, of Parsons. For a comic actor he had a very tragical method of life—indicated by a bottle of rum and another of brandy being among the furniture of his breakfast table. From 1780 to 1805 he was a favorite low comedian; he killed his audiences with laughter, and then went home (the tavern intervening) to bed, where his sleep was merely a night of horror caused by hideous dreams, and mental and bodily agony. John Kemble appreciated him, in Weazle particularly, which he played to the tragedian's Penruddock, and by his

VOL. II.—15

impertinent and persevering inquiries, peering into Penruddock's face, used to work him up into a condition of irritability required by the part. He was tall, thin, and ungainly; addicted to grimace and interpolations; given to practical jokes on his brother actors on the stage; and original in every thing, even to encountering death with a pun excited by a sign of its dread approach. Suett was one of those perversely conscientious actors, that when he had to represent a drunkard, he took care, as Tony Lumpkin says, to be in " a concatenation accordingly."

In 1809 Lewis withdrew, in his sixty-third year. He was a Lancashire man, well descended, though a draper's son, and was educated at Armagh. He left linen-drapery for the stage, played with success in Dublin and Edinburgh, and came to Covent Garden in 1773, where, however, he did not displace Barry, as in Dublin he had vanquished Mossop. He remained at Covent Garden from 1773, when he appeared in Belcour (a compliment to Cumberland, who had helped to bring him thither), till the 29th of May, 1809, when he took his farewell in the Copper Captain, the best of all his parts. He died in 1813, and out of part of his fortune bequeathed to his sister, the beautiful new church at Ealing was chiefly erected. His various styles are indicated by some of the parts he created. Pharnaces and Sir Charles Racket; Arviragus (Caractacus) and Millamour; Percy and Doricourt; Sir Thomas Overbury and Count Almaviva; Herodian and Lackland; Aurungzebe ("Prince of Agra") and Young Rapid; Faulkland and Jeremy Diddler: he played Carlos in the "Revenge," and created the Hon. Tom Shuffleton in "John Bull;" acted Posthumus, and originated Vapid; began his course of original parts with Witmore, in Dr. Kenrick's "Duellist;" and ended them with Modern, in Reynolds's "Begone Dull Care"—both of which plays were failures.

In Morton and Reynolds's comedies, his breathless and restless style told well; but Lewis's reputation is connected with the authors of an older period. His Copper Captain was a masterpiece; and Cooke recorded of him, that during the last thirty years of his life, he was the unrivalled favorite of the comic muse, in all that was frolic, gay, humorous, whimsical, eccentric, and at the same time elegant." During twenty-one years he was manager of Covent Garden; and the same writer testifies that Lewis was "a model for making every one do his duty, by kindness and good treatment." As early as 1802, he had been warned by an epileptic fit, while rehearsing Sapling, in Reynolds's "Delays and Blunders;" but he recovered, played two years longer, and in less than two years more died, leaving a handsome fortune to his wife, children, and other members of his family.

The greatest loss to the stage, in the early years of the present century, was in the person of Miss Pope, the only real successor of Kitty Clive. She withdrew on the 26th of May, 1808, after playing Deborah Dowlas in the "Heir at Law," for the first and last time. She had played as a child when Garrick was in the fullest of his powers; won his regard, and the friendly counsel of Mrs. Clive; played hoidens, chambermaids, and half-bred ladies, with a life, dash, and manner, free from all vulgarity; laughed with free hilarity that begot hilarious laughing; and the only question about her was not if she were an excellent actress or not, but as an actress, in what she most excelled. She gave up young parts for old as age came on, and would have done it sooner, but that managers found her still attractive in the younger characters. In them she had been without a rival; and when she took to the Duennas and Mrs. Heidelbergs, she became equally without a rival. She was the original Polly Honeycombe, Miss Sterling, Mrs. Candour, Tilburina, and of two or threescore other parts, less known.

Miss Pope was as good a woman, and as well bred a lady, as she was a finished actress, and was none the less a friend of Garrick for having little theatrical controversies with him touching costume, salary, or other stage matters. In the year she played Cherry, Polly Honeycombe, Jacinta, Phædra, Beatrice, Miss Prue, Miss Biddy, and other buoyant ladies and lasses, a poet said of her:—

> "With all the native vigor of sixteen,
> Among the merry groups conspicuous seen,
> See lively Pope advance to jig and trip,
> Corinna, Cherry, Honeycombe, and Snip!
> Not without art, but yet to nature true,
> She charms the town with humor, just, yet new,
> Cheered by her promise, we the less deplore
> The fatal time when Clive shall be no more."

Such was she in Churchill's eyes, in 1761. The fairy of that day; but, in 1807, the fairy had expanded into "a bulky person, with a duplicity of chin." Such was she in the eyes of Horace Smith, to whom she told her love for handsome but fickle Holland, losing,—or casting off whom,—she never after heeded suit of mortal man.

In the drawing-room of her and her brother's house in Queen Street, Lincoln's Inn Fields, two doors east of the Freemason's Tavern, in that richly furnished apartment, where, for forty years Miss Pope lived,—among choice portraits of Mrs. Oldfield and her little son, afterwards General Churchill; of Lord Nuneham, who, as Earl of Harcourt, visited Miss Pope with as much ceremonious courtesy as if she had been a princess; of Garrick and of Holland,—the old lady told the tale of her young love, her hopes and her disappointment, to Horace Smith. Garrick, or "Mr. Garrick," as Miss Pope, with the old habit of reverence, used to call him, had observed the intimacy and growing attachment between the young actor and actress, and, guardian of the happiness of those whom he regarded, he warned the lady of the waywardness, instability, and recklessness of the swain. But Holland could persuade in his own cause more successfully than Garrick could urge against him; and Miss Pope, trusting the man she loved, looked confidently forward to the day when she would become his wife. Ere that day arrived, she went in the old Richmond coach, on her way to pay a visit to Mrs. Clive, at Twickenham; and on the road, she passed a post-chaise, in which were Holland and a lady. The perplexed Miss Pope rode thoughtfully on, and, alighting at Richmond Bridge, walked meditatively along the meadows to Strawberry Hill. Her jealous attention was attracted by a boat on the river, opposite Eel Pie Island, the rower of which could not so hurriedly but confusedly pull through the weeds to the Richmond side, before she saw that he was her faithless swain, Holland, making a day of it with that seductive piece of mischief, Mrs. Baddeley. Poor Miss Pope might fairly confess to the "pang of jealousy," which she then endured.

Shortly after, they met at rehearsal. He, being conscious of wrong and incapable of confessing it, assumed a haughty bearing, but the injured woman was as proud as he; and from that time they never exchanged a word, except in acting. The foolish, weak, and ungrateful fellow, went philandering on; "but I have reason to know," said Miss Pope, "that he never was really happy." And forty years after this rude waking from a happy illusion, and in presence of the counterfeit presentment of her faithless lover, the lady, whose heart at least never grew old, shed tears as she told the one love passage of her life, and thought of the dream of the bygone time.

Out of life she faded gradually away; and one of the merriest and most vivacious actresses of her day lost, mutely, sense after sense ere she expired. Previous to this, she had left her old familiar house in Queen Street; much as she was attached to it, she found the Freemasons too lively neighbors. "From the Tavern, on a summer's evening, when windows are perforce kept open, the sounds of 'Prosperity to the Deaf and Dumb Charity!' sent forth a corresponding clatter of glasses, which made everybody in Miss Pope's back drawing-room, for the moment, fit objects of that benevolent institution." Mr. James Smith alludes to the pleasant parties she gave at the house in Newman Street, in which she died. She was attacked by "stupor of the brain;" and gradually passed away. "She sat quietly and calmly in an arm-chair by the fireside, patting the head of her poodle dog, and smiling in what passed in conversation, without being at all conscious of the meaning of what was uttered."

Miss Pope had a sort of *doublure* in Mrs. Mattocks, granddaughter of the Hallam unhappily killed by Macklin. Her father was the founder of the English drama in America. Under his management, the first play ever regularly performed beyond the Atlantic, was at Williamsburg, in Virginia, on the 5th of September, 1752, namely, the "Merchant of Venice," in which Malone acted Shylock; Hallam, Launcelot Gobbo; and Mrs. Hallam, Portia. During Mrs. Mattocks's long career, from 1752, when a child, to 1808, she played a variety of characters, commencing with tragedy; but, as she used to say, in her old age,— "so long ago I have almost forgotten it." She thence passed through light, young, comic characters, to old women; and played the latter very happily. In her widowhood, she bestowed a rich marriage dowry on her daughter, reserving for herself the interest of £6,000 in the five per cents, on which to live, at Kensington. Her son-in-law held her general power of attorney, and received her dividends; but he one day made away with both interest and principal, and the old actress was left penniless. A free benefit, however, produced upwards of £1,000, with which a life annuity was purchased, on which the aged player lived till 1826. If human art could have prolonged her life, it would have been done by her friend and medical adviser, the late Mr. Merriman, to whom, in testimony of her respect, Mrs. Mattocks bequeathed her portrait.

I add a passing word to record the passing away of Mrs. Litchfield, in 1806, after a brief career in London, of nine years. She came at a time when competition with Mrs. Siddons was impossible; but Mrs. Litchfield was pre-eminent in having the finest voice that was ever heard on the stage,—from an actress.

Bannister, Charles or John, father or son,—the name had a pleasant sound in our fathers' ears. The elder was a bass singer, with a voice that would crack a window pane. "A *pewtiful foice!* your father had," said a German Jew to the son; "so deep, so deep! He could go so low as a bull!" Handsome Jack played in his salad days, with Garrick; in his glowing maturity, with Edmund Kean,—in whose brilliancy, as he said, he almost forgot his old master, David. John Bannister might have been a painter, but he chose to be a player; and, in his line, he was one of the best. He felt, and made feel; could exact tears as easily as laughter; and was never out of temper but once, when a critic denounced him for acting ill, on a night when he was too ill to act. For this malicious deed, the player recovered damages from his assailant.

There was nothing he could not do *well*. There were many things he did inimitably. His Hamlet belonged to the first—a host of comic parts to the second category. His author was never dissatisfied with him, however exigent; and he engaged the immediate attention of the audience, by seeming to care nothing about it. Applause interrupted his speech—never his action. In depicting heartiness, ludicrous distress, grave or affected indifference, honest bravery, insurmountable cowardice, a spirited young, or an enfeebled old fellow, yet impatient; mischievous boyishness, good-humored vulgarity,—there was no one of his time who could equal him. In every thing he acted he was natural, except in Mercutio, which, strangely enough, did not suit him:—he made of that elegant and vivacious gentleman, simply an honest, jolly fellow. In parts, combining tragedy and comedy, he was supreme. Such was his Walter; such, too, his Sheva,—though in some parts of the latter he was, perhaps, surpassed by Dowton. His features were highly expressive and flexible, and he had them in supreme command. In 1772, he played Calippus, in the "Grecian Daughter," and then had a time of probation; but, from 1778, when he played Zaphna, in "Mahomet," to 1815, when the curtain finally descended on him, as Walter,—a part which he created in 1793,—there was no more pleasant actor before an audience. Walpole thus speaks of the last-named part in the year just named:

"I went on Monday evening, with Mrs. Damer, to the Little Haymarket, to see the 'Children in the Wood,' having heard so much of my favorite, young Bannister, in that new piece, which, by the way, is well arranged, and near being fine. He more than answered my expectation, and all I had heard of him. It was one of the most admirable performances I ever saw. His transports of despair and joy are incomparable; and his various countenances would be adapted to the pencil of Salvator Rosa. He made me shed as many tears as I suppose the old original ballad did, when I was six years old. Bannister's merit was the more striking, as, before the 'Children in the Wood,' he had been playing the sailor, in 'No Song, No Supper,' with equal nature. I wish I could hope to be as much pleased to-morrow night, when I am to go to Jerningham's play, the 'Siege of Berwick;' but there is no Bannister at Covent Garden."

He left the stage with a handsome fortune, the fruits of his labor; and younger actors visited him and called him "father!" Among the very long list of characters he created at Drury Lane or the Haymarket, were Don Ferolo Whiskerandos, Inkle, Sir David Dunder, Robin ("No Song, No Supper"), Leopold ("Siege of Belgrade"), Lenitive ("Prize"), Walter ("Children in the Wood"), Will Steady, Sheva, Michael ("Adopted Child"), Sylvester Daggerwood, Three Singles, Wilford ("Iron Chest"), Sponge,

Frank Heartall, Rolando ("Honey Moon"), Ali Baba, Storm, and Sam Squib, in "Past Ten o'Clock." A print, from a miniature, by Edridge, shows how goodly was his presence in young manhood off the stage; his well-known portrait, as Colonel Feignwell, reveals a handsome presence on the stage; and in his features, which Leslie borrowed for his "Uncle Toby," we may see (in the picture at Kensington) a presence fine, frank, and simple, which was that of his older age.

Mrs. Jordan was another of the players whose youth belonged to the last century, but who did not retire till after Edmund Kean had given new life to the stage. She came of a lively mother, who was one of the many olive branches of a poor Welsh clergyman, from whose humble home she more undutifully than unnaturally, eloped with, and married a gallant Captain, named Bland. The new home was set up in Waterford, where Dorothy Bland was born in 1762; and nine children were there living when the Captain's friends procured the annulling of the marriage, and caused the hearth to become desolate.

Dorothy was the most self-reliant of the family, for at an early age she made her way to Dublin, and under the name of Miss Francis, played every thing, from sprightly girls to tragedy queens. As she produced little or no effect, she crossed the Channel to Tate Wilkinson, who inquired what she played,—tragedy, comedy, high or low, opera or farce? "I play them all!" said the young lady,—and accordingly she came out as Calista, in the "Fair Penitent;" and Lucy, in the "Virgin Unmasked." Previously to this, Wilkinson, addressing her as Miss Francis, was interrupted by her,—"my name," she said, "is Mrs. Jordan,"—her Irish manager had called her flight over the Channel, "crossing *Jordan*," and she took the name with the matronly prefix. Wilkinson looked at her, and saw no reason why she should not.

Three years after, she was acting some solemn part, at York, when Gentleman Smith saw her, and forthwith recommended her to the managers of Drury, as a good *second* to Mrs. Siddons; and in that character she was engaged. But Dorothy Jordan was not going to play second to anybody; she resolved to be first in comedy, and came out in 1785, as the heroine of the "Country

Girl." Her success raised her from four to eight, and then twelve pounds a week. Her next character was among her best; namely, Viola; in which the buoyant spirit oppressed by love and grief was finely rendered. Equal to it was her Hypolita. Rosalind, also one of her great achievements, she did not play till the next season; and Lady Contest ("Wedding Day"), which was born with, and which died with her, she did not create till the season of 1795-6.

When she first appeared in London, she was in her twenty-fourth year. Just previous to the commencement of the Drury Lane season of 1789-90, the season in which she added Polly Honeycombe, Laetitia Hardy, and Lydia Languish, to her parts; and created Little Pickle, in the "Spoiled Child," I find indications of another condition which she had reached. On the 4th of September, 1789, Walpole writes from Strawberry Hill to the Miss Berrys: "The Duke of Clarence has taken Mr. Henry Hobart's house (Richmond), point blank over against Mr. Cambridge's, which will make the good woman of that mansion cross herself piteously, and stretch the throat of the blatant beast at Sudbrook (Lady Greenwich), and of all the other pious matrons *à la ronde;* for his royal highness, to divert loneliness, has brought with him ————, who being still more averse to solitude, declares that any tempter would make even Paradise more agreeable than a constant *tête-à-tête.*" The Duke's companion is not named; but Mrs. Jordan is supposed to be alluded to. But in September, 1791, Walpole writes to the same ladies: "Do you know that Mrs. Jordan is acknowledged to be Mrs. Ford?" They could not know it, for Ford (the magistrate) never married her, though he kept household with her, where all the signs of matrimony were at least abundant.

In the previous March of that year Mrs. Jordan played Cœlia, in an adaptation of the "Humorous Lieutenant," called the "Greek Slave," for her benefit. Cœlia is the mistress to a king's son; and this, coupled with a prophetic allusion in the modern epilogue, to a future condition in her life, which was not then, in the remotest degree, contemplated, is noted in Mr. Boaden's life of the actress, as a coincidence. At whatever period she first became the intimate friend of the Duke, she certainly was never married to Ford. "Her husband," the wits used to say, "was killed in the battle of Nubibus."

When she said that "laughing agreed with her better than crying," and gave up tragedy, she both said and did well. John Bannister declared that "no woman ever uttered comedy like her;" and added, that she was perfectly good-tempered, and possessed the best of hearts." She partook of the fascination of Mrs. Woffington, having a better voice, with less beauty. She surpassed Mrs. Clive and Miss Farren, in some parts, but fell short of the former in termagants, and of the latter in fine, well-bred ladies. Her voice was sweet and distinct, and she played rakes with the airiest grace and the handsomest leg that had been seen on the stage for a long time. Simple, arch, buoyant girls,—with sensibility in them; or spirited, buxom, lovable women,—in these she excelled. She liked to act handsome hoidens, but not vulgar hussies. In later days she grew fat, but still dressed as when she was young. The hints of critics were unheeded by her, as were those of her friends, that "she should assume an older line." Mr. Charlton, the Bath manager, once proposed to her to play the "Old Maid." "No," she answered: "I played it in a frolic, for my benefit, but do not mean to play such parts in a common way."

After a London career of little less than thirty years,—long after her home with the Duke had been broken up, she suddenly left London, without any leave-taking. Her finances, once so flourishing, had become embarrassed,—and the old actress with whom "laughing used to agree," withdrew without friend or child or ample means, to St. Cloud, in France, where she assumed her third pseudonym, Mrs. James. She was neglected, but she was not destitute; for at the time of her death, in 1815, she had a balance of £100 at her bankers. She was buried without a familiar friend to follow her, and the police seized and sold her effects,—"even her body-linen," says Genest, who wrote her epitaph, "was sold amidst the coarse remarks of low Frenchwomen." Her wealth had been largely lavished on the Duke of Clarence and their family; and she had calls upon it from other children. In the days when she was mistress of the house at Bushey she was often, with more or less ill humor, saluted as

"Duchess." When the Duke became King, he ennobled all their children, raising the eldest of Mrs. Jordan's sons to the rank of Earl of Munster, and giving precedence to the remaining sons and daughters. Thus the blood of this actress, too, runs in the English peerage,—in the line of the Earls of Munster, and by her daughter Sophia, whom the King raised to the rank of a Marquis's daughter, in that of the Lords De L'Isle and Dudley. If the portrait of the Monarch hangs from the walls of their mansions, that of Dora or Dorothea Bland should not be absent; for, despite appearances, the worth, the virtue, and the endowments of the mother were, in many respects, greater than those of the sire.

ROBERT WILLIAM ELLISTON, like Mrs. Jordan and some others, belongs to two centuries. Born in Bloomsbury, in 1744, he had, in due time, the choice of two callings,—that of his father, a watchmaker; or of his uncle, the Rev. Dr. Elliston, master of Sidney Sussex College, Cambridge,—"the Church." He declined both; and having been applauded in his delivery of a thesis, at St. Paul's School, on the subject: "Nemo confidat nimium secundis," he threw up his own happy prospects, and ran away to Bath, at sixteen, to seek an engagement on the stage. While waiting for it, he engaged himself as clerk in a lottery-office; but he eagerly changed his character, when opportunity was afforded him to act Tressel, in "Richard III." Between that and the Duke Aranza, the greatest of his parts, he had far to go; but his energies were equal to the task.

The first success was small, and Elliston resorted to Tate Wilkinson, at York; where he had few opportunities of playing leading characters; and in disgust and want, he came up to London. Kemble advised him to study Romeo, and in that character he charmed a Bath audience, and laid the foundations of a future prosperity. Subsequently, after playing a few nights at Covent Garden, he appeared at the Haymarket, in 1797, as Octavian and Vapor. In the first part, a rival to the throne of Kemble was recognized; in the latter, one who had gifts which were wanting even in Bannister. A few nights later, he played Sir Edward Mortimer, and obtained a triumph in the character in which Kemble had signally failed. From that time, the "greatness" of Elliston was an accepted matter in his lofty mind. But it suffered much mutation between that time and 1826, when, at the end of nearly thirty years, after being proprietor of the Olympic, the Surrey, and Drury Lane, disregarding the prudence of Kemble in refraining from such an attempt, he tried Falstaff, failed thereby to recover his ruined fortunes, and sank again to the Surrey. Famous for putting the best face on every thing, he comforted himself, by observing, that he had "quite an opera pit!"

For a brief period after his first appearance, Elliston was held to have excelled Kemble in truth and inspiration. Elliston's Hamlet was accounted superior in two points, the humor of the Dane, and his princely youth;—but in the deep philosophy of the character, Robert William was not above respectability. And yet, by his universality of imitation, he was pronounced to be the only genius that had appeared since the days of Garrick. Perhaps he never manifested this more clearly than when, on the same night, he played Macbeth and Macheath!

His soliloquies were too declamatory: he forgot that a soliloquy is not an address to the audience, but simply a vehicle to enable them to be familiar with the speaker's thoughts. His voice was here too pompously deep, and a certain catching of his breath, at the end of energetic words, sounded like sobbing. Nevertheless, it was said that Elliston was not less than Kemble in genius;—but only in manner. With study and a more heroic countenance he would have been on the same level. As it was, *in general excellence*, he may be said, when in his prime, to have been one of the greatest actors of the day.

A more complete stage "gentleman," our fathers and some of ourselves never knew. He was well made; had a smile more winning and natural than any other actor; and perhaps a lover so impassioned never made suit to a lady; one so tender never watched over her; one so courteous never did her offices of courtesy; the *gentleman* was never forgotten. He was never a restless gentleman, like Lewis, nor a reserved or languid one, like Charles Kemble. All the qualities that go to the making of one, were conspicuous in his Duke Aranza,—self-command, kindness, dignity, good humor, a dash of satire, and true amatory fire. The only fault of Elliston's low comedy was that he could not get rid of his gentility. The only fault of his real gentlemen was that he dressed them uniformly. Summer or winter, day or night, they were always in blue coats, white waistcoats, and white knee-breeches.

Leigh Hunt loved the actor; Charles Lamb reverenced the man,—that is, the actor also: for Robert William, wherever he might be, was in presence of an audience; it was his nature to be artificial; or he was so great an artist that all things in his bearing seemed natural; that is, natural to him, Robert William Elliston. When he seemed to be enacting the "humbug," he was perfectly consistent, without being the thing at all. Young Douglas Jerrold saved the Surrey with his "Black-eyed Susan," and Elliston thought such service worthy of being acknowledged by the presentation of a piece of plate. The anxious author wondered in what form Mr. Elliston would make the gift; but Mr. Elliston only asked him, if he, the author, could not get his friends to do him this service? He was not joking. He thought the young fellow's friends ought to be proud of him, and ought to manifest their pride by endowing him with testimonial plate,—towards which he, Robert William, had largely contributed by starting the idea.

Of his lofty remonstrances with audiences, his magnificence of matter and of manner, the awe with which he inspired the humbler actors of his company by believing in his own lofty manner, —there are samples enough to fill a volume. The "bless you my people!" which he uttered as George IV., in the coronation procession, sprung, it was said, from a vinous excitement; but it was thoroughly in his manner. He would have believed in the efficacy of a sober benediction of the pit! He outlived his fame, as he did his fortune; his powers to act well failed, but not his acting. He was imposing to the last; and, perhaps beyond that limit, if we might accept that gracefully fantastic sketch which Charles Lamb has addressed to his shade,—the "joyousest of once embodied spirits!"

There were few actors on the stage for whom Elliston had more regard than he had for the veteran, Hull. In 1807, worn out with a career which dated from 1759, heavy, useful, and intelligent Hull played his last character, the Uncle, in "George Barnwell," and he died soon after. Mason had a good opinion of him, for in consigning the Chief Bard, in "Caractacus," to be played by him, the poet remarked: "Any instruction from me will be unnecessary; your own taste and judgment will direct you." To Hull is owing the establishment of the Covent Garden fund for the benefit of decayed actors. He proposed that sixpence in the pound should be contributed weekly from each actor's salary, and that such contributors only should have claim upon the fund. From this proposal issued the two "funds,"—once so useful, and now so rich. Hull never acted so well as during the Lord George Gordon riots, when a mob assembled in front of his house, roared for beer, and threatened dire results, if the roar was unheeded. Hull appeared on the balcony, bowed thrice, assured the "ladies and gentlemen" that the beverage should be immediately forthcoming, and in the mean time asked them for "their usual indulgence."

To the last century, too, and to this, belong Holman, Munden, and Dowton. All began their careers as tragedians. Holman was graceful, but in striving to be original fell into exaggeration, and excited laughter. His London course only lasted from 1784 to 1800, when he wandered abroad with his daughter, whose mother was a grand-daughter of the famous Lady Archibald Hamilton, the daughter of the sixth Earl of Abercorn. Thus a family, into which had married the daughter of Miss Santlow, "famed for dance," gave to the stage the Miss Holman, who soon ceased to figure there.

Munden was the most wonderful of grimaciers. He created laughter on the London stage, from 1790, when he appeared at Covent Garden, as Sir Francis Gripe, to 1823, when he quitted it, in good condition, financially, as Sir Robert Bramble and Dozey. It was said of him that he lost half his proper effect, by the very strength of his powers. The breadth of his acting is now hardly conceivable, so farcical was its character. Of another trait of his disposition, an incident, on his farewell night, affords an illustration. As he was bowing, and retiring backwards, from the audience, and wishing to avoid coming into collision with the wings, he once or twice asked in a whisper, of those standing there: "Am I near?" "Very!" answered Liston, "nobody more so!"

Dowton, who came to us in 1796, as Sheva, backed by a

recommendation from Cumberland, retired less richly endowed than Munden. He was most felicitous in representing testy old age, but especially where extreme rage was combined with extreme kindness of heart; and he acted the opposite of this just as felicitously,—as they will acknowledge who can remember both his Sir Anthony Absolute and his Dr. Cantwell, the composure and rascality of which last are exasperating in the very memory of them.

Willy Blanchard, who opens the period commencing with the year 1800, was as natural as Dowton; but he was a mannerist, always walking the stage with his right arm bent, as if he held it in a sling. I find him often preferred to Fawcett, whom I remember as a superior actor, to whom some stern critics denied all feeling,—but they had not seen his Job Thornbury; and of whose famous Caleb Quotem they could say no more than that the actor of it was a speaking harlequin.

Mathews, who first appeared in London, at the Haymarket, in 1803, as Jubal to Elliston's Sheva, was as superior to Dowton in many parts as he was to Bannister in a few. As a mimic, he has never been excelled in my remembrance. Through the whole range of lower comedy he was supreme ; and his *M. Malet* showed what power this great artist could exercise over the most tender feelings. No comedian ever compelled more hearty laughter, or, when opportunity offered, as in *M. Malet*, more abundant tears.

Liston, who followed him at the Haymarket, in 1805, making his *début* as Sheepface, belonged rather to farce than comedy. Like Suett, he excited more laughter than he ever enjoyed himself. He suffered from attacks of the nerves, and, in his most humorous representations, was the more humorous from his humor always partaking of a melancholy tone. He seemed to be comic under some great calamity, and was only upheld by the hilarity of those who witnessed his sufferings, and enjoyed his comedy under difficulties. Perhaps, he had a settled disappointment in not having succeeded in tragedy ; or some remorse, as though he had killed a boy when, under the name of Williams, he was usher at the Rev. Dr. Burney's, at Gosport; as he subsequently was at the old school in St. Martin's. However this may be, he ever and anon wooed the tragic muse, with a comically serious air, and on three several occasions I trace him playing, for his benefit, Romeo, Octavian, and Baron Wildenheim! It was more absurd than Mrs. Powell's mania for acting Hamlet.

Two years later, in 1807, appeared Young, as Hamlet, at the Haymarket, and Jones, as Goldfinch, at Covent Garden. If the word "respectable" might be used in a not disparaging sense, I would apply it to Young, who was always worthy of respect,—whether he played Hamlet, Rienzi, which he originated, Falstaff, or Captain Macheath. He belonged to the Kemble school, but he never delivered soliloquies in that ludicrous, self-approving style which I find laughingly noticed by the critics, as a great blot in John Kemble's acting. Young had more natural feeling, and he liked to play with those who could feel in like manner,—whereas I have read of John Kemble that, in a love scene, he was not only coldly proper himself, but insisted on the same coldness of propriety in the lady who played his mistress. As for Airy Jones, I have only space to remark, that he acted rakes, at night, and taught clergymen to read their prayers decently, by day? Jones was a naturally serious man; but his combination of callings was something incongruous.

Of other actors, mention will be made incidentally in other places. There are some ladies of the time before Edmund Kean who will receive, or have received like notice,—my eye falls but upon three others, of whom I need make record here. One is that beautiful Louisa Brunton,—member of a gifted family, who, in the bud of her brilliant promise, was "crept the stage" by honorable love, and died but the other day,—Countess of Craven. The other lady is Miss Duncan, subsequently Mrs. Davison, the original Juliana to Elliston's Duke Aranza; and who, when she came upon the town as Lady Teazle, satisfied her audiences that Miss Farren had a worthy successor, and that Mrs. Jordan's possession of certain characters must thenceforth be surrendered. The dramatic life of this admirable actress commenced as soon as she could walk, and lasted almost with her natural life. I have a Margate bill before me, of the year 1804, where the bright and gifted young actress, the "Little Wonder," as Miss Farren called her, was playing high comedy. The music there was led by Frederick Venua, who, at the distance of threescore years, still delights his friends with the memories of that period, and with its music, in the rendering of which, Time has strengthened and improved the hand of the artist.

With a passing notice of a survivor of all these,—coming on the stage near fourscore years ago, with the honored name of Betterton, and leaving it, or dying on it, but the other day, as Mrs. Glover, I close this section of my labor. From youth to old age she acted appropriate parts, and acted all in a way that would require Cibber, Hazlitt, and Leigh Hunt to describe, analyze, and grow pleasantly fanciful upon. Her life was one of self-denial, unmerited suffering, and of continual gratification to others. She was the support of three generations, the evidences of which she bore in her face,—in its beautiful expression of a felicity it knew not wherefore.

With a pleasanter name, a more finished actress, or a truer woman, I could not bring this chapter to a close. The list which follows by way of supplement, will enable the reader to trace what the poets were doing for the drama, and who the actors were that carried out their intentions,—between the commencement of the century and the night when Edmund Kean flashed upon the town.

LIST OF THE PRINCIPAL NEW PIECES PRODUCED BY THEIR MAJESTIES' SERVANTS, FROM THE BEGINNING OF THE CENTURY TILL THE APPEARANCE OF EDMUND KEAN.

### 1801.—*Drury Lane.*

"Deaf and Dumb" (Holcroft; from the French). De l'Epée, Kemble, Theodore, Miss De Camp; St. Alme, C. Kemble; Mdme. Franval, Miss Pope.
"Julian and Agnes" (Sotheby). Julian, Kemble; Agnes, Mrs. Siddons.
"Adelmorn" (*Monk* Lewis). Adelmorn, C. Kemble; Innogen, Mrs. Jordan.

### 1801.—*Covent Garden.*

"Poor Gentleman" (Colman, Jun.) Sir Robert Bramble, Munden; Ollapod, Fawcett; Emily, Mrs. Gibbs.
"Perouse" (Fawcett). Kanko, Farley; Umba, Mrs. Mills.
"Blind Girl" (Morton). Sligo, Johnstone; Clara, Mrs. H. Johnstone.

### 1801-2.—*Drury Lane.*

"Lovers' Resolutions" (Cumberland). Worthiman, J. Bannister; Mapletoft, Suett; Mrs. Mapletoft, Miss Tidswell.

### 1801-2.—*Covent Garden.*

"Integrity" (Anonymous). Herman, H. Siddons, his first appearance; Albert Voss, Brunton; Julia, Miss Murray.

"Folly as it Flies" (Reynolds). Peter Post Obit, Munden; Georgiana, Mrs. Gibbs.

"Alfonzo" (*Monk* Lewis). Orsino, Cooke; Ottilia, Mrs. Litchfield.

"Cabinet" (T. Dibdin). Prince Orlando, Braham; Lorenzo, Incledon, Curvoso, Emery; Floretta, Signora Storace.

### 1802-3.—*Drury Lane.*

"Hear Both Sides" (Holcroft). Fairfax, Dowton; Eliza, Mrs. Jordan.

"Hero of the North" (Dimond). Gustavus, Pope; Frederica, Mrs. Mountain.

"Marriage Promise" (Allingham). Merton, C. Kemble; Emma, Mrs. Jordan.

### 1802-3.—*Covent Garden.*

"Delays and Blunders" (Reynolds). Henry Sapling, Lewis; Lauretta, Mrs. H. Siddons.

"Tale of Mystery" (Holcroft). Romaldi, H. Johnston; Francisco, Farley; Fiametta, Mrs. Mattocks.

"Family Quarrels" (T. Dibdin). Charles, Braham; Foxglove, Incledon; Mrs. Supplejack, Mrs. Davenport.

"John Bull" (Colman, Jun.) Job Thornberry, Fawcett; Peregrine, Cooke; Hon. Tom Shuffleton, Lewis; Mary, Mrs. Gibbs.

### 1803-4.—*Drury Lane.*

"Wife of Two Husbands" (Cobb). Carronade, Bannister, Jun.; Montenero, Kelly; Eugenia, Mrs. Mountain.

"Hearts of Oak" (Allingham). Ardent, Dowton; Fanny, Mrs. Harlowe.

"Caravan" (Reynolds). Arabbo, Dignum; Rosa, Miss De Camp.

"Soldier's Daughter" (Cherry). Governor Heartall, Dowton; Widow Cheerly, Mrs. Jordan.

"Sailor's Daughter" (Cumberland). Varnish, Russell; Julia, Mrs. H. Johnston.

### 1803-4.—*Covent Garden.*

"Raising the Wind" (Kenney). Diddler, Lewis; Sam, Emery.

"English Fleet in 1342" (Dibdin). Valentine, Braham; Fitzwalter, Incledon; Katherine, Signora Storace.

"Valentine and Orson" (T. Dibdin). Valentine, Farley; Orson, Dubois; Eglantine, Mrs. St. Leger.

### 1804-5.—*Drury Lane.*

"Matrimony" (Kenney, from the French). Delaval, Elliston; Clara, Mrs. Jordan; Lisetta, Mrs. Bland.

"Land We Live In" (Holt). Melville, Elliston; Probert, Mathews; Lady Lovelace, Mrs. Jordan.

"Honeymoon" (Tobin). Duke Aranza, Elliston; Juliana, Miss Duncan; Volante, Miss Mellon.

## LIST OF NEW PLAYS. 355

### 1804–5.—*Covent Garden.*

"Blind Bargain" (Reynolds). Giles, Emery; Mrs. Villars, Mrs. Gibbs.
"School of Reform" (Morton). Tyke, Emery; General Tarragon, Munden; Ferment, Lewis; Julia, Miss Brunton.
"To Marry or Not to Marry" (Mrs. Inchbald). Sir Oswin, Kemble; Lord Danberry, Munden; Lady Susan, Mrs. Glover.
"Who Wants a Guinea" (Colman, Jun.) Solomon Gundy, Fawcett; Oldskirt, Simmons; Mrs. Glastonbury, Mrs. Mattocks.

### 1805–6.—*Drury Lane.*

"Weathercock" (Allingham). Tistram Fickle, Bannister.
"School for Friends" (Miss Chambers). Matthew Daw, Mathews; Lady Courtland, Miss Pope.
"Travellers" (Cherry). Koyan, Braham; Celinda, Mrs. Mountain.
"Forty Thieves" (Colman, Jun.) Ali Baba, Bannister; Morgiana, Miss De Camp; Cogia, Mrs. Bland.

### 1805–6.—*Covent Garden.*

"Rugantino" (*Monk* Lewis). Rugantino, H. Johnston.
"Delinquent" (Reynolds). Delinquent, Kemble; Nicolas, Liston.
"We Fly by Night" (Colman, Jun.) Bastion, Munden.
"Hint to Husbands" (Cumberland). Lord Transit, C. Kemble.
"Edgar" (Manners). Edgar, Miss Smith; Emma, Miss Brunton.

### 1806–7.—*Drury Lane.*

"Vindictive Man" (Holcroft). Goldfinch (from the "Road to Ruin"), De Camp; Charles, Bartley.
"Tekeli" (Theodore Hook). Tekeli, Elliston; Christine, Mrs. Bland.
"Mr. H——" (Charles Lamb). Mr. H——, Elliston.
"False Alarms" (Kenney). Sir Damon, Wroughton.
"Curfew" (Tobin). Fitzharding, Elliston; Florence, Miss Duncan.
"Adelgitha" (*Monk* Lewis). Lothair, Elliston; Adelgitha, Mrs. Powell.

### 1806–7.—*Covent Garden.*

"Town and Country" (Morton). Reuben Glenroy, Kemble; Rosalia Somers, Miss Brunton.

### 1807–8.—*Drury Lane.*

"Faulkener" (Godwin). Faulkener, Elliston; Countess Orsini, Mrs. Powell.
"World" (Kenney), Index, Mathews; Lady Bloomfield, Mrs. Jordan.
"Jew of Mogadore" (Cumberland). Nadab, Dowton; Zelina, Mrs. Mountain.

### 1807–8.—*Covent Garden.*

"Blind Boy" (Hewetson). Edmund, Mrs. C. Kemble; Kalig, Farley.
"Wanderers" (C. Kemble, from Kotzebue). Sigismund, C. Kemble.
"Begone Dull Care" (Reynolds). Modern, Lewis.

### 1808–9.—*Drury Lane.*

"Venoni" (*Monk* Lewis, from Monvel). Venoni, Elliston.

"Man and Wife" (Arnold). Sir Willoughby and Lady Worrett, Dowton, and Mrs. Harlowe.

Theatre burned down 24th February, 1809. The Company played at the Opera House and the Lyceum during the remainder of the season.

### 1808–9.—*Covent Garden.*

Theatre burned down 19th September, 1808, after the play of "Pizarro." The Company acted at the Opera House, where the only new piece of any merit that was produced was the "Exile" (Reynolds). Daran, by Young, from the Haymarket.

### 1809–10.

The Drury Lane Company continued at the Lyceum without producing any novelty of mark.

### 1809–10.

Covent Garden opened at increased prices for admission on the 18th of September. No new piece deserving of record was produced throughout the season.

### 1810–11.

The Drury Lane Company played at the Lyceum, but without bringing forward any piece of particular merit. The same may be said of Covent Garden, where, however, the season was rendered memorable and profitable by the run of "Blue Beard" and "Timour the Tartar," with horses. Before these Shakspeare, and all other of the tuneful brethren gave way.

### 1811–12.

The Drury Lane Company were still at the Lyceum, where they produced Moore's "M. P." the more successful "Devil's Bridge," by Arnold, with Braham as Count Belino, and Mrs. Dickens as the Countess Rosalvina. The greatest success was with a piece called "Quadrupeds," altered from the "Tailors; or, a Tragedy for Warm Weather," and intended to ridicule the equestrian performances at Covent Garden. The corresponding season at Covent Garden saw no new piece which is now remembered; but it is remarkable as the one in which an Elephant made its first appearance as an actor— after which Mrs. Siddons withdrew, but not on that account, from the stage.

### 1812–13.—*Drury Lane.*

The season opened on the 10th of October, 1812, in the present house, built by Wyatt. Mr. Whitbread and a committee erected the house, and purchased the old patent rights, by means of a subscription of £400,000. Of this, £20,000 was paid to Sheridan, and a like sum to the other holders of the patent. The creditors of the old house took a quarter of what they claimed, in full payment; and the Duke of Bedford abandoned a claim of £12,000. With the remainder of the sum subscribed, the house was established—Elliston, Dowton, Bannister, Rae, Wallack, Wewitzer, Miss Smith, Mrs. Davison, Mrs. Glover, Miss Kelly, and Miss Mellon, leading. Except Coleridge's "Remorse," which was acted about a score of times, they brought out no new piece. Covent Garden was equally unproductive, its most profitable drama being "Aladdin, or the Wonderful Lamp" (Aladdin, Mrs. C. Kemble; Kazrac, Grimaldi). In the next season, as in this, Covent Garden had a stronger company, with John and Charles Kemble, Conway, Terry, Mathews, and a troup of vocalists, than Drury Lane possessed. At the latter house, neither new pieces nor new players succeeded, till, on the 20th of January, 1814, the playbills announced the first appearance of an actor from Exeter—whose coming changed the evil fortunes of the house, scared the old, correct, dignified, and classical school of actors, and brought back to the memories of those who could look back as far as Garrick—the fire, nature, impulse, and terrible earnestness—all, in short, but the versatility of that great master in his art.

While Kean is dressing for Shylock, I will briefly notice a few incidents connected with both sides of the curtain, and which chiefly belong to that part of the century when he was not yet known in London.

## CHAPTER XXV.

NEW IDEAS; NEW THEATRES; NEW AUTHORS; AND THE NEW ACTORS.

EARLY in the present century, Mr. Twiss published his *Verbal Index to Shakspeare:* and this led to an attack upon the poet and the stage, as fierce, if not so formidable, as the onslaught of Prynne and the invective of Collier. The assailant, in the present case, was an anonymous writer, in the *Eclectic Review,* for January, 1807. As an illustration of the feeling of dissenters towards the bard and players, generally, this attack deserves a word of notice. The writer, after denouncing Mr. Twiss as a man who had no sense of the value of time, in its reference to his eternal state; sneering at him as one who would have been more innocently employed in arranging masses of pebbles on the seashore; and bewailing "the blind devotion which fashion requires to be paid at the shrine of Shakspeare," professes to recognize "the inimitable excellencies of the productions of Shakspeare's genius;" and then proceeds to illustrate the sense of the recognition, and to pour out the vials of his wrath, after this fashion:

"He has been called, and justly, too, the 'poet of Nature.' A slight acquaintance with the religion of the Bible will show, however, that it is of human nature in its worst shape, deformed by the basest passions and agitated by the most vicious propensities, that the poet became the priest; and the incense offered at the altar of his goddess will continue to spread its poisonous fumes over the hearts of his countrymen till the memory of his works is extinct. Thousands of unhappy spirits, and thousands yet to increase their number, will everlastingly look back with unutterable anguish, on the nights and days in which the plays of Shakspeare ministered to their guilty delights. And yet these are the writings which men, *consecrated* to the service of Him who styles Himself the Holy One, have prostituted their pens to illustrate! such this writer, to immortalize whose name, the resources of the most precious arts have been profusely lavished! Epithets, amounting to blasphemy, and honors, approaching to idolatry, have been and are shamelessly heaped upon his memory, in a country professing itself Christian, and for which it would have been happy, on moral considerations, if he had never been born. And, strange to say, even our religious edifices are not free from the pollution of his praise. What Christian can pass through the most venerable pile of sacred architecture which our metropolis can boast, without having his best feelings insulted, by observing, within a few yards of the spot from which prayers and praises are daily offered to the Most High, the absurd and impious epitaph upon the tablet raised to one of the miserable retailers of his impurities? Our readers who are acquainted with London, will discover that it is the inscription upon David Garrick, in Westminster Abbey, to which we refer. We commiserate the heart of the man who can read the following lines, without indignation:

"'And till eternity, with power sublime
Shall mark the mortal hour of hoary time,
Shakspeare and Garrick like twin stars shall shine
And earth irradiate with a beam divine.'

"' *Par nobile fratrum!*' your fame *shall* last during the empire of vice and misery, in the extension of which you have *acted* so great a part!"

There is much more in this style, and it seems rather overstrained, however well meant. I must confess, too, that the writer had some provocation to express himself strongly, not in the writings of Shakspeare, nor in Twiss's Concordance, but in the meanness and blasphemy which Mr. Pratt, or Courtenay Melmoth, infused into his wretched epitaph on Garrick's monument. Charles Lamb has hardly gone further in attacking the monument itself. "Taking a turn the other day, in the Abbey," he says, "I was struck with the affected attitude of a figure which I do not remember to have seen before, and which, upon examination, proved to be a whole length of the celebrated Mr. Garrick. Though I would not go so far, with some good Catholics abroad, as to shut players altogether out of consecrated ground, yet I own, I was not a little scandalized at the introduction of theatrical airs and gestures, into a place set apart to remind us of the saddest realities. Going nearer, I found inscribed, under this harlequin figure, a farrago of false thoughts and nonsense."

Such falsehood and nonsense helped to bring the stage into disrepute; and the pulpits, for seven or eight years, often echoed with disparaging sentiments on the drama—and quotations from Shakspeare. Nevertheless, those who never worked, as well as those who were overworked, needed amusement; and what was to be done?

"The devil tempts the industrious; idle people tempt the devil," was a saying of good Richard Baxter. Good men took it up, in 1815. Well-intentioned preachers denounced the stage, and recommended rather an unexceptional relaxation;—the sea-side, pure air, and all enjoyments thereon attending. But, while audiences were preached down to the coast, and especially to Brighton, there were zealous pastors at the latter place, who preached them back again. One of these, the Rev. Dr. Styles, of Union Street, Brighton, did his best to stop the progress of London-on-sea. He left the question of the stage for others to deal with; but, in his published sermons, he strictly enjoined all virtuously minded people to avoid watering-places generally, and Brighton in particular, unless they wished to play into the devil's hands. He denounced the breaking up of homes, the mischief of minds at rest, and the consequences of flirting and philandering. He looked upon a brief holiday as a long sin,—at the sea-side; and, with prophecy of dire results attending on neglect of his counsel, he drove, or sought to drive, all the hard workers, in search of health and in the enjoyment of that idle repose which helps them in their search, *back* to London! Then, as now, England stood shamefully distinguished for the indecorum of its sea-coast bathers; but, with certain religious principles, whereby to hold firmly, the good Doctor does not think that much ill may befall therefrom; and he sends all erring sheep with their faces towards London, and with a reference to Solomon's Song, above all things!—bidding them to await for the south wind of the Holy Spirit to blow over their spices!

On the other hand, good men in France were then seeking to render theatrical amusements universally beneficial; and a pamphlet, by Delpla, suggested a few reforms which evoked notice in this country. In some respects, the project was a development of that proposed in England, in 1732, when the idea of turning Exeter Change into a theatre and college, was first started. M. Delpla held, that the public required stage exhibitions, but that they did not always know what was good for them. He thought, that in every country there ought to exist a theatrical board, or censorship, composed, not of government officials, but of poets, reviewers, retired actors, and men of letters, generally. There would then be, he thought (poor man!) a reconstruction of theatrical literature;—the beautiful, preserved; the exceptionable omitted; and the instructive, imported. Historic truth was never to be departed from; local costume was to be strictly observed; dénoûements, in which virtue looked ridiculous, or vice seemed triumphant, were to be severely prohibited; and poets, critics, and ex-actors, were to be charged with this responsibility! M. Delpla considered that, by such means, the theatre and the pulpit would be on a level, as public instructors; or, if any difference could be between them, the greater efficiency of instruction would rest with the stage. If they were simply equal, the writer concluded that bishops themselves would show their exemplary presence in the side boxes!

The French Government only adopted that part of M. Delpla's project which spoke of a censorship; but as the censors were not competent persons,—poets, critics, actors, literary men,—but "officials," they often came to grief. Their greatest calamity, I may notice here, though it befell them at a later period, when a new law rendered the old censorship more stringent. To the authorized officials two well-known dramatic writers sent a new tragedy for examination and approval. It was returned in a few days, with 1,500 erasures. The authors were required to modify 300 lines, replace 500 words, shorten 12 scenes, and change a score of names, all of which, in the original, was considered obnoxious to public tranquillity, political order, and dramatic propriety. On receiving the corrected manuscript, the rebuked authors addressed the following note to the censors: "Gentlemen, we have the honor to acknowledge the receipt of our censured manuscript, with an accompanying letter. We agree with you in thinking that the passages marked for erasure may be of that perturbative character which you suppose; but as we do not dare to cut or modify the verses of Pierre Corneille, we prefer foregoing the representation of 'Nicomède' at the 'Théâtre Français.'"

But let us go back to our own theatres, and to the manners of audiences, between the commencement of this century and the coming of Edmund Kean. Such manners are most strikingly illustrated by the O. P., or *old price* riots of 1809. In ten months a new Covent Garden Theatre had risen, at an expense of £150,000. Smirke had taken for his model the Acropolis of Athens, and in a narrow, flat street, had built, or hidden, his imitation of the mountain fortress of the Greeks. The house was unnecessarily large, and attendant costs so heavy, that the proprietors raised the price of admission to the boxes from 6s. to 7s., and to the pit, from 3s. 6d. to 4s. They had also converted space, usually allotted to the public—the third tier, in fact—into private boxes, at a rental of £300 a year for each. The pit and box public resolved to resist, and the gallery public having a grievance in its defective construction,—the view being impeded by solid divisions, and the *run* of the seats being so steep that the occupants could see only the legs of the actors at the back of the stage,—joined the insurrection.

The house opened on the 18th of September, 1809, with "Macbeth," and the "Quaker." The audience was dense and furious. They sat with their backs to the stage, or stood on the seats, their hats on, to hiss and hoot the Kemble family especially; not a word of the performance was heard, for when the audience were not denouncing the Kembles, they were singing and shouting at the very tops of their then fresh voices. The upper gallery was so noisy, that soldiers, of whom 500 were in the house, rushed in to capture the rioters, who let themselves down to the lower gallery, where they were hospitably received. The sight of the soldiers increased the general exasperation. "It was a noble sight," said the *Times*, "to see so much just indignation in the public mind;" and that paper scorned the idea that the prices were to be raised, to pay for such vanities as were exhibited by Mrs. Siddons and John Kemble, who were on the stage "with clothes on their backs worth £500."

Such was the first of nearly seventy nights of riot, out of which the public issued with a cry of "victory," but under a substantial defeat. In alluding to this matter, it is only necessary to notice the additions to, or the variations in, the riot,—in the conduct of which the proceedings of the first night were imitated, with this exception, that the insurrectionists did not enter the theatre till half-price.

First came the introduction of placards and banners, for furnishing pins to affix one of which, in front of the boxes, a lady received an ovation; then speeches were made against the exorbitant salaries of the Kembles, and prisoners were made of the speakers; magistrates appeared on the stage to read the riot-act; and the public, preparing for a rush on the stage itself, were deterred by the sudden opening of all the traps.

The proprietors then assembled partisans by distributing *orders*, and this introduced fighting. Between the combats, post-horns confounded the confusion. Pigeons were let loose,—symbols that the public were pigeoned, and Kemble, compelled at last to come forward, only gave double fury to the storm, by asking "what they wanted," and, on being told, by replying that such demand was not reasonable, and they would think better of it! Lawyers addressed the house from the boxes, encouraging the rioters, and, in allusion to the expensive engagements of Catalani and others, declared that "the British stage should not be contaminated by Italian depravity and French duplicity,"—at which declaration the modest and candid public flung some highly-seasoned aspersions at the immoral private-boxes, and retired, cheering.

Watchmen's rattles and "artillery whistles" next added to the storm which tore the public ear. Placards increased. Cheers were given for the British Mrs. Dickens, and groans for Madame Catalani. The very name seemed to give birth to cat-calls. The actors in no way interrupted the uproar. The *Times* remarked that this was kind, as the public had so often sat without interrupting them.

Kemble made stiff-necked speeches, and the house called him

"fellow" and "vagrant," said his head was "full of *a-ches*," declared they would obey King George and not King John, and protested that they would be sung to by "native nightingales, not foreign screech-owls." The boxes looked like booths, so hung were they with placards and banners,—the most loudly cheered of which former was one which announced that the salaries of the Kembles and Madame Catalani amounted, for the season, to £25,575. "Mountain and Dickens, no Cats, no Kittens!" Such is a sample of the poetry of the O. P. row,—the first series of which ended by Kemble announcing, on the sixth night, that Catalani's engagement had been cancelled, and that the house would be closed till the accounts of the proprietors had been examined by competent gentlemen. "Britons who have humbled a prince will not be conquered by a manager!"—in that form was reply made by huge placard; and, next day, the *Times* told the public that they would not be bound by the report of the examiners of the accounts, as the people had no voice in the choice of arbitrators.

The report appeared in a fortnight. In few words, it amounted to this: If the present prices were reduced, the proprietors would lose three-fourths per cent. on their capital; but as the reporters could not even guess at the possible profits, the award was null. Meanwhile, the *Times* suggested that it would be better to reduce the exorbitant salaries. There was Mrs. Siddons with £50 per night! Why, the Lord Chief Justice sat every day in Westminster Hall, from 9 to 4, for half the sum.

The house reopened on the 4th of October, with the "Beggars' Opera!" and "Is he a Prince?" The war was resumed with increase of bitterness in feeling, and-of fury in action. Jewish pugilists, under the conduct of Dutch Sam, were hired to awe and attack the dissentients. The boxer, Mendoza, distributed orders, by dozens, to people who would support the pugilists. The speech-makers were dragged away in custody, and Bow Street magistrates sat, during the performances, ready to commit them to prison-companionship with the worst class of thieves; and they lent Bow Street runners to the managers, and these runners, armed with bludgeons, charged and overwhelmed the dauntless rioters in the pit. Dauntless, I say; for, on a succeeding night, they fell upon the Jews in great numbers, and celebrated their triumph in a bloody fray, by hoisting a placard with the words, "And it came to pass that John Bull smote the Israelites sore!"

The incidents present themselves in such crowds, that it is hardly possible to marshal them. Among them I hear the audience called a "mob," from the stage; and I see Lord Yarmouth and Berkley Craven fighting in the pit, on the part of the managers; and there are "middies" and "gallant tars," or people so attired, addressing the house, in nautical and nonsensical, and rather blackguard style, from upper boxes and galleries; and Brandon is rushing in to point out rioters, and rushing out to escape them; and gentlemen, with "O. P.," in gold, on their waistcoats, laugh at him; and there is up above an encounter between two boxes, the beaten party in which slide down the pillars to the tier below; and, suddenly, there is a roar of laughter at an accident on the stage. Charles Kemble, in Richmond, has stumbled in the fight, with Mr. Cooke as Richard, and fallen on his nose, and the house is as delighted as if he had been their personal enemy!

Then, the ear is gratefully sensible of a sudden *hush!* and the voices of the actors, for once, are heard; but it is not to listen to them the house is silent. A gentleman in the boxes has begun playing "*Colleen*" on the flute; the piece goes on the while, but it is only the instrumentalist who is listened to and cheered. Then there is an especially noisy night, when rows of standing pittites are impelled one row over the other, in dire confusion. Anon, we have a night or two of empty houses; the rioters seem weary, and the managers' friends do not care to attend to see a Jubilee procession in honor of George III., in which the cars of the individualized four quarters of the globe are drawn by scene-shifters and lamplighters, in their own clothes!

Because the public were thus kept away, the proprietors thought they had gained a victory; and on the first appearance of a Mrs. Clark, in the "Grecian Daughter," Cooke alluded, in a prologue, to the late "hostile rage." This little scrap of exultation stirred the house to fury again; and when Charles Kemble died as Dionysius, the half-price rioters shouted as if one of their most detested oppressors had perished.

Then came the races up and down the pit benches, while the

play was in progress; and the appearance of men with huge false noses, making carnival, and of others dressed like women, who swaggered and straddled about the house, and assailed the few bold occupants of private boxes in terms of more coarseness than wit. Then, too, was introduced the famous O. P. war dance in the pit, to see which alone,—its calm beginning, its swelling into noise and rapidity, and its finale of demoniacal uproar and confusion, even Princes of the Blood visited the boxes; and having beheld the spectacle, and heard the Babel of roaring throats, laughed, and went home.

Not so the rioters; these sat or danced till they chose to withdraw, and then they went in procession through the streets, howling before the offices of newspapers which advocated the managerial side, and reserving their final and infernal serenade for John Kemble himself, in front of his house, No. 89 Great Russell Street, Bloomsbury.

The lack of wisdom on the part of the management was remarkable. The introduction of Jewish pugilists into the pit had been fruitless in good; and now I find them and other questionable looking people admitted to the boxes. Of course, increase of exasperation followed. The rioters celebrated the jubilee of their row on its fiftieth night. Ladies who came wearing O. P. medals were cheered as if they had been goddesses, and gentlemen who had lost hats in the previous night's fray came in cotton night-caps, or with kerchiefs round their heads. The pit was in a frenzy, and so was the indefatigable Brandon, who captured two offenders that night, one of whom he charged with calling "Silence!" and the other with "unnaturally coughing!" The Bow Street runners also carried off many a prisoner, half-stripped and profusely bleeding, to the neighboring tribunal; and altogether the uproar culminated on the jubilee night.

The acquittal of leading rioters gave a little spirit to some after-displays; but it led to a settlement. Audiences continued the affray, flung peas on the stage to bring down the dancers, and celebrated their own O. P. dance before leaving; but, at a banquet to celebrate the triumph of the cause in the acquittal of the leaders, Mr. Kemble himself appeared. Terms were there agreed upon; and on the sixty-seventh night, a banner in the house, with "We are satisfied" inscribed on it, proclaimed that all was over.

After such a fray the satisfaction was dearly bought. The 4s. rate of admission to the pit was diminished by 6d., but the half-price remained at 2s. The private boxes were decreased in number, but the new price of admission to the boxes was maintained. Thus, the managers, after all, had more of the victory than the people; but it was bought dearly. In a few years the prices were lowered, but the audiences, except on particular occasions, were not numerous enough to be profitable. In fact, the house was too large. The public could not hear with ease what was uttered on the stage, and spectacle was more suited to it than Shakspeare or old English comedy;—and huge houses, high prices, and exorbitant salaries, soon brought the British Drama to grief in the patented houses. Into this melancholy question I do not wish, however, to enter. I have only noticed the O. P. affair, as it marks an improvement in the manners and customs of our audiences. In the preceding century, at Lincoln's Inn Fields and Old Drury, rioters on less provocation went more desperate lengths. Destruction even by fire was often resorted to by them. In the O. P. matter, the insurrectionists did not even break a bench. Mixed with the fury of fight there was an under-current of fun. The combatants declared that they would attain their end by perseverance. They persevered, and did *not* attain it!

I have previously shown that the second George did not dislike to witness an insurrection of a theatrical audience. The third George was of a more placid temperament, and not only laughed at clowns who swallowed sausages, but at allusions to his own agricultural tendencies, which he accepted with a half delighted— "I! I! good; they mean *my* sheep!" or some equally bright exclamation. As *guests*, he did not invite actors to his house; but his eldest son was more, and unnecessarily, condescending.

When Prince of Wales, and subsequently as Prince Regent, actors and managers were not unfrequently invited to Carlton House. The former seem to have appreciated their position better than the latter, at least as far as we may learn from instances afforded by the elder Bannister and the younger Colman. Charles Bannister told Mr. Adolphus, who had questioned him as to the

Prince's bearing, whether it resembled that of Prince Hal amid his boon companions? "The Prince never assumed familiarity with us, though his demeanor was always most gracious. We public performers sat all together, as all guests took their places according to their rank; our conversation was to ourselves, and we never mixed in that of the general party, further than to answer questions. At proper moments, with inimitable politeness, he would suggest that he should be pleased with a song, and the individual selected received his highest reward in praises which his royal highness bestowed with an excellent judgment, and expressed with a taste peculiar to himself."

When the younger Colman obtained a day-rule from the King's Bench, in 1811, to dine at Carlton House, whither he was conveyed by the Duke of York, dramatic literature was not so pleasantly represented as the stage had previously been in the persons of Charles Bannister and his comrades. The guest behaved like a boor, the host still like a gentleman. Among the offensive queries put by the former to the Duke, was—" Who is that fine-looking fellow at the head of the table?" The Duke urged him to be silent, lest he get into a scrape. Colman would not be any thing but ruffianly, and raising his voice, he exclaimed,—" No! no! I want to know who that fine square-shouldered, magnificent-looking, agreeable fellow is, at the end of the table!" The Duke remonstrated; saying, " You know it is the Prince." " Why, then," said George, " he is your elder brother! I declare he doesn't look half your age. Well! I remember the time when he sang a good song, and as I'm out for a lark, for one day only, he will not refuse an old play-fellow, if he is the same good fellow that he used to be." The Prince, with more condescension than was warrantable, laughed, and then sang a song, which, being done, Colman roared out applause at the magnificent voice, and with a round oath, expressed his determination to engage the singer for the next season at his own theatre! Peake, who tells the story in fuller detail, in his *Memoirs of the Colman Family*, adds that that the Prince was not offended, and that Colman was subsequently his guest. If so, the former had forgotten, since Charles Bannister's days, that propriety which the actor so justly admired.

To the list of pieces by which this chapter is preceded, I direct the attention of those who desire to know the character of our stage literature half a century ago. I will not go so far as Gifford, who, on contemplating a similar list, remarked: "All the fools in the kingdom seem to have risen up and exclaimed, with one voice,—LET US WRITE FOR THE THEATRES!" But the censure of Leigh Hunt is almost as strong, when he says, that being present at the comedies of Reynolds and Dibdin, he laughed heartily at the actors; but, somehow or other, never recollected a word of the dialogue!" The truth is, that the actors, tragic as well as comic, were superior to the authors, especially to those who wrote parts expressly for them, and composed tipsy grimaciers for Munden, and chatterers for Fawcett, and voluble gentlemen for Lewis; and, let the scene of the play be in what remote part of the world it might, always introduced an Irishman, because Johnston was there, ready and richly able, to play it. The authors thus depended on the actors, and not on themselves; and this was so much the case that Leight Hunt remarked, that the loss of Lewis would be as rheumatism to Reynolds; and the loss of Munden, "who gives such agreeable variety of grin, would affect him little less than lock-jaw!" The old sentimental comedy was bad enough, and we rejoice to this day that Goldsmith overthrew it; but he was followed by writers who mingled sentiment and farce together, who extorted tears, exacted rude laughter, and violated nature in every sense. With all this, however,—vapid in the reading, as some of these productions now appear, they reflected, with great distortion, no doubt, the manners of the times, and suggested, with some awkwardness, how those manners might be improved. The more intrusively loyal such writers affected to be, the more loudly their *clap-traps* were applauded. The absence of servile sentiment, and the suspicion of the author being led by liberal principles in politics, could only bring down upon him condemnation. Poor Holcroft, who went through so many painful varieties of life, and who was a radical before the radical era, was one of the ablest writers of what was then called comedy, but he often failed, because of his politics, and was then taunted for his failure, and that by brother-dramatists. "Holcroft has done nothing for literature," says Charles Dibdin; "because, perhaps,

16*

he has done little for morality, less for truth, and nothing for social order!" Holcroft belongs, indeed, to two centuries; but if the Administration had hanged him, as they wished to do, in 1794, when he took his trial for high treason, the author of the *Road to Ruin* would not have added his adaptation of "Deaf and Dumb," and the very first of melodramas, the "Tale of Mystery," to the list of his deserved successes.

The younger Colman justified the writing of nonsense, by metrically asking:

> "If we give trash, as some poor critics say,
> Why flocks an audience nightly to our play?"

Nevertheless, there were authors who, in the French phrase, had frequently to "sup at the 'Bagpipes,'" like the minor French playwright, Dancourt, who was accustomed to failure, but who used to find solace under the catastrophe by supping joyously with his friends, at an inn with the above sign. One night, his candid daughter was present at the first representation of one of Dancourt's little comedies. At the close of the second scene, the sibillations commenced, and mademoiselle thereupon turned gayly to her sire, with the pleasant remark, "Papa, you are going to sup to-night at the 'Bagpipes!'" The Regent Duke of Orleans was less tender toward a dramatist who bitterly complained to him, not merely that his piece had been hissed, but that he had been horsewhipped by some of the audience, who disliked the coarse raillery of his satire. "Well," said the duke, having listened to the complaint, "what is it you now want?" "Justice," answered the author. "I think," replied his highness, coolly, "I think you have had that, already!"

English managers found authors quite as unreasonable. Early in the present century, there existed a writer of tragedies, named Masterton. Failing to get any of them represented, he printed one, the "Seducer," in 1811;—promising to publish all his rejected pieces, if his specimen tragedy obtained approval. His object, of course, was to shame the managers. Like most of the authors of this century, Mr. Masterton took Otway for his model,—but he did it after this wise:

"Beware, Olivia, of the wiles of man!—
You've seen one suck an orange in the street;
And when he's feasted, fling the rind away?
So will a man, who has despoiled a woman,—
When all's ta'en from her, cast her in the dirt."

Hayley was angry enough when the public damned his "Eudora," which act, he thought, manifested only the bad taste of the public, seeing that his play had received the sanction of Lieutenant-General Burgoyne; but if Hayley knew little of practical triumphs of temper, and exhibited small discretion in printing his rejected tragedy, he at least showed that his tragedy was free from such nonsense as we find in Mr. Masterton's.

The two authors who most strongly contrast with each other as to their feelings under a disagreeable verdict, were Charles Lamb and Godwin. The former was present on the night that his farce, "Mr. H." was played, and he heartily joined in the shower of hisses with which it was assailed by the audience. This was in juster taste than the conduct of Godwin, who sat in the pit, stoically indifferent, in all appearance, to the indifference of the audience to his tragedy—"Antonio." As the act-drop descended, without applause or disapprobation, the author grimly observed that "such was exactly the effect he had labored to produce." And as the piece proceeded amid similar demonstrations of contemptuous indifference, "I would not for the world," said poor Godwin, have the excitement set in too early."

I question, however, if any thing superior to "Antonio" was produced between 1800 and the first appearance of Edmund Kean. Soon after that event came Sheil, Maturin, Proctor, and a greater than any of them, Sheridan Knowles. Sheil wrote his tragedy, "Adelaide," expressly for Miss O'Neill; every thing was sacrificed to one character,—and "Adelaide" proved a failure. The poem, however, contained promise of a poet. There was originality, at least, there was no servile imitation in the style, which was not indeed without inflation, and thundering phrases, and conceits,—but there was, withal, a weakness, from which, if the writer ever extricated himself, it was only to fall into greater defect. The story is romantic, and something after the fashion of the day, in which there was an apotheosis for every romantic villain. Such a villain is Lunenberg, who, as he remarks in an early part of the play, had lured Adelaide's unsuspecting innocence,—

> 'And with a semblance of religious rites,
> Abused thy trust, and plunged thee into shame,"

This sorry rascal treats the lady so ill that she is driven to take poison, and Lunenberg, after fighting her brother Albert, and heroically running on his sword, dies with sentimental phrases in his mouth of pure and hallowed happiness to come, and with the prophecy that "when the sound of heaven shall raise the dead," he and Adelaide would "awake in one another's arms," which is a very bold image, to say the least of it.

Adelaide herself is so feeble a personage, in nothing superior to the heroines of the Leadenhall Street romances of the time, that she fails to win or to exact sympathy. How very silly a young lady she is, may be seen by her dying speech to the villain who had deceived her by a false marriage:

> "When I am dead,
> As speedily I shall be, let my grave
> Be very humble in that mournful spot.
> I pray thee, sometimes visit it at eve,
> And when you look upon the fading rose
> That grows beside a pillar down the aisle,
> And watch it drooping in the twilight dews,
> Then think of one who bloomed a little while,
> E'en as that sickly rose, and bloomed to die."

There is more here of the small sweets of Anna Matilda than of the pathos and harmony of Otway, or the vigor of Lee.

Whatever promise this first tragedy gave, there was nothing of realization in the author's next tragedy, the "Apostate." In this piece, Hermeya, the Moslem hero, renounces his faith, for love of the Christian lady Florinda, who is so perplexed between love and duty, even more than he between love and patriotism, that she at length finds expression for her condition in the unusually majestic line—"This is too much for any mortal creature!"—a line which was echoed by more than one critic. "Adelaide" was feeble; the "Apostate," in place of being stronger, was only furious.

There was the bombast of Lee, but none of his brilliancy; the hideousness of his images without any thing of their grand picturesqueness. Florinda, looking on at the execution of Hermeya, exclaims :

> "Lo! they wrench his heart away:
> They drink his gushing blood!"

—and when a compassionate gentleman requests that the lady may be removed, she sets forth this series of screaming remarks:

> "You shall not tear me hence; No!—Never! never!
> He is my lord!—My husband!—Death!—'twas death!
> Death married us together!—Here I will dig
> A bridal bed, and we'll lie there forever!
> I will not go!—Ha! You may pluck my heart out,
> I will never go!—Help!—Help!—Hermeya!
> They drag me to Pescara's cursèd bed!
> They rend the chains of fire that bind me to thee!
> Help!—Help!"

—and so, screaming, she dies. Not thus, despite some raving, was Belvidera frantic, calling on Jaffier;—and the audience failed to see a second Otway in Lalor Sheil.

It has hardly fared better with Maturin, who wrote especially for Edmund Kean. The year 1816 produced this new dramatic writer, and also a new actress of great promise, in Miss Somerville, who made her first appearance at Drury Lane, in Maturin's tragedy of "Bertram, or the Castle of St. Aldobrand;" which was played for the first time on May the 9th. The plot is of the romantic school. Imogine, loving and loved by an exiled ruffian (Bertram), marries, in his absence, Bertram's enemy, St. Aldobrand, in order to save her sire from ruin. Bertram, the outcast, is wrecked near the castle of the wedded pair; and of course the old lovers encounter each other. From this time, with some hesitations of decency, all goes wrong. Imogine forgets her duty to her husband, whom Bertram kills, after seducing his wife. He, moreover, treats the lady very ungallantly; and Imogine, gaining nothing by her lapse from righteousness of life, goes mad, and dies; whereupon, Bertram, finding the world emphatically unpleasant, kills himself, with considerable self-exultation that he, captain of a robber-band, who had lived with desperate men in desperate ways,—

"Died no felon's death;
A warrior's weapon freed a warrior's soul!"

There is no moral to this piece; but there is some beauty of language, with a load of bombast, and an old-world amount of fierce sentiment and grotesque horrors. Among the last may be enumerated, Bertram sitting with the body of the murdered Aldobrand; and Imogine sitting with that of her child,—who had been a good angel, of the best intentions, but never in time to save his mother from mischief. The German element,—in story, style, speech, and minute stage-directions,—prevails throughout the piece, which had a greater success than it deserved.

If Maturin, in this tragedy, followed the German model rather than strove to imitate the touching melody of Rowe, and the unaffected but energetic tenderness of Otway,—he brought back to the stage some of the grosser features of the dramas of the preceding centuries, which lowered the standard of woman, and made her not less eager to be won than dishonest lovers were to woo. The same villianous spirit marked the epilogue, furnished by the Hon. George Lamb (afterwards Viscount Melbourne). In it, the villainous Bertram was covered with the dignity of a hero; and of woman, generally, it was said by the writer, that—" Vice, on her bosom, lulls remorseful care."

As in the case of Sheil, Maturin's second tragedy, "Manuel," did not fulfil even the small promise of his first; and, after "Bertram," "Manuel" was found insipid,—but more pretentious, roaring, and bombastic. The interest of the play hangs on one incident. Manuel's son is reported as slain in battle; but Manuel accuses his kinsman, and once heir, before that son was born (De Zelos), of having murdered him. Trial by battle ensues, between Torrismond, son of De Zelos, and a stranger, who offers himself as champion of Manuel. This champion (Murad) is vanquished: and he confesses to have been the murderer, at the instigation of De Zelos; but, having been uneasy in his mind ever since, he had come to risk and render his own life, by way of expiation. The instigator stabs himself; Manuel dies; and of course there is no wedding for Victoria, the daughter of the latter, and her lover (Torrismond), the son of De Zelos.

A droll, minor incident, in this tragedy, is that in which De Zelos, when hiring the assassin, and very much desiring to be unknown, gives him a dagger, with the owner's name upon the haft. Thereby, of course, he is ultimately known and betrayed; and it was suggested, that the incident might have authorized the writer to call his tragedy a comedy, and to give it the name of the "Absent Man." For violation of nature, common sense, and I may add, sound, this tragedy of Maturin's equals any thing of the kind produced in the earliest ages of the drama. To Edmund Kean, in the very bloom of his fame and best of his strength, was raving, like the following, consigned. De Zelos has just died,— hiding his face,—probably ashamed of the whole business, whereupon Manuel exclaims, spasmodically:

"False!—Falso!—ye cursèd judges!—do ye hide him?
I'll grasp the thunderbolt! rain storms of fire!
There!—There! I strike! The whizzing bolt hath struck him.
He shrieks! His heart's blood hisses in the flames!
Fiends rend him! lightnings sear him! hell gapes for him!
Oh! I am sick with death! (*Staggering among the bodies.*)
Alonzo! Victoria!—I call and none answer me!
I stagger up and down, an old man, and none to guide me!
"Not one! (*Takes Victoria's hand.*) Cold! cold! That was an icebolt!
I shiver! It grows very dark! Alonzo! Victoria!—Very—very dark!
(*Dies.*)"

There is no such nonsense as this in the tragedies of Proctor, Milman, or Sheridan Knowles. "Mirandola," "Fazio," and "Virginius," will never want readers; and "Virginius," especially, will never want an audience, if it be but fittingly represented. The principal character in "Virginius" was written expressly for Edmund Kean; but mere and lucky accident conveyed it to Mr. Macready, who found therein golden opportunity, and knew how to avail himself of it. To the former, with a sketch of whose career I close my contributions towards a History of the English Stage, may be happily applied the lines of the French poet:

"Ce glorieux acteur,
Des plus fameux héros fameux imitateur;
Du Théâtre Anglais, la splendeur et la gloire,
Mais si mauvais acteur dedans sa propre histoire."

## CHAPTER XXVI.

### EDMUND KEAN.

"IT is, perhaps, not generally known," says Macaulay, when closing his narrative of the death of the great Lord Halifax, in 1695, "that some adventurers who, without advantages of fortune or position, made themselves conspicuous by the mere force of ability, inherited the blood of Halifax. He left a natural son, Henry Carey, whose dramas once drew crowded audiences to the theatres, and some of whose gay and spirited verses still live in the memory of hundreds of thousands. From Henry Carey descended that Edmund Kean who, in our own time, transformed himself so marvellously into Shylock, Iago, and Othello."

This reminds me of an anecdote of Louis Phillippe, when Duke of Orleans, who happened one day to speak of Louis XIV. as "my august ancestor." The remark was made to a young clerk in his household,—a future novelist and dramatist, Alexander Dumas. This gentleman opened his eyes in amazement, knowing that the duke was legitimately descended from the brother of the "Grand Monarque." The duke, however, was thinking of the intermarriages between members of his family and the illegitimate descendants of Louis XIV.; but he noticed the surprise of Dumas, and then calmly added: "Yes, Dumas; *my august ancestor, Louis XIV.;* to descend from him, only through his bastards, is, in my eyes at least, an honor sufficiently great to be worth boasting of!"

In like manner Edmund Kean might have boasted of his descent from George Saville, Marquis of Halifax; but I think he was prouder of what he had achieved for himself through his genius, than of any oblique splendor derived to him from the author of the *Maxims* and the great chief of the Trimmers,—if, indeed, he knew any thing about him.

A posthumous son of Henry Carey,—well known as George

Saville Carey, inherited much of his father's talents. After declining to learn the mystery of printing he tried that of playing; —produced little effect, but by singing, reciting, and above all by his imitations, lived a vagabond life, and managed to keep his head above water, with now and then a fearful dip into the mud below, for forty years; when paralysis depriving him of the means to earn his bread, he contrived to escape further misery here, by strangling himself. He was a man of great genius not unmixed with a tendency to insanity.

He was cursed in one fair and worthless daughter, "Nance Carey," whose intimacy with Aaron Kean,—a tailor,—or as some say, Edmund Kean, a builder, but at all events brother to Moses Kean, a tailor, and as admirable a mimic as George Kean himself, —resulted in her becoming the mother of a boy, her pitiless neglect of whom seems to have begun even before his birth.

Whether that event took place in an otherwise unoccupied chamber in Gray's Inn, which had been lent to her vagabond father, or in a poor room in Castle Street, Leicester Square, or in a miserable garret in Ewer Street, Southwark,—for all of which there are respective claimants, Miss Carey's son had a narrow escape from being born in the street. But for Miss Tidswell, the actress, and another womanly gossip or two, this would have happened. It seemed all one to "Nance Carey," who having performed *her* part in this portion of the play, deserted her child, and left him to the cruelty, caprice, or humanity of strangers.

Little Edmund Kean, born in 1787, or in the following year, for the date is uncertain, had a hard life of it from the first. In a loving arm he never was held,—a loving eye never looked down upon him. Had he not been a beautiful child, perhaps the charity of Miss Tidswell and of whomsoever else extended it to him, would have failed. It is certain that they took the earliest opportunity of deriving profit from him ; and before he was three years old, Edmund Kean figured as a Cupid in one of Noverre's ballets at the Opera House. He owed his election to this dignity to his rare personal beauty, an endowment which went for nothing in his subsequent appointment, when four or five years of age, to act as one of the imps attendant on the witches in "Macbeth." John Kemble was then supreme at Drury Lane, and, of course, little conscious that among the noisy and untractable young imps, the wildest by far would prove to be, what Mrs. Siddons would have called,—one of those new idols which the public delight to set up, in order to mortify their old favorites!

One night the goblins fell over one another in the cavern-scene, Edmund going down first, out of weakness, or of mischief. This led to the dismissal of the whole troop; and some good Samaritan then sent young Kean to school. In Orange Court, Leicester Square, was the fountain whence he drew his first and almost only draught of learning. In that dirty locality may be found the shrine of three geniuses. There, Holcroft was born, Opie was housed, and Edmund Kean instructed.

Thereafter comes Chaos; and it is only by glimpses that the whereabouts of the naturally-gifted but most unhappy lad can be detected. A little outcast, with his weak legs in "irons," day and night, he sleeps between a poor married couple whose sides are hurt by his fetters. Miss Tidswell takes him, ties him to a bed-post, to secure his attention, teaches him elocution, and corrects him a little too harshly, though out of love. He dances and tumbles at fairs and in taverns, performs wonderful feats, is kicked and starved, thrives nevertheless,—and conceives that there is something within him which should set him above his fellows in hard work and lean fare. And then, when he is becoming a bread-winner, he is claimed by his evil genius, Nance Carey.

His mother has been a stroller; she is a vagabond still; tramps the country with pomatums, and perfumes, and falballas, and her son is her pack-horse;—and the bird, to boot, that shall lay golden eggs for her. He is savage at having to plod through mud and dust, but he has a world of his own beyond it all; and he not only learns soliloquies from plays, but recites them in gentlemen's houses. To the audiences there, he goes confident but sensitive; proud and defiant even when wounded by many a humiliation. By reciting, selling the wares in which Nance Carey dealt, and exhibiting in every possible and impossible play and posture, at fairs, he earned and received some small but well-merited wage. "She took it *all* from me!" cried the boy, in his anguish and indignation.

A London Arab leads an easier life. It was a dark and hard

life to Edmund,—Miss Tidswell occasionally appeared to do him a kindness, to give him bread, and more instruction for the stage. Of his father, we hear nothing save his rascal gallantry with Miss Carey; of his mother, nothing but her rapacity; of his uncle, Moses Kean, only that Miss Tidswell turned his wooden leg to account. When her young pupil, studying Hamlet, had to pronounce the words, "Alas, poor Yorick!" she first made him say, "Alas, poor uncle!" that the memory of the calamity the latter had suffered might dispose Edmund's face to seriousness!

And then he is abroad again; not easily to be followed. His sensitive pride renders him hasty to take offence, and then he rushes from some friendly roof, and disappears, sinks down some horrible gulf, issues not purified, nor softened, nor inclined to give account of himself. A more sober flight took him to Madeira as a cabin-boy, whence he returned, disgusted with Thalatta. Finally, he runs the round of fairs again, and starves and has flashes of wild jollity, as such runners have; and pauses in his running at Windsor. He was just then the property of crafty old Richardson, and at Windsor Fair made such a local reputation by his elocution, that King George sent for him, and so enjoyed a taste of his quality that the young player carried away with him the bright guerdon of two guineas,—either to his manager or his mother, I forget which.

I think, however, this speaking in presence of royalty was the getting the foot on the first round of the slippery ladder which he was so desirous to ascend. He spoke a speech or two at some London theatres, when benefit nights admitted of extraordinary performances; and he now went the round of country theatres, and not of country fairs. It was not a less weary life; he starved as miserably as before, and he began to find a means of reinvigoration in "drink." Had his labor been paid according to its worth, the devil could not have flung this temptation in his way. "A better time will come by-and-by," said the poor stroller, who was always promising to himself, or to others, a happy period in which all would be right.

In the course of his wanderings he played at Belfast. Mrs. Siddons passed that way too, and acted Zara and Lady Randolph. Edmund Kean, not then, I believe, nineteen, played Osmyn and

Young Norval. In the first part I think he was imperfect, and the Siddons shook her majestic head at the apparent cause. Nevertheless, her judgment was, that he played "well, *very* well; but there was too little of him wherewith to make a great actor!"

If painstaking could do it, he was resolved to be one. No amount of labor to this end daunted him. However poor the task intrusted to him, he did his utmost for it. When playing some worthless fifth-rate character at the Haymarket, a generous colleague remarked: "Look at the little man, he is trying to make a part of it."

I find by the bills of the Haymarket Theatre, which Mr. Buckstone kindly placed at my disposal, that Dubbs, in the "Review," to Fawcett's Caleb Quotem, was about the best character he played. Considering that he was at this time under twenty, his position was not a very bad one; but it seemed to him to promise no amendment—and he again passed to the country, to play first business, and to be hungry three or four days out of the seven.

He could not earn enough to enable him to travel from one place of engagement to another. He journeyed on foot, and when he came to a river, swam it (particularly when a press-gang was near), as readily as an Indian would have done. In some towns his Hamlet was not relished, but his Harlequin filled the house. The Guernsey critics censured his acting, on the ground that he would rudely turn his back on the audience, and make no more account of them than if they were the fourth side of a room in which he was meditating! When the Guernsey pit hissed him in Richard III., his cry, pointedly addressed to them: "Unmannered dogs! Stand ye, when I command!" rendered them silent. He tried the same trick, and not without effect, when the pit of Drury Lane was hissing him, not for being a bad actor, but an immoral man.

"Who is that shabby little man?" said Mary Chambers, a young Waterford girl, who had been a governess, and who was going through her probationary time as an actress at Gloucester. "Who the devil is she?" asked Kean, after being soundly rated by her for spoiling her performance through his unsettled memory. She was what Kean never thoroughly knew her to be—his good genius—worth more than all the kinsfolk he had ever possessed, including Miss Tidswell, who once gave him a home and the stick. The imprudent young couple, however, fell in love; they married; and the manager paid his congratulations to them, by turning them out of his company.

They loved, slaved, and starved. The misery of their lives is unparalleled, except by the heroic uncomplainingness with which it was endured by Mrs. Kean. *His* industry was really intense; his study of every character he had to play careful, earnest, conscientious; and after acting with as much anxiety as if he had been performing before a jury of critics, he would return to his miserable home, saddened, furious, and unsober. "I played the part finely; and yet they did not applaud me!"

Gleams of good fortune occasionally lit up their path. An engagement at Birmingham at a guinea a week to each, was comparative wealth to them; and there Kean found the applause for which he sighed. His Octavian was preferred to Elliston's; and Stephen Kemble told him that his Hotspur and Henry IV. were superior to those of his brother, John Kemble. Kean thought of London. "If I could only get there, and succeed! If I *succeed*, I shall go mad!"

There was much to be suffered by Kean and his wife before that triumph came. For lack of means, they have to walk from Birmingham to Swansea. Two hundred miles, and that poor lady may be a mother before she accomplishes half of them! They wend painfully on, pale, hungry, and silent; twelve miles a day; not asking alms, but not above receiving that hospitality of the poor which is true, because self-denying charity. Needing many things, and obtaining none of those she most needed, Mrs. Kean reached Bristol more dead than alive. A cast in a boat, more weary suffering, a son born, and an audience at Swansea who preferred Bengough, an elephantine simpleton, with large, unmeaning eyes, to Edmund—tells the outline of his tale before they crossed from Wales to Waterford.

Soon in this troop, under Cherry, at Waterford, there were two men, destined to be at the very head of their respective vocations, as player and dramatic poet—Edmund Kean and Sheridan Knowles. At present they are only strolling players. The training of the two men had been totally different. Kean was "Nobody's

Son," and had passed through the misery, degradation, and black-guardism attendant on such a parentage—his genius not slumbering, but ready to flash, like the diamond, when light and opportunity should present themselves.

Knowles, on the other hand, was the son of a scholar, and a trainer of scholars. He came of a literary race; his sire compiled a dictionary. Sheridan, the lexicographer, was his uncle; Richard Brinsley, his cousin. At an early age he was removed from his native city, Cork, to London, where the boy wrote boyish plays, and the youth grew up in friendship with Hazlitt, Coleridge, and Lamb. Then he went into the world, to fight his fight, and at four-and-twenty, that is, in 1808, I find him, a tolerable actor, on the old Dublin stage in Crow Street, and a very acceptable guest at firesides where merit, wit, and a harmonious voice were appreciated. Subsequently he joined the troop of vivacious Cherry, in Waterford. There he met with the little, bright-eyed, swarthy young man, who was Richard in the play, and Harlequin in the pantomime, on the same evening; who, in short, could do any thing and did every thing well. For him, Edmund Kean, Knowles wrote his first serious play, a melodramatic tragedy, "Leo, the Gypsy;" and in that piece Kean achieved so notable a triumph, that he would have chosen it for his first appearance in London, but that luckily for him, he had lost the copy.

Edmund seems to have worked steadily in the ancient Irish city. Of the general business I can say nothing, except that Mrs. Kean played a Virgin of the Sun, at a time when the character least suited her; but for a reminiscence of a benefit night, I take half a page from Mr. Grattan.

"The last thing I recollect of Kean in Waterford, was the performance for his benefit. The play was Hannah More's tragedy of "Percy," in which he of course played the hero. Edwina was played by Mrs. Kean, who was applauded to her heart's content. Kean was so popular, both as an actor, and from the excellent character he bore, that the audience thought less of the actor's demerits than of the husband's feelings; and besides this, the *débutante* had many personal friends in her native city, and among the gentry of the neighborhood, for she had been governess to the children of a lady of good fortune, who used all her influence at this benefit. After the tragedy, Kean gave a specimen of tight-rope dancing, and another of sparring with a professional pugilist. He then played the leading part in a musical interlude, and finished with Chimpanzee, the monkey, in the melo-dramatic pantomime of La Pérouse, and in this *character* he showed agility scarcely since surpassed by Mazurier or Gouffe, and touches of deep tragedy in the monkey's death scene, which made the audience shed tears."

What cause broke the connection of the Keans with Cherry, I do not know; but the former were one day without an engagement, and among the separations that ensued was that of Kean and Knowles. They were both to find what they thirsted for in London; but for the former many were the trials, and terrific the ascent, before he was to reach that pinnacle which he occupied so gloriously, and so briefly.

From Waterford Edmund and his wife took with them no more than they had brought, except an additional son, the day of whose birth was a happy day in the mother's calendar of sorrows. They suffered, and the children with them, all that humanity could suffer and yet live. I find them at Dumfries, depending for food and shelter upon the receipts at an "entertainment," given by Kean, in a room at a tavern. There was *one* auditor, and he paid sixpence! There were even worse disappointments than these; and, under their accumulation, I do not wonder that Kean broke into curses at his perverse destiny; or that Mrs. Kean, looking at her children, prayed to God that He would remove them, and her!

And so from town to town they pursued their hapless pilgrimage. *He* sometimes driven to fury and to drink; she only asking for death to her and the two younger sufferers. Now and then, a divine charity enabled them to rest and refresh; and *once*, a divine by profession, in a country town, forbade them the use of a school-room, because they were actors! The reverend gentleman himself, probably, thought it very good amusement to listen to his own boys enacting the "Eunuchus" of Terence.

Famine, rage, drink, and tears marked the way of the wanderers. Brief engagements enabled them to exist, just to keep themselves out of the grave; and then came vacation and want to let them slip back again to the very brink of that grave. Amid it all, Kean *did* succeed in making a reputation. Passing through London, he saw John Kemble and Mrs. Siddons, in Wolsey and Constance, —and he registered a vow that *he would* be there a great actor, too! And so again to the country, to work hard, gain little, and wait; but also to enjoy some antepast of metropolitan triumph at Exeter, where his success was great, but not remunerative; where, with a great coat flung over his stage-dress, he might too often be seen at the bar of the tavern near the theatre, and where he enlarged his means by teaching dancing and fencing, elocution and boxing,—or "a word and a blow," as some wag styled the latter two accomplishments. Exeter foretold that he would not have to wait long, but all the prophetic patronage of Exeter did not furnish him with means to get to Dorchester by any other process than on foot, and with his son Charles on his back. The poor sick little Howard, the elder son, had to be conveyed thither by his mother. Howard had shown some promise of histrionic talent already, and he helped to win a little bread for the family before he died. For this, perhaps, the father loved him; and toiled on till the tide came in his affairs which promised to raise him at its flood to highest fortune. The tide began to flow, after Dr. Drury had seen him act, and reported well to the Drury Lane Committee of his acting; it was running fast in the same direction when Kean saw a gentleman, in the boxes at Dorchester, so attentive to his playing, that Edmund acted to him alone, as Booth had done in his day, but under other influences, to Mr. Stanyan, the judicious gentleman from Oxford. Kean's gentleman was Arnold, stage-manager of Drury Lane, and he commenced negotiations with Kean for an engagement before they parted for the night. The poor player rushed home, hysterical with agitation and delight, and all his good impulses uppermost. He announced the glad intelligence to his wife, with the touching comment,—" If Howard only get well, we shall be all happy yet!"

Howard died, and Kean played, danced, sorrowed, and hoped, —for the time at which he was to go up to London was at hand; and thither they went, at the close of the year 1813. When that season of 1813–14 opened, Drury was in a condition from which it could be relieved only by a genius;—and there he stood, in that cold hall, a little, pale, restless, dark-eyed man, in a coat with two or three capes, and nobody noticed him. In Cecil Street, his family was living on little more than air; and he was daily growing sick, as he stood, waiting in that hall, for an audience with the manager; and subject to the sneers of passing actors. Even Rae, handsome and a fool, affected not to know him, though they had played together, when Rae's mother was matron at St. George's Hospital, and they had acted together at the Haymarket, in 1806, when Rae led the business, and Kean was but a supernumerary. Arnold treated him superciliously, with a "*young man !*"—as he condescended to speak, and put him off. Other new actors obtained trial parts, but there was none for that chafed, hungry, restless little man in the capes. Even drunken Tokely, like himself, from Exeter, could obtain a " first appearance," but Kean was put off. Stephen Kemble played Shylock, and failed ! why not try a new actor ? The Committee did so, and Mr. Huddart, from Dublin, went on as Shylock, and was never heard of more. And the poor stroller looked through the darkness of that miserable passage the while, and murmured, " Let me but get my foot before the floats, and *I'll* show them— !"

The permission came. Would he,—no, he *must* play Richard. " Shylock, or nothing !" was his bold reply. He was afraid of the littleness of his figure,—which he had heard scoffed at, being exposed in the " trunks" of Glo'ster. He hoped to hide it under the gown of Shylock. The Jew, or nothing ! The young fellow, he was not yet six-and-twenty, was allowed to have his way.

At the one morning rehearsal he fluttered his fellow-actors, and scared the manager, by his independence and originality. " Sir, this will never do !" cried Raymond, the acting manager. " It is quite an innovation; it cannot be permitted." " Sir," said the poor, proud man, " I wish it to be so ;" and the players smiled, and Kean went home, that is, to his lodgings, in Cecil Street, on that snowy, foggy, 26th of February, 1814, calm, hopeful, and hungry. " To-day," said he, " I must *dine.*"

Having accomplished that rare feat, he went forth alone, and on foot. " I wish," he remarked, " I was going to be shot !" He had with him a few properties which he was bound to procure for himself, tied up in a poor handkerchief, under his arm. His wife remained, with their child, at home. Kean tramped on beneath the falling snow, and over that which thickly encumbered the ground,—solid here; there in slush; and, by and by, pale, quiet, but fearless, he dressed in a room shared by two or three others, and went down to the wing by which he was to enter. Hitherto no one had spoken to him, save Jack Bannister, who said a cheering word; and Oxberry, who had tended to him a glass, and wished him good fortune. "By Jove!" exclaimed a first-rater, looking at him, "Shylock in a black wig! Well!!"

The house could hold, as it is called, £600; there was not more than a sixth of that sum in front. Winter without, his comrades within;—all was against him. At length, he went on, with Rae, as Bassanio, in ill-humor; and groups of actors at the wings, to witness the first scene of a new candidate. All that Edmund Kean ever did, was gracefully done; and the bow which he made, in return to the usual welcoming applause, was eminently graceful. Dr. Drury, the head master of Harrow, who took great interest in him, looked fixedly at him as he came forward. Shylock leant over his crutched stick, with both hands; and, looking askance at Bassanio, said: "Three thousand ducats?" paused, bethought himself, and then added: "Well?" *He is safe*, said Dr. Drury.

The groups of actors soon after dispersed to the green room. As they reached it, there reached there, too, an echo of the loud applause given to Shylock's reply to Bassanio's assurance that he may take the bond. "I *will be* assured I may!"—later came the sounds of the increased approbation bestowed on the delivery of the passage ending with,—" and for these courtesies, I'll lend you thus much moneys." The act came to an end gloriously; and the players in the green room looked for the coming among them of the new Shylock. He proudly kept aloof; knew he was friendless; but felt that he was, in himself, sufficient.

He wandered about the back of the stage, thinking, perhaps, of the mother and child at home; and sure, now, of having at least made a step towards triumph. He wanted no congratulations; and he walked cheerfully down to the wing where the scene was about to take place between him and his daughter, Jessica, in his very calling to whom :—" Why, Jessica! I say"—there was, as some of us may remember, from an after night's experience, a charm, as of music. The whole scene was played with rare merit; but the absolute triumph was not won till the scene (which was marvellous in his hands) in the third act, between Shylock, Salanio, and Salarino,—ending with the dialogue between the first and Tubal. Shylock's anguish at his daughter's flight; his wrath at the two Christians who make sport of his anguish; his hatred of all Christians, generally, and of Antonio in particular; and then his alternations of rage, grief, and ecstasy, as Tubal relates the losses incurred in the search of that naughty Jessica, her extravagances, and then the ill luck that had fallen upon Antonio;—in all this, there was such originality, such terrible force, such assurance of a new and mighty master,—that the house burst forth into a very whirlwind of approbation. "What now?" was the cry in the green room. The answer was, that the presence and the power of the genius were acknowledged with an enthusiasm which shook the very roof. How so select an audience contrived to raise such a roar of exultation, was a permanent perplexity to Billy Oxberry.

They who had seen Stephen Kemble's Shylock, and that of Huddart, this season, must have by this time confessed, that the new actor had superseded both. He must himself have felt, that if he had not yet surpassed Cooke, and Henderson, and Macklin, he was tending that way; and was already their equal. Whatever he felt, he remained reserved and solitary; but he was now sought after. Raymond, the acting manager, who had haughtily told him his innovations "would not do," came to offer him oranges. Arnold, the stage manager, who had *young-manned* him, came to present him, "sir!" with some negus. Kean cared for nothing more now, than for his fourth and last act; and in that his triumph culminated. His calm demeanor at first; his confident appeal to justice; his deafness, when appeal is made to him for mercy; his steady joyousness, when the young lawyer recognizes the validity of the bond; his burst of exultation, when his right is confessed; his fiendish eagerness, when whetting the knife;—and then, the sudden collapse of disappointment and terror, with the words,—" Is *that*—the LAW?"—in all, was made manifest, that a noble successor to the noblest of the actors of old, had arisen. Then, his trembling anxiety to recover what he had before refused; his sordid abjectness, as he finds himself foiled, at every turn; his subdued fury; and, at the last (and it was always the crowning glory of his acting in this play), the withering sneer, hardly concealing the crushed heart, with which he replied to the jibes of Gratiano, as he left the court;—all raised a new sensation in an audience, who acknowledged it in a perfect tumult of acclamation. As he passed to his dressing room, Raymond saluted him with the confession, that he had made a hit; Pope, more generous, avowed that he had saved the house from ruin.

And then, while Bannister was dashing through Dick, in the "Apprentice," I seem to see the hero of the night staggering home through the snow, drunk with delicious ecstasy, all his brightest dreams realized, and all his good impulses surging within him. He may be in a sort of frenzy, as he tells of his proud achievement; but, at its very wildest, he exclaims: "Mary, you shall ride in your carriage yet!" and, taking his son, Charles, from the cradle, swears he "shall go to Eton;" but therewith something overshadows his joy, and he murmurs, "If Howard had but lived to see it!"

That poor wife and mother must have enjoyed, on that eventful night, the very brightest of the few gleams of sunshine that fell upon her early hapless life. Thenceforth, there was never to be misery or sorrow, in that household, again! Poor lady! She did not, perhaps, remember that Edmund had said, "*If* I succeed,—it will drive me mad!"

But not yet: all was triumph for awhile; and worthily it was won. His audiences rose, from one of a £100 to audiences of £600; and £20 a week rewarded efforts, for far less than which, he subsequently received £50 a night. He was advanced to the dignity of having a dressing-room to himself. Legislators, poets, nobles, thronged his tiring room, where Arnold took as much care of him, as if on his life hung more than the well-being of the theatre. Friends flocked to him, as they are wont to do, where there is an opportunity of basking in pleasant sunshine, imparted, by genius. And old Nance Carey turned up, to exact £50 a year from her not too delighted son, and to introduce a Henry Darnley, who *would* call Edmund, "dear brother!"

Some years later, in 1829, Moore was talking with Mrs. Kean

of this critical period in Edmund's career. The poet suggested, that some memorial of his first appearance should be preserved. "Oh!" exclaimed Mrs. Kean; "will you write his life? You shall have half the profits;" adding, as she probably remembered the dark time which had come upon her since the sunshine,— "if you will only give me a little."

But success was not to be considered as achieved, by playing one character supremely well. Kean had, in the general memory, shaken Macklin from his supremacy in Shylock. He was now summoned to show himself worthy of being the successor of Garrick,—by acting Richard III. A few nights before he played that part it was performed at Covent Garden, by John Kemble; and a short time after Kean had triumphed, it was personated by Young; but Kemble could not prevent, nor Young impede, the triumph of the new actor, who now made Richard his own, as he had previously done with Shylock.

His Richard settled his position with the critics; and the criticism to which he was subjected was, for the most part, admirably and impartially written. He is sometimes spoken of as "this young man;" at others, "this young gentleman." "Even Cooke's performance," says one, "was left at an immeasurable distance." A second adds, "it was the most perfect performance of any that has been witnessed since the days of Garrick." Of the grand effects followed by a storm of applause, a third writes that "electricity itself was never more instantaneous in its operation." They are, however, occasionally hypercritical. The able critic of the *Morning Chronicle* objected that in the young man's Richard "too great reliance was placed on the expression of the countenance, which is a language intelligible only to a part of the house;" and a contemporary thought that when the young gentleman, as Richard, crossed his hands behind his back, during his familiar colloquy with Buckingham, the action was altogether *too natural!* Others point to attitudes which Titian might have painted. Such use of eye, and lips, and muscle, had never had any thing comparable to it since the best days of Garrick. Even Sylvanus Urban aroused himself, and declared, that Mr. Kean's success had given new interest to the biography of Richard III.

Indeed, this second glory was greater than the first, for the difficulties were greater, and they were all surmounted. Joyous and sarcastic in the opening soliloquy; devilish, as he passed his bright sword through the still breathing body of Lancaster; audaciously hypocritical, and almost too exulting, in the wooing of Lady Anne; cruelly kind to the young Princes, his eye smiling while his foot seemed restless to crush the two spiders that so vexed his heart;—in representing all this there was an originality and a nature which were entirely new to the delighted audience. Then they seemed to behold altogether a new man revealed to them, in the first words uttered by him from the throne,—"Stand all apart!" from which period to the last struggle with Richmond, there was an uninterrupted succession of beauties; even in the bye-play he found means to extort applause, and a graceful attitude, an almost silent chuckle, a significant glance,—even so common-place a phrase as "Good-night, my lords," uttered before the battle of the morrow, were responded to by acclamations such as are awarded to none but the great masters of the art.

The triumph was accumulative, and it was crowned by the tent-scene, the battle, and the death. Probably no actor ever even approached Kean in the last two incidents. He fenced with consummate grace and skill; and fought with an energy that seemed a fierce reality.

Rae had sneered at the "little man," but Rae now felt bound to be civil to the great tragedian, and referring to the passage of arms in "Richard III.," he, having to play Richmond, asked, "Where shall I hit you, sir, to-night?" "Where you can, sir," answered Kean; and he kept Richmond off, in that famous struggle, till Rae's sword-arm was weary with making passes.

His attempt to "collar" Richmond when his own sword had fallen from him was so doubtful in taste that he subsequently abandoned it; but in the faint, yet deadly-meant passes, which he made with his swordless arm, after he had received his death-blow, there was the conception of a great artist; and there died with him a malignity which mortal man had never before so terribl portrayed. Young, in his dying scene of Richard, used to fling his sword at Richmond, a trick which the critics, very properly, denounced.

They who said that Mr. Kean's figure and voice were against him, unconsciously exalted the genius which had triumphed over the difficulties of Shakspeare and Cibber's Richard. They who accepted rather than rejoiced in his triumph, called him "The Fortunate Actor!" They did not know that under slavery, starvation, and every disadvantage but despair, Kean had silently and solitarily studied these characters, and had come to conclusions which he hoped would enable him to achieve a success which, *if* accomplished, he was, after all, afraid would drive him mad.

At this time, 1814, Moore speaks of "poor Mr. Kean," as being "in the honeymoon of criticism;" and then the bard speaks disrespectfully of the critics. "Next to the pleasure," he says, "of crying a man down, your critics enjoy the vanity of writing him up; but when once up, and fixed there, he is a mark for their arrows ever after."

His other characters this season were Hamlet, when to John Bannister was assigned the first of the two Grave-diggers, whom he had restored to the stage from which they had been abolished by Garrick; Othello, to the Iago of Pope; and Iago, to the Othello of Sowerby, Pope, Rae, and Elliston; Miss Smith, who refused to play the Queen, in "Richard," being his Desdemona. He also acted Luke, in "Riches" ("City Madam"), to the Lacy of Wallack, and the Lady Traffic of Mrs. Edwin. Of these, he was always inclined to think Hamlet his best character. He had, perhaps, studied it more deeply than the others, and Mrs. Garrick took such especial interest in his representation of it, that on comparing it with her husband's she saw only one great defect, in the closet scene. Garrick was severer with the Queen of Denmark than Kean, and Mrs. Garrick persuaded him, though unconvinced by her, to throw more sternness into this celebrated scene. The good old lady merited *some*, yet not *such* concession; but then she invited Kean to Adelphi Terrace, and sent him fruit from Hampton, and made him a present of Garrick's stage-jewels. The young man was in a fair way of being spoiled, as Pope said of Garrick, when thinking of the laborious, but splendid time of his friend and favorite, Betterton.

Tenderness to Ophelia, affection for his mother, reverential awe of his father, and a fixed resolution to fulfil the mission confided to him by that father, were the distinct "motives," so to speak, of his Hamlet.

The critics, especially, dwell on the tender vibration of his voice, when uttering the word "father" to the Ghost; they approve of his sinking on one knee before the solemn spirit, and they are lost in admiration of his original action when, instead of keeping the Ghost off with his sword, when he bids it, "go on," he pointed it back at his friends to deter them from preventing his following the visionary figure. This, and another original point, have become stage-property. I allude to the scene in which he seems to deal so harshly with Ophelia. At the close of it, Kean used to return from the very extremity of the stage, take Ophelia's hand, kiss it with a tender rapture, look mournfully loving upon her, with eyes full of beautiful significance, and then rush off. The effect never failed, and the approbation was tumultuous.

Gracefully and earnestly as his Hamlet was played, it yielded in attractiveness to his Othello, which, despite some little exaggeration of action, when told to beware of jealousy, was, perhaps, the greatest of his achievements. In the tender scenes,—and love for Desdemona was above all other passion, even when for love he jealously slew her, he had as much power over his "bad voice," as his adversaries called it, as John Kemble over his asthmatic cough, and attuned it to the tenderness to which he had to give expression. In the fiercer scenes he was unsurpassable,—and in the great third act none who remember him will, I think, be prepared to allow that he ever had, or is ever likely to have, an equal.

John Kemble himself said of Kean's Othello: "If the justness of its conception had been but equal to the brilliancy of execution it would have been perfect; but," added the older actor, with some sense, perhaps, of being disturbed by the younger player, "the whole thing is a mistake; the fact being that Othello was a slow man,"—to be moved, he was; but being moved, swift and terrible in moving to consequent purpose.

Iago, curiously enough, was not so welcome a part to Kean as Othello. Its characteristic was the concealment of his hypocrisy, and in the delineation of such a part Kean was usually unrivalled. Some of his admirers considered his Iago as fine as his Richard, but he never played the two with equal care and equal success. On the other hand, he was pleased with the strong *oppositions* in the character of Luke, but his audiences were not satisfied in the same degree, and it fell out of his repertory. He of course thought them in the wrong; lamented on the few competent judges of acting, and limited these to lawyers, doctors, artists, critics, and literary men. He was then the (often unwilling) guest of noblemen who, I doubt not, were excellent judges, too; but Kean thought otherwise: "They talk a great deal," he said, "of what I don't understand,"—politics, and equally abstruse matters; "but when it comes to plays, they talk such nonsense!"

I am not about to follow this actor through his score of seasons, but as a sample of his value to the treasury of Drury Lane, at this time, and therefore to the stage, I may just make record of the fact that in this first season, he played Shylock fifteen times, Richard twenty-five, Hamlet eight, Othello ten, Iago eight, and Luke four; and that in those seventy nights, the delighted treasurer of Drury Lane struck a balance of profit to the theatre, amounting in round numbers, to £170,000. Previous to the appearance granted to him so tardily, there had been one hundred and thirty-nine nights of continual loss. Mr. Whitbread, a proprietor, might well say of him that "he was one of those prodigies that occur only once or twice in a century."

In this same season, Kemble stood his ground against Kean in the one character played by both,—Hamlet; but two new actors,— tall, earnest, handsome, but ungainly Conway, from Dublin, and Terry, from Edinburgh,—only took a respectable position. The Othello of the first, and the Shylock of the second, were never heard of after Kean had played and made them his own.

In Kean's second season, he added to his other characters, Macbeth, which had some magnificent points, but in which Kemble had personal advantages over him; Romeo, which continues the traditional glory of Barry; Reuben Glenroy and Penruddock, in neither of which he equalled Kemble; Zanga, played in a style which made the fame of Mossop pale, and shook Young and Kemble from an old possession; Richard II., in an adaptation by Merivale, acted with a new grace to the expression of melancholy; Abel Drugger, concerning which he answered the legendary—"I know it," to the "you can't play it," of Mrs. Garrick; Leon, performed with moderate success, and Octavian, with rare sweetness, but not with such rare ability as to make John Kemble uneasy.

Kean also acted his first original character, Egbert, in the tragedy of that name, by Mrs. Wilmot. His prestige suffered a little in consequence, for Egbert was condemned on the first night. He had compensation enough in Zanga. As one who stood among the crowd in the pit passage heard a shout and clamor of approbation within, he asked if Zanga had not just previously said, "Then lose her!" for that phrase, in the country, when uttered by Kean, used to make the walls shake; and he was answered that it was so. I remember having read that some one was with Southey, when the "Revenge" was played, and that when Zanga consummated his vengeance in the words, "Know then 'twas I,"—lifting up his arms, as he spoke, over the fainting Alonzo, and seeming to fill the theatre,—the same image was simultaneously presented to the minds of the two friends. "He looks like Michael Angelo's rebellious Archangel!" thought one. "He looks like the Arch-Fiend himself," said the other.

Covent Garden struggled nobly, with its old and strong company, against the single power of Kean at the other house; but found its best ally in a new actress. On the 13th of October, 1814, Miss O'Neill made her first appearance in Belvidera. It is not my intention to do more than record the names of the players who made their *début* after the coming of Edmund Kean, but there is something so singular in the lucky chance which led to Miss O'Neill's well-merited fortune, that I venture to tell it in the words of Michael Kelly.

Let me first remark that, no doubt, some of us are old enough to have seen, as many of us have heard, of Miss Walstein, that "sort of Crow-Street Bonaparte," who struggled so bravely, though so briefly, at Drury Lane against Miss O'Neill, when the latter carried the town by her superior charms and talents. Miss O'Neill was furnished by her undoubtedly great rival with the means of supplanting her. Had not Walstein been arrogant, the famous Juliet of our infantine days might never have sighed on the Covent Garden balcony. Her first step, however was made on the stage at Crow Street, and Miss Walstein unwittingly helped her to obtain a secure footing. The story is thus told by garrulous Mike Kelly:—"Miss Walstein, who was the heroine of the Dublin stage, and a great and deserved favorite, was to open the theatre in the character of Juliet. Mr. Jones received an intimation from Miss Walstein that without a certain increase of salary, and other privileges, she would not come to the house. Mr. Jones had arrived at the determination to shut up his theatre sooner than submit to what he thought an unwarrantable demand, when Mac Nally, the box-keeper, who had been the bearer of Miss Walstein's message, told Mr. Jones that it would be a pity to shut up the house; that there was a remedy if Mr. Jones chose to avail himself of it. 'The girl, sir,' said he, 'who has been so often recommended to you as a promising actress, is now at a hotel in Dublin with her father and brother, where they have just arrived, and is proceeding to Drogheda, to act at her father's theatre there. I have heard it said by persons who have seen her, that she plays Juliet extremely well, and is very young and very pretty. I am sure that she would be delighted to have the opportunity of appearing before a Dublin audience, and if you please, I will make her the proposal.' The proposal was made, and accepted; and on the following Saturday, 'the girl,' who was Miss O'Neill, made her *début* on the Dublin stage as Juliet. The audience was delighted; she acted the part several nights, and Mr. Jones offered her father and brother engagements on very liberal terms, which were thankfully accepted. 'In Dublin,' adds Kelly, 'she was not only a great favorite in tragedy, but also in many parts of genteel comedy. I have there seen her play Letitia Hardy; she danced very gracefully, and introduced my song, 'In the rough Blast heave the Billows,' originally sung by Mrs. Jordan, at Drury Lane, which she sang so well as to produce a general call for its repetition from the audience. She was in private life highly esteemed for her many good qualities. Her engagement in Dublin wafted Miss Walstein from Dublin, where she had been for many years the heroine of Crow Street, to Drury Lane, where she made her appearance as Calista, in 'The Fair Penitent,' on the 15th November, 1814, but only remained one season."

It would seem as if Drury Lane were weary by this time of its success, for early in 1815-16 that excellent actor, Dowton, who disliked seeing Kean's name in large type, tried to extinguish him by playing Shylock! The Kentish baker's son could play Sheva and Cantwell, and many other parts, admirably; but Shylock!— No, let us pass to more equal adversaries; in a contest between whom, Kean did fairly extinguish his antagonist. In this season Kean acted all his old and many new parts, among the latter, Shakspeare's Richard II., Bajazet, Duke Aranza (in which Elliston had the better of him), Goswin ("Beggars' Bush"), Sir Giles Overreach, and Sforza. Among these, Sir Giles stands pre-eminent for its perfectness, from the first words, " Still cloistered up," to the last convulsive breath drawn by him in that famous *one* scene of the fifth act, in which, through his terrible intensity, he once made so experienced an actress as Mrs. Glover faint away,—not at all out of flattery, but from emotion.

Now, Sir Giles had been one of Kemble's weaknesses; and he affected it as he might have done Coriolanus. He had played it since Mr. Kean had come to London, but as no comparison could be drawn, his performance was accepted, as even an indifferent but honest effort by a great artist deserves to be. But after Edmund Kean had added another rose to his chaplet, by his marvellous impersonation of Sir Giles, Kemble played it again, as if to challenge comparison. I am sorry to say it, but John Kemble was hissed! No! It was his Sir Giles that was hissed. Two nights later he acted Coriolanus, the merits of which were acknowledged with enthusiasm by his audience. But he never ventured on Sir Giles again! In this last character, all the qualities of Kean's voice came out to wonderful purpose, especially in the scene where Lovel asks him,

> "Are you not moved with the sad imprecations
> And curses of whole families, made wretched
> By your sinister practices?"

to which Sir Giles replies:—

> "Yes, as rocks are
> When foamy billows split themselves against
> Their flinty ribs; or as the moon is moved
> When wolves with hunger pined, howl at her brightness."

I seem still to hear the words and the voice as I pen this passage; now composed, now grand as the foamy billows; so flute-like on the word "moon," creating a scene with the sound; and anon sharp, harsh, fierce in the last line, with a look upward from those matchless eyes, that rendered the troop visible, and their howl perceptible to the ear;—the whole serenity of the man, and the solidity of his temper, being illustrated less by the assurance in the succeeding words than by the exquisite music in the tone with which he uttered the word "brightness."

It was on the night he played Sir Giles for the first time in London, that Mrs. Kean, who seems to have been too nervous to witness his new essays, asked him what that hanger-on at the theatres, Lord Essex, had thought of it. You know the jubilant reply:—"D—— Lord Essex, Mary! The pit rose at me!"

But to Sir Giles were not confined Kean's triumphs of this year. He created the part of Bertram, in Maturin's tragedy of that name; and he alone stands associated with the part. It suited him admirably,—for it is full of passion, pathos, wild love, and tenderness. One great point made by the actor (whose Imogine was Miss Somerville, afterwards Mrs. Bunn) was in the exquisite delivery of the words, "God bless the child!" They have made many a tear to flow, and he acquired the necessary pathos and power by first repeating them at home, while he looked on his sleeping boy; and I do not know a prettier incident in the life of this impulsive actor. Would there were more of them!

In the season of 1816–17 John Kemble withdrew, full of honors, though his laurels had been a little shaken. As opponents to the now well-established actor at Drury Lane, two gentlemen were brought forward, Mr. Macready, from Dublin, and Mr. Junius Booth, from Worthing. The former is the son of the respectable actor and dramatic author, whose abandonment of upholstery, in Dublin, did something towards giving to the stage the son who long refined and adorned it. Mr. Macready made all the more progress by not coming in contrast, or comparison, with Kean. He was of the Kemble school, but with ideas of his own, and he made his way to fame, independently. But Booth was so perfectly of the Kean school that his Richard appeared to be as good as his master's. Indeed, some thought it better. Whereupon,

Kean counselled the Drury Lane management to bring him over to that theatre. It was done. They played in Othello,—the Moor, by Kean: Iago, by Booth. The contact was fatal to the latter. He fell ingloriously, even as a Mr. Cobham had done before him in an audacious attempt on Richard; but both gentlemen became heroes to transpontine audiences.

Kean's other achievements this season were his fine interpretation of Timon, after Shakspeare's text, " with no other omissions than such as the refinement of manners has rendered necessary ;" his creation of Maturin's " Manuel," and his last triumph over Kemble, in doing what the latter had failed to do, stirring the souls, raising the terror, and winning the sympathy of his audience by one of the most finished of his impersonations,—Sir Edward Mortimer. Oronooko, Selim, and Paul, were the other characters newly essayed by him during this season. The last two were for his benefit, and therewith he closed the season,—the last very fruitful in great triumphs, but not the first in the chronicle of his decline.

He was now the oft invited guest of people with whom he did not particularly care to associate. Moore chronicles his name as one of the guests with Lord Petersham, Lord Nugent, the Hon. William Spencer, Colonel Berkeley, and Moore, at an "odd dinner," given by Horace Twiss, in Chancery Lane, in 1819, in " a borrowed room, with champagne, pewter spoons, and old Lady Cork." Lord Byron was reluctant to believe in him, but after seeing him in Richard, he presented the actor with a sword, and a box adorned by a richly-chased boar-hunt; when Lord Byron had seen his Sir Giles, he sent to the player a valuable Damascus blade. His compliments, at Kean's benefit, took the shape of a fifty-pound note; and he once invited him to dinner, which Kean left early, that he might take the chair at some pugilistic supper!

## CHAPTER XXVII.

#### EDMUND KEAN—CONTINUED.

BETWEEN the last named period, and the time when Edmund Kean played Virginius, there is but one character in which he produced any extraordinary effect—namely, King Lear. This sustained, but I do not think it increased, his glory. His other characters only seem to glide past, and disappear. Such are Richard, Duke of York, in a compilation from several of Shakspeare's plays; Barabbas, in Marlowe's "Jew of Malta," the heaviness of which he relieved by a song, sweetly warbled; Selim, in Dimond's melodramatic "Bride of Abydos;" Young Norval, in which he was graceful and affecting; King John, which did not disturb the repose of Kemble; and Alexander the Great, which could as little stir the dead sleep of Verbruggen. Something more effective was his Brutus, in Payne's compilation. The scene of his simulated folly was skilfully played; that with the son whom he condemns to death, full of tenderness and gravity. He could not sustain Miss Porter's "Switzerland," and he would not support Mr. Bucke's "Italians." Soane literally measured him for Malvesi, in the "Dwarf of Naples," and misfitted him grievously. Mr. Twiss had no better success with the "Carib Chief," in which Kean played Omreah; and my recollections of his Rolla are not so agreeable as those which I have of Young, and even Wallack. Well do I remember his Coriolanus, for which he was physically unfitted; but only a great actor could have played the scene of the candidateship, and that of the death, as Kean did—who, however, gave more pleasure to the followers of the Kemble school by this performance, than he did to his own. He made up for all, by the grandeur, the touchingness, and the sublimity of his King Lear. It was throughout thoroughly original, in conception and in execution, and by it he maintained his pre-eminency, and sustained, as I have said, without increasing his old glory. He did not quite realize his own assertion : " I will make the audience as mad as I shall be."

His laurels were menaced. Frederick Yates came from the camp, and flashed a promise in tragedy which moved the hearts of playgoers, who saw his later devotion to comedy with early regret, but an ultimate delight. Mr. Macready was steadily rising from melodrama to the highest walks of tragedy, and his golden opportunity came in Virginius. Hitherto, Kean had been shaking the secondary actors of the old Kemble type, into fits of jealousy, fear, disgust, and admiration. Expressly for him did Knowles write the " Virginius," which gave a lasting celebrity to Mr. Macready. Already, however, had a play on the subject, by Soane, been accepted at Drury Lane, and in the Roman father Kean was for the first time designedly opposed to the younger actor. He utterly failed; while Mr. Macready, in the part written expressly, and by an able hand, for Kean, won a noble victory. Kean might have said as the captured French Marshal said to Marlborough :—" Change sides with me, and I'll fight it out again, to a very different issue."

A range through his principal parts, and a running salute of thundering puffs on the part of Elliston, heralded his visit to America in 1820. He played at Liverpool before embarking, and like George Frederick Cooke, had a hit at the audience before he left them. They were the coldest people, he said, in whose presence he had ever acted. That was true; but though Liverpool was chary of approbation, it had applauded ungrateful Edmund more cordially than any other actor.

From his first trip to America he brought back much solid gold, a detestation of the Boston people, who would not patronize the theatre at an unfashionable season of the year, and one of the toe-bones of Cooke, over whose translated and mutilated remains, he raised the monument of which I have already spoken.

Some ill-health he brought back with him too; but he rallied, drank, relapsed, and struggled into strength again. It was wasted on Miss Baillie's " De Montfort;" though parts of this were played in his grandest style. He seemed conscious that something was expected of him by the public, and he flung himself, as it were, at every thing. He played Hastings to the Jane Shore of a Miss

Edmiston—whose success was predicted by aristocratic poets, and who is now, I believe, painfully "strolling." With Sir Pertinax he did not move the dead Macklin as his Shylock may have done; though it was better played, save in the accent, than any living actor could have played it. His Osmond gave some dignity to the "Castle Spectre," and his Wolsey but little to Henry VIII."

For Miss Tidswell's farewell benefit, after forty years of useful subalternship, he attempted Don Felix. He would have done more for her had he been asked; for in his breadless, boyish days, she had beaten, taught, fed, and clothed him—till Nance Carey claimed him for her own, and stole *all* his earnings. Edmund's good impulses made him fail in affection to this parent. Thinking of Miss Tidswell, he used to say—"If she wasn't my mother, why was she kind to me?"

For his own benefit, in this season of 1821-2, he played the Roman actor, Octavian, and Tom Tug—the song in which last part he sang with great feeling. The whole proceeds of this benefit he gave to the fund for the starving Irish. It was not exactly like Mrs. Haller's charity, who gives her master's wine to the sick poor; but that virtue, which is said to begin at home, might have sent the amount in a different direction.

In November, 1822, he played out the first of his two great struggles with Young, at Drury Lane. Since Quin and Garrick, or Garrick and Barry, no conjunction of great names moved the theatrical world like this. Both men put out all their powers, and the public profited by the magnificent display. Kean and Young acted together—Othello and Iago, Lothaire and Guiscard, Jaffier and Pierre, Alexander and Clytus, Posthumus and Iachimo, eliciting enthusiasm by all, but by none so much as by Othello and Iago. The two great wrestlers won equal honor; but that was not enough for one of them. "How long sir," said Kean to Elliston, the manager, "How long am I to play with that—*Jesuit*, Young?"

Certainly, if he feared competition with experienced actors, Kean was very encouraging to beginners. "You are the best Iago I ever played to," he once remarked to an earnest, youthful, gentleman at Edinburgh. The latter smiled; and Kean asked him *wherefore?* " Because, sir," was the answer, " I know of seven poor Iagos, to whom you have kindly said the same thing !"

In a revival of *Shakspeare's* " King Lear," Kean showed good taste, sublime acting, and an appreciation of opportunity for self-distinction. He was not always equally in the vein, but on some nights he excelled all he had done before. Genest says, that " his personal appearance was better than Kemble's or Young's, and his manner more natural. In the mad scenes he seemed to copy Murphy's account of Garrick." The only drawback I have heard of to this noble, and last of his noble and complete performances was, that he was neither tall enough nor strong enough to carry off the body of Cordelia (Mrs. W. West.)

He might have begun a fresh career, however, from this new starting-point, had he been so minded. But this success did not brace him to new effort, except a quietly ineffectual one to make the world forget the Stranger of John Kemble. His failing strength was probably the chief cause of his avoiding or refusing to appear in the same piece with Mr. Macready, of whom he rather rudely remarked,—" He is no actor, sir; he is a player!"

But the satirist himself was fast ceasing to be either. He had never recovered from the madness which he prophesied would follow his success in London. Gradually he lost all self-control, plunged into terrible excesses, courted rather than fell into evil company, took tribute, indeed, most willingly of the noble and intellectual who heaped rich gifts upon him, but he scorned or feared their society. He affected to feel that they invited him simply to stare at him, and that they would have despised him as a poor actor. He had not common sense enough to see that when the noble and intellectual opened their doors to him they rendered graceful homage to his genius,—and I have heard that where he *did* accept such homage, and was himself subdued to the refinements of the society where it was liberally, yet delicately rendered, his easy bearing was that of a man who had not lost his self-respect, and his manners and conversation emphatically " charming."

But this was under restraint, and to be thus " charming" was irksome to Edmund Kean;—by this time it had become almost impossible, and he could charm only those on whom the magic was not worth expending. He had not broken his word to his wife—that she should ride in her carriage, nor to his son—that he should go to Eton,—but he had not made the first happier, nor the second the more attached to him. His home, indeed, was broken up, and in the season of 1824–5, after failing in the poor melodramatic part of Masaniello, came out the great scandal—that he loved his neighbor's wife better than his own. All its necessary consequences followed,—a fierce, an almost ruffianly hostility on the part of his audiences, damage to his fortune, and irretrievable ruin to his reputation. Reckless and defiant as he was, he was glad to endure exile, for such was his voyage to, and sojourn in, America during this and the following year.

Let me notice that he bore himself in presence of a cruel audience, with an almost ferocious courage. His pride was greater than his humiliation. As at Drury, he applied every strong epithet in his part to the howling pit, so, when running his erratic course through the minor theatres, he could treat audiences that were ignorant, as well as insolent, with strong terms and lofty contempt. He had one night played Othello to a "Coburg" public. Iago was acted by Cobham, the performer who had once vainly attempted to dethrone him, by acting Richard at Covent Garden to a house, however, which would not listen to him, to the end. The New-Cut costermongers adopted him; they applauded him, on this particular night, more than they did the great Kean, who received £50 for condescending to exhibit himself in Othello. Nevertheless, at the fall of the curtain, there was such an uproar in front, apparently a call for Kean, that he came slowly forward, and bluntly asked, "What do you want?" A thousand voices answered, "You! you!" Well, said Kean after a slight peroration, "I have played in every civilized country where English is the language of the people; but I never acted to an audience of such unmitigated brutes as you are!" He walked slowly off, as Cobham, to a shout for him from the sweet voices of his Lambeth-marsh patrons, rushed on the stage, proud and radiant, to tell Edmund's "unmitigated brutes" that they were the most enlightened and liberal audience that had ever sat as judges of acting, and that the happiest night of his life was that on which he had the opportunity of telling his friends and admirers that incontrovertible truth. A cry that might have been heard across St. George's Fields proclaimed him to be "a trump!" —and Cobham won the honors of the night!

Kean, as before recorded, betook himself again to America. Since his previous visit to the Northern States he was greatly changed; but that the seeds of insanity were in him at the earlier period, a passage from Dr. Francis's *Old New York* will mournfully show. Some hospitable friends exerted themselves to render his earlier stay agreeable, and this is an incident of the time,—one out of many :

" A few days after, we made the desired visit at Bloomingdale. Kean, with an additional friend and myself, occupied the carriage for a sort of philosophical exploration of the city on our way there. On the excursion he remarked, he should like to see our Vauxhall; we stopped, he entered the gate, asked the door-keeper if he might survey the place, gave a double somerset through the air, and in the twinkling of an eye stood at the remote part of the garden. The wonder of the superintendent can be better imagined than described. Arriving at the Asylum, with suitable gravity he was introduced to the officials, invited to an inspection of the afflicted inmates, and then told if he would ascend to the roof of the building a delightful prospect would be presented to his contemplation; many counties, and an area of sea, rivers, and lands, mountains, and valleys, embracing a circuit of forty miles in circumference. His admiration was expressed in delirious accents : ' I'll walk the ridge of the roof of the Asylum,' he exclaimed, ' and take a leap! it's the best end I can make to my life;' and forthwith started for the western gable end of the building. My associate and myself as he hurried forward seized him by the arms, and he submissively returned. I have ever been at a loss to account for this sudden freak in his feelings; he was buoyant at the onset of the journey; he astonished the Vauxhall door-keeper by his harlequin trick, and took an interest in the various forms of insanity which came before him. He might have become too sublimated in his feelings, or had his senses unsettled (for he was an electrical apparatus) in contemplating the mysterious influences acting on the minds of the deranged, for there is an attractive principle, as well as an adhesive principle, in madness; or a crowd of thoughts might have oppressed him, arising from the disaster which had occurred to him a few days before with the Boston audience, and the irreparable loss he had sustained in the plunder of his trunk and valuable papers, while journeying hither and thither on his return to New York. We rejoiced together, however, when we found him again safely at home at his old lodgings at the City Hotel."

That the fit had not decreased by lapse of time, another extract from the same volume will amply demonstrate. Kean was not so satisfied with the success he achieved professionally, as he was of a visit to an Indian tribe who had enrolled him among their chiefs. It was a freak which he took seriously, as will be seen by what follows:

" Toward the close of his second visit to America Kean made a tour through the northern part of the State, and visited Canada; he fell in with the Indians, with whom he became delighted, and was chosen a chief of a tribe. Some time after, not aware of his return to the city, I received at a late hour of the evening a call to wait upon an Indian chief, by the name of Alantenaida, as the highly finished card left at my house had it. Kean's ordinary card was *Edmund Kean*, engraved; he generally wrote beneath '*Interger vitæ scelerisque purus*.' I repaired, to the hotel, and was conducted up stairs to the folding doors of the hall, where the servant left me. I entered, aided by the feeble light of the moon; but at the remote end I soon perceived something like a forest of evergreens, lighted up by many rays from floor-lamps, and surrounded by a stage or throne; and seated in great state was the chief. I advanced, and a more terrific warrior I never surveyed. Red Jacket or Black Hawk was an unadorned simple personage in comparison. Full dressed, with skins tagged loosely about his person, a broad collar of bear-skin over his shoulders, his leggings with many stripes, garnished with porcupine quills; his moccasins decorated with beads, his head decked with the war-eagle's plumes, behind which flowed massive black locks of dishevelled horse-hair, golden-colored rings pendent from the nose and ears, streaks of yellow paint over the face, massive red daubings about the eyes, with various lines in streaks about the forehead, not very artistically drawn. A broad belt surrounded his waist, with tomahawk; his arms with shining bracelets, stretched out with bow and arrow, as if ready for a mark. He descended his throne, and rapidly approached me. His eye was meteoric and fearful, like the furnace of the Cyclops. He vociferously exclaimed, ALANTEN-AIDA, the vowels strong enough. I was relieved, he betrayed something of his raucous voice in imprecation. It was Kean. An explanation took place. He wished to know the merits of the representation. The Hurons had honored him by admission into their tribe, and he could not now determine whether to seek his final earthly abode with them, for real happiness, or return to London and add renown to his name by performing the Son of the Forest. I never heard that he ever after attempted in his own country the character. He was wrought up to the highest pitch of enthusiasm at the Indian honor he had received, and declared that even old Drury had never conferred so proud a distinction on him as he had received from the Hurons."

I shall not soon forget that January night of 1827, on which he reappeared at Drury Lane, in Shylock. A rush so fearful, an audience so packed, a reconciliation so complete, acting so faultless, and a dramatic enjoyment so exquisite, I never experienced. Nothing was heeded,—indeed, the scenes were passed over till Shylock was to appear; and I have heard no such shout since, as that which greeted him. Fire, strength, beauty;—every quality of the actor seemed to have acquired fresh life. It was all deceptive, however. The actor was all but extinguished, after this convulsive, but seemingly natural effort. He lay in bed at the Hummums' hotel, all day, amusing himself melancholily with his Indian gewgaws, and striving to find a healthy tonic in "cognac." While immolating himself, he still clung to a hope of rescue; and he strove to create one more new character, Ben Nazir, in Mr. Colley Grattan's tragedy of that name. His power of memory was gone; but he had a fatuitous idea that he had mastered his part, and this is how he figured in it, as told by the author of that hapless drama, himself. The picture has been often exhibited; but it must needs be looked upon once more:

"He did at length appear. The intention of the author, and

the keeping of the character, required him to rush rapidly on the stage, giving utterance to a burst of joyous soliloquy. What was my astonishment, to see him as the scene opened, standing in the centre of the stage, his arms crossed, and his whole attitude one of thoughtful solemnity. His dress was splendid; and thunders of applause greeted him from all parts of the house. To display the one, and give time for the other, were the objects for which he stood fixed for several minutes, and sacrificed the sense of the situation. He spoke; but what a speech! The one I wrote, consisted of eight or nine lines; *his*, was of two or three *sentences*,—but not six consecutive words of the text. His look, his manner, his tone, were to *me* quite appalling; to any other observer, they must have been incomprehensible. He stood fixed; drawled out his incoherent words, and gave the notion of a man that had been half hanged and then dragged through a horse pond. My heart, I confess it, sank deep in my breast. I was utterly shocked. And as the business of the play went on, and as *he* stood by, with moveless muscle and glazed eye, throughout the scene which should have been one of violent, perhaps too violent exertion,—a cold shower of perspiration poured from my forehead, and I endured a revulsion of feeling which I cannot describe, and which I would not for worlds, one eye had witnessed. I had all along felt, that this scene would be the touchstone of the play. Kean went through it like a man in the last stage of exhaustion and decay. The act closed; a dead silence followed the fall of the curtain; and I felt, though I could not hear, the voiceless verdict of 'damnation.' . . . . . When the curtain fell, Mr. Wallack, the stage manager, came forward, and made an apology for Kean's imperfection in his part, and an appeal in behalf of the play. Neither excited much sympathy; the audience was quite disgusted. I now, for the first time during the night, went behind the scenes. On crossing the stage toward the green-room, I met Kean, supported by his servant and another person, going in the direction of his dressing-room. When he saw me, he hung down his head, and waved his hand, and uttered some expressions of deep sorrow, and even remorse. 'I have ruined a fine play, and myself; I cannot look you in the face,' were the first words I caught. I said something in return, as cheering and consolatory as I could. I may say, that all sense of my own disappointment was forgotten, in the compassion I felt for him."

The descent now was rapid, but it was not made at one leap. Penniless, though he might have been lord of "thousands," he caught at an offer to provide for his son by a cadetship; but the son refused to accept the offer,—as such acceptation would have exposed his mother to worse than the destitution of her earlier days,—before hope of a bright, though closing future, had died away. To lose her son, was to lose the best friend she had; for she had none, now, in her faithless and suicidal husband. Edmund Kean heard of his son's determination to go on the stage, in order to support his mother, with grim dissatisfaction, and, I should hope, some sense of reproach and abasement. They parted in anger, it is said, as far as the father was concerned; the more angry, perhaps, that in his temporary wrath he cast off the son whom he, in his heart, must have respected.

Consequently, the season of 1827-8, at Drury Lane and Covent Garden, had a singular incident to mark them;—the struggle of the son to rise, at the former; the struggle of the father not to fall, at the latter. Mr. Charles Kean opened the season, in Norval. Mr. Cole, in his biography of the son, quotes a letter, written by a friend of the father, to the latter, in which the writer, who had watched the attempt, remarks:—"The speech, 'My name is Norval,' he hurried, and spoke as though he had a cold, or was pressing his finger against his nose."

The attempt, in short, was unsuccessful; so had that of many an aspirant been who subsequently reaped triumphs at his will; and Mr. Charles Kean might find consolation. The attempt, at all events, enabled him to fix his foot on the first step of the giddy ascent; and, let it be said, he owed the possibility of doing so, entirely to his father's name. So young a man, without a great name, would have found no access to Drury open to him; and I like to think, that if he missed the fortune which his half mad, yet kindly impulsive father, had promised him, he owed to that father the foundations on which he raised another. He inherited a great name and a great warning.

While the son was anxiously and painfully laying these foundations, the sire was absolutely electrifying audiences at Covent Garden by old flashes of his might, or disappointing them by his incapacity, or his capricious absence. He reminded me of Don Juan, who, though he went with open eyes recklessly to destruction, flung off the fiends, who at last grasped him, with a fearful, but vainly expended energy. On one night, when he played Othello to Young's Iago, the Cassio of Charles Kemble, the Roderigo of Farley, and the Desdemona of Miss Jarman, I saw strong men clamber from the pit, over the lower boxes, to escape suffocation, and weak men, in a fainting condition, passed by friendly hands towards the air, in the same way. I remember Charles Kemble, in his lofty, bland way, trying to persuade a too-closely packed audience to fancy themselves comfortable, and to be silent, which they would not be till *he* appeared, who, on that, and some after nights, could subdue them to silence or stir them into ecstasy, at his will.

To those who saw him from the front, there was not a trace of weakening of any power in him. But, oh ye few who stood between the wings where a chair was placed for him, do you not remember the saddening spectacle of that wrecked genius,—a man in his very prime, with not merely the attributes of age about him, but with some of the infirmities of it, which are wont to try the heart of love itself. Have you forgotten that helpless, speechless, fainting mass bent up in that chair; or the very unsavory odor of that very brown, very hot, and very strong brandy-and-water, which alone kept alive the once noble Moor? Aye, and *still* noble Moor; for when his time came, he looked about as from a dream, and sighed, and painfully got to his feet, swayed like a column in an earthquake, and in not more time than is required for the telling of it, was before the audience, as strong and as intellectually beautiful as of old;—but only happy in the applause which gave him a little breathing space, and saved him from falling dead upon the stage.

During a few nights of another year or two, he acted under the exacting conditions of a nature that had been violated. He gained a little strength from his island home in Bute, and even acted in Glasgow, Cork, and Dublin, with his son, in whose success he took a father's part. Thrice he essayed fresh study, and once he nearly conquered; his Virginius, in Knowles's play, was superbly affecting, in fragmentary passages, but he tried it at too late a period, not of his natural life, but of his professional career. Richard II. was magnificently got up for him, but as the curtain was about to rise, it was discovered that he was not in the house, and days passed before he emerged into the world and decency. His last essay in a new part was in "Henry V.;" but he broke down, addressed the audience deprecatorily, muttered something about being the representative of Shakspeare's heroes, and lamented, at little more than forty, what Macklin did not plead till he was past ninety,—his decaying memory.

Now and then, the town saw him, but his hold on it was nearly gone. He was now at the Haymarket; and then, uncertainly, at Drury Lane; and again at the Haymarket in 1832, where I saw him for the last of many times, in Richard. The sight was pitiable. Genius was not traceable in that bloated face; intellect was all but quenched in those once matchless eyes; and the power seemed gone, despite the will that would recall it. I noted in a diary, that night, the above facts, and, in addition, that by bursts he was as grand as he had ever been,—that though he looked well as long as he was still, he moved only with difficulty, using his sword as a stick. I find, and perfectly remember, that there was a murmur of approbation at the pause and action of his extended arm, as he said—" In the deep bosom of the ocean,— BURIED!"—as if he consigned all lowering clouds to the sea. At —"The dogs bark at me, as I halt by them:" the action was so expressive as to elicit a round of applause; and in the last of the lines—

> "Why what a peevish fool was he of Crete,
> Who taught his son the office of a fowl,
> And yet for all his wings, the fool was drowned,"

the playful yet fiendish sarcasm was delivered with marvellous effect. His words, after "Die, prophet, in thy speech,"—"For this among the rest was I *ordained*," seemed like a devilish joke after a burst of fury. In—

> "Villains, set down the corse, or by St. Paul,
> I'll make a corse of him that disobeys,"—

his voice was scarcely distinguishable; but his old attitude of leaning at the side scene, as he contemplated Lady Anne, was as full of grace as ever,—save that the contemplator had now a swollen and unkingly face. Then—

"Shine out fair sun, till I have bought a glass,
That I may see my shadow as I pass,"—

was sportive in accent as in the very action of saluting; and there was a world of argument and resolution in the delivery of the simple words—" The tower?—*Aye;* the TOWER!" The chuckle at "So much for *Buck*ingham!" I always considered wanting in dignity, but it brought a roar of applause. In the scene with the Mayor and Buckingham, he displayed talent unsurpassable;—the scarcely-subdued triumph that lurked in his eyes, as he refused the crown; his tone in "Call him again;" his acceptance of the throne, and his burst of joy, when he had dismissed the petitioners, were perfect in their several ways; but he was exhausted before the fifth act, and when, after a short fight, Richmond (Cooper) gave him his death wound in Bosworth Field, as he seemed to deal the blow, he grasped Kean by the hand, and let him gently down, lest he should be injured by a fall.

The end was at hand. He could no longer even venture, after the play, to Offley's symposium, in Henrietta Street, Covent Garden, that lively singing-room, with a window looking into the mouldiest of churchyards,—where, however, slept some noble actors. To and from Richmond he occasionally travelled,—a feeble bundle of humanity, that seemed to lie unconsciously in one corner of his carriage. But, I think, conscience was there, too, and rage, and remorse,—that a life had been so wasted, and mighty powers, almost as divine as the poet's, so irretrievably abused. He aroused himself to make his last appearance, as it proved, on the stage, in conjunction with his son, in Othello, Mr. Charles Kean playing Iago. The night was the 25th of March, 1833. Edmund Kean was so shattered in frame, that he had scarcely strength to pass over him the dress of the Moor; so shattered in nerve, that he dreaded some disaster. Brandy gave some little heart to the greatly fallen actor, but he anxiously enjoined his son to be ever near him, in case of some mischance, and he went through the part, dying as he went, till after giving the sweet utterance, as of old, to the celebrated " Farewell," ending with " Othello's occupation's gone !" he attempted to utter the next speech, and in the attempt fell on his son's shoulder, with a whispered moan, " I am dying,—speak to them for me !" The curtain here descended on him forever, and the rest was only slow death, with intervals of hope. He, the faithless, and now helpless, husband sent a note, which sounds as a cry of anguish, to that good Mary Chambers of old, who had had the ill-luck to listen to his wooing. But, having so listened, she would not now be deaf to the wail of the man who said that he had gone wrong in judgment, not in feeling; in head, not in heart, and who cried, " Come home; forget and forgive !" She went, and forgave; an angel could not, however, have forgotten all; but she acted as if she had, and the true-hearted young partner of his early miseries was the gentle alleviator of his last sufferings. She stood by him till, on the 15th of May, death came upon the unconscious man after some old tag of Octavian had passed his restless lips, of " *Farewell Flo—, Floran the !*"

*Come home!* was the dying actor's cry to his wife. Dead; there was no home for the widow; for creditors took possession of it, and its contents. To such end had come the humble and hapless wedding of Mary Chambers and Edmund Kean at Gloucester, the brief glory after long suffering,—sorrow and want at the end as at the beginning; with him, an added shame; with her, uncomplainingness. Yes, and consolation. The happiness she lacked with her husband was vouchsafed to her through her son, and the union of the two strolling players at Gloucester was thus not altogether barren of good and happy fruits.

And over the grave of one of the greatest of actors something may be said in extenuation of his faults. Such curse as there can be in a mother's indifference hung about him before his birth. A young Huron, of whose tribe he subsequently became a member, could not have lived a more savage,—but certainly enjoyed a more comfortable and better-tended boyhood. Edmund Kean, from that very time of boyhood, had genius, industry, and ambition,—but, with companionship enough to extinguish the first, lack of reward sufficient to dull the second, and repeated visitations of disappointment that might have warranted the exchange of high hopes for brutal despair,—he nourished his genius, maintained his industry, and kept an undying ambition, under circumstances when to do so was a part of heroism. Compare his young and hard and blackguard life with the disciplined boyhood of Betterton, the early associations of Booth, the school career of Quin, the decent but modest childhood of Macklin, the gentlemanly home of the youth Garrick, the bringing up of Cooke, and the Douay College life of the Kembles. Kean was trained upon blows, and curses, and starvation, and the charity of strangers. It was enough to make all his temper convert to fury, and any idea of such a young, unnurtured savage, ever becoming an inheritor of the mantle worn by the actors I have named, would have seemed a madness even to that mother who soon followed him in death, Nance Carey. But Edmund Kean cherished the idea, warm in his bosom, never ceased to qualify himself for the attempt, studied for it while he starved,—and when about to make it, felt and said that success would drive him mad. I believe it did; but whether or not, I can part from *the* great actor of my young days only with a tender respect. I do not forget the many hours of bright intellectual enjoyment for which I, in common with thousands, was indebted to him, and in the contemplation of this actor's incomparable genius, I desire to forget the errors of the man.

Over his remains, in Richmond churchyard, a plain tablet arrests the eye. I never look at it without a crowd of memories of the old and brilliant scene he for a while adorned, nor without thinking of the words of Lesingham, in the Elizabethan drama:

> "Oh! what our wills will do,
> With over-rash and headlong peevishness,
> To bring our calm discretion to repentance!"

## Epilogue.

I leave the history of the great players who rivalled or succeeded Edmund Kean, to other chroniclers. They belong—the *great* players—to a vocation which is next in dignity to that of the poet. In the far-off Ionian Islands, Demodocus first inspired his countrymen with that taste for dramatic representation which has overrun the world. Five centuries later, Thespis invented tragedy; and after seven centuries more had elapsed, and there was a new dispensation upon earth, and heathenism was fiercely fighting out its last struggle with Christianity, the stage yielded two of the noblest martyrs to the faith, in the persons of the then renowned actors,—Genesius of Rome, and Gelasinus of Heliopolis.

Looking, recently, at the old patent granted by Charles II. to Killigrew and Davenant (now in Drury Lane Theatre), I could not help remarking, that the parchment for which so many hundreds of thousands of pounds had been given, was now virtually worthless, save for the superb portrait of Charles, within the gigantic initial letter of his name. When that patent for two theatres was granted, London was less populous than Manchester is now; and as the population increased, theatres (beginning with that in Goodman's Fields) sprung up in spite of the patent or Lord Chamberlain. The latter granted licenses to a few, with great restrictions. At the Lyceum, for instance, not even a tragedy could be produced, unless there were at least five songs or concerted pieces in each act; and the tragedy even then must be called a *burletta.* The licenser's powers did not extend to St. George's Fields, where political plays, forbidden on the Middlesex side of the river, were attractive merely because they were forbidden.

Subsequently, at the minor theatres, plays, which could only be legally acted at the patent houses, were performed, without being converted into burlettas. The proprietors of the patents prosecuted the offenders; but the levying of penalties (£50 nightly) against Englishmen, for producing or acting in Shakspeare's plays, seemed so absurd, that after some toying with the question, in

1842, the government brought forward the bill of 1843, which passed both houses, after Lord Campbell had deprived it of some tyrannic authority it conferred upon the Lord Chamberlain. A "free trade" principle was thereby introduced. The patent houses lost all their privileges, save that of being exempt from a yearly renewal of license to act; and the legitimate drama could be performed in any licensed theatre. At Sadler's Wells, for instance, it was long and worthily upheld by Mr. Phelps, without fear of every actor therein incurring a penalty of £300 weekly, as when he played every night, contrary to law.

Since 1843, then, the term of "Their," or "Her Majesty's Servants," is a mere formality, as there is no especial company now privileged to serve or solace royalty. Mr. Webster, who occupies Garrick's chair, in the management of the Theatrical Fund, tells me, that Baddeley was the last actor who wore the uniform of scarlet and gold, prescribed for the "gentlemen of the household," who were patented actors; and that he used to appear in it at rehearsal. He was proud of being one of their "Majesties' servants;"—a title once coveted by all nobly-aspiring actors. They were sometimes nearest to the desired end when they seemed farthest off. "Have you ever heard," asks Garrick, in an unpublished letter to Moody, then at Liverpool, "of a Mrs. Siddons, who is strolling about somewhere near you?" Four months later, Garrick brought her out at Drury Lane. That space of time intervened, between the periods when Edmund Kean was starving and triumphing. And now, in the green-room of Drury Lane Theatre, the busts of Mrs. Siddons and Kean face each other; while that of Shakspeare, opposite Garrick, seems to smile on all three,—*his* great interpreters, as well as THEIR MAJESTIES' SERVANTS.

# INDEX TO VOL. II.

## A.

Abington, Mrs., life and career, 208–11.
Actor, qualifications for, 23; the only one elected a member of White's, 27; combination to make a great one, 55.
"Agis," Home's, 38.
Ailesbury, Lord, and Mrs. Siddons, 243.
"Almida," by Mallett's daughter, 68.
Arne, Tom, and his sister, 51.
Arnould, Sophie. 53.
Aristophanes, 127.
Audiences, treatment of, by Mrs. Woffington, 10; liberty taken with, by Holland and Powell, 148; of the last half of the 18th century, 163–183; encore a prologue. 173; French, 179; the trunkmaker, 180; Foote on English, 182.
Authors, list of, with their plays, from 1776 to 1800, 136–143; condemned authors, and how they bore the condemnation, 144–162; first fashion of calling for, 174; dramatic, of the early part of the 19th century, 369–375.

## B.

Baddeley, Mrs. career of, 197–8; Baddeley, Mr., 416.
Baillie, Joanna, dramatist, 149.
Bannister, J., accused of disloyalty, 167; Charles, 342; John, 342–44.
Barry. his attraction in Dublin, 88–9; last nights, 58; his decay, 74; depreciation of, by Walpole, 74; comment on Garrick, 98; estimation of Garrick, 100; sketch of his life and professional career, 96–103.
Barry, Mrs., re-appears after her husband's death, 103; maiden name. Miss Street, account of, 103–4; marries Dancer, an actor, 104; married to Spranger Barry, 104; prefers comedy to tragedy, 104; married to Crawford, barrister and actor, 105; rivalry with Mrs. Siddons, 105; original characters, 106; her parallel between the Garrick and Kemble schools, 106.
Barsanti, Miss, aversion to male costume, 196.
Barresford, Mrs. (Bulkeley), original Julia, 204.
Barnwell, George, as played by Rose, 223.
Beard, actor, marries daughter of the Earl of Waldegrave, 46.
Bellamy, Mrs., arouses the King of Denmark, 166; sketch of life and career, 199–203.
Belfille, Mrs., 203.
Bensley, actor and barrack-master, 226–7.
Bentley, his "Philodamus," 145; Bentley, at the condemnation of his own play, 171.
Benefits, incidents of, 316, 332, 336.
Betterton and Garrick, comparative labors of, 90; honor rendered to Betterton, 94.
Betty, Master, 296–301.
Bisse. Rev. P., 17.
Bickerstaffe, his operas, 37.
Blanchard, 351.
Booth and Quin, in Cato, 74.
Boaden, his "Aurelio and Miranda," 146.
Brandon, Countess of, patronizes the Irish stage, 40.
Brand, Hannah, dramatist and actress, 149.
Brunton, Louisa, 204.
Brereton (actor), inspired by Mrs. Siddons, 254.
Brooke, Mrs., dramatist, 149.
Brown, Anthony, his quarrel with Quin, 155.
Brown, Miss (vocalist), her effect on a sentimental captain, 181.
Buckingham, Sheffield, Duke of, on Cibber, 26.
Bulkeley, Mrs., her acts and audiences, 230.
Burgoyne, his "Maid of the Oaks," 72.
Burke and Garrick, 84.
Buxton, Jedediah. 87.
Byron, Lord, and Mrs. Bellamy, 200.

## C.

Cadogan, Dr. Garrick's remark to, on his death-bed, 93.
Calcraft, Mr. and Mrs. Bellamy, 201.
Canning, Mrs., married Reddish, 219; her career as an actress, 219, 244.
Canning, George, the statesman, son of the actress, 221.
Cautherley, alleged son of Garrick, 219.
"Careless Husband," Cibber's account of, 21–2.
Carmontelle, his double portrait of Garrick, 84.
"Caractacus," by Mason—by D'Egville, 145.
Cargill, Mrs., tragic point in Macheath, 150.
Carlton House, actors at, 307.
"Castle Spectre." Sheridan's estimate of, 151.
Catherine. Czarina, invites Garrick to Prussia, 85.
Catley, Miss, conduct in front of the house, 198.

18*

Celisia, Madame, 68.
Centlivre, Mrs., impatient under failure, 152.
Charke, Mrs., her melancholy career, 30, 31.
Charles I. portrayed in Home's "Agis," 33.
Charlotte, Queen, at the play, 168; in state, 170; appoints Mrs. Siddons preceptress in English reading to the princesses, 248.
Chesterfield, his advice to Dodsley, 35; thought Garrick poor in comedy, 79; on Garrick's marriage, 90; on Barry, 101.
"Chinese Festival," cause of a riot, 164.
Cholmondeley, Hon. Mrs. (Mary Woffington), 8.
Chudleigh, Miss, at the opera, 173.
Churchill, abused by Foote, 133.
Cibber, Theophilus, his wit, 29; death, 31.
Cibber Colley, sketch of his life, 15-32; instructs his daughter-in-law, 52.
Cibber,' (Susanna Maria), sketch of life of, 51-56; her original characters, 53; salary, 56.
Clairon, Mdlle., and Garrick, 63; off the stage, 263.
Clairval de Passy, Viscount and Viscountess (actors), 208.
"Clandestine Marriage" (Colman and Garrick), 36.
Clarence, Duke of, dresses Bannister, 169.
"Cleone," Dodsley's, 34-5.
Clive, Mrs., first appearance as Ismenes, 108; her marriage, when Miss Raftor, with Mr. Clive, 108; testimony to, by Fielding, 108; by Isaac Reed, 110; her career and characteristics, 109; a mimic, 109; attempts serious parts, 110; her farewell, 110; Walpole provides a home for her, 111; scenes at Strawberry Hill, 111-12; her opinion of Mrs. Siddons, 112; original characters and death, 113; as Portia, gives imitations of the leading lawyers, 158.
Cole, Mrs., idea of, taken from Reed, 131.
Colman, his opinion of the Fool in "King Lear," 68; and Garrick, 87; his delicacy of stage-feeling, 205.
Comedies of the 18th century, 146.
Commons, House of, suspends rule respecting strangers in favor of Garrick, 84; compliment to Master Betty, 299.
Converts, theatrical, Mrs. Woffington, 11; Melmoth, Mrs., 313.
Cooke, G. F., life of, 236-295.
Cork Theatre, incidents at, 176.
Copenhagen Theatre, hissing forbidden at, 176.
Costume, Mrs. Lisley's in Arionelli, 196; of the Barrys in Dublin, 98, 101; Woodward's, 115; Bannister's dress rearranged by the Duke of Clarence, 169; Catley, Miss, in Macheath, 198; Belfille, splendor of her stage wardrobe, 203; Mrs. Robinson, as Statira, 215; Kemble's in Othello, 266; anachronisms in, exemplified, 302, 309, 316.
Coventry, Earl of, and Sarah Kemble, 242.
Cowley. Mrs., "Anna Matilda," originator of "At Homes," 148.
Cradock's "Zobeide," 68.
Craven, Lady, "in form," 177; her " Princess of Georgia," 179.
Crawford, Mrs.; Mrs. Siddons's jealousy of, 346.

Critics in Cibber's time, 26.
Crouch, Mrs., and John Kemble, 266.
Cumberland, his "Timon," 68; "West Indian," 70; his merits and defects, 70; "Brothers," 70; "Wheel of Fortune," 70; his "Choleric Man," 72; his "Carmelite," 145; "Jew," 147; defence of himself, 162; his description of Garrick and Quin in the "Fair Penitent," 80-1.
Curtis, Mrs., alleged sister of Mrs. Siddons, 247.

D.

Darby, Miss, 212.
Davies, on Garrick and Quin in the same play, 79.
Deaths—Woffington, Mrs., stricken by paralysis on the stage, 12; Cibber, Theophilus, drowned, 31; in what company, 31; Delane, allegedly of broken heart, at Garrick's mimicry of him, 76; Middleton, of destitution, 103; Mossop, of pride and want, 107; Baddeley, when dressed for Moses, 230; Palmer, on the stage at Liverpool, 234.
Dedications, samples of dramatic, 323-332.
De Camp, Miss, dramatist and actress, 149; (De Fleury), 281.
Deighton, actor and artist, 312.
Delaney, Mrs., describes Garrick at home, 92; on Barry, 97.
Delaney, Dr., 56.
Delavals, Foote's intimacy with, 120, 126, 163, 172, 134.
Denmark, King of, at the play, 166-7.
Derby, Earl of, 207.
Descendants from actresses—Earl of Munster and Lords De l'Isle, from Mrs. Jordan and William IV., 347; Wilton, from Earl of Derby and Miss Farren, Countess of Derby, 208; Bellinghams in Ireland, from Mary Woffington and Hon. Mr. Cholmondeley, 9.
Desdemona, by Mrs. Siddons, 255.
Desnoyers teaches Barry dancing, 100.
Dexter, on the night of his début, 182.
Diet of actors, 101, 107; Garrick's, 239; Henderson's, 239.
Digges, a speech encored, 38; alleged conduct towards, of Foote, 132; and Mrs. Bellamy, 201; the original Norval, 226.
"Discovery," Mrs. Sheridan's, why revived, 86.
Dow, as dramatist, 67.
Dodd, actor, 229, 230.
Dowton, 350.
Dublin Theatre, rudeness and gallantry at, 175; a night in the, 97.
Ducis, double dénouement to his "Othello," 159.
Duclos, Madame, 182.
Du Fresne, 182.
Duels—Baddeley and George Garrick, 197; Mossop and a Major, 175; Aiken and John Kemble, 225, 269; Baddeley challenges Foote, 231.
Duncan, Miss, (Mrs. Davison), 352.
Drury Lane, grand night at, in 1751, 163.

INDEX. 419

## E.

"Earl of Essex," Brookes's, 36.
Edward III., the Maximin of Home's "Siege of Aquileia," 86.
Edwin, his first appearance, 186, 225.
"Elfrida," Mason's, cast of, 68-9.
Elliston, 347-9.
Erskine and Mrs. Siddons, 262.
Esten, Mrs., 204.
Essex, Earl of, and Mrs. Robinson, 213.
Evander, one of Barry's great parts, 102.
Epilogue, 415.

## F.

"False Delicacy," Kelly's, 57.
Falstaff, John Kemble and Munden, desirous of playing it, 240.
Farces, 36-7.
Farren, Miss (Countess of Derby), her life and career, 204-8.
"Fate of Sparta," Mrs. Cowley's, epigram on, 148.
Fielding, his indifference under failure, 154.
Fitzhenry, Mrs., 312.
Flecnoe, as a condemned author, 151.
Foote, worsted at joke-making, 133; —, life and character, 119-135; on Garrick, 75, 76; mimicry of, 81.
Fox, Charles, and O'Brien the actor, 48; as Horatio, 177.
Franklin, Dr., his "Matilda," 73.
Francis, Miss, 265.
French stage, 361.
French actors, traits of,—Rachel, 62; Lekain. 61; Clairon, 63; Arnould, Sophie, 63; Preville, 83; Montfleury, 86; Du Fresne, 182; Mdlle. Fleury (Mdme. Sainville), 208.

## G.

Garrick, Mrs., a guest of Bp. Porteus, 94; refuses an offer of marriage from Lord Monboddo, 94.
Garrick and Mrs. Woffington, 7; his last night, 73; sketch of his professional career, 75-95; his anonymous critics, 77; founds his "Lethe," on Miller's "Hospital for Fools," 156; his house assailed, 106.
Gay, described by Cibber, 25; reading his condemned play, at Leicester House, 153.
George III., stage jokes at his expense, 167: indirect cause of Mrs. Cibber's death, 54; fired at by Hatfield, 169.
Gloucester, Duke and Duchess of, at the play, 177.
Glover, Mrs., 353.
Godwin, his "Antonio," 144.
Goldsmith, his "Good-Natured Man," 57. 67; "She Stoops to Conquer," its first night, 70; unsuccessful dramatist, 157.
Goodman, opinion of Cibber, 17, 22.
Goodere, family of, 119.
Graham, Mrs. (afterwards Mrs. Yates), 193.
Greathead, Mr., and Mrs. Siddons, 242.
Greatbead, B., dramatist, 161.

Green, Mrs., the original Mrs. Malaprop, 197.
Griffith, Mrs., her "Platonic Wife," 148.
Grimm, his criticism on Garrick, 85.
Grimaldi, Signor, 87.
"Guardian," Garrick's, 84.
Gunnings, Misses, 5.

## H.

Hallam, killed by Macklin, 186.
Hamilton, Mrs., 312.
Hardy, French dramatist, 160.
Harlequin, the old actors, on, and players of, 44-5.
Hartley, Mrs., 69; her love-passage with Gentleman Smith, 69; her death, 197.
Havard, death of, 66; effect of his "Charles I.," 66.
Haymarket, catastrophe at, 169; the old lower gallery at, 164.
"Heiress," Mozeen's, 84.
Henderson, John, life and stage career of, 235-240; Kemble's opinion of, 275.
"Henry VII.," by Macklin, 188.
Hill, Dr., his aspersions answered by Garrick, 89.
Hill, Aaron, under condemnation, 152.
Hollingsworth, actor, accident to, 181.
Holland and Powell, their joint career, 66; Holland's funeral, 180.
Holman, 350.
Home, fate of his "Fatal Discovery" and "Alonzo," 67.
Hoole, a dramatist, 67, 73; generous behavior of, 160.
Hopkins, Priscilla (Mrs. Brereton, afterwards Mrs. John Kemble), 267.
Horton, Miss P. (Mrs. German Reed), 68.
Home, at the representation of "Douglas," 297.
Hull, his Edward and Eleonora," 73.

## I.

Inchbald, Mrs., dramatist and actress, 148-9 ; and John Kemble, 266.
Individuals referred to in dramatic pieces:—
Charles I. in Agis, 33; Edward III. as Maximin, in "Siege of Aquileia," 86; Douglas, Mother, as Mrs. Cole, by Foote, 122; Whitfield, Rev. G., as Shift (Minor), by Foote, 122; Kingston, Duchess of, as Kitty Crocodile, by Foote, 123; Faulkner, Alderman ("Orators"), by Foote, 123; Newcastle, Duke of, as Matthew Mug ("Mayor of Garratt"), by Foote, 123; Melcombe, Lord, as Sir Thomas Lofty ("Patron"), by Foote, 123; Arne, Dr., as Catgut ("Commissary"), by Foote, 124; Brocklesby, Dr., as Squib ("Devil on Two Sticks"), by Foote, 124; Browne, Sir William ("Devil on Two Sticks"), by Foote, 124; Long, Walter, as Flint ("Maid of Bath"), by Foote, 125; Smith, General, as Sir Matthew Mite ("Nabob") by Foote, 125; Grieve, Mrs., as Mrs. Fleecem ("Cozeners"), by Foote, 126; Dodd, Mrs.,

as Mrs. Simony ("Cozeners"), by Foote, 127; Jackson, Rev. Mr., as Viper ("Capnchin"), by Foote, 127; Barrowby, Dr., in Foote's Entertainment, 121; Taylor, the oculist, by Foote, 121; Cocks, the auctioneer, by Foote, 121; Henly, by Foote, 121; De Veal, Sir Thomas, by Foote, 121; Ap Rice, Mr., by Foote, 122; Longford, the auctioneer, in the "Minor," by Foote, 122.

## J.

"Jealous Wife," Colman's, 36.
Jephson, his "Braganza," 73; his "Law of Lombardy," 145.
Johnson, Miss, first wife of Theophilus Cibber, 148.
Johnson at Mrs. Woffington's, 7; criticises Brookes's "Earl of Essex," 36; Goldsmith, 58; attack on Garrick in the *Rambler*, 78, 79; his praise of Garrick, 79, 94; his dislike of Foote, 129.
"John Bull," how written, 289.
Jordan, Mrs., Mrs. Siddons's opinion of, 256, 257; in Imogen, 344-7.

## K.

Kean, Moses, as Glumdalca, 73.
Kean, Edmund, and Mrs. Garrick, 90; his Shylock, 191; Kemble's criticism on, 270; sketch of his life, 377-414.
Kelly, killed by Ryan, 42; Kelly, (Hugh,) his "False Delicacy," 67; "Clementina," 68, 69, 71.
Kemble, John, in Mark Anthony, 180, 283; life of, 264-278; Colman's opinion of, 277.
Kemble, Sarah, playing Ariel in harns, 64.
Kemble, Elizabeth (Mrs. Whitelock), 243, 255, 265.
Kemble, Frances, (Mrs. Twiss), 243, 255.
Kemble, Anne, (Mrs. Hutton), 255.
Kemble, Roger, 242, 243, 247.
Kemble, Henry, 279.
Kemble, Charles, 276-281; Mrs., 281-2
Kemble, Stephen, 265, 278.
King, 337.
Kitty Fisher and Henderson's brother, 239.
Kirk, general assembly of the, and Mrs. Siddons, 250.

## L.

Laureate, the only actor nominated to the post, 27.
Leo, Sophia, her "Chapter of Accidents," 149.
Lee, Lewes, actor, 226.
Leinster, Duchess of, and Miss Farren, 207.
Lewis, descended from Harley's secretary, 98, 333.
"Liar," Foote's, whence derived, 131.
Le Kain, the French Garrick, sketch of, 81-2, Llanover, Lady, on lack of refinement in actors, 92.
Liston, 351.
"Love à la Mode," Macklin's, 190.

"Love's Last Shift," Cibber's, 19-20; Southerne and Lord Dorset's criticism on, 20; Congreve's, 24.
Lyttelton, Lord, counsels Garrick to enter parliament, 89.

## M.

Macbeth, Lady, by Mrs. Pritchard and Mrs. Siddons, 252-4.
Macklin, sketch of life and career, 184-196; his first night in Macbeth, and consequent riots, 71-2; counsel to Reynolds, 145; generosity of Garrick to, 85; his criticism on Barry and Garrick, 189.
Macklin, Rev. Charles, his eccentricity, 191.
Macklin, Miss, her character, 195; death, 195.
Macklin, Mrs., death of, 35.
Mallett, his flattery disregarded by Garrick, 88.
"Man of the World," Macklin's, 190.
Marriages—Parsons and Dorothy Stewart, niece to the Earl of Galloway, 232; Miss Farren and the Earl of Derby, 207; Gentleman Smith and the daughter of Lord Hinchinbroke, 224; Woffington, Mary, with Hon. Mr. Cholmondeley, son of Earl Cholmondeley, 8; Beard with Lady Henrietta Herbert, daughter of the Earl of Waldegrave, 46; O'Brien with Lady Susan Strangways, daughter of the Earl of Ilchester, 46; Pritchard, Miss, with the elder John Palmer, 64; with Lloyd, the political writer, 64; Dancer with Miss Street, afterwards Mrs. Barry and Mrs. Crawford, 104; Dancer, Mrs., with Spranger Barry, 104; Barry, Mrs., widow of Spranger Barry, with Mr. Crawford, 104; Cibber, Theophilus, and Miss Johnson, 108; secondly, with Susanna Maria Arne, 52; Raftor, Miss (Kitty Clive), with Mr., brother of Mr. Baron Clive, 108.
Mason, his "Caractacus," 74, 145; his "Elfrida," 68.
Mattocks, Mrs., granddaughter of Hallam, 186, 341.
Mathews, 351.
"Mayor of Garratt," 131.
Medea—Mrs. Yates and Mrs. Siddons, 254.
Melmoth, Mrs. (Pratt), 313.
Mercier, on Garrick and Lekain, 82.
Merchant Tailor's School, life at, 115.
Metham, Mr., carries off Mrs. Bellamy, 201.
Middleton (Magnan), follows Barry, 103.
Mitchell, Joseph, as a condemned playwright, 159.
Montagu, Mrs., her freedom with audiences, 188.
Montfleury, 86.
Monimia, played by Macklin, 185.
Moody, actor, his career, 227-9, 416.
More, Hannah, seriousness of her "Percy," 148.
Mossop, opposed to Barry, 39; his merits and manners, 107; rivalry with Barry, 107; excelled by Lewis, 98.
Murphy, 33, 34; his "Alzuma," 68.
Murray, Charles, 314.
Munden, 350.
Mexborough, Lord, entertains Foote, 133.

# INDEX.

## N.

Northumberland, Duke of, and John Kemble, 274.

## O.

O'Brien, first appearance, 34; marries Lady Susan Strangways, 47; original characters, 47; descent of, 48-9; his plays, 49.
Opera, English, progress of, 150.
O. P. Row, 362-7.
"Orphan of China," Murphy's, 34.
Orestes, never played by Garrick in London, 100.
Ossory, Lord, on Garrick in company, 92.
Owenson, actor, father of Lady Morgan, 227-8.

## P.

Palmer, John, the elder, 64.
Palmer, John, (the second), career of, 232-4; stabbed on the stage by Mrs. Barry, 233.
Palmerston, Lord, and Macklin, 185.
Parsons, his stage career, 231-2.
Pelham, Henry, at Barry's house, 102.
Pertinax, Sir, Macsycophant—Cooke's, compared with Macklin's, 192.
Players, loyalty of, *temp.* George III., 168.
Plays, new, produced between 1801-1814, 853-7.
Pope, Miss, 339.
Pope, Mrs. (Miss Younge), death of, 208.
Pope, why he abused the actors, 152.
Powell, Jane, and Lady Hamilton, 131.
Powell, Mrs. Jane, retort of, 146.
Powell, Thomas, a timid playwright, 156.
Powell, William, first appearance of, 35.
Powlett, Lady Nassau, intimacy with Foote, 126.
Pritchard, Miss Mrs. John Palmer, afterwards Lloyd, 62-4.
Pritchard, Mrs., her family, 59; character, 59; principal parts played by her, 60; as the Comic Muse, 61; Walpole's, Johnson's, and Churchill's estimation of her, 61; her ignorance, 62; death, 64.
Preville and Garrick, 83.
Prologues and Epilogues, 318-23.
"Provoked Husband," opposition to, 153.
Purvor, Grace (Mrs. Macklin), 186.
Pye, his "Adelaide," 144.

## Q.

Quarrels of actors, 12; Macklin and Reddish, 217; Quin and Macklin, 193.
Quin, beats an adverse critic, 89; encored in the soliloquy in "Cato," 74; ignorance of, 62; on Macklin, 185; retort by, 26.

## R.

Readings, Public, first instituted by Henderson and Sheridan, 238; of Mrs. Siddons, 262.
Rachel, Mdlle., ignorance of, 62.

Randolph, Lady, Mrs. Crawford and Mrs. Siddons in, 248.
Reddish, Samuel, his career, 217-221; "Regent," tragedy, criticised by Mrs. Siddons, 253.
"Register Office," Reed's, plagiarized by Foote, 131.
Reynolds's "Werter," "Eloisa," 145.
Rich, John, the rare qualities of his Harlequin, 43-45; his humor, 44.
Ridley, Dr., the critic, 154.
Robinson, Mrs (Perdita), her career, 212-16.
Rolla, Pitt and Kemble's, 270.
Roman and Greek characters declined by Garrick, 81.
"Rose," most absurd of the sentimental pieces, 71.
"Route," Dr. Hill's, 34.
Ross, his stage career, 221-3.
Rowe, 144; as a condemned author, 151.
Ryan, life of, 41-2.

## S.

Saurin, a condemned French author, 155; his play with double *denouement*, 158.
"School for Lovers," Whitehead's, 87.
"School for Scandal," 146-7.
Scottish Stage, New Edinburgh Theatre, 222.
Seward, Miss, on Mrs. Cibber, Pritchard, and Siddons, 64.
Shakspeare, patronage of, by Prince Frederick, 170.
Shakspeare—Tinkers, 25, 59, 68, 266.
Shelburne, Lord, on Lord Carlisle, 161.
Sheridan and Cumberland, 167; his Irish management, 38; reception of the "Rivals," 73; his "Duenna," 73.
Sheridan, Mrs., 36; her "Discovery," 87; "Dupe," 58.
Shift, in the "Minor," first intended for Wilkinson, not Whitfield, 134.
Shuter, Edward, his birth, education, and his stage career, 116-118; his piety and death, 117, 118; his freedom with audiences, 183.
Shylock—played as a serious character by Macklin, 187.
Siddons, Henry, 289; correspondence with his mother and uncle, 261.
Siddons, Mrs., after leaving the stage, 285; disparagement of Garrick, 86; her life and career, 241-263; "Siege of Aquileia," Home's, 86.
Sloper, Mr., the "friend" of Mrs. Cibber, 55.
Smith, Charles, 233-4; stabbed on the stage by Reddish, 213.
Southerne, his philosophy when unsuccessful, 153.
Spencer, Lady G., on Mrs. Abington, 210.
Stage, English, condition of, in eighteenth century, 57, 61.
Strolling, incidents of, 314-17.
Suett, 337-8.

## T.

Talma, first appearance of in Selde, 82; his restoration of Othello, 159.

Teddington, its debt to Mrs. Woffington, 8.
Theatre, French, armed guard in, 179; critics at, 179; the eccentric Swiss, 180.
Theobald, angry under failure, 152.
Townley, Mr., Rev., dramatic author, 86.
Tracy, an unsuccessful playwright, 153.
Tricks in acting exemplified, 309–12.
Twiss, stage attacked through him, 358–9.
Tyrawley, Lord, 200.

## U.

Unrehearsed Stage effects, 9, 41, 69, 99, 105, 172, 173, 174, 180, 215, 218, 220, 238, 234, 238, 244, 246, 259, 260, 261, 304, 311, 312, 314, 315, 317.
Upholsterer, Murphy's, 33.

## V.

Violante, Madame, 5.
Violetti, Eva Maria, her noble friends, 91; marries Garrick, 91.
"Vortigern," first night of, 271–2.

## W.

Waldron, Francis Godolphin, bookseller, actor, and editor of pieces by Johnson and Father Southwell, 71.
Wales, Prince of, and "Perdita," 213.
Wallace, Lady, dramatist, 149.
Walpole, (Horace), describes Garrick at home, 91, 92; grounds of his dislike of Garrick, 157; on Home's "Alonzo," 67; on Burgoyne, 72; on Barry, 74; on Garrick, 76, 77; on Mrs. Siddons, 106; on Mrs. Abington, 210; on Mrs. Siddons's Isabella, 251; on Mrs. Woffington, 6,—Sir Robert chastises an actor, 167.
Ward, father of Mrs. Roger Kemble, 241.
Wedderburn, on the stage, 135.
Wells, Mrs., comic actress, rival of Mrs Siddons, 204.
Whalley, Dr., one of the condemned, 160.
White's Club, reception of Cibber, 23.
Whitfield and Foote, 122, 131, 132; Shuter's religious instructor, 117.
Whitlock, Mrs. (Elizabeth Kemble), jealous of Mrs. Belfille, 203.
Wilkinson aided by Garrick, 87; his inability to imitate Mrs. Cibber, 53; mimics Foote, 134; Tate and Garrick, 224.
Woffington, life of Margaret, 5–14.
Woffington, Mary, 5; marriage, 8; death, 9.
Wolsey, Kemble's, founded on that of Digges, 273.
Woodward, Henry; original characters, 113; early life, 113–14; education, 114; his career and qualities as an actor, 115–16; defended by Garrick, 115.

## Y.

Yates, Mrs., gallantry of Garrick to, 79; in Medea, 198; as Violante, 199; as Constance, 199; her last appearance, 203.
Yates, Richard, 223.
York, Duke of, amateur actor, 172.
Young, Charles, 294, 308, 352.
Younge, Miss, her acting, 145; marriage with Mr. Pope, 256; the last Cordelia to Garrick's Lear, 94.

www.ingramcontent.com/pod-product-compliance
Lightning Source LLC
Chambersburg PA
CBHW022107290426
44112CB00008B/582